Inclusive Community Development Through Tourism and Hospitality Practices

Vipin Nadda
University of Sunderland in London, UK

Faithfull Gonzo
University of Sunderland in London, UK

Ravinder Batta
Shimla University, India

Amit Sharma
Shimla University, India

A volume in the Advances in Hospitality, Tourism, and the Services Industry (AHTSI) Book Series

Published in the United States of America by
 IGI Global
 Business Science Reference (an imprint of IGI Global)
 701 E. Chocolate Avenue
 Hershey PA, USA 17033
 Tel: 717-533-8845
 Fax: 717-533-8661
 E-mail: cust@igi-global.com
 Web site: http://www.igi-global.com

Copyright © 2023 by IGI Global. All rights reserved. No part of this publication may be reproduced, stored or distributed in any form or by any means, electronic or mechanical, including photocopying, without written permission from the publisher.
Product or company names used in this set are for identification purposes only. Inclusion of the names of the products or companies does not indicate a claim of ownership by IGI Global of the trademark or registered trademark.

 Library of Congress Cataloging-in-Publication Data

Names: Nadda, Vipin, 1970- editor. | Gonzo, Faithfull, 1974- editor. |
  Batta, Ravinder Nath, editor. | Sharma, Amit, 1978- editor.
Title: Inclusive community development through tourism and hospitality
  practices / edited by Vipin Nadda, Faithfull Gonzo, Ravinder Nath Batta,
  Amit Sharma.
Description: Hershey, PA : Business Science Reference, [2023] | Includes
  bibliographical references and index. | Summary: "The objective of this
  book is explore various viable strategies for the adoption of a
  sustainable approaches which can eventually boost economic growth and
  poverty reduction all over the world. Sustainable tourism should not
  only be limited to environmental preservation, but the socio-cultural
  and economic sides should also be considered. It is expected to
  highlight the need for an integrated approach recognizing that
  resources, facilities, and infrastructures are interrelated with the
  social, cultural, and natural environment within the respective
  communities"-- Provided by publisher.
Identifiers: LCCN 2022044517 (print) | LCCN 2022044518 (ebook) | ISBN
  9781668467961 (hardcover) | ISBN 9781668467978 (paperback) | ISBN
  9781668467985 (ebook)
Subjects: LCSH: Sustainable tourism. | Community development. | Sustainable
  development. | Green marketing.
Classification: LCC G156.5.S87 I54 2023 (print) | LCC G156.5.S87 (ebook)
  | DDC 338.4/791--dc23/eng20221230
LC record available at https://lccn.loc.gov/2022044517
LC ebook record available at https://lccn.loc.gov/2022044518

This book is published in the IGI Global book series Advances in Hospitality, Tourism, and the Services Industry (AHTSI) (ISSN: 2475-6547; eISSN: 2475-6555)

British Cataloguing in Publication Data
A Cataloguing in Publication record for this book is available from the British Library.

All work contributed to this book is new, previously-unpublished material.
The views expressed in this book are those of the authors, but not necessarily of the publisher.

For electronic access to this publication, please contact: eresources@igi-global.com.

Advances in Hospitality, Tourism, and the Services Industry (AHTSI) Book Series

Maximiliano Korstanje
University of Palermo, Argentina

ISSN:2475-6547
EISSN:2475-6555

MISSION

Globally, the hospitality, travel, tourism, and services industries generate a significant percentage of revenue and represent a large portion of the business world. Even in tough economic times, these industries thrive as individuals continue to spend on leisure and recreation activities as well as services.

The Advances in Hospitality, Tourism, and the Services Industry (AHTSI) book series offers diverse publications relating to the management, promotion, and profitability of the leisure, recreation, and services industries. Highlighting current research pertaining to various topics within the realm of hospitality, travel, tourism, and services management, the titles found within the AHTSI book series are pertinent to the research and professional needs of managers, business practitioners, researchers, and upper-level students studying in the field.

COVERAGE

- Customer Service Issues
- Travel Agency Management
- Tourism and the Environment
- Service Training
- Leisure & Business Travel
- Service Management
- Destination Marketing and Management
- Sustainable Tourism
- Cruise Marketing and Sales
- Food and Beverage Management

IGI Global is currently accepting manuscripts for publication within this series. To submit a proposal for a volume in this series, please contact our Acquisition Editors at Acquisitions@igi-global.com or visit: http://www.igi-global.com/publish/.

The Advances in Hospitality, Tourism, and the Services Industry (AHTSI) Book Series (ISSN 2475-6547) is published by IGI Global, 701 E. Chocolate Avenue, Hershey, PA 17033-1240, USA, www.igi-global.com. This series is composed of titles available for purchase individually; each title is edited to be contextually exclusive from any other title within the series. For pricing and ordering information please visit http://www.igi-global.com/book-series/advances-hospitality-tourism-services-industry/121014. Postmaster: Send all address changes to above address. Copyright © 2023 IGI Global. All rights, including translation in other languages reserved by the publisher. No part of this series may be reproduced or used in any form or by any means – graphics, electronic, or mechanical, including photocopying, recording, taping, or information and retrieval systems – without written permission from the publisher, except for non commercial, educational use, including classroom teaching purposes. The views expressed in this series are those of the authors, but not necessarily of IGI Global.

Titles in this Series

For a list of additional titles in this series, please visit: http://www.igi-global.com/book-series/

Sustainable Growth Strategies for Entrepreneurial Venture Tourism and Regional Development
Andreas Masouras (Neapolis University, Cyprus) Christos Papademetriou (Neapolis University, Cyprus) Dimitrios Belias (University of Thessaly, Greece) and Sofia Anastasiadou (University of Western Macedonia, Greece)
Business Science Reference • © 2023 • 320pp • H/C (ISBN: 9781668460559) • US $250.00

Measuring Consumer Behavior in Hospitality for Enhanced Decision Making
Célia M.Q. Ramos (CinTurs, ESGHT, University of the Algarve, Portugal) Carlos M.R. Sousa (ESGHT, CiTUR, University of the Algarve, Portugal) Nelson M.S. Matos (CinTurs, ESGHT, University of the Algarve, Portugal) and Rashed Isam Ashqar (CinTurs, ESGHT, University of the Algarve, Portugal)
Business Science Reference • © 2023 • 295pp • H/C (ISBN: 9781668466070) • US $225.00

Global Perspectives on the Opportunities and Future Directions of Health Tourism
Oğuz Doğan (Antalya Bilim University, Turkey)
Business Science Reference • © 2023 • 319pp • H/C (ISBN: 9781668466926) • US $270.00

Leadership Approaches in Global Hospitality and Tourism
Ahmet Baytok (Afyon Kocatepe University, Turkey) Özcan Zorlu (Afyon Kocatepe University, Turkey) Ali Avan (Afyon Kocatepe University, Turkey) and Engin Bayraktaroğlu (Anadolu University, Turkey)
Business Science Reference • © 2023 • 341pp • H/C (ISBN: 9781668467138) • US $250.00

Handbook of Research on Sustainable Tourism and Hotel Operations in Global Hypercompetition
Hakan Sezerel (Anadolu University, Turkey) and Bryan Christiansen (Global Research Society, LLC, USA)
Business Science Reference • © 2023 • 677pp • H/C (ISBN: 9781668446454) • US $315.00

701 East Chocolate Avenue, Hershey, PA 17033, USA
Tel: 717-533-8845 x100 • Fax: 717-533-8661
E-Mail: cust@igi-global.com • www.igi-global.com

Table of Contents

Preface xiii

Chapter 1
Advocating Empowerment and Gender Equality: A Study of Community-Based Tourism Initiatives 1
    Isabella Roveri, University of Aveiro, Portugal
    Rita Fernandes, University of Aveiro, Portugal
    Rita Pereira, University of Aveiro, Portugal
    Vitória Plácido, University of Aveiro, Portugal
    Nina Szczygiel, University of Aveiro, Portugal

Chapter 2
Community Development Through Ecotourism: A Stakeholder Analysis of Botevgrad, Bulgaria 20
    Anna Daneva, University of Sunderland in London, UK
    Vipin Nadda, University of Sunderland in London, UK

Chapter 3
Green Marketing Applications in Hospitality Businesses 49
    Mehmet Tekeli, Karamanoğlu Mehmetbey University, Turkey
    Gülsüm Kasap, Isparta University of Applied Science, Turkey

Chapter 4
Impacts of Tourism Development in Developing Countries: A Namibian Perspective 71
    Faithfull Gonzo, University of Sunderland in London, UK

Chapter 5
Indigenous and Tribal Tourism 107
    Amit Sharma, Shimla University, India

Chapter 6
Pro-Poor Tourism and Poverty Alleviation 125
    Faithfull Cecilia Gonzo, University of Sunderland in London, UK

Chapter 7
Prospects of Tea Tourism in India: Tea Culture With Its Influence Towards
Tourists Along With the Destination 160
    Shuvasree Banerjee, Chandigarh University, India

Chapter 8
Reinforcing Tourism Carrying Capacity Assessments: Holistic Approach and
Future Research Directions 185
    Ravi Sharma, Symbiosis Institute of International Business, Symbiosis
        International University (Deemed), Pune, India

Chapter 9
The Impact of Small Island Sports Events on Developing Sustainable
Tourism 212
    Ian Arnott, University of Westminster, UK

Chapter 10
The Impact of Tourism Development on Community Quality of
Life (QoL) 234
    Latif Oztosun, University of Sunderland in London, UK

Chapter 11
The Role of Ecotourism in Sustainable Development 250
    İrem Yıldırım, Nevşehir Hacı Bektaş Veli University, Turkey
    Ezgi Kırıcı Tekeli, Karamanoğlu Mehmetbey University, Turkey

Chapter 12
Using Indigenous Sport and Games for Sustainable Community Tourism in
Barbados 273
    Wendy Cynthia Sealy, Institute of Psychology, Business, and Human
        Sciences, University of Chichester, UK
    Paul Wheeler, Institute of Sports, University of Chichester, UK

Compilation of References 298

About the Contributors 355

Index 359

Detailed Table of Contents

Preface xiii

Chapter 1
Advocating Empowerment and Gender Equality: A Study of Community-Based Tourism Initiatives 1
    Isabella Roveri, University of Aveiro, Portugal
    Rita Fernandes, University of Aveiro, Portugal
    Rita Pereira, University of Aveiro, Portugal
    Vitória Plácido, University of Aveiro, Portugal
    Nina Szczygiel, University of Aveiro, Portugal

The UN 2030 Agenda for Sustainable Development acknowledges that economic growth that countries are seeking need to be accompanied by same-degree efforts to combat inequality, eradicate poverty, and protect the planet's environment and climate, and has been recognized by organizations and individuals for its quest of sustainable development. This study focuses on the fifth sustainable development goal: gender equality, applied into the tourism industry. Tourism has become one of the main sectors for today's economy, thanks to its weight in the GDP, as well as its contribution to job creation and employment rate translated into local populations' well-being. The chapter aims to analyze and discuss the role and importance of entrepreneurship allied to tourism to achieve gender equality. The analysis of case studies comprises a series of community-based tourism initiatives developed in four different continents and selected on the basis of specific criteria, such as the role of women, and the rural, tourist, and community environment.

Chapter 2
Community Development Through Ecotourism: A Stakeholder Analysis of
Botevgrad, Bulgaria 20
> Anna Daneva, University of Sunderland in London, UK
> Vipin Nadda, University of Sunderland in London, UK

According to UNWTO, annual ecotourism revenues worldwide are estimated to grow from approximately $800 billion to one trillion in 2025. About 11 million people are employed in the tourism sector and related activities. The current growth of ecotourism is 10% to 12% per year and is the fastest-growing sector. The average age of travellers has become lower, and more and more young people are now interested in environmentally friendly forms of tourism. Ecotourism travellers cost less in infrastructure per income unit than any other type of tourist. In the last 30 years, no other type of tourism has generated such growth and popularity and become fundamentally important in the tourism sector and the world economy. Last year, nearly 9.5 billion tourists visited ecotourism destinations and raised awareness of the ecotourism concept and invested heavily to gain a sustainable travel experience. Currently, ecotourism is preferred by 71% of people under 30.

Chapter 3
Green Marketing Applications in Hospitality Businesses 49
> Mehmet Tekeli, Karamanoğlu Mehmetbey University, Turkey
> Gülsüm Kasap, Isparta University of Applied Science, Turkey

Industrial activities significantly affect the environment, which makes environmental sensitivity one of the most critical issues in the national and international arenas. As in other areas, the green approaches adopted in the tourism sector aim to reduce the negative environmental impact. The current study discussed the meaning of green marketing practices for hospitality businesses, the green marketing practices adopted by these businesses, and the results. In addition, the study presented a holistic perspective by presenting examples from hospitality businesses and gave general information about the green marketing concept, its scope, the reasons to turn to green marketing, and the benefits of such practices. In the study, which deals with the elements of the green marketing mix in hospitality businesses and touches on the examples of green hotels, green marketing practices were evaluated in the tourism sector.

Chapter 4
Impacts of Tourism Development in Developing Countries: A Namibian
Perspective 71
Faithfull Gonzo, University of Sunderland in London, UK

Tourism development has been viewed in terms of its contribution to economic growth. Thus, most developing countries have declared tourism as an important economic sector. Tourism is also envisaged to provide economic benefits to communities through the provision of employment. Due to the increase in tourist numbers, environmental changes to the natural resources have been a cause for concern to nations. Tourism stakeholders have incorporated environmental issues in their tourism development plans to ensure that the tourism products are sustainable, and communities are benefitting. For the communities to benefit from tourism development, the analysis of socio-cultural impacts has become of paramount importance. Governments have emphasised increasing tourism numbers to influence economic growth. The local community would then benefit from the tourism increase through multiplier effects. Thus, the chapter explores the impacts of tourism development in developing countries with a focus on Namibia as a developing country.

Chapter 5
Indigenous and Tribal Tourism..107
Amit Sharma, Shimla University, India

The interest in indigenous and tribal tourism is increasing rapidly in the new era of technologically savvy, thoughtful, and responsible travellers looking to explore less-travelled regions. This type of tourism is classified as "niche tourism," which falls under the umbrella of the sustainable tourism domain. Changed consumer behaviour has created the demand for a coherent market, which is related to the aforementioned business stream. Indigenous people are living in the natural environment in the hinterlands, which stems from inherent traditional knowledge, sustainable practices, and mystery traditions. This mysticism has led to the creation of the niche segment of indigenous and tribal tourism among the travel-savvy population around the world. Different marketing and business strategies are required to cater to different subsets of clients who may be suitable for this type of tourism.

Chapter 6
Pro-Poor Tourism and Poverty Alleviation..125
Faithfull Cecilia Gonzo, University of Sunderland in London, UK

Tourism has been utilised as a tool for poverty alleviation globally, and its growth is envisioned to directly or indirectly impact the lives of the local communities. The dialogue on poverty alleviation led to the formulation of pro-poor tourism (PPT). PPT is defined as tourism that generates net benefits to the poor, and it should be economically, socially, environmentally, or culturally beneficial. Although PPT has the potential to benefit the poor, it is not clear how the different types of tourism impact the poor. The tourism industry is mainly driven by the private sector, particularly large international companies. Therefore, their interest in ensuring that poverty is alleviated between local communities is not guaranteed. Thus, with this view, PPT has been criticised for over-emphasising local initiatives. Similarly, the understanding of the poverty concept has been overtly debated. Hence, this chapter intends to explore the concept of PPT and its effect on poor communities.

Chapter 7
Prospects of Tea Tourism in India: Tea Culture With Its Influence Towards Tourists Along With the Destination 160
Shuvasree Banerjee, Chandigarh University, India

The social shifts in Indian society towards tea are pervasive, and they are now being seen through tourism, where local tea customs, cultures, services, and attractions are part of several tourist activities. The delightful and enjoyable experience of tea tourism might pique visitors' interests. The chance to access all knowledge and experiences linked to tea is provided by tea tourism. In the context of global tourism, tea tourism is a relatively new specialty. By generating jobs and increasing the rural economy, the development of tea tourism would assist the area and lessen insurgency and other socioeconomic issues while also protecting the environment, heritage, and culture. In order to draw tourists and increase revenue, tea farms and the government are proposing to build more amenities inside the tea garden. In the tea garden, there are various homestays where visitors may stay and enjoy all the amenities.

Chapter 8
Reinforcing Tourism Carrying Capacity Assessments: Holistic Approach and Future Research Directions 185
Ravi Sharma, Symbiosis Institute of International Business, Symbiosis International University (Deemed), Pune, India

Carrying capacity assessment assists in estimating human intervention thresholds bearable to natural-social ecosystems, specifically in tourism. Earlier studies implemented isolated determining system combinations, namely physical-ecological, socio-cultural, political-economic, and perceptual-psychological, impacting carrying capacity assessments. Results obtained through experts' opinion and systematic literature review meta-analysis suggest a lack of policy-governance components. Imperatively, policy matters governing environmental issues are crucial; especially in tourism, policy-governance systems form holistic components for achieving resilience and enhanced thresholds. This must be well-integrated into the carrying capacity assessment framework, as proposed and outlined as an outcome of this review and in the best interest of society. Validation of the framework using accurate data from the tourism domain through further research will motivate researchers and practitioners.

Chapter 9
The Impact of Small Island Sports Events on Developing Sustainable Tourism 212
    Ian Arnott, University of Westminster, UK

Small islands rely heavily on tourism as a way of an economic boost, as well as a way of growth for business development, in particular, hospitality. One of the ways that several islands around the world have excelled in this is through hosting sports events as a way of sustainable tourism and there are many examples of this such as Hawaii that have $200 million dollar source of revenue and 94% of inbound tourists coming to the island for this type of tourism. This is just one example that is discussed within the chapter along with others as such stakeholders as the International Island Games that takes place every two years on 24 small islands around the world. Key areas that will be discussed as how the community must be involved in any type of tourism development due to the number of potential tourists who may visit the island and its potential positive or negative impact that this might have.

Chapter 10
The Impact of Tourism Development on Community Quality of Life (QoL) 234
    Latif Oztosun, University of Sunderland in London, UK

The impact of planners' development operations on host governments and residents has emerged as a growing subject of study in recent years, as it has become widely accepted that planners and entrepreneurs must consider the perspectives of the host community if the sector is to be successful in the long-term. However, there has been insufficient emphasis on local communities, their needs, and, most crucially, their assessment of the impact on their quality of life. This chapter discusses why and how tourism and hospitality planners must consider inhabitants' attitudes and opinions, particularly when it comes to legislation that may affect their way of life.

Chapter 11
The Role of Ecotourism in Sustainable Development 250
    İrem Yıldırım, Nevşehir Hacı Bektaş Veli University, Turkey
    Ezgi Kırıcı Tekeli, Karamanoğlu Mehmetbey University, Turkey

As a concept, development was evaluated only as an economic goal until the 1970s, and its physical, social, and cultural environment elements were ignored and left in the background. The concept of development has turned into a sustainable development phenomenon, which includes physical, social, and cultural factors, as people notice environmental pollution over time. Sustainable development, which integrates the mission of many industries interacting with the environment, has also gained ground in the tourism industry and has led to sustainable tourism understanding. Therefore, destinations have developed different tourism types within the sustainable tourism framework. Ecotourism has come to the forefront as a tourism type that can minimize physical, social, and cultural damage of tourism to the environment. Therefore, the current study, aiming to reveal the impact of ecotourism on sustainable development, covered the subjects of sustainability, sustainable development, sustainable tourism, ecotourism, and the relationship between sustainable development and ecotourism.

Chapter 12
Using Indigenous Sport and Games for Sustainable Community Tourism in Barbados 273
    Wendy Cynthia Sealy, Institute of Psychology, Business, and Human Sciences, University of Chichester, UK
    Paul Wheeler, Institute of Sports, University of Chichester, UK

Sustainable tourism development in the Caribbean is inhibited by several challenges, such as diseconomies of scale and scope and other structural and resource constraints. These challenges are further exacerbated by the heavy prominence of transnational conglomerates. As a result, many Caribbean islands do not appropriate the full value from tourism with the majority of the revenues and profits accruing to companies based outside the region. Many tourists who visit these islands do not venture into the local communities as they are encouraged to stay in the all-inclusive enclaves. Researchers have long recognised that indigenous sports tourism can be a tool that would allow marginalised communities to achieve greater control of their livelihoods. This chapter will focus on sports and games that are deeply rooted in Barbadian culture and history. Using a case study approach, the authors will show how they can be monetised and fused with other aspects of community culture to attract a different type of tourists who will venture into the local communities and spend their money there.

Compilation of References 298

About the Contributors 355

Index 359

Preface

The tourism industry is a leading and robust economic sector in the world generating US$1.7 trillion in export earnings, international tourist arrivals increased from 25 million in 1950 to 278 million in 1980, 674 million in 2000, 1186 million in 2015 and 1.5 billion in 2019 (UNWTO, 2019). Although the tourism industry has been growing, the industry experienced peaks and troughs over the years. Negatively, the COVID-19 pandemic caused a 22% decline in international tourist arrivals, however, these numbers are anticipated to increase at a faster pace after the pandemic because the industry is resilient. Tourism is an important sector for governments and regions searching for economic development, improvement of community services and employment creation.

Development is a continuous increase of income per person to empower the community to distribute its yield quicker than the population growth. Whilst tourism development is a dynamic process which involves matching tourism resources to the demands and preferences of tourists. Tourism development includes developing approaches, policies and plans that influence the increase and development of tourism at a destination. Therefore, tourism development regulated by the community will not only economically benefit the community but can also be utilised as an essential device for reducing poverty. However, the community should be part of tourism development by being involved in decision-making. From an international perspective, inclusion is one of the main principles behind the United Nations' Sustainable Development Goals (SDGs). However, a lot of people are excluded from development because of their gender, ethnicity, age, or poverty. Development can be inclusive if the communities contribute to creating opportunities, share the benefits of development and participate in decision-making.

This book: *Inclusive Community Development Through Tourism and Hospitality Practices* is designed for various audiences-students and educators of higher education, community leaders, government officials, librarians, researchers, and academics. It provides an overview of the global tourism industry and attempts to address various issues that have an effect on community development. The book consists of twelve chapters that underline the importance of inclusive community development. Chapter 1 focuses on the fifth Sustainable Development Goal (SDG): gender equality, applied into the tourism industry. The chapter analyses the role and importance of entrepreneurship in relation to tourism to achieve gender equality. Furthermore, it explores a series of Community-Based Tourism (CBT) initiatives developed in four different continents. Chapter 2 provides an insight into concept of eco-tourism and discuss how local communities and governments can benefit from adopting eco-tourism initiatives, whilst chapter 3 discusses environmental impacts initiated by tourism and hospitality business practices. It further explores the green marketing concept, its scope, and the benefits of such practices. Chapter 4 acknowledges the importance of tourism development in terms of economic growth. The chapter highlights the importance of communities benefitting from tourism increase through multiplier effects. It utilises Namibia as a case study and provides an in-depth analysis of economic, environmental, and socio-cultural impacts of tourism development.

Approximately 370 million indigenous and tribal people live in 70 countries who speak about 7,000 languages worldwide and represent 5,000 distinct cultural entities. Hence, the biggest challenge faced by these communities in relation to sustainable development is to ensure territorial security, legal recognition of ownership and control over customary land. Chapter 5 focuses on indigenous and tribal tourism as a niche tourism, it highlights that indigenous people should be directly involved in the tourism activities through control and/or by having their culture serve as the essence of the attraction. Chapter 6 explores the poverty concept (SDG1) and analyses how Pro-Poor Tourism (PPT) can be adopted to alleviate poverty. This chapter further explores how PPT strategies can be utilised to open opportunities for poor people through their involvement in decision making. Chapter 7 further utilises India as a case study to explore the potential of tea tourism and stresses how travelling and consuming tea may increase people's perceptions of tea plantations and their overall tea tourism experiences, which will benefit the tea industry as a whole. Hence, the chapter significantly links tea tourism and sustainable development.

Carrying Capacity Assessment (CCA) assists in estimating human intervention thresholds bearable to natural-social ecosystems, specifically in tourism. Earlier studies implemented isolated determining system combinations, namely physical-ecological, socio-cultural, political-economic, and perceptual-psychological, impacting CCA. Chapter 8 therefore evaluates critical components that influence the tourism carrying capacity along with their inter-relationships and proposes a comprehensive Tourism Carrying Capacity Assessment Framework. Chapter 9 analyses the impact of small Islands sports events on developing sustainable tourism. It further explores how the community must be involved in any type of tourism development due to the number of potential tourists who may visit the island. Whilst chapter 10 emphasises the importance of considering the perspectives of the host

Preface

community in tourism development and further discusses why and how tourism and hospitality planners must consider inhabitants' attitudes and opinions, particularly when it comes to legislation that may affect their way of life. Chapter 11 focuses on the impact of ecotourism on sustainable development and explores the relationship between sustainable development and ecotourism. Chapter 12 utilises Barbados as a case study to investigate the extent to which traditional games and sport in Barbados could be used to stimulate local community engagement to minimise the oligopolistic powers that appropriate the majority of the wealth made from tourism.

It is our pleasure to offer this book of *Inclusive Community Development Through Tourism and Hospitality Practices*. We hope readers will benefit from this detailed coverage of community development, which addresses the challenges and opportunities offered by various tourism and hospitality practices.

Vipin Nadda
University of Sunderland in London, UK

Faithfull Gonzo
University of Sunderland in London, UK

Ravinder Batta
Shimla University, India

Amit Sharma
Shimla University, India

Chapter 1
Advocating Empowerment and Gender Equality:
A Study of Community-Based Tourism Initiatives

Isabella Roveri
University of Aveiro, Portugal

Rita Pereira
University of Aveiro, Portugal

Rita Fernandes
University of Aveiro, Portugal

Vitória Plácido
University of Aveiro, Portugal

Nina Szczygiel
University of Aveiro, Portugal

ABSTRACT

The UN 2030 Agenda for Sustainable Development acknowledges that economic growth that countries are seeking need to be accompanied by same-degree efforts to combat inequality, eradicate poverty, and protect the planet's environment and climate, and has been recognized by organizations and individuals for its quest of sustainable development. This study focuses on the fifth sustainable development goal: gender equality, applied into the tourism industry. Tourism has become one of the main sectors for today's economy, thanks to its weight in the GDP, as well as its contribution to job creation and employment rate translated into local populations' well-being. The chapter aims to analyze and discuss the role and importance of entrepreneurship allied to tourism to achieve gender equality. The analysis of case studies comprises a series of community-based tourism initiatives developed in four different continents and selected on the basis of specific criteria, such as the role of women, and the rural, tourist, and community environment.

DOI: 10.4018/978-1-6684-6796-1.ch001

Copyright © 2023, IGI Global. Copying or distributing in print or electronic forms without written permission of IGI Global is prohibited.

INTRODUCTION

In 2015, the United Nations (UN) approved a new 2030 Agenda for countries and societies. Successors to the eight Millennium Development Goals (MDGs) of the 2015 Agenda, the new 17 Sustainable Development Goals (SDGs) add more subjects and aim to address a greater number of social problems. The SDGs are more comprehensive, easily measurable and with concrete target objectives (UN, 2018). The countries covered by this agenda acknowledge that their initiatives, such as eradication of poverty in all its manifestations, need to be accompanied by strategies linked to economic growth that address at the same time social needs, such as education, health, employment, climate change and environmental protection (Portales, 2019). This is because such a multidimensional challenge as poverty requires a multidimensional response through education, work, markets, and social and employment protection.

The World Tourism Organization (UNWTO), a UN institution, has incorporated this agenda into its activity, with a premise that, through tourism, the sustainable development goals can be achieved. In fact, as an economic activity, tourism represents a large percentage of the Gross Domestic Product (GDP) of many countries and is a source of employability worldwide, making the sustainable development of this sector a necessity (Peña-Sánchez et al., 2020) rather than a mere recommendation. In light of these tendencies, entrepreneurship presents itself as a fundamental element for the tourism activity, and, together, they are believed to play an important role in achieving the SDGs. Despite its importance, entrepreneurship rates vary (sometimes significantly) between countries, particularly in regard to the number of female entrepreneurs, which is in most of the cases significantly lower than that of males (Bastian et al., 2019). Although local economies are now including the female workforce on their agendas for economic development (Koutsou et al., 2009), there is still a lot of work to be done. In tourism, female empowerment can be achieved through community-based initiatives (McCall & Mearns, 2021). Therefore, it is important to understand how community-based tourism (CBT) supports gender equality and what role entrepreneurship plays in this process.

The present chapter is based on the fifth SDG, gender equality, and focuses specifically on the role of entrepreneurship and female empowerment in tourism. The methodology of this study is mainly qualitative. In order to analyze and discuss the role and importance of entrepreneurship allied to tourism as a means to achieve gender equality, four international cases of community-based tourism were selected, with 'tourism', 'entrepreneurship' and 'female empowerment' being the center of the business model.

BACKGROUND OF THE STUDY

Entrepreneurship and Sustainable Development

The issue of sustainable development has been gaining greater notoriety as an academic and research subject since the late 1980's (Eusébio et al., 2014). Although the concept was first mentioned in 1972 by the United Nations, it only earned greater prominence in 1987 thanks to a publication of the World Commission on Environment and Development (Hall et al., 2010), a report entitled 'Our common future'. From that report, the following definition of sustainable development emerged: "sustainable development is development that meets the needs of the present without compromising the ability of future generations to meet their own needs" (WCED, 1987).

This definition has been subject to continuous changes and improvements, not only from a theoretical or practical viewpoints, but also in regard to the precision with which the constructs of sustainability and sustainable development are approached. At the European level, for instance, in 2001 the European Union adopted a strategy in favor of sustainable development which has been so far revised a few times (EurLex, n.d.). However, it is now generally acknowledged that the main objective of sustainable development is to find the balanced interaction between economic, human, environmental and technological systems (Kardos, 2012).

Since sustainability has become a fundamental aspect of contemporary research, work on merely commercial objectives and resources optimization without considering a priori the aspects of sustainable development has been left quite behind (Peña-Sánchez et al. al., 2020). But the concern about sustainability goes well beyond academic research. For example, in some companies, sustainability is now seen as a part of corporate strategy (Hall et al., 2010). For example, for Konda et al. (2015), a successful enterprise is focused on sustainable development and leverages technological and social innovation, which derives largely from the entrepreneurial mindset and entrepreneurial venturing.

The link between entrepreneurship and sustainable development is salient in the research of several scholars, such as Kardos (2012), Hall et al. (2010), Morozova et al. (2018), Liguori & Bendickson (2020), Ogamba (2018), and Portales (2019). All of the above acknowledge the role and importance of entrepreneurship in achieving sustainable development, and unanimously recognize it as a vehicle for social transformation.

Morozova et al. (2018) believe that entrepreneurship is one of the most promising means of overcoming the consequences of global crises, as well as preventing future crises of economic systems, since it allows to ensure greater optimization of production and distribution processes. Hall et al. (2010), refer to entrepreneurship as a catalyst for the creation of sustainable products, processes and businesses, considered as the solution to various current social and environmental concerns. In turn, Kardos (2012) argues that innovation done in a sustainable way is attained when entrepreneurial agents achieve competitive advantages through economic success arising from good environmental and/or social practices considered innovative. In this view, entrepreneurship may be seen as a consequence of social responsibility and of pursuit of sustainable development.

For activities that address the problem of a group of people, a community, or a society at large, a specific type of entrepreneurial activities has emerged. Social entrepreneurship is regarded as an approach of individuals, groups, companies or individual entrepreneurs, in which they develop and implement solutions to specific social and environmental causes. Social entrepreneurship is a process that can occur in different organizational contexts, public or private, with commercial objectives defined by profit or non-profit. It is characterized by the simultaneous action of creating the public good (by identifying social problems) and the use of entrepreneurial principles to achieve a positive social change (Konda et al., 2015), thus achieving sustainable development.

Community-Based Tourism

Formal origins of community-based tourism or community tourism reach the beginning of the 1980's. CBT refers to (sustainable) tourism experiences hosted and managed by local communities. Simply put, residents invite travelers to visit or stay in their communities, which allows the travelers to connect, participate and be involved with the local population living in tourism destinations. For Cox (2009), CBT corresponds to tourism development based on a socio-organizational model and process that favors the ancestry and participation of indigenous, peasant and/or urban communities. According to UNWTO (2021), CBT "offers visitors a unique opportunity to meet locals, experience and learn about local culture, ways of life and natural environment – through locals. Their activities are usually led by the community of local guides and members of the host family." The main objective of CBT is to reduce poverty in small communities through the exploration of different types of tourism: ecotourism, experience tourism and cultural tourism.

Community-based tourism follows a self-management model as an alternative to the existing hierarchical models (Roveri, 2019). The relevance of CBT can be analyzed from different perspectives. As Roveri (2019) has pointed out, this type of tourism management goes against the flow of normalized mass tourism in today's society, aiming to strengthen the ties between the local population and visitors, thus contributing to the valorization of the culture of both parties. The target audience of CBT are, therefore, tourists looking for original, culturally rich and unique experiences.

It is important to emphasize that CBT is also work methodology, where the expected results are the improvement in quality of life of the people who live in the receiving community. In the position of CBT, tourism should not become the main source of local income, but should rather be an alternative income tool, bringing direct benefits to the community (Mielke & Pegas, 2013). In this way, CBT can directly contribute to sustainable local development (DLS) in five areas: economic, by generating income for the local population; ecological, by contributing to the awareness of visitors in relation to preservation of the local environment; social, by reducing socio-territorial exclusion in the community; cultural; and political, by increasing the decision-making role of the local population (Almeida & Emmendoerfer, 2022).

Gender (In)Equality

In recent decades, growing concerns about systemic gender inequalities have been addressed by policy makers, legislators and NGOs (Worsdale & Wright, 2020). The study of these inequalities contemplates their origin in several contexts; therefore, gender inequality is not considered as a homogeneous phenomenon, but rather as a set of problems that are interconnected (Sen, 2001). In a broad sense, there are four basic effects of gender inequality: health; education and employment; decision-making and leadership; and violence.

In many ways, these effects are universally present, regardless of the geographic or socio-economic context. However, for some authors, in some regions of the globe, these inequalities are more incisive. For Jayachandran (2015), for instance, the inequalities are more prominent and notable systematically in countries with a low GDP per capita. This perspective could refute the idea that the poorest countries are the only ones to suffer from gender inequality but, at the same time, it would argue that these are the poorest countries that experience its effects more sharply. Thus, in developing economies, prevalence of corruption and the extent of gender inequality is expected to be greater when compared to advanced economies (Forgues-Puccio & Lauw, 2021).

These effects, albeit in different forms and shapes, are expected to be present universally, independently from the socio-economic or geographic context. For Osmani and Sen (2003), in some regions of the globe, such as the African and Asian continents, the inequality comes to the point that it involves questions of life and death. An example of this are high mortality rates in countries in these aforementioned regions, and with greater expression in the female population. For Osmani and Sen (2003), this panorama can be related to difficulties in women's access to some resources and less attention and health care as compared to the other gender.

School dropout and consequent difficult access to education is greater, resulting in a lower competitiveness of women in the labor market. In a still patriarchal society, the role of women remains centered on domestic work, focusing on motherhood and informal caretaking. According to the 2020 Sustainable Development Goals Report, women spend three times more hours as caregivers and on unpaid domestic work than men (UN, 2020). Whether in the public or private sector, discrimination regarding remuneration is still a reality, with substantial wage differences related to gender (Forgues-Puccio & Lauw, 2021).

The representation of women in leadership and decision-making positions is also uneven in several public administration institutions, which poses further challenges for public policies in many countries (Johnston, 2018). Globally, women only represent 25% of national parliament members and 36% of local governments (UN, 2020). Johnston (2018) also argues that there are specific barriers in the labor market and for gender parity, such as discrimination, prejudice, harassment, gender role stereotypes, conflicts between personal life and work, organizational culture, to name a few.

Women's empowerment is influenced by international tourism indicators and since these indicators are presented in a general way, they lack specific references to women's conditions. That is why it is appropriate to stand up for tourism indicators from financial intermediaries who implicate women's empowerment in CBT (Nassani et al., 2019).

Violence remains present in women's lives, and can be physical, sexual or psychological and, in countries with a lower GDP per capita, it has a particular impact on two phenomena: early marriage in childhood, and female genital mutilation, both violations of the basic human rights. Upsettingly, while covered by the 2020 Sustainable Development Goals Report, violence against women has actually worsened with the Covid-10 pandemic. According to this report, the number of cases of domestic violence has further increased by 30%, due to confinement and greater family involvement (UN, 2020). As violence against women is an obvious violation of human rights, Goldblatt (2019) emphasizes women's right to life, dignity, physical integrity and autonomy, as well discusses how violence and fear prevent women from having access to health care, education, employment and financial resources, returning to Sen's (2001) idea that these problems are interrelated to a high degree, which can be compared to a "snowball effect". Although poverty is not a direct cause of violence, for Goldblatt (2019), it increases women's vulnerability and has an impact on their access to mechanisms of support and capacity to mitigate the effects.

National governments and international organizations have made several commitments in regard to gender equality, such as the Convention on the Elimination of All Forms of Discrimination against Women (CEDAW), the Beijing Declaration and Platform for Action and the Agenda for Sustainable Development, with the fifth SDG, which is the main focus of this work. All these commitments are fundamental for developing and sustaining a fair society. The problem of gender inequality is not limited to the female gender, but it represents a societal and economic cost, thus also harming men (Osmani & Sem, 2003) in general.

Gender Equality and Tourism

In 2010, the first Global Report on Women in Tourism was published and was considered a pioneering report in the study of the presence of women in tourism. In its second edition, launched in 2019, the report emphasized the correlation between gender equality, various thematic goals and the SDGs (UNWTO, 2019). Its main areas of study and thematic objectives were employment, entrepreneurship, leadership, education and community. In this report, UNWTO has recognized the role of tourism in achieving the 2030 Agenda, especially the fifth SDG – gender equality and female empowerment without leaving anyone behind.

At an academic level, the number of studies on gender equality and tourism has increased in terms of 'gender', 'tourism' and 'sustainable development' topics, with a notable agreement that the tourism sector contributes to achieve gender equality and fosters women's empowerment (Ramos et al., 2021). For Alarcón (2018), studying and analyzing tourism from a gender perspective helps consolidate the sector's role in sustainable development. Legitimizing women in tourism, especially in places where tourism is the main economic activity, allows for giving them the power to decide on economic, social and environmental aspects related to the sector, as well as improving their legal, relational, cultural, social and economic position in the community. Moreover, according to McCall & Mearns (2021), "SDG 5, related to the empowerment of women, can be achieved through economic empowerment, which, in turn, allows women to socially empower the communities in which they operate" (p. 157).

According to the European Institute for Gender Equality, tourism assists gender equality in a number of ways, such as the creation of employment, promoting performance and participation of women in the community's life and increasing access to resources as well as women's economic empowerment (EIGE, 2018). Especially if one looks at the statistics of the sector compared to the others (UNWTO, 2019), tourism seems to be an engine of equality. For example, in terms of employability, 54% of positions in the sector are occupied by women, while, in the general economy, only 39% of women are employed. Also, in terms of remuneration, women in tourism earn 14.7% less than men, however, in the case of the general economy, this number is higher (16.0%), showing a less accentuated wage gap in the tourism sector. Finally, in terms of female representation in leadership and decision-making positions, 23% of tourism ministries are chaired by women compared to an average of 20.7% of other ministries worldwide (UNWTO, 2019).

Methodology

The methodology used to carry out the empirical component of this chapter was qualitative. Specifically, in the first stage, a literature review of articles, reports, books, and digital documents and platforms was carried out with the objective to collect relevant sources and establish the background of the study. In the second stage of the study, case studies (associations, companies and organizations related to community-based tourism) were selected and analyzed. The entities were selected with the following inclusion criteria:

- Entities in different organizational contexts, as long as women are in evidence.
- Entities whose activity is inserted in some way or contributes to the tourism sector.
- Entities inserted in rural contexts and with a strong focus on the community (in order to frame CBT).
- Entities in different geographical contexts (for example, on different continents).

The analysis also allowed for mapping the relationships between the bibliographic review and the selected case studies. The approach used by the researchers can be considered exploratory, descriptive and comparative.

RESULTS

Case 1: Maggie's Tours e Dare Women's Foundation

Although they are two different entities, Maggie's Tours (MT) and Dare Women's Foundation (DWF) have the same founder and follow the same principles of social entrepreneurship. Initially, Maggie Simbeye founded DWF in 2005, an NGO working exclusively with female target audience in Tanzania. In 2008, Maggie began her career as a tourist guide in Tanzanian safaris and, having realized that she was one of the very few female guides, she founded the African Women's Stories and Tour Company (better known as Maggie's Tours) and established a commitment with the local community (the organization is not an NGO), especially women (Maggie's Tour Company, 2021).

In Tanzania, a country whose main economic activity of the population is agriculture (mostly because of the lack of other possibilities), poverty is still associated with rurality. Although over the last 25 years, the inequality in access to education and distribution of wealth has been decreasing, the question of equality, in the economic sphere, gender, employability, among others, continues to be a great challenge in the country (Maliti, 2018). In this sense, the presence of NGOs in Tanzania is not unknown either unexpected, especially those that aim to empower women.

In tourism, Simbeye invested in two projects with different logics, although with clear objectives of female empowerment and rural social transformation. The first of them, DWF, aims to empower women and girls and to help alleviate poverty, achieve economic empowerment and gender equality. The projects are inserted in the tourism sector and related to education for sustainability, environmental and cultural heritage conservation, entrepreneurship and micro-loans, nutritional education and access to school (Maggie's Tour Company, 2021). The second project, MT, develops commercial activity, that is, tourists can buy tours and guided tour packages led by women and local tribes. This project has also an important social aspect. At MT, women have an opportunity to receive training and mentoring to become guides, having all the support for continuous learning, supporting their emancipation, self-efficacy and autonomy, as they become sources of income for their families.

With these projects inserted in social entrepreneurship, Maggie has become an example of the spirit of a woman entrepreneur, sharing her experience, knowledge and reaching more women in the tourism sector through the entrepreneurial approach. This is a great example of how the tourism industry can evolve through female cooperation and entrepreneurship and can bring benefits that go well beyond the sector itself, and reach economic, social, and cultural dimensions, among others.

These two projects developed by Maggie are transversal and can serve as support to promote more than one SDG: they help empower local women, create employment and promote education and training; teach about sustainability, and contribute into ending poverty.

Case 2: The Empowerment of Women Involved in Tourist Activities in Arraias – Tocantins

Arraias is a municipality in the state of Tocantins, northern Brazil. Most of its population has a vulnerable financial situation, and most of the income comes from agriculture. The city offers only a few job opportunities. This generates a triple working day for women: working in the field, performing domestic work and selling products at fairs (Xavier, 2018).

This case study was presented and analyzed by Xavier (2018). The author reports that the city has two events that attract a considerable number of visitors to the municipality and where women have a substantial participation. The first event is organized by the Catholic Church, the Pilgrimage of *Nossa Senhora dos Remédios*, while the second event was created by university professors and students, and is called the Gastronomic Festival of Arraias.

The Pilgrimage of *Nossa Senhora dos Remédios* is an event organized by the church to celebrate the patron saint's day. In practice, it is a more diversified fair, offering for sale everything from household products to clothing, and attracts a large female audience. On the other hand, there are also many women exhibitors. Therefore, the event is important for the local population as it can bring additional income and financial autonomy to the families.

In 2017, the Arraia Gastronomic Festival was created as part of the course "Gastronomy, Management and Culture" taught in the Heritage and Socio-environmental Tourism program, by one of the professors at the University of Tocantins – Arraia campus – Thamyris Andrade and her students, in partnership with the Municipality of Arraias. The main objective of this festival is to give value to regional cuisine and the fruits of the *cerrado* (local flora) and promote it. Importantly, it is also a way of preserving the culture and way of life of the local population.

The festival attracts a significant number of visitors. In its first edition, there were about 1,500 people, in the second there were about 3,500 and raised more than R$15,000.00 (Xavier, 2018). This celebration contributed significantly as an extra income for participants because, despite the event exhibitors paying a low registration fee, this amount was reverted to the awards for the best dishes of the night, all in cash and profits were 100% for each seller. At the moment, the importance of women in participating in the project is emphasized, since in its second edition (held in 2018) all awards went to women.

Arraias is still in a process of developing tourism and the contribution of women is of enormous relevance, as in addition to collaborating with the performance of festivals, they also contribute with handicrafts, gastronomy and local commerce.

Xavier (2018) argues that this project has great potential to be developed within community-based management, as all knowledge and practices come from the community itself. According to her, "to ensure the development of local tourism and unite the proposals for empowering these women, it would be necessary to apply community-based tourism as a form of involvement to seek to articulate activities to better receive visitors" (p. 34).

Finally, it is important to mention that these types of initiatives can empower those involved in an interpersonal and personal way, as well as a means to guarantee their participation in the organization and entrepreneurial aspects of the event. Cooking has always been seen by the society as a domestic task predestined to be performed solely and exclusively by women and manifestations such as these can be seen as a public demonstration of the social appreciation of this sort of work, and promote its valorization also in terms of remuneration, as well as the activity itself.

Advocating Empowerment and Gender Equality

Case 3: Female Micro Entrepreneurship Project in Rural Tourism

PCN – Persone Come Noi, is an Italian NGO based on a basis of solidarity and international cooperation with developing countries. PCN aims to contribute to make a social change so that the signs of extreme poverty, hunger, exploitation, disease, illiteracy and violations of basic rights are minimized and, subsequently, extinguished (PCN, 2021).

This organization teamed up with another NGO across borders, the Women's Organization of Cape Verde (OMCV) and together they developed the project "Support for Environmentally Sustainable Female Micro Entrepreneurship in the Scope of Rural Tourism Aiming at the Resilience of Vulnerable Sectors", which operates in Cape Verde, on the islands of Santiago, Fogo and Santo Antão, and receives financial support from the Italian Agency for Development Cooperation.

The s project aims to improve living conditions of the population in the rural areas and to empower women in the territory, in order to promote greater gender equality and environmental sustainability. So far, it has benefited more than 400 people, mostly females (Brito, 2021).

The project presents several areas of action to achieve its objectives, focusing essentially on awareness-raising actions and cleaning campaigns for the protection of the environment and the species, workshops on sustainable tourism in protected areas, qualified training of communities to provide services in rural tourist areas, obtaining spaces to receive tourists and sell local products, in order to establish partnerships with national and international agencies and tour operators (Varela, 2021).

With the creation of this project by the two non-governmental organizations, Cape Verdean can minimize the existing national socio-economic imbalance, increasing the tourist flow into the islands that are associated to the project, valuing the sustainable territory and its endemic plants, selling local products and showing their culture, in addition to defending women's rights and being able to empower them, especially in the tourism sector.

Case 4: Community Homestay Network

The Community Homestay Network (CHN) is a public company dedicated to supporting a network of homestays in Nepal in diverse communities. The company acts as an intermediary between tourists and the communities of Nepal, providing a unique experience for both, the tourist and the host. The tourist has the opportunity to be welcomed by a Nepalese family and to experience life as it is in these communities, from cooking typical dishes of the region to participating in local festivals. Host communities, on the other hand, can share their culture and landscapes with tourists, while gaining access to a sustainable income from tourism (Community Homestay Network, 2021).

The company aims to impact Nepalese communities, especially women and their families, as well as tourists themselves, in a positive way. It is clearly a n example of empowering women through tourism, especially in situations where they may be economically vulnerable. The company offers Nepalese women an opportunity to become entrepreneurs, as the vast majority of hosts are women. The CHN provides women with a salary and further training. The initiative started in 2012, with a house and a woman in Panauti (Community Homestay Network, 2021). Stays are booked through the website: www.communityhomestay.com.

According to the Community Homestay Network (2021), there are four fundamental elements of its project:

- **To Establish Valuable Partnerships:** The company creates partnerships between themselves, hosts and other entities. They offer the service from various partners and through this, these and the hosts establish a connection with each other, thus benefiting.
- **To Provide Education/Training:** Mostly, in hospitality management and English.
- **To Create an Impact on Communities:** 85% of the money invested in the company reverts to helping Nepalese communities. 20% of the 85% reverts to the community fund and is used for the development of infrastructure, scholarships, and the payment of services to volunteer teachers. The remaining 80% of those 85% reverts to the host household, both in terms of children's education, personal development, social obligations, and stable salary.
- **To Reinvest:** Participate in various loans and help communities with the development of housing construction and infrastructure.

The project is, therefore, clearly related to the sustainable development goals. It is focused on gender equality, eradication of poverty (since involved people can earn a sustainable wage) and promoting quality education (since they can receive training and learn new skills and competences), decent work and economic growth and cities and sustainable communities.

Discussion

The analyzed cases were selected on the basis of a set of criteria that would allow for framing the general scope of the study. During the analysis, some relevant properties have been identified. They are shown in Figure 1.

Figure 1. Evaluation criteria and attributes of case studies
Note ○ - present; Δ - not present; x - to be developed.

Criteria/Incidences	MT & DWT	Mulheres de Arraias	PNC & OMCV	CHN
Female participation	○	○	○	○
Rural areas and/or of low population density	○	○	○	○
Tourism setting	○	Δ	○	○
Community involvement	○	○	○	○
State presence	x	x	x	○
Entrepreneurship	○	Δ	○	○

In all the analyzed cases, female participation was present. The CBT initiatives were located and developed in rural areas or areas with low population density, and they were part of the tourist industry in some way (although their business model was not necessarily focused exclusively on this sector). A strong participation of women and local community, as well as prevalence of gender inequality in less favored areas were salient. In this context, Eusébio et al. (2014) has recognized a significant role of rural tourism in the development of these communities through the active participation in the tourism process and the positive economic impacts with several multiplier effects.

A relevant feature was the absence of the State, that is, the creation and management of these entities was carried out by local communities autonomously and in a process of self-management, as stated by Roveri (2019), a characteristic of CBT. In addition to the absence of the State, in some cases the entities had either sprung from academic organizations or community organizations (e.g., the Church), as in the case of PCN and the Women of Arraias, or they had originated from an individual entrepreneurial action of women from the local communities, as the case of DWF and CHN. Having the majority of organizations founded by women was considered a great advantage to improve gender equality, as well as female employment and empowerment, however, for public organizations and other entities to have this vision remains challenging (Freund & Hernandez-Maskivker, 2021).

An interesting phenomenon was that, in addition to these women being considered entrepreneurs, they were also responsible for training other women in their community and providing them with entrepreneurial tools. Thus, the presence of entrepreneurship in these cases can be considered both, a key activity and the value proposition for its target market. Analyzing examples of entrepreneurial women within communities is extremely enriching when having in mind increasing the entrepreneurial intentions of other women (Bastian et al., 2019).

Finally, the researchers recognize that when developing their activity in developing countries, the involved women did not enjoy the same resources. The same holds true in the case of local social entrepreneurial networks that had different structures and operating modes. In other words, resources and structures that could leverage traditional entrepreneurial ventures (Konda et al., 2015) were lacking. According to Konda et al. (2015), what differs between social and traditional entrepreneurs is mostly the radical innovation of financing, management, and marketing. In the analyzed cases, the activity is rather focused on everyday products, but it also relates to health, employment, water, education, among others.

CONCLUSION

Entrepreneurship is at the basis of the struggle against gender inequality in the tourism sector, especially in what concerns its role in financial independence and female empowerment. The cases presented and analyzed in this chapter fall within the framework of community-based tourism and demonstrate the importance of the entrepreneurial mindset, skills and activity in the development of the tourism sector, especially in rural development, and in the promotion of gender equality. The empowerment of local women, mainly through community-based tourism, results in the return of value to the community, as they reciprocate and share their achievements with others and help the rest of the local community (McCall & Mearns, 2021) move forward.

This chapter proposes that there is a clear contribution of entrepreneurship allied to tourism in the pursuit of female empowerment. This is especially evident in rural areas where, through innovation and creativity, local development and significant social transformation can be achieved. It is recommended that future studies evaluate the specific factors in the relation between entrepreneurship, other SDGs and the tourism sector. It would be particularly interesting to do that in the lens of sustainability.

REFERENCES

Alarcón, D. (2018). *Cómo elaborar un diagnóstico de género y turismo en un contexto rural*. Alba Sud.

Almeida, T., & Emmendoerfer, M. (2022). Turismo de base comunitária e desenvolvimento local sustentável: Conexões e reflexões. *Revista De Turismo Contemporâneo*, *11*(1). Advance online publication. doi:10.21680/2357-8211.2023v11n1ID29163

Bastian, B. L., Metcalfe, B. D., & Zali, M. R. (2019). Gender inequality: Entrepreneurship development in the MENA Region. *Sustainability*, *11*(22), 64–72. doi:10.3390u11226472

Brito, K. (2021, May 15). *PNC e OMCV promovem projeto ambiental e de microempreendedorismo feminino para beneficiar 400 pessoas*. Mindel Insite. https://mindelinsite.com/social/pnc-e-omcv-promovem-projeto-ambiental-e-de-microempreendedorismo-feminino-para-beneficiar-400-pessoas/

Community Homestay Network. (2021). *Community Homestay Network Nepal*. https://www.communityhomestay.com/about

Cox, J. R. (2009). *Turismo indígena y comunitario en Bolivia: Un instrumento para el desarrollo socio-económico e intercultural*. Plural Editores.

EIGE. (2018). *Tourism: Relevance of gender in the policy area*. European Institute for Gender Equality. https://eige.europa.eu/gender-mainstreaming/policy-areas/tourism

EURLex. (n.d.). *Sustainable development*. https://eur-lex.europa.eu/EN/legal-content/glossary/sustainable-development.html

Eusébio, C., Kastenholz, E., & Breda, Z. (2014). Turismo e desenvolvimento sustentável de destinos rurais: Uma visão dos stakeholders. *Revista Portuguesa de Estudos Regionais*, *36*(36), 13–21. doi:10.59072/rper.vi36.418

Figueroa-Domecq, C., de Jong, A., & Williams, A. M. (2020). Gender, tourism & entrepreneurship: A critical review. *Annals of Tourism Research*, *84*, 102980. doi:10.1016/j.annals.2020.102980

Forgues-Puccio, G. F., & Lauw, E. (2021). Gender inequality, corruption, and economic development. *Review of Development Economics*, *25*(4), 2133–2156. doi:10.1111/rode.12793

Freund, D., & Hernandez-Maskivker, G. (2021). Women managers in tourism: Associations for building a sustainable world. *Tourism Management Perspectives*, *38*, 100820. doi:10.1016/j.tmp.2021.100820

Goldblatt, B. (2019). Social and economic rights to challenge violence against women – examining and extending strategies. *South African Journal on Human Rights*, *35*(2), 169–193. doi:10.1080/02587203.2019.1615351

Hall, J. K., Daneke, G. A., & Lenox, M. J. (2010). Sustainable development and entrepreneurship: Past contributions and future directions. *Journal of Business Venturing, 25*(5), 439–448. doi:10.1016/j.jbusvent.2010.01.002

Jayachandran, S. (2015). The roots of gender inequality in developing countries. *Annual Review of Economics, 7*(1), 63–88. doi:10.1146/annurev-economics-080614-115404

Johnston, K. (2018). Women in public policy and public administration? *Public Money & Management, 39*(3), 155–165. doi:10.1080/09540962.2018.1534421

Kardos, M. Research on European Union Countries. (2012). The relationship between entrepreneurship, innovation and sustainable development. Research on European Union countries. *Procedia Economics and Finance, 3*, 1030–1035. doi:10.1016/S2212-5671(12)00269-9

Konda, I., Starc, J., & Rodica, B. (2015). Social challenges are opportunities for sustainable development: Tracing Impacts of Social Entrepreneurship Through Innovations and Value Creation. *Economic Themes, 53*(2), 211–229. doi:10.1515/ethemes-2015-0012

Koutsou, S., Notta, O., Samathrakis, V., & Partalidou, M. (2009). Women's entrepreneurship and rural tourism in Greece: Private enterprises and cooperatives. *South European Society & Politics, 14*(2), 191–209. doi:10.1080/13608740903037968

Liguori, E., & Bendickson, J. S. (2020). Rising to the challenge: Entrepreneurship ecosystems and SDG success. *Journal of the International Council for Small Business, 1*(3–4), 118–125. doi:10.1080/26437015.2020.1827900

Maggie's Tour Company. (2021). *Meet Maggie.* https://maggiestourcompany.com/introducing-maggies-tour-company/meet-maggie/

Maliti, E. (2018). Inequality in education and wealth in Tanzania: A 25-year perspective. *Social Indicators Research, 145*(3), 901–921. doi:10.100711205-018-1838-y

McCall, C. E., & Mearns, K. F. (2021). Empowering women through community-based tourism in the Western Cape, South Africa. *Tourism Review International, 25*(2), 157–171. doi:10.3727/154427221X16098837279967

Mielke, E. J. C., & Pegas, F. V. (2013). Turismo de base comunitária no Brasil. Insustentabilidade é uma questão de gestão. *Revista Turismo Em Análise, 24*(1), 170–189. doi:10.11606/issn.1984-4867.v24i1p170-189

Morozova, I. A., Popkova, E. G., & Litvinova, T. N. (2018). Sustainable development of global entrepreneurship: Infrastructure and perspectives. *The International Entrepreneurship and Management Journal, 15*(2), 589–597. doi:10.100711365-018-0522-7

Nassani, A. A., Aldakhil, A. M., Abro, M. M. Q., Islam, T., & Zaman, K. (2019). The impact of tourism and finance on women empowerment. *Journal of Policy Modeling, 41*(2), 234–254. doi:10.1016/j.jpolmod.2018.12.001

Ogamba, I. K. (2018). Millennials empowerment: Youth entrepreneurship for sustainable development. *World Journal of Entrepreneurship, Management and Sustainable Development, 15*(3), 267–278. doi:10.1108/WJEMSD-05-2018-0048

Osmani, S., & Sen, A. (2003). The hidden penalties of gender inequality: Fetal origins of ill-health. *Economics and Human Biology, 1*(1), 105–121. doi:10.1016/S1570-677X(02)00006-0 PMID:15463967

PCN. (2021). *Who We Are - Persone Come Noi*. https://www.personecomenoi.org/who-we-are-pcn-busca

Peña-Sánchez, A. R., Ruiz-Chico, J., Jiménez-García, M., & López-Sánchez, J. A. (2020). Tourism and the SDGs: An analysis of economic growth, decent employment, and gender equality in the European Union (2009–2018). *Sustainability, 12*(13), 54–80. doi:10.3390u12135480

Portales, L. (2019). Alignment of social innovation with Sustainable Development Goals. *Social Innovation and Social Entrepreneurship*, 193–204. doi:10.1007/978-3-030-13456-3_13

Ramos, D., Malta, A., & Costa, C. (2021). Uma perspetiva teórica sobre o turismo, género e objetivos de desenvolvimento sustentável. *Revista Turismo e Desenvolvimento, 2*(36), 619–629. doi:10.34624/rtd.v36i2.26034

Roveri, I. (2019). *Desenvolvimento do turismo de base comunitária no assentamento Ipanema – Iperó/SP* [Degree dissertation, Universidade Federal de São Carlos, Campus Sorocaba]. Repositório Institucional.

Samad, S., & Alharthi, A. (2022). Untangling factors influencing women entrepreneurs' involvement in tourism and its impact on sustainable tourism development. *Administrative Sciences, 12*(2), 52. doi:10.3390/admsci12020052

Sen, A. (2001). The many faces of gender inequality. *New Republic*, 35–40.

UN. (2018). *From MDGs to SDGs*. https://www.sdgfund.org/mdgs-sdgs

UN. (2020). *The Sustainable Development Goals report*. doi:10.18356/214e6642-en

UNWTO. (2019). *Global report on women in tourism* (2nd ed.)., doi:10.18111/9789284420384

UNWTO. (2021). *Community based tourism training workshop - World Tourism Day (27)*. https://www.unwto.org/node/12238

Varela, J. M. (2021). *OMCV promove workshop para apresentação da carta europeia do turismo sustentável nas áreas protegidas*. INFORPRESS. https://inforpress.cv/omcv-promove-workshop-para-apresentacao-da-carta-europeia-do-turismo-sustentavel-nas-areas-protegidas/

WCED. (1987). *Our common future*. Oxford University Press.

Worsdale, R., & Wright, J. (2020). My objectivity is better than yours: Contextualising debates about gender inequality. *Synthese, 199*(1–2), 1659–1683. doi:10.100711229-020-02835-5

Xavier, M. D. (2018). *O trabalho da mulher em Arraias: Desafios e possibilidades para o turismo* [Degree dissertation, Universidade Federal do Tocantins]. Repositório Institucional da Universidade Federal do Tocantins. https://repositorio.uft.edu.br/handle/11612/2615

ADDITIONAL READING

Bagheri, F., Ghaderi, Z., Abdi, N., & Hall, C. M. (2022). Female entrepreneurship, creating shared value, and empowerment in tourism; the neutralizing effect of gender-based discrimination. *Current Issues in Tourism*, 1–18. doi:10.1080/13683500.2022.2126749

Cole, S. (Ed.). (2018). *Gender equality and tourism: Beyond empowerment*. CABI. doi:10.1079/9781786394422.0000

Franco, I. C., Suárez, M. A., & García, A. P. (2020). Marine Tourism as an option for sustainable local development based on female empowerment. *Cuadernos de Turismo, 46*, 649–652.

Moswete, N., & Lacey, G. (2015). "Women cannot lead": Empowering women through cultural tourism in Botswana. *Journal of Sustainable Tourism, 23*(4), 600–617. doi:10.1080/09669582.2014.986488

Scheyvens, R., & van der Watt, H. (2021). Tourism, empowerment and sustainable development: A new framework for analysis. *Sustainability*, *13*(22), 12606. doi:10.3390u132212606

Tajeddini, K., Ratten, V., & Denisa, M. (2017). Female tourism entrepreneurs in Bali, Indonesia. *Journal of Hospitality and Tourism Management*, *31*, 52–58. doi:10.1016/j.jhtm.2016.10.004

Zhang, J., & Zhang, Y. (2020). Tourism and gender equality: An Asian perspective. *Annals of Tourism Research*, *85*, 103067. doi:10.1016/j.annals.2020.103067

KEY TERMS AND DEFINITIONS

Empowerment: Degree of power, autonomy and self-determination in people, organizations, and societies.

Entrepreneur: A person who operates in a financial world and takes on financial risks in the hope of profit.

Entrepreneurship: Ability to develop, organize and implement a business idea.

Gender: A socially constructed characteristic of men and women.

Inequality: An imbalanced relation between two parties. At socio-economic level refers to the situation in which resources are distributed unevenly resulting in reduced opportunities.

Poverty: A state or condition of lacking basic resources to live a healthy and safe life at, at least, minimum level.

Sustainable Development: Development that meets the needs of the present generation without compromising the same ability in future generations.

Chapter 2
Community Development Through Ecotourism:
A Stakeholder Analysis of Botevgrad, Bulgaria

Anna Daneva
University of Sunderland in London, UK

Vipin Nadda
University of Sunderland in London, UK

ABSTRACT

According to UNWTO, annual ecotourism revenues worldwide are estimated to grow from approximately $800 billion to one trillion in 2025. About 11 million people are employed in the tourism sector and related activities. The current growth of ecotourism is 10% to 12% per year and is the fastest-growing sector. The average age of travellers has become lower, and more and more young people are now interested in environmentally friendly forms of tourism. Ecotourism travellers cost less in infrastructure per income unit than any other type of tourist. In the last 30 years, no other type of tourism has generated such growth and popularity and become fundamentally important in the tourism sector and the world economy. Last year, nearly 9.5 billion tourists visited ecotourism destinations and raised awareness of the ecotourism concept and invested heavily to gain a sustainable travel experience. Currently, ecotourism is preferred by 71% of people under 30.

DOI: 10.4018/978-1-6684-6796-1.ch002

INTRODUCTION

According to Bruno (2021), annual ecotourism revenues worldwide are estimated to grow from approximately $800 billion to one trillion in 2025. The current growth of ecotourism is 10% (TIES) to 12% (UNWTO, 2021) per year and is the fastest-growing tourism industry sector. The average age of travellers has become lower, and more and more young people are now interested in environmentally friendly forms of tourism. Ecotourism travellers cost less in infrastructure per income unit than any other type of tourist. More than 90 nations are currently promoting places and events for sustainable tourism at the national or regional level. In the last 30 years, no other type of tourism has generated such growth and popularity and become fundamentally important in the tourism sector and the world economy. Last year, nearly 9.5 billion tourists visited ecotourism destinations and raised awareness of the ecotourism concept and invested heavily to gain a sustainable travel experience. Currently, ecotourism is preferred by 71% of people under 30 (Bruno, 2021).

Nowadays, following the world trends, Bulgaria develops and renews the opportunities for the successful development of ecotourism. Representative of sustainable tourism, ecotourism is a form of environmentally safe nature exploration, and its goal is to preserve nature and at the same time promote this form of tourism. It offers consumers a variety of outdoor activities such as hiking, eco-tours, climbing, cave visits, animal exploration, cultural and local customs. Bulgaria is a unique country, offering tourists incredible nature - forests, large and small rivers, lakes, beaches, caves, and thermal springs. Every tourist passionate about the beauty of nature and outdoor activities is more than welcome to come and visit this paradise. (Kitt,2020)

Statement by the Minister of Tourism Nikolina Angelkova (2020) considers the current development of ecotourism in Bulgaria as a potential opportunity to present the country on the world tourism market as "The jewel of ecotourism destinations in the Balkans." The government is currently focusing its efforts on promoting, developing, and recreating Bulgaria as an ecotourism destination and this will lead the country to annual growth in the tourism market and make it a popular representative of sustainable tourism. (The ministry of Tourism, Bulgaria, 2020)

Resources for Eco-Tourism Development in Botevgrad

Botevgrad area is in a valley with 507 sq.m, 46 km from the capital of Bulgaria, Sofia. Its strategic location is rounded out by the Vitinya pass, which connects Bulgaria's southern and northern parts. This area is famous and rich in natural resources, and the relief is known for its incredible biological diversity. The municipality includes the following features: Botevgrad valley, the foothills of Botevgrad, part of the mountain

- Ryazana Golyamata mountain, ridge and peak Murgash. There is a fillet between the Great Mountain and the Northern Balkans. The bottom of the valley is a river terrace on the river Bebresh. Murgash Peak is 1687 m and is the highest part of the mountain, located in the country's southwestern region. (Botevgrad Guide, 2019).

Geographical Location and Transport Accessibility

Botevgrad Municipality is in Northern Bulgaria. It is located at the eponymous valley with an elliptical shape in the northwest-southeast direction between the Balkan Mountains and the Fore-Balkans on an area of about 500 square kilometers. with an average altitude of 348 m. Administratively, it borders the municipalities: Pravets, Etropole, Gorna Malina, Elin Pelin, Svoge, Mezdra and Roman, the first two of which are established destinations on the map of Bulgarian tourism. The municipality consists of 13 settlements - the municipal center Botevgrad and twelve villages: Bozhenitsa, Vrachesh, Gurkovo, Elovdol, Kraevo, Lipnitsa, Litakovo, Novachene, Radotina, Rashkovo, Skravena and Trudovets.

Geological Features

Botevgrad is in the Botevgrad Valley - a natural depression in the Western Fore-Balkans, located between the mountains Bilo and Murgash to the south, Golema Mountain to the southwest and Rzhana Mountain to the northwest, which are part of the Western Stara Planina. This flat-valley relief passes in the periphery to the steep surrounding slopes, which is a favorable prerequisite for the development of hiking and cycling.Of the landforms, caves are important for tourism. In the municipality of Botevgrad more than 50 caves have been studied near the villages of Skravena, Novachene, Bozhenitsa and Lipnitsa, most of which are up to 12 m long and do not have interesting formations.

Climatic Resources

The Botevgrad valley belongs to the temperate-continental climatic region. The average annual temperature is about 12.6 ° C, with rainfall - between 750 and 1000 mm. The annual maximum of the daily precipitation amounts is 128.5 mm during the summer season, and the minimum - in the winter months. Traditionally for the valleys in Bulgaria and here during the winter season temperature inversions are often observed, which leads to the formation of fog and ice. This state of the climate is not particularly favorable for tourist visits to the valley area during the summer and winter months.

Water Basins

The Botevgrad valley is drained by the Bebresh River and its tributaries for 46 km. The river springs 1 km northwest of Zvezdets peak in the Etropole Mountains, at 1,430 m above sea level. Next to the village of Vrachesh it flows in a deep wooded valley between the mountains Bilo to the northeast and Murgash to the southwest, after which it enters the Botevgrad valley. In the territory of the village of Novachene it turns sharply to the east, crosses the ridge Gola glava of the Fore-Balkans through the Novachena gorge, passes under the village of Bozhenitsa through a picturesque canyon, suitable as a site for rock climbing, to flow a little further into the river Malki Iskar.

Surface and groundwater are rain-snow fed and depend on the climatic conditions. In the municipality of Botevgrad has a dam "Bebresh" - in the village of Vrachesh, which is used mainly for water supply to the population, but is also subject to fishing: catfish, pike, perch, white fish, rainbow trout, bleak, carp, maple and caracuda. The much smaller Mali Lag Dam was used for sport fishing, was a suburban recreation area, and operated a campsite, but now these opportunities to attract tourists have disappeared. The most suitable for fishing are Bebresh Dam and the river of the same name in the village of Bozhenitsa. Objects of catch are perch, white and black (Balkan) barbel, maple (river mullet), skobar, ukley, common melon, caracuda. Rainbow trout, European catfish and pike are more difficult to catch and rare.

Protected Areas

In the municipality of Botevgrad there are 1 maintained reserve, 6 protected areas and 2 natural landmarks: the maintained reserve "School Forest" is on the land of the village of Bozhenitsa. It was declared to protect natural oak forests. A total of 62 species of birds can be observed during the nesting period on the territory of the reserve, including: white and black stork, osprey, great hawk, common buzzard, red-breasted kestrel, orc falcon and peregrine falcon, and many others.

The protected areas are:

1. "Dreneto" is located on the land of the village of Litakovo. It was created to protect natural meadows and oak forests. The area is also of ornithological interest, as there are regularly about 28 nests of herons and about 14 of storks.
2. "Muhalnitsa" or "Frog Swamp", as it is known among the local population, is located on the land of the town of Botevgrad in the villa zone Zelin. It was declared to protect the swamp and its adjacent territories and is known for the unique worldwide migration of the mountain frog Rana temporaria.

3. "Urvich" in the land of the village of Bozhenitsa near the fortress Bozhenishki Urvich. It was established as a forest park and declared to protect oak seed forests. There is a preserved group of ancient trees on the territory.
4. "Rudinata" in the land of the town of Botevgrad, where centuries-old beech forests are preserved.

Landmarks:

1. "Elaka" – for protection of centuries-old beech forests and rock formations in the land of the village of Vrachesh,
2. "Water furnace" – for protection of bats and characteristic formations in the land of the village of Lipnitsa. Without the status of a natural landmark, but attractive enough are the Bear Holes (rocks) in the village of Novachene.

The chapter includes research of the ecotourism potential of Botevgrad municipality and the possibilities for the attractiveness of offering of ecotourism products. The region presents various options for available development opportunities related to the extraction and use of natural resources from protected areas. Based on the findings, specific proposals for new ecotourism products are presented, contributing to the transformation of the Municipality of Botevgrad into an attractive tourist destination and the sustainable development of the local community. The territory has not been studied in detail in terms of natural resources and protected areas. That requires individual studies of biodiversity in the region and field studies and studies of good practices in the country and abroad to prepare for the practical implementation of specific proposals for ecotourism development (The ministry of Tourism, Bulgaria, 2020).

Although the tourism industry is constantly growing, this growth does not always positively impact destinations and their resources. On the one hand, the increased influx of tourists can endanger the ecosystem and natural resources in one place. The high number of visitors could have a negative impact on nature. Another disadvantage of mass tourism is that a small part of the tourism revenue is invested locally, despite the significant financial turnover (Stefanov, Petrov & Alexova, 2018). It is essential to examine awareness of ecotourism to measure the impact on the environment and how sensitive the local economy is to it. That means that the legal ecotours might not increase the revenue of the multinational companies but will help the local population. For that reason, tourism research is essential to research and how they affect local communities, both humans and natural resources.

MAIN DISCUSSION

The tourism industry is the fastest growing and most important area of financial income for institutions and enterprises in the world (Singh, 2010). Thus, with the steady progress of the tourism industry, countries seeking instruments for financial improvement continue to increase their interest in the tourism industry. Before the official coronavirus epidemic, tourist arrivals worldwide were just over 630 million for international visitors in 2019 (Oxford Economics, 2020). This number of visitors has dropped dramatically since the beginning of the pandemic.

Attempts to define tourism most often include visits to certain places for sightseeing, vacations and weekends (Goeldner and Ritchie, 2009). However, they do not exhaust the characteristics of tourism, as the definition may include trips related to conferences or other business or professional activities, as well as those that take a study trip under expert guidance or to perform some kind of research or studies. Tourism, as an element of leisure time, involves the movement of people away from their usual place of residence, i.e., it can also be defined as a process that usually requires some costs, although this is not mandatory. It is possible to do tourism without incurring costs such as camping, where everyone brings their own food and may not contribute to the economy of the area in which they travel, but can still be considered a tourist. There are many other examples in which the costs of the tourist are minimal. According to Holloway (2009) tourism is an aspect of leisure that usually, but not necessarily, brings some income to the local community.

Among the most common definitions of the tourism industry is the United Nations Conference on Trade and Development. It is defined as "a set of productive, non-productive and commercial activities which create goods and services intended wholly or partly for consumption by foreign or domestic visitors" (UNCTAD, 1972).

According to Evans, Campbell, and Stonehouse (2003), the five major components of the tourism industry are as follows: accommodation of tourists; landmarks; transportation; travel organizers; destination organizations.

Given the above definitions and approaches, it can be concluded that tourism is an activity composed of those who offer tourist services and those who require tourist services and have the desire and ability to pay for them. In this sense, the tourism industry can be considered as a specific business activity that is related to the supply and demand at the same time and in the same place, of specific products and services. For the purposes of this study, we assume that the scope of the tourism industry includes all manufacturing and non-manufacturing organizations involved in the service of tourists or producing goods consumed by them.

According to the UNWTO (2015), there are three basic forms of tourism: domestic tourism, inbound tourism, and outbound tourism. The tourism activities are classified according to different criteria such as: origin and nationality of tourists; the purpose of the trips and nature of tourist activities; socio-demographic characteristics of tourists; location preference; nature of activity; duration of trip and distance travelled; product, etc. (IRTS 2008). According to the tourist product, there are two main types of tourism: mass tourism (package tour) and alternative tourism (ecotourism) (IRTS 2008).By nature of the activity, there are: Active tourism: (Adventure tourism, Ecotourism,Golf etc.) and Passive tourism:(Sightseeing, Beach holiday and cruise etc. (IRTS 2008). By location preference there are: coastal tourism; city tourism; rural tourism; mountain's tourism, etc. (IRTS 2008). According to duration of trip and distance travelled tourism activities are classified into the following categories: day trip; weekend break; annual holiday etc.

THE CONCEPT OF ECO-TOURISM

Ecotourism is a tourism activity that develops without changing the balance of the environment and seeks to avoid damage to nature. This is a trend that aims to make the tourism industry compatible with the environment.

In the early 1970s, first the environmental, and later the social and economic problems caused by tourism in developed destinations, led to a more balanced attitude towards the tourism industry. The view that excessive pressure on the environment reduces its attractiveness and leads to an inevitable decline in tourism development has gained popularity. The concept of recreational capacity, based on the notion that the growth of tourism must comply with the permissible load limits (environmental, social and economic), beyond which its negative effects are beginning to manifest itself in destinations, has become crucial. The question of the industry's long-term interest in sparing the resources on which it prospers has become increasingly widespread. An idea for development aimed not at maximizing growth and profits, but at environmental and humanitarian needs has emerged (de Kadt, 1979).

In the 1980s, the main focus gradually shifted from the tourism industry and tourists to an environment where tourism is an environmentally sustainable and socially responsible industry. Numerous concepts have been formulated aimed at launching such forms of tourism that will bring the greatest benefit to the local population, tourists and the tourism industry, while causing the least possible environmental and social burdens - "soft tourism", "smart tourism"," responsible tourism ", etc. (Getz, 1986). In the 1980s, the important role of tourism policy and planning as a means of managing a rapidly changing industry and directing its development in the right direction was widely accepted. Along with the traditional economic approach, environmental and socio-cultural approaches have begun to be applied, taking into account the impacts of tourism on the natural and social environment in destinations (Gunn, 1988).

Since the beginning of the 1990s, the need for an integrated approach to tourism planning and policy, aimed at "fitting" tourism into the general framework of socio-economic development at all levels, has been increasingly emphasized (Churchill, 1995). The tourism industry itself has changed dramatically in the late twentieth century under the influence of these ideas and new public attitudes and trends in demand. The growing concern of tourists about the environment, the increased interest in healthy recreation, cultural and historical sites and close contact with the local population in tourist destinations, give reason to define "greening" as one of the most characteristic features of tourist demand since the mid 80's (Gunn, 1988). Its manifestation is associated with new models of tourist behavior and new requirements for the tourist product. The industry responded to these trends by proposing new forms of tourism, alternative to the mass ones - ecological, green, rural, adventure, etc.

Entrepreneurs in tourism gradually realized their long-term interest in tourism development, resource-saving and tolerant of the environment in the broadest sense. A number of tourism companies have adopted the idea that in tourism "ecology is a long-term economy" and consider the protection of the natural and social environment as a factor in increasing competitiveness and long-term investment (Churchill, 1995). From this brief review of the evolution of concepts of tourism development and their practical dimensions, it can be concluded that they are changing in parallel with the processes that took place in the 70s and 80s at all levels in the scientific, political and social spheres and led to the formulation of the general concept of sustainable development and in particular the concept of ecotourism in the late 1980s.

Many authors associate the concept of ecotourism with the Mexican ecologist Hector Ceballos-Lascurrain, who coined the term in the 1980s. He defined ecotourism as:

tourism that consists in travelling to relatively undisturbed or uncontaminated natural areas with the specific object of studying, admiring and enjoying the scenery and its wild plants and animals, as well as any existing cultural manifestations (both past and present) found in these areas (Ceballos-Lascurain, 1987).

Butler (1992) formulated the basic principles of eco-tourism, namely:

1. It must be consistent with a positive environmental ethic, fostering preferred behaviour.
2. It does not denigrate the resource. There is no erosion of resource integrity.
3. It concentrates on intrinsic rather than extrinsic values.
4. It is biocentric rather than homocentric in philosophy, in that an ecotourist accepts nature largely on its terms, rather than significantly transforming the environment for personal convenience.

5. Ecotourism must benefit the resource. The environment must experience a net benefit from the activity, although there are often spin-offs of social, economic, political, or scientific benefits.
6. It is first-hand experience with the natural environment.
7. There is, in ecotourism, an expectation of gratification measured in appreciation and education, not in thrill-seeking or physical achievement. These latter elements are consistent with adventure tourism, the other division of natural environment (wildland) tourism.
8. There are high cognitive (informational) and effective (emotional) dimensions to the experience, requiring a high level of preparation from both leaders and participants.

Ecotourism was officially characterized as a type of tourism industry in the 1980s (Parks, 2006; Page and Dowling, 2002). From that moment on, ecotourism is constantly growing and benefits local communities that general tourism cannot.

Ecotourism is defined as the responsible travel of visitors or tourists to areas with natural habitats for environmental protection and provides sustainable protection in the interests of residents (Jones, 2005). Through ecotourism, the tourist area of interest can create professions, provide protection against the climate, and reduce pollution.

Ecotourism first appeared in the mid-1990s and soon became a well-known method in the tourism industry. From that point on, it became a much more advanced concept in the application, especially in parallel development to the awareness of the need to protect the environment from pollution (Briedenhann and Wickens, 2004). Although this is anything but a well-known method of travel, it took a long time to expand the scope of the ecotourism industry. In any case, with growing concerns about our natural impact, ecotourism can continue to be seen as a more significant industry in 2018 (Tseng, 2019). It enables visitors and residents of tourist areas to have more open positions, ensure their regular risk-free habitat, and reduce poverty.

The World Tourism Organization (UNWTO) defines tourism activities aimed at monitoring natural resources, wildlife, and fauna on two levels:

1. Nature-friendly tourism, which aims to reflect "forms of tourism in which the main motivation of the tourist is the observation and aesthetic perception of nature" (Fotiadis, 2009).
2. Ecotourism, which is used to denote forms of tourism with the following characteristics: all forms of nature tourism, where the primary motivation of tourists is the observation and perception of nature and traditional cultures typical of natural areas; has an educational and interpretive character (related to the specific perception and understanding); usually organized, but not always,

by specialized tour operators for small groups; partners providing services in tourist places are generally at the level of their own small business; minimizes the negative impacts on the natural and socio-cultural environment, helps maintain the natural areas used to attractions in ecotourism such as:

a. Generates economic benefits for the host societies, organizations and bodies managing natural areas for nature protection.
b. Provides alternative employment and income opportunities for local communities.
c. Raises awareness of the protection of natural and cultural values, both among local people and tourists (Fotiadis, 2009).

In the context of sustainable development, ecotourism is seen as a "responsible journey to natural areas that protect the environment and improve the well-being of local people" (TIES, 2019). From that definition, ecotourism takes place in a natural environment and, at the same time, seeks to change it as less as possible. At the same time, the business aims to support the local population. That creates a scheme for sustainable development with minimal use of resources and at the same time investing in their protection.

According to the International Society for Ecotourism (TIES), those who carry out and participate in ecotourism activities must adhere to the following principles:

- Minimize the impact.
- Building environmental and cultural awareness and respect.
- Providing positive experiences for both visitors and hosts.
- Providing direct financial benefits for conservation.
- Providing financial benefits and empowering local people.
- Increasing the sensitivity to the host countries' political, environmental, and social climate.

According to the International Union for Conservation of Nature (IUCN), ecotourism is an "environmentally responsible visit to relatively unspoilt natural areas to enjoy and appreciate nature (and all the accompanying cultural features - both past and present), which promotes conservation. low negative impact on visitors and ensures favorable active socio-economic participation of the local population". (Hector, 1996).

The essential elements that are emphasized in both definitions are: minimizing the negative impacts on the natural and socio-cultural environment, generating economic benefits for local communities, and protecting the environment by creating employment, raising awareness among tourists and local people, implementing the concept of protected areas, inside and out, addressing sustainability and capacity issues. An essential element that distinguishes ecotourism is the educational and interpretive elements.

The main characteristics that determine ecotourism are:

- Actively contributes to the protection of the natural and cultural heritage, has a minimal negative impact on the environment (natural and socio-cultural) environment and provides an opportunity for conservation and sustainable use of nature.
- Engages local communities and contributes to increasing their well-being, provides alternative employment and additional income, brings income for nature protection.
- Provides information to tourists about the natural and cultural heritage, has an educational and interpretive character.
- It is more suitable for individual tourists and organized small groups - most often specialized tour operators participate in its organization, and representatives of their own small business provide tourist services in the tourist place.

STAKEHOLDER ANALYSIS AND THE ROLE OF ECOTOURISM IN COMMUNITY DEVELOPMENT

According to Uran and Juvan (2010),

The stakeholders in tourism destination are: local residents, local companies, media, employees, government, competitors, tourists, business associations, activists and tourism developers.

TOUR OPERATORS AS STAKEHOLDERS

Tour operators specializing in ecotourism base their activities on nature conservation and community support in the respective places. In addition, they seek to convey this to consumers through their marketing and advertising activities. They are small companies with a small advertising budget, targeting targeted advertising channels, such as special fairs, trade fairs and advertisements in specialized magazines. Groups with similar interests such as environmental organizations, organizations for the so-called responsible tourism. Over the last decade, a new kind of cooperation has emerged around the idea of "fair tourism". The British NGO Travindy developed the International Fair-Trade Network. The European Charter for Fair and Sustainable Tourism is based on the principle of "fair trade" and calls for:

- Mutually beneficial and equal cooperation with local communities and service providers.
- Fair pay and good working conditions.
- Development of local business run by local people, good management positions. (European Charter for Sustainable and Responsible Tourism)

Most ecotourism trips are made as part of a nature vacation. Tour operators classify "being in pristine nature" and "observing wildlife" as critical elements of an ecotourism trip. The characteristic qualities of the landscape, the preserved environment, the national parks are also indicated as necessary. The cultural component is essential as nature and culture are strongly linked. "Meetings with local people", "to get acquainted with cultural traditions and local life", "discovery of local products and cuisine" are part of ecotourism tours and are second only to the component related to nature. Sports activities and tourism are also mentioned as part of the motivation for undertaking tourist excursions in nature.

There are various tourist excursions such as tourism and mountaineering and observing wildlife, fauna, and flora. Other special tours are also available in relatively smaller quantities. British and German operators have developed special excursions on interests such as ornithology, national parks, and conservation. In France, Italy and Spain, tour operators remain with a generalized profile. Ecotourism excursions are based on mixed programs that offer sports activities or cultural events related to nature. There is also a growing importance of other niche markets related to nature tourism, such as agritourism in Italy and rural tourism in Spain. There are already established tour operators in Bulgaria focused on offering ecotourism: responsible attitude towards the environment, the so-called "cause trips", in which part of the revenue is generated for nature protection, "Penguin Travel", "Spacia Tours". "Pandion", "Odyssey-In" - aimed at organized foreign groups, mountain tourism and more.

Tour operators significantly influence the main components of the tourist product, both in quantitative and qualitative terms. They determine the routes, travel periods, range, standards and quality parameters of the product. They also ensure the functioning of the routes, organize advertising, calculate and determine the prices of travel agencies. During the preparation and implementation of the tourist route, the tour operators enter into various contracts with carriers, hoteliers, restaurateurs, services and enterprises for tourist and excursion services and others involved in the process of implementation of the tourist route.

GOVERNMENT AND LOCAL BUSINESS AS STAKEHOLDERS

Global demand for tourism, in general, is focused on the market for more diverse, complex, and complementary products. There is a growing demand for non-traditional tourist services and types of tourism other than mass tourism. According to the UNWTO, 65-70% of the UK, Germany, the Netherlands, and the Nordic countries need tourism. (Trends in tourism of the European Union. 2020).

In Bulgaria, the development of tourism still does not correspond to the country's natural, historical, and cultural realities. There are difficulties in selling tourist products for specialized types of tourism, including ecotourism in the open world market. That is why consumption is still focused on domestic tourism. Favorably reflected are the tendencies for diversification and improvement of the material base, striving for prolongation of the tourist season and increasing the quality of the service. There is a desire to win positions in many European countries. Russia and Ukraine have the most significant market shares in Germany, followed by Greece, the United Kingdom, Russia, Israel, Sweden, Poland, the Czech Republic, Slovakia, Ukraine, and Denmark.

The weak competitiveness of the Bulgarian market is due to external and internal factors, mainly related to planning: lack of a working strategy for ecotourism development at the national level, project financing and lack of coherence, lack of commitment from local authorities. Some of the reasons for the unsuccessful outcome of ecotourism performance are:

1. The government lack appropriate investment orientation
2. Poor infrastructure and organization of public transport in the remote regions of the country,
3. About 90% of the employees are without the necessary qualification,
4. Deteriorating age structure of the population in ecotourism destinations,
5. Lack of specialized centers for tourist information, limited financial opportunities,
6. Limited range of tourist products and services are offered, weak advertising on the foreign market,
7. Lack of marketing strategy for issuing specialized advertising materials, most of which do not meet the requirements of tourists.
8. Lack of information leads to short stays and loss of customers.

Ecotourists love nature, but their expectations for such trips are not limited to being in nature and observing wildlife, but a general desire for change and a specific desire to experience the culture and way of life of local people. From the point of view of most customers, ecotourism routes should not be entirely dominated by eco-activities, but on the contrary - should be accompanied by cultural and other activities, especially sports. Wildlife monitoring is considered the most common activity among nature-oriented tourism internationally, but only 10-15% of ecotourists are bird watchers with significant knowledge or experience and expect more specific services (Chatzigeorgiou, Simelli & Tsagaris, 2015). Most tourists want to watch adorable animals or have other exciting adventures in a beautiful natural environment without special knowledge or skills.

There are challenges in developing and marketing an ecotourism product-too many products fail. Some ecotourism products fail due to unprofitability because of lack of market response, lack of a good business plan, and reasonable feasibility assessment. Other possible reasons might be difficulties accessing the market for small businesses and local community products and the quality of the tourist experience and care for the environment. Visitors' contribution to natural areas to local communities and environmental protection may be more significant. However, society is not yet aware of or interested in the problems of sustainable development.

About these challenges, Government can identify the following priority areas for action:

- Creation of appropriate structures for joint work in developing and marketing ecotourism products.
- Pre-connect products and markets and supply and demand through better understanding and access to markets.
- Paying attention to all aspects of product quality to reconcile market interests with sustainable development goals.
- Adequate support for those communities and businesses that need technical assistance. The local government should do that at the local level and according to the local community's needs.
- Greater publicity of messages and products in ecotourism. There is still work to be done globally and locally to make ecotourism a concept and facilitate consumer access to the product.

Local communities, private sector enterprises, NGOs, local authorities and protected areas, national governments, and international agencies have a role in developing ecotourism and its marketing and are invited to work closely together. Ecotourism includes new techniques in the following areas: package development and pricing; agreements with local partners; arranging tours; negotiating with clients; leading groups (Ribeiro, & Ferreira, & Silva, 2011).

Ecotourism marketing has several characteristics that must be considered when developing ecotourism strategies, plans and programs, namely:

- Increasing the abundance of new products in most markets makes consumers more demanding in what they want.
- The success of marketing strategies is related to the degree of satisfaction, not the number of sales.
- Effective market sharing is key to identifying the right ecotourism users.
- There is a strong link between inclusion in tourist travel and the provision of information.
- Market research in the form of advertising is more likely to attract consumers to reach a decision based on the target market's characteristics.
- The increase of groups united by common interests, particularly of various environmental organizations, creates an opportunity for direct marketing.
- Creating solid ideas that are a realistic reflection of the product is extremely useful for review.
- It is first necessary to determine the exact allowable load and then decide on marketing strategies.
- Pricing is more demand-oriented than supply-oriented. Selection of target markets and target niches by announcing promotions.
- Sensitivity to the environment by tourists and tour operators.

Concerning advertising and information channels, the "oral recommendation" is emerging as one of the most fundamental ways of transmitting information to ecotourism operators. The Internet and online sales are increasingly being used for advertising purposes. The fact that eco-tour operators are small companies with a small advertising budget is considered, so they focus on targeted channels for advertising purposes, such as special fairs, trade fairs and ads in professional magazines. Groups with similar interests, such as environmental organizations, organizations for the so-called responsible tourism and the development of ecotourism, have a small advertising role in Bulgaria and Europe.

LOCAL COMMUNITY AS A STAKEHOLDER

Local job vacancies are just one of the benefits of ecotourism. In addition to receiving income for organizations working in ecotourism destinations, it also allows them to gain preparatory skills. Employees can move them to different work areas to use the local site. For example, ecotourism in South Africa accelerates financial development by creating professions and affecting relatives in mechanical support (Kakar, 2018). That directly contributes to the political and monetary strengthening of close networks. Ecotourism in South Africa creates more than $ 8 billion a year and 5,000 positions. The benefits of ecotourism extend to various means of travel, such as aeroplanes, cafes, accommodation and the general framework.

Pennsylvania, for example, expands so many employment opportunities through ecotourism (Mooney, 2018). Today, guests spend nearly $ 1.8 billion each year in Pennsylvania's wildlife tourism areas. In another case, countries such as Indonesia use ecotourism to transfer much of the trade links to nearby globalized networks, especially for the city and local travel agencies (Tshomo, 2018). In the future, more than 90% of households say that ecotourism has supported the local area with financial investments allocated to areas in need. Considering the camp tourism, almost 90% of the respondents in the survey stated that the covered regions had benefited significantly from the improvement caused by ecotourism development. Therefore, these advances can ensure that people in local areas can get more business opportunities from ecotourism. However, there is an established stagnation resulting from COVID-19 in progress, as pointed out by Buckley (2020).

The ecotourism industry helped improve the local community in countries such as the United States, Indonesia, China, and other areas such as Scotland, which is also the focus of this research proposal. The last aspect that has been improved by tourism development is poverty. In Indonesia, for example, the local government supports the development of camps which is a source of income for the locals. (Tshomo, 2018). Zhemgang and Paro have the highest incomes, earning more than $ 300,000 a year.

That example was followed by household groups from Wangdu, Timfu and Luence, with annual salaries ranging from $ 6.8 million to about $ 13.8 million. In addition, the total payment for these areas is about 18.8 million and is increasing. The covering regions have benefited economically in terms of business development, job creation, office improvement and progress, and the development of the framework. Ecotourism invests in people's everyday environment in countries actively implementing it. For example, in the wilds of Pennsylvania, the area is poor before ecotourism appearance. Through ecotourism, the local Government attracts many tourists and improves the financial turnover through ecotourism developments and organization of events (Mooney, 2018).

Many people with minor financial support live in rural areas on their land. (Hakim, Siswanto and Makagoshi, 2017). Such land is often considered biologically delicate. However, more than 16 million people live in South Africa, and ten of them need more income because there is not enough rural land to use as a source of food and potential revenue. For these people, ecotourism offers a realistic chance to earn money and support their families (Kakar, 2018). Therefore, more people can use the land for agriculture growth in rural areas. Ensuring sound use of the environment and strengthening biological cycles will broaden the guidelines for work and play in agriculture. Through these changes, people in local areas have more income and have a better lifestyle.

ENVIRONMENTALISTS AS STAKEHOLDERS

Ecotourism provides common areas and improves environmental aspects such as thick forests, minerals, and rural lands (Cengiz and Çalışkan, 2009). Regular promotion of these assets means changing or destroying untamed housing and excellent ordinary scenes and networks to boost their economy without harming the local and national environment, as Wondirad, Tolkach and King (2020) noted.

In general, the goal is to turn the territorial dream of the tourism industry to zero in terms of ecotourism resources, and interestingly, the company provides the climate. Second, ecotourism in nations like Scotland allows neighboring and unfamiliar tourists to perceive Scotland's common heritage (Kakar, 2018). According to Adom (2019), there is no uncertainty about the effect of ecotourists on the climate. In particular, the author emphasizes that climate impacts have financial benefits for countries such as Ghana. Their trend attracts many travel agents, making them more aware of the need to ensure that tourists do not harm ecological areas. In the same way, different countries, such as Indonesia, provide their impeccable climate (Tshomo, 2018). About 95% of households worldwide agree that the payment made by the family has helped the local population acquire various sources of income and has seen the improvement of rich practices and culture, just like improving the security of the environment and this protection.

Ecotourism in Botevgrad, Bulgaria

Given the requirement of ecotourism to offer a highly individualized product in areas with preserved natural resources, the diverse nature of Bulgaria gives it several advantages compared to the more industrialized regions of Europe. The country offers mainly hikes and mountain tourism, excursions of interest for wildlife observation and less often tours related to speleology, extreme experiences and more. An interesting eco-tourist product is the many marked trails in mountainous, semi-mountainous and flat-hilly places. A comparative novelty for Bulgaria is the ecological paths built with natural materials in an attractive natural environment with a high degree of biological diversity.

A valuable resource for developing ecological tourism and an opportunity to diversify the tourist product is the nature protection centres, specialized in research and protection of rare species, informing about the natural diversity and tourist routes, conducting training programs. Botevgrad Municipality has no traditions in the field of tourism. The tourism services sector is not developed according to national proportions, at the expense of a well-functioning economy with an industrial-agrarian structure. The well-being and standard of living of the population have a significant impact on the consumption of tourist services. The increase of incomes in recent years in Bulgaria, the proximity of Botevgrad to the capital, the excellent transport accessibility and the preserved natural environment represents a favourable opportunity to expand the tourist offer of alternative types of tourism, including the development of ecotourism in the municipality.

In the context of the political environment in Bulgaria, the municipality of Botevgrad is in a relatively favourable position. The municipality's mayor demonstrated political will for the development of the tourism sector and readiness for targeted actions in this direction. The writer took the need to apply a research approach in studying the potential of the municipality and building administrative capacity in the sector into account. The local government is also aware that creating an attractive and competitive destination requires significant potential in the tourist resources of the territory, as well as a public environment whose management is constantly supporting the tourism business to its sustainable development. That could be seen in "Situational Analysis of the Tourist Environment in the Municipality of Botevgrad"(2017). Study of the tourist potential, conditions, and opportunities for tourism development in the Municipality of Botevgrad. Situational analysis of the tourist environment in the Municipality of Botevgrad. (July 2017).

The mission of ecotourism in the municipality of Botevgrad coincides with the plan „National Strategy and Action Plan for Ecotourism Development in Bulgaria" (2004), where the expected results are related to the prices of the diversity, uniqueness, and authenticity of the natural and cultural resources. This product should be intended for Bulgarian and foreign tourists who treat nature responsibly and with concern and support the preservation of biological diversity and cultural and historical heritage.

For Bulgaria and in particular, the Municipality of Botevgrad, ecotourism is essential and is related to:

- Growth of the local economy and social development.
- Attracting foreign tourists with good financial opportunities for more extended periods throughout the year.
- Year-round contribution to the market share of domestic tourism.
- Development of positive attitudes and knowledge in the local communities towards the protection of the biological diversity and the cultural and historical heritage.
- Expanding the range of instruments and financial mechanisms for the protection of natural and cultural wealth.

- Directing the infrastructure development to be appropriate, environmentally friendly solutions.

POTENTIAL FOR DEVELOPMENT OF ECOTOURISM IN BOTEVGRAD

The preserved natural environment and the attractiveness of the landscape in the Botevgrad valley and the hills of the Fore-Balkans in combination with the biological diversity is a very good precondition for the development of ecotourism. The villages of Lipnitsa, Bozhenitsa, Elov dol, Kraevo, Litakovo, Rashkovo, Radotina, Gurkovo provide opportunities for offering complex tourist products, including wildlife monitoring, hiking, fishing, adventure tourism, including horseback riding and cycling. A limitation for a long stay is the lack of enough guest houses, family hotels and other accommodation. In some of the smaller villages there are no restaurants.

Comprehensive human activity and intervention in the development of ecosystems integrates the components of the natural and social environment into a single environment. In the context of tourism development, this means that natural resources are very often associated with the anthropogenic environment in a single product, ie. the elements of nature and climate are in constant interaction with human activities.

Over time, health has become essential, and tourists are increasingly concerned about it. This will certainly affect your travel decision. Destinations that are not considered environmentally friendly will gradually be avoided by tourists. The demand for active vacations in areas with a clean natural environment will form the need to build suitable facilities for active sports. Botevgrad as a destination with traditions in sports, appropriate altitude, and climate parameters, as well as built material sports facilities has the prerequisites to provide conditions for short-term recreation and tourism related to sports activities.

According to the 2014 national report "Analysis and assessment of the risk and vulnerability of sectors in the Bulgarian economy to climate change", climate change can lead to wider heat waves, as well as more frequent floods and droughts. Almost all sectors are sensitive to such meteorological phenomena, but the three most vulnerable sectors are water management, agriculture, and tourism. In addition to climate change, the constant pressure on the environment from other economic sectors is also a threat. The generation of insufficiently treated wastewater, the presence of solid waste outside the landfill, the quality of the air during the winter months affects the components of the environment and lead to serious environmental problems that either threaten the tourist site / product or reach more large scale and affect the image of the whole region.

Some polluting productions on the territory of the municipality also have a negative impact, which results in periodic gassing of the city. The selection of a destination also includes significant factors such as the quality of drinking water and environmental pollution. Outdated and depreciated water supply and sewerage infrastructure, frequent accidents, deteriorating drinking water quality, non-functioning treatment plants, which currently pose a problem for the living standard of the local community, will have an adverse impact on the tourist supply and quality of the tourist product.

Despite the problems, the nature in the municipality of Botevgrad is well preserved and suggests opportunities for ecotourism visits, combined with potential sites of cultural and historical heritage. (Situational analysis for the development of tourism in the Municipality of Botevgrad, 2017)

Representatives of local authorities are unanimous that the development of tourism in the region is one of the main goals that must be set before the public. Therefore, they recognize that it is necessary for its development to move gradually, purposefully and focused on the main tourist resource - nature, culture, living environment, etc. In addition, they do not ignore the fact that consumer demand is constantly changing, and the ability of the destination to adapt quickly and in a timely manner to these changes makes it sustainable and competitive.

According to them, the sustainability of the municipality and the improvement of the quality of life of its inhabitants, as well as the protection of natural resources in the region depends on the following factors:

- **Ecological Sustainability:** Compatibility between the main ecological processes, biological diversity, and biological resources.
- **Socio-Cultural Sustainability:** Synergy between people, culture, and history, used for the development of cultural and historical values and the destination itself.
- **Economic Sustainability:** Effective economic development, efficient use of resources for future development.

The analysis of the focused group interview outlines the path to be followed, namely: to combine the strengths and capabilities of the territory; to initiate processes for obtaining the most favourable result and to plan actions to prove that users identify the destination, clearly understanding the image of the place and how the factors that shape it distinguish it and help preserve local cultural identity.

CONCLUSION AND RECOMMENDATIONS

In conclusion, the reader could summarize that the successful development of ecotourism in Botevgrad is related to the inventory of tourist resources and conducting systematic marketing research. However, construct thematic routes and specialized ecotourism infrastructure (nature protection centres, bird watching shelters, etc.). A good suggestion for increasing productivity should be the introduction of uniform standards for servicing tourists, categorization, and voluntary certification of tourist sites ("ecohotel", "greenhouse", etc.) along with diversification of the tourist product by offering additional services. The use of opportunities for a standard regional tourist product with neighbouring municipalities, coordination between stakeholders, and establishing public-private partnerships also need to be implemented. Trends related to tourist demand require more extensive use of the Internet and individual websites and digitalization of tourist sites. In this regard, we recommend providing information through online brochures, making online reservations, using e-marketing to bring together local providers, domestic agencies and external tour operators. Exploration tours or workshops where local providers invite external tour operators to give their expertise and develop new packages based on equality and partnership should play an important role. The sightseeing tours in poorly researched areas, such as Botevgrad, aim to acquaint the tour operators with the destination and the product, visit interesting sites and submit offers, and establish business relations and cooperation between local service providers and specialized tour operators.

Restrictions for tourism development in the municipality are mainly related to the lack of specialized tourist infrastructure: There is no eco-trails or facilities for bird watching, no signboards and other information and advertising materials. Such stuff needs to be placed on-site near tourist trails and sites, online or print. The small number of places for recreation and the insufficient number of beds adversely affect the more extended stay of tourists.

The proximity to Vrachanski Balkan Nature Park and the Iskar Gorge through Rzhana Mountain provides opportunities for the joint offering of ecotourism routes and products with the municipalities of Mezdra, Vratsa and Svoge. Still, to visit ecotourists, the area of Botevgrad needs to have favourable conditions for stay and complex tourist offers. The municipality can achieve this through original tourist attractions for the region, such as the proposed for the authors of this study sites for feeding and shelters for bird watching, the construction of a conservation centre, the creation of protected landscapes and green infrastructure. The unique worldwide migration of the mountain frog in the protected area "Muhalnitsa", although observed during a brief period of the year, with responsible and systematic actions by the municipal leadership related to conservation and communication activities, has the opportunity to highlight Botevgrad on the map of Bulgaria as a preserved ecotourism destination.

The improvement of the tourist infrastructure, marketing, and advertising, as well as the combination of the new proposals for ecotourism with horse and bicycle hikes, speleotourism, geological tours in the area of Elov dol, adventure and extreme experiences, promoted in an appropriate way to the target tourists, will contribute to the creation of the Botevgrad brand as a green destination with preserved natural resources. That requires a targeted and consistent tourism policy, planning and sustainable development of alternative tourism in the municipality of Botevgrad, part of which is ecotourism.

Opportunities for tourism development in the municipality of Botevgrad include both existing routes and tourist locations and new eco-tourist attractions. Based on systematic observations and field studies, the authors propose the following forms of ecotourism products:

1. Ecotourism location Dreneto Protected Area - Gurkovo micro-dam - Rzhana mountain, where grey herons, black-breasted kestrel, red-legged (evening) kestrel, osprey, common white-tailed buzzard, small bald eagle, great hawk, small hawk, the hawk can be observed bee-eater, hoopoe, corncrake, white stork, crows, starling, anglerfish, Spanish sparrow, black-headed oatmeal, as well as in wolf, badger, fox, deer, deer, wild boar, jackal, badger, wild rabbit, ferret, weasel, rat, mouse, shrew, bats.

2. . Ecotourism location Bozhenitsa - Lipnitsa, with opportunities for combination with speleotourism and mountaineering, including undeveloped caves and climbing rocks, where interesting birds nest. In the area of the climbing rocks near Bozhenitsa nests a black stork. At the reserve "School Forest", the fortress Bozhenishki Urvich, there is a pedestrian alley, and there is a separate recreation area with a fountain and gazebos. The visitors could see an owl, a forest owl, veiled owl, barn owl, vulture, black stork, cinderella, stag deer, beech woodpecker, great woodpecker, spiny-tailed tortoise. In the village centre, there is an opportunity to use premises in the building of the town hall or the former post office, where to create a nature protection centre with a thematic exposition, carrying out conservation activities, conducting training and offering tourist services.

3. Development of niche ecotourism: ecotourism product related to the unique migration of the mountain frog in the protected area "Muhalnitsa". The Muhalnitsa area, also known as the Frog Swamp or the Zelina Swamp, is located 1 km south of the town of Botevgrad, in the Zelin villa zone. In the first sunny and warm days of spring, there is a unique worldwide migration of mountain frogs (Rana temporaria), which descend on the riverbeds of

three rivers - Echemishka, Zelinska and Chervena Kiselitsa, passing 6 km. they remain in the swamp until they breed. After developing metamorphoses, the little frogs leave the swamp and return to the Balkan Mountains along the riverbeds. This migration is unique and remarkable because of its duration - according to scientists, it is unchanged from about 10-12 thousand years. This phenomenon can attract visitors engaged in zoology or fauna lovers and animal behaviour. Student groups may be involved. Tour operators can offer specialized day trips for student groups or nature lovers interested in animal watching. The local authority can provide a technical ecotourism product Zoomarshut in Botevgrad municipality, which includes a visit to the Frog Swamp, observing and photographing frogs, then groups to visit the protected area "Dreneto" and wetlands near the village of Gurkovo to watch different species of birds.

4. Ecotourism in Botevgrad. The park of the Technical College in the city provides excellent opportunities for Observation of different birds, such as black woodpecker, green and grey woodpecker, capercaillie, cuckoo, dove, woodpecker, small and large hawk, barn owl, blackbird, southern nightingale, great black-headed nettle, Observation of waterfowl near the small lag dam: coot, whistle (fish), green-headed duck, small diver, a small cormorant, forest eared owl, fisherman eagle (migratory), grey heron.

5. Construction of shelters for bird watching and feeding grounds In the past, there were four species of vultures - griffon vulture, Egyptian, black and bearded on the territory of Bulgaria. These vast and beautiful birds feed only on the carcasses of dead animals. In this way, they prevent diseases, infections and parasites in wildlife, domestic animals and humans. In other words, these birds can be called - "Sanitarians" of nature. Unfortunately, only two of the four species - Griffon and Egyptian - currently breed in Bulgaria, and their populations have significantly decreased. The other two species - black and bearded - have entirely disappeared from the territory, and it is possible to observe single black vultures from a colony in northern Greece. These species are extinct for three main reasons - their pursuit by humans, poisonous baits for predators and the lack of enough food. All species are protected by the Biodiversity Act and are included in the Red Data Book of Bulgaria. In Vratsa Balkan for years, specialists have been trying to reintroduce vulture species, and currently, there are about 45-55 birds, some of which raise young. Their number cannot be increased too much because there is not enough food in the area. That enables the two municipalities to join forces and build a vulture feeder in Botevgrad municipality. The city can expand the size of the vultures in the direction of the town of Botevgrad by providing them with favourable conditions and especially food, which the local authority should place in a specially designated area - a site for feeding vultures. Local authorities can

do that by working in partnership with local farmers, ranchers, farms, and slaughterhouses to provide unnecessary scraps and dead pets to feed the sites. The benefits of this feeding will not only be for vultures, but also for farmers, who will be able to get rid of the carcasses of dead animals without having to dig pits, burn them or throw them into the wild as often happens, risking the spread of infections. In parallel with the feeding, year-round monitoring of the site will be carried out to determine what birds visit and use it. Vultures reintroduced in the Vratsa Balkan National Park (Directorate of Vratsa Balkan Nature Park. 2010. "Restoration of the Griffon Vulture as a nesting species in Vratsa Mountain". https://www.vr-balkan.net/bg/vr-balkan113/) are marked with GPS transmitters. Thus tourists will know where they are and make additional observations and conclusions about their behaviour. Visiting the feeding site will be attractive and generate more visitors who otherwise would have chosen another destination. This method is also applied in other parts of the country. Good practices have been studied in Madzharovo, Kotel and Trigrad, which show that this type of ecotourism can attract ornithologists, biologists, student groups, school groups, and tourists interested in seeing these majestic animals, whose scale of the wingspan reaches 2.80 meters. The observation is done with the help of binoculars, scopes, and other optical devices. Another target for tourists attracted is wildlife photographers, slang for "photo hunters". Photo hunting is no less attractive and appealing than rifle hunting. Its most significant advantage is that it does not harm populations or kill animals, and the trophy is the fascinating photographs of majestic birds. That achieves harmony with wildlife in the context of sustainable development, and at the same time, tourists enjoy it and see it in all its glory.

6. Another relevant suggestion is the Creation of protected landscapes (to protected areas "Etropole - Baylovo" and "Bebresh"). During the last 80 years, since the existence of legislation for protected areas in Bulgaria, the aesthetic value of the municipality of Botevgrad is not considered, and its specific landscape is not included in a significant protected area.

The existing protected areas -"Visoka Mogila", "Dreneto", "Muhalnitsa", "Romania" and "Urvich" natural landmarks "Elaka" and "Vodnata Peshta" as well as the "School Forest" are small as autonomous areas. That cannot guarantee (in the long run) if they will be under protection and maintenance of the local landscape. The municipality of Botevgrad includes a significant part of the Protected Area "Bebresh", and small amounts of protected areas "Etropole - Baylovo" and "Iskar Gorge - Rzhana", which are attractive for the development of ecotourism, but no tools have been developed for their protection. According to the Bulgarian legislation, goals for the conservation of biodiversity and landscape are achieved by implementing the Protected Areas Act, the Biodiversity Act and the Spatial Planning Act. Within the framework of the implementation of the Spatial Planning Act (SPA), there are three instruments for achieving the objectives related to landscape protection:

- Designation of territories with special territorial protection for which a special regime of planning and control is determined by specific rules and regulations for the device (according to art. 10 para. two and art. 12 para. 2 of the Spatial Development Act).
- Determination of territories with a regime of preventive structural protection" (according to Article 10, paragraph 3 of the Spatial Development Act). Concepts and schemes for development plans define them. They include territories with a high natural landscape and ecological and cultural value but are not protected by a particular law. A special regime of structure and control is determined for them through specific rules and norms for structure (according to art. 13 para. 2 of the Spatial Development Act).

The local authorities can also guarantee the preservation of the existing landscape through the measures of the device itself. The Art. 45 of Ordinance N° 7 of 2003(on rules and norms for the development of the different types of territories and development zones) states that the authorities agree that the general development plans determine the structure and possibly the construction of the forest and agricultural environments outside the borders (of the settlements and settlement formations). The writer believes that government can use these tools of the general development plans within the future General Development Plan (GDP) of the Municipality of Botevgrad to protect some of the important and essential for the community landscapes and thus stimulate the development of ecotourism.

The authors proposes in the future Master Plan of the Municipality of Botevgrad to use this tool for spatial planning and to set the following opportunities for landscape protection:

Creation of a separate protected landscape for the Protected Landscape "Zvezdets" in the municipality of Gorna Malina, which should include the boundaries of the protected area "Etropole - Baylovo" in the municipality of Botevgrad. This relatively small area will create a green connection between the two towns. The territory will include mainly forest areas around the Arabakonak pass with existing bans on use and construction due to the regime of the natural landmark Elaka and the Forests at the old age phase of Botevgrad forestry.

REFERENCES

Adom, D. (2019). The place and voice of local people, culture, and traditions: A catalyst for ecotourism development in rural communities in Ghana. *Scientific American*, 6, e00184.

Briedenhann, J., & Wickens, E. (2004). Tourism routes as a tool for the economic development of rural areas—Vibrant hope or impossible dream? *Tourism Management*, 25(1), 71–79. doi:10.1016/S0261-5177(03)00063-3

Buckley, R. (2020). Pandemic Travel Restrictions Provide a Test of Net Ecological Effects of Ecotourism and New Research Opportunities. *Journal of Travel Research*.

Butler, J. R. (1992). *Ecotourism: Its changing face and evolving philosophy*. Paper presented to the IVth World Congress on National Parks and Protected Areas, Caracas, Venezuela.

Ceballos-Lascurain, H. (1987). The future of ecotourism. *Mexico Journal*. Available at: https://booksite.elsevier.com/samplechapters/9780750668781/9780750668781.pdf

Ceballos-Lascurain. (1996). *Tourism, Ecotourism and Protected Areas*. IUCN. Available at www.iucn.org/content/tourism-ecotourism-and-protected-areas-state-nature-based-tourism-around-world-and-guidelines-its-development

Cengiz, T., & Çalışkan, E. (2009). Ecological approach in sustainable tourism: Şavşat district example. *Scientific Research and Essays*, 4(5), 509–520.

Cherkaoui, S., Boukherouk, M., Lakhal, T., Aghzar, A., & El Youssfi, L. (2020). Conservation Amid COVID-19 Pandemic: Ecotourism Collapse Threatens Communities and Wildlife in Morocco. *E3S Web of Conferences*, 183.

Chryssoula, C., Ioanna, S., & Apostolos, T. (2015). *Bird Watching and Ecotourism: An Innovative Monitoring System to Project the Species of Lesvos Island to Potential Ecotourists*. Available at: https://ceur-ws.org/Vol-1498/HAICTA_2015_paper54.pdf

Churchill, G. A., & Peter, J. P. (1995). *Marketing: creating value for customers*. Irwin McGraw Hill.

Cooke, H., & Tate, K. (2011). *Project management*. Mcgraw-Hill.

Economics, O. (2020). *Global city travel: 2019 to 2025*. Oxford Economics. Available at: www.oxfordeconomics.com/recent-releases/global-city-travel-2019-to-2025

European Union Tourism Trends. (2020). Available at: https://www.e-unwto.org/doi/pdf/10.18111/9789284419470

Evans, N., Campbell, D., & Stonehouse, G. (2003). *Strategic Management for Travel and Tourism*. Butterworth-Heinemann.

Fotiadis, A. (2009). *The role of tourism in rural development through a comparative analysis of a Greek and a Hungarian rural tourism area*. Available at: https://pea.lib.pte.hu/bitstream/handle/pea/14945/fotiadis-anestis-phd-2009.pdf?sequence=1&isAllowed=y

Getz, D. (1986). Models in tourism planning: Towards integration of theory and practice. *Tourism Management, 17*(1), 21–32. doi:10.1016/0261-5177(86)90054-3

Goddard, W., & Melville, S. (2017). *Research methodology*. Juta & Co., Repr.

Goeldner, Ch. R., & Ritchie, B. J. R. (2009). *Tourism: Principles, Practices, Philosophies* (11th ed.). John Wiley & Sons Inc.

Government of Bulgaria. (2021). *Analysis and assessment of the risk and vulnerability of sectors in the Bulgarian economy to climate change*. Available at: https://www.moew.government.bg/bg/analiz-i-ocenka-na-riska-i-uyazvimostta-na-sektorite-v-bulgarskata-ikonomika-ot-klimatichni-promeni/

Gunn, C. A. (1988). *Tourism Planning* (2nd ed.). Taylor & Francis.

Hakim, L., Siswanto, D., & Makagoshi, N. (2017). Mangrove Conservation in East Java: The Ecotourism Development Perspectives. *Journal of Tropical Life Science, 7*(3), 277–285. doi:10.11594/jtls.07.03.14

Heerkens, G. R. (2015). *Project management*. McGraw-Hill Education.

Higham, J. (2007). *Ecotourism: Competing and conflicting schools of thought*. Available at: www.researchgate.net/publication/283378699

Holloway, J. Ch. (2012). *The business of tourism* (9th ed.). Pearson.

Ihtimanski, I., Nedkov, S., & Semerdzhieva, L. (2019). *Mapping the natural heritage as a source of recreation services at national scale in Bulgaria*. I.K. International Pub. House.

Jing, Y., & Fucai, H. (2011). Research on Management of Ecotourism Based on Economic Models. *Energy Procedia, 5*, 1563–1567. doi:10.1016/j.egypro.2011.03.267

Jones, S. (2005). Community-Based Ecotourism: The Significance of Social Capital. *Annals of Tourism Research, 32*(2), 303–324. doi:10.1016/j.annals.2004.06.007

Kadt, E. (1979). *Tourism: Passport to Development?* Oxford University Press. European Charter for Sustainable and Responsible Tourism. Available at https://www.ceeweb.org/wp-content/uploads/2011/12/Commented_Tourism_Charter_CEEweb.pdf

Kakar, N. (2018). Success Story: Ecotourism in South Africa. *Borgen Magazine*. Available at:www.borgenmagazine.com/ecotourism-in-south-africa

Kiper, T. (2012). *Role of Ecotourism in Sustainable Development*. Available at: https://www.intechopen.com/chapters/45414

Mitova, R., Borisova, B., & Koulov, B. (2021). Digital Marketing of Bulgarian Natural Heritage for Tourism and Recreation. *Sustainability, 13*, 13071. Available at:https://www.mrrb.bg/static/media/ups/articles/attachments/838602eca62db5f279ff6321a7a55608.pdf

Mooney, S. (2018) *Ecotourism can benefit Rural communities*. Available at www.sustainablecitynetwork.com/topic_channels/community/article_c7a6f70a- ccb0-11e8-bf4e-efa2f0cbd95b.html

Osland, G., & Mackoy, R. (2012). *Education and Ecotourism. Scholarship and Professional Work - Business*. Available at: https://digitalcommons.butler.edu/cob_papers/236

Page, S., & Dowling, R. K. (2002). *Ecotourism*. Prentice Hall.

Parks, P. J. (2006). *Ecotourism*. Kidhaven Press.

Ribeiro, M.F., Ferreira, J., & Silva, C. (2011). The Sustainable Carrying Capacity as a Tool for Environmental Beach Management. *Journal of Coastal Research*, 1411–1414.

rKrasnokutskiy, E. (2016). The Main Trends and Prospects of Development of International Tourism. *International Journal of Economics and Financial Issues, 6*(S8), 257-262.

Sowicz, T. J. (2017). Mixed methods designs. *Pain, 158*(4), 760. doi:10.1097/j.pain.0000000000000806 PMID:28301401

Stefanov, N., Petrov, G., & Alexova, D. (2018). *Factors and opportunities for development of ecotourism at Botevgrad Miunicipality, Bulgaria*. Available at: www.researchgate.net

The International Ecotourism Society. (2019). Available at: www.bsc.smebg.net/ecotourguide/best_practices/articles/files/TIES.pdf

Travingdy, A. (2017). *Thirty years on the front line - the inside story of Tourism Concern*. Available at: www.travindy.com

Tseng, M.-L., Lin, C., Remen Lin, C.-W., Wu, K.-J., & Sriphon, T. (2019). Ecotourism development in Thailand: Community participation leads to the value of attractions using linguistic preferences. *Journal of Cleaner Production, 231*, 1319–1329. doi:10.1016/j.jclepro.2019.05.305

Tshomo. (2018). *Study finds positive impact of ecotourism on local communities*. Available at:www.kuenselonline.com

Uran, M., & Juvan, E. (2010). The stakeholders role within tourism strategy development: The local residents viewpoint. *Organizacija, 43*(5).

Wearne, N., & Baker, K. (2002). *Hospitality Marketing in the e-commerce Age* (2nd ed.). Hospitality Press. Available at www.osea-cite.org

Wisdom, J., & Creswell, J. (2013). *Mixed Methods: Integrating Quantitative and Qualitative Data Collection and Analysis While Studying Patient-Centered Medical Home Models*. PCMH Resource Center. Available at: www.pcmh.ahrq.gov

Wondirad, A., Tolkach, D., & King, B. (2020). Stakeholder collaboration as a major factor for sustainable ecotourism development in developing countries. *Tourism Management, 78*, 104024. doi:10.1016/j.tourman.2019.104024

Chapter 3

Green Marketing Applications in Hospitality Businesses

Mehmet Tekeli
Karamanoğlu Mehmetbey University, Turkey

Gülsüm Kasap
Isparta University of Applied Science, Turkey

ABSTRACT

Industrial activities significantly affect the environment, which makes environmental sensitivity one of the most critical issues in the national and international arenas. As in other areas, the green approaches adopted in the tourism sector aim to reduce the negative environmental impact. The current study discussed the meaning of green marketing practices for hospitality businesses, the green marketing practices adopted by these businesses, and the results. In addition, the study presented a holistic perspective by presenting examples from hospitality businesses and gave general information about the green marketing concept, its scope, the reasons to turn to green marketing, and the benefits of such practices. In the study, which deals with the elements of the green marketing mix in hospitality businesses and touches on the examples of green hotels, green marketing practices were evaluated in the tourism sector.

INTRODUCTION

The ever-increasing industrial activities, technological developments, rapid increase in the population, and unconscious use of resources negatively impact the environment. Corrective policies and discourses at various levels have become common to reduce

DOI: 10.4018/978-1-6684-6796-1.ch003

Copyright © 2023, IGI Global. Copying or distributing in print or electronic forms without written permission of IGI Global is prohibited.

these adverse–sometimes even irreversible–effects on the environment. In this context, environmental management approaches such as green marketing, green management, green production, and green innovation have become closely followed by organizations to eliminate environmental pollution and destruction problems (Chen et al., 2006).

The environment is a necessary resource for tourism activities (Lim & McAleer, 2005). The natural environment, historical texture, and cultural values are the most prominent attractions of the tourism industry. However, while tourism develops, unplanned tourism investments devastate the natural environment (Deng et al., 2002). The deterioration in the natural environment means the disappearance of the most important source of tourism. In this respect, ensuring the environmental awareness of the tourism industry is one of the most significant issues. In this direction, the concept of sustainable tourism, which expresses the preservation and use of tourism resources and their successful transfer to future generations, comes to the fore (Tekeli & Kırıcı Tekeli, 2020; Yetiş, 2018).

The sustainable tourism approach, which overlaps with the primary purpose of tourism, aims to use the resources correctly, develop steadily and improve the life quality, as well as highlights the concepts such as green management, green marketing, green production, and green innovation. The green marketing notion, one of these concepts, has become a prominent tool, especially in the competitiveness of hospitality businesses. In other words, environmental pollution, imbalanced ecology, changing consumer trends, competitive pressure, legal sanctions, and touristic consumers' more conscious preferences have urged tourism enterprises to adopt green marketing practices (Chen et al., 2006: Dilek, 2012).

With the increasing environmental problems, green practices have become widespread in all sectors, especially in the tourism sector, which is closely associated with the environment. Day by day, tourism enterprises show more interest in green marketing practices (Atay & Dilek, 2013; Gryshchenko, 2022). This is because green marketing practices have benefits, such as protecting touristic resources, saving money, increasing competitiveness, and being an important marketing tool (Sert, 2017).

The current study deals with green marketing applications in hospitality businesses. In this direction, at the outset, the research deals with the green marketing notion and the factors that are effective in adopting green marketing approaches comprehensively. Then, the benefits of green marketing practices to businesses are emphasized. In addition, the concepts of green products, green price, green promotion, green distribution, and green consumer, which are crucial for tourism businesses, are included. Finally, green marketing practices in hospitality businesses are discussed via examples and generally evaluated.

CONCEPT AND SCOPE OF GREEN MARKETING

The emergence of social marketing in the 1970s changed the scope of the traditional marketing concept. Along with the increasing environmental issues since the 1990s, consumer interests and concerns about the environment have increased (Kaya, 2009; Sert, 2017). The increase in environmental concerns and the expectations of consumers from businesses have been influential in developing environmental awareness and sensitivity in the 2000s. With the developing environmental awareness, various strategies, rules, and regulations have become widespread in the national and international arena to reduce environmental problems, minimize the use of natural resources and increase clean technology applications (Giraldo & Castro, 2014). Increasing sensitivity to environmental issues, covering unconscious natural resource use and global climate change, has improved the environmentalist understanding in marketing as in many other areas (Kocagöz, 2011). Thus, the green marketing approach, which emphasizes environmental awareness against environmental problems, has emerged.

First brought to the agenda in the "ecological marketing" seminar organized by the American Marketing Association in 1975, the green marketing concept involves "studies on the positive or negative effects of marketing activities on environmental pollution and energy and other resource consumption" (Polonsky, 1994). In other words, green marketing is "meeting the desires and needs of people in a way that causes the least damage to the environment." This definition emphasizes that businesses should pay attention to protecting the environment while meeting consumer demands in green marketing (Polonsky, 1994). Green marketing refers to commerce activities, policies, and procedures that consider the natural environment in generating profits from a product or business and meeting corporate and individual goals (Menon et al., 1999).

Green marketing is the activity of developing and promoting environmentalist products (Clow and Baack, 2007). Kozak (2014), who deals with the concept of green marketing in the tourism sector, defines green marketing as "managing all resources to meet the needs of today's people, considering the protection and development of the living resources of future generations" (Kozak, 2014: 176). Definitions of green marketing change and develop over time according to the conditions. In this direction, the American Marketing Association redefined green marketing in 2017 as "the activities carried out to produce, promote, package and then recycle products that are sensitive to environmental concerns and safe for the environment" (American Marketing Association, 2017).

Green marketing covers designing and implementing changes with minimum environmental impact while meeting human desires and needs (Polonsky, 1994). Therefore, green marketing closely relates to the business issues such as eco-efficiency, responsibilities, material use, resource flow, and life cycle analysis in terms of environmental sustainability and industrial ecology. In this respect, green marketing widely impacts business strategies and business policies (Prakash, 2002). All in-house controls should be within the green marketing approach to ensure minimum environmental impact in the business activities (Polonsky & Rosenberger III, 2001).

Businesses generally implement green marketing practices within three principles: social responsibility, sustainability, and integrity. The *social responsibility* of a business means having social obligations as much as economic interests. In this respect, enterprises should contribute to solving the social problems they cause. Moreover, companies are responsible for a large social segment and should provide services for humanitarian values (Peattie, 1995). The *sustainability* principle is about using natural resources, allowing them to renew themselves, or turning to sustainable alternative resources. In addition, it aims that wastes do not harm the natural environment (Peattie, 1999). The *holistic approach* aims at a holistic perspective by dealing with the businesses–handled in a technological and economic framework so far–from a social and environmental perspective, as a part of the ecological system (Peattie, 1995). In general, businesses carry out activities by adopting these three principles within the framework of green marketing understanding.

Businesses with a green marketing approach highlight activities that aim to reduce environmental pollution, waste, excessive consumption of natural resources and energy, encourage the use of recycling and renewable resources, make products safer in the eco-system, and encourage the use of environmentally friendly products. These activities include correctly using social resources, selecting and using raw materials, protecting the environment and the consumers besides economic interests, planning and controlling product policies, and the processes such as controlled production, packaging, distribution, promotion, sale, disposal, and recycling (Chamorro & Bañegil, 2006; Eser et al., 2011; Karaca, 2013; Türk & Gök, 2010). In addition, businesses with environmental awareness have to manage technological risks holistically, and they also need to protect the health of employees and society (Ay & Ecevit, 2005).

Environmentally friendly businesses adopt the green marketing approach in four stages. In the first stage, environmentally friendly products are designed for environmentalist consumers. In the second stage, green strategies are developed for environmental measures such as lowering waste and increasing energy efficiency. The third stage emphasizes producing environmentally friendly products rather than non-environmentally friendly ones. At this stage, businesses adapt to the changing environmental needs. In the last step, businesses reach responsibility awareness in every social field besides environmentalism. In general, business culture and environmental factors are the dynamic factors in green marketing awareness in enterprises (Uydacı, 2016).

Green marketing should be adopted throughout the corporation as a strategy. Unlike traditional marketing, green marketing does not just deal with the marketing department. The green marketing approach applies to all departments, such as production, marketing, purchasing, human resources, finance, and accounting. More generally, the company's success in green marketing closely relates to integrated marketing efforts (Varinli, 2012). On the other hand, in green marketing, businesses should not overemphasize (marketing myopia) environmental features in the way of causing customer dissatisfaction. In other words, the understanding of green marketing should focus on both improving environmental quality and ensuring customer satisfaction (Ottman et al., 2006).

The Green marketing approach focuses on long-term corporate environmental strategies and senior management policies and follows proactive environmental procedures with stakeholders (Papadas et al., 2017). Integrating such an approach into the corporate strategy will increase sales and profitability. In other words, by providing long-term cost and sustainable competitive advantage to businesses, the green marketing approach positively affects consumers' purchasing behavior. This situation causes enterprises to adopt green understandings and show more interest in green practices over time (Dilek, 2012; Khan et. al., 2021).

FACTORS LEADING TO GREEN MARKETING

Increased adverse effects on the natural environment and ecological destruction are global problems today. Therefore, social and political pressures on industrial activities have become widespread. This situation leads businesses to produce green products, implement clean production technologies and methods, make environmentally friendly packaging and designs, and expand recycling (Ay & Ecevit, 2005). Besides their intentions of reducing the negative impact on the environment, businesses have various additional reasons for adopting green marketing practices: In general, macro factors, such as the pressure of consumers, environmental organizations, and governments, and competition, (Polonsky, 1994) and micro factors, such as organizational management characteristics, value judgments, property status, and organizational culture, (Leonidou et al., 2013) are influential in the spread of green marketing practices.

The increasing number of environmentally sensitive and conscious consumers, and their environmentally friendly product preferences, impact the adoption and spread of green marketing practices in businesses (Eren & Yılmaz, 2008). Indeed, a study conducted on the tourism sector states that customers are conscious of environmentally friendly practices in hotels and prefer such hospitality businesses (Manaktola & Jauhari, 2007). In addition, environmental organizations formed to defend against environmental threats, increase environmentalist movements in society and fight against pollutants (Duymaz, 2013) also support the emergence of green marketing practices.

The certifications given by the state, local government, or other stakeholders promote the enterprises to carry out social and environmental practices (Porter & Kramer, 2006). In addition, legal regulations and government promotions for environmental sensitivity lead businesses to green practices (Rivera, 2004). A study on hospitality businesses in Mexico has revealed that legal and political sanctions are more persuasive than customer demands on managers in adopting green practices (Revilla et al. 2001). Another factor in the spread of green marketing practices is the competitive pressure in the sector. Businesses observe the environmental behavior of their competitors and try to imitate them. This situation becomes widespread in the whole market and causes green practices to be adopted more (Polonsky, 1994). Apart from the factors above, the benefits of green marketing practices to businesses also promote this adoption (Ottman, 1998; Polonsky, 1994).

BENEFITS OF GREEN MARKETING FOR BUSINESSES

The most prominent factor for enterprises in adopting the green marketing approach is the increasing environmental awareness of the consumer and their tendency to prefer green products. These green marketing practices provide businesses with various attractive benefits, such as reducing costs in the long term, a competitive advantage, a high environmentalist image, and sustainable development opportunities (Lumbaraja et al., 2019; Polonsky, 1994).

The adoption of green practices, such as waste management, energy saving, and reuse of materials, reduces costs in the long run, increases profitability, and contributes significantly to the businesses' sustainable development in severe competitive conditions (Polonsky, 1994; Khan et. al., 2021). Besides the cost advantage, businesses achieve a competitive advantage with their green practices. In the market, strengthening the company's financial structure by saving money and influencing consumer preferences with green practices are the two most important elements of gaining a competitive advantage (Dilek, 2012).

Embracing green marketing practices significantly increases the environmentalist image of businesses as an indicator of their social responsibility understanding. In addition, taking such environmental steps ensures that companies be more secure against the law (Sert, 2017). In general, developing green marketing strategies and conducting environmentalist activities provides many benefits to businesses, such as reducing costs, creativity, increasing brand image, recovering resources, and sustainable competitive advantage (Khan et. al., 2021). However, green marketing practices should not be evaluated only in terms of the economic benefits and public image. The primary purpose of such processes is to act consciously and sensitively within the social responsibility framework for a sustainable environment and human future (Özcan & Özgül, 2019).

GREEN MARKETING MIX IN TOURISM SECTOR

The continuity of sustainable tourism activities is possible when businesses organize their activities and strategies in accordance with the environment. The concept of sustainability, which has become much more significant recently–especially in tourism businesses where the environment is an indispensable factor–should be included in all business strategies. One of these strategies is the marketing mix elements that the marketing department frequently uses. In this context, the marketing mix is "all the marketing tools used by a company in the target market to carry out its marketing objectives" (Çakıcı et al., 2002: 295). Jerome McCarthy, who introduced the concept of the marketing mix as 4P, brought this concept to the literature for the first time in 1964 using the initials of the product, price, place, and promotion words (Mosavichechaklou, 2017).

Tourists' environmental sensitivities have steadily increased depending on their changing living standards, expectations, and rising consciousness along with globalization and technological developments. Considering this situation, Bradley was the first person to develop the traditional marketing mix (4P) already applied by businesses by combining it with green practices towards the end of the 1980s (İpar, 2018). This effort started by Bradley enabled other researchers to focus on this issue. In the end, the practices in the traditional marketing mix have been made more environmentally friendly, and the concepts of green product, green price, green place, and green promotion have emerged. These significant concepts are detailed as follows:

Green Products

Product, one of the significant elements of the marketing mix, is "the presentations of commercial enterprises or non-profit organizations to their current and potential customers" (Tenekecioğlu, 2004). In other words, a product is anything introduced to the market for consumption, use, or possession to satisfy a desire or need. Products are among the main variables controlling the position of companies in the market (Tek, 1999). It is crucial for a business that the products offered to the market are environmentally friendly (Baki & Cengiz, 2002). People demonstrate a massive reaction against environmentally harmful products because of the rapid environmental pollution stemming from excessive industrialization. Since consumers reflect these reactions to their purchasing behaviors, businesses feel obligated to produce and develop green product policies (Kaur et al., 2022; Uydacı, 2016;).

In general, green products are "products that contribute to protecting the natural environment by saving energy and resources, and reducing harmful effects on the environment" (Ottman et al. 2006: 24). Uydacı considers them as "products not over-packaged, free of unnecessary waste, produced with no animal testing, environmentally friendly from production to disposal" (Uydacı, 2016: 187). In short, green products allows the decomposition and recycling processes after the products have expired (Ottman et al. 2006). In addition to the definitions above, a green product should have the following characteristics (Çabuk et al. 2008; Günay, 2017; Onurlubaş & Dinçer, 2016):

- It should not be health-threatening,
- It should not contain environmentally harmful materials,
- It should not have excessive energy and resource consumption during the manufacture, use, or disposal process,
- It should not cause unnecessary use and should be produced with no animal testing,
- It should be ecologically packaged and not contain excessive packaging.

The product concept has a much broader scope in the tourism sector, as it corresponds to all the goods and services demanded and purchased by tourists during their travels. The touristic product means a series of services such as transportation, accommodation, food and beverage, rest, and entertainment (İstanbullu Dinçer & Muğan Ertuğral, 2009). In the tourism sector, which is intertwined with the environment, green marketing practices have made the use of green products widespread. For example, reducing waste, recycling, or reusing are indicators of green product activities in hospitality businesses. These applications provide water and energy savings in hotels (Sert, 2017). In addition, recycling food and beverage wastes, using solar and wind for energy generation, choosing recycled stationeries for reception uses, and choosing reusable shampoo boxes are among the green applications in accommodation establishments.

Green Price

Price is among the significant decisions for businesses that produce or use green products in their service processes. In short, price is "the sum of the values exchanged by the consumer for the products or services obtained or utilized" (Tenekecioğlu, 2004: 8). Another study defines the price notion as "the exchange rate of a good or service with another good or service" (Üstünel, 2000: 109). In green marketing, the price concept has gained a different dimension. Businesses incur additional costs to produce a green product and include it in the selling price (Günay, 2017). In this context, the green price arises through "the addition of green marketing costs to the product price" (Varinli, 2012).

Businesses should accurately consider whether they should price their environmentally friendly products more expensive or cheaper than other products. Here, three different methods are available: First, environmentally friendly products can be more economical than other products. Such a case encourages consumers to purchase environmentally friendly products at a lower price. The second approach is to keep the selling prices of ordinary and environmentally friendly products at the same level. When consumers are torn between two products, they usually prefer the environmentally friendly product. The third way is to set the environmentally friendly product prices higher than the ordinary products. Businesses generally prefer the third way and add extra expenses to their costs. It is widely believed that green consumers tend to pay more for environmentally friendly products and do not focus on the product or service prices but on their benefit (Aytekin, 2007; Kaur et al., 2022; Peattie & Crane, 2005).

The price factor steadily becomes much more critical in tourism enterprises. Tourists generally have limited time and budget and try to get the most satisfaction with the least cost. Tourists use many touristic products during their travels and have to pay for them. On each voyage to touristic destinations, transportation, accommodation, food and beverage, entertainment, and other activities have a cost. Some studies show that environmentally friendly people can bear additional costs during their holidays (Tabak & Güneren Özdemir, 2019). Touristic businesses should consider these factors to determine correct price policies (Olalı & Timur, 1988).

Green Place

Place, one of the four fundamental marketing mix elements, refers to transferring the products from the supply point to the consumption point and providing service to customers after this transfer (Rushton et al., 2006). In other words, the activities carried out in conveying the products from the production place to the consumers mean *place* (Dülgeroğlu et al., 2016: 7). Environmentally friendly activities impact the distribution activities, as do all commercial activities. The primary purpose of the *green place* is to use methods and practices that cause minimal harm to the environment during distribution (Djaadi, 2016). However, the distribution system in the tourism sector works in reverse. Distribution in tourism means "taking the consumer to the place where the goods and services are produced, instead of taking the goods and services to the consumer" (Usta, 1992: 158). Distribution channels in tourism are in two stages. The first stage conveys all kinds of information about the touristic product to the consumer, and the second ensures the consumers reach the destination where the touristic product is available (Hacıoğlu, 2008: 57).

Green Promotion

Promotion refers to "all activities related to providing the target market with product information and persuading the consumers to buy" (Kozak, 2010: 11). After product, price, and place activities to exchange a commodity, a promotion activity is carried out (Tenekecioğlu, 2004). Marketing management uses a promotion mix including advertising, sales development, personal selling, public relations, publicity, and direct marketing applications to achieve the determined goals. Whatever tools businesses use, the primary purpose should be to create a positive image and value in the eyes of potential and current customers (Ural, 2003). Firms frequently use the green promotion to make a positive impression by highlighting environmentally friendly activities. The green promotion covers all activities to accurately inform consumers about the environmental characteristics of the business and product, raise consumer awareness, remind them of the advantages of green products, and draw an environmentally friendly business image (Dilek, 2012).

Promotion activities in the tourism sector have particular importance because product information and perception significantly affect the purchasing decisions of tourists. In other words, the general impression of the tourism destination or product affects the purchasing decision (Sanchez et al. 2006). While a positive image positively affects the purchase decision on the product, negative opinions or insufficient information may cause the consumer to give up buying (Sarkım, 2007). Many hospitality businesses with various environmental certificates such as green star, green pine, and blue flag also announce these to the public and seek to create a positive impression about their establishment.

GREEN PRACTICES IN HOSPITALITY SECTOR

The increasing domestic and international tourism movement is a significant resource for world economies. Although they sound to be income-generating activities at the first stage, intensive tourism investments and the severe use of the environment for tourism purposes adversely affect nature and cause environmental problems for the next generation (Dolmacı & Bulgan, 2013). Yet, tourism enterprises are more sensitive to the environment than others because attractive environmental conditions are the most indispensable factor for the touristic development in a region. Natural beauties and an unspoiled ecology are the factors that significantly affect the purchasing preferences of tourists. Therefore, while the regional development of tourism depends on high environmental quality, its sustainability depends on the management of touristic activities in a way that will increase the ecosystem quality (Demir & Çevirgen, 2006; Kaur et al., 2022).

The effects of tourism businesses on the environment and ecological balance are very diverse and complex. Rising environmental awareness and preferences for more environmentally friendly products have led tourism businesses to develop strategies toward these factors. When considering the touristic activities such as swimming pools, baths, restaurants, lighting, cleaning, air conditioning, and irrigation of gardens, the daily resource consumption of visitors using hotels globally is very high (Mastny, 2001). The unconscious use of resources both brings a considerable cost to accommodation businesses and has adverse effects on the sustainability of tourism. Depending on the reasons above, "environmentally sensitive business" or "green business" notions have emerged (Mesci, 2014; Nemli, 2001). A typical example of green management in tourism is green hotels. Green hotels are "environmentally friendly businesses willing to protect the world by saving water and energy and reducing solid waste and thus saving money" (Yeşil Oteller Birliği, 2015).

While the understanding of environmentally sensitive hotel management tries to keep the energy used by hospitality businesses at the lowest level, on the other hand, tries to reduce the wastes that harm nature. In this context, hotels take steps to use recycled materials (Eren & Yılmaz, 2008; Tavmergen & Meriç, 1999). In addition, they adopt many applications, such as protecting water resources, ensuring air quality, preventing noise pollution, providing environmental training to personnel, and expressing environmental policies in writing (Kahraman & Türkay, 2012; Rivera, 2002). In addition, some applications adopted by hospitality businesses are listed below (De Fran, 1996; Erdogan & Tosun, 2009; Mensah, 2006):

- The air conditioners and other unnecessary electrical appliances used in the rooms should automatically turn off when the customer leaves the room.
- The exterior door and window glasses should be double-glazed to preserve heat.
- Energy-efficient electrical appliances should be preferred in common areas and rooms.
- In order to prevent the water from overflowing in swimming pools, raceway should be built around the pool sides and the water level in the pool should be kept a little low.
- Cotton sheets and towels that contain no bleach and chemicals should be preferred.
- Buildings should be constructed using recycled materials and carefully isolated.

- Sensors should be used in lighting sparsely used areas.
- Waste water should be used in garden irrigation after treatment.
- The employees should get general environmental education.
- Meanwhile, guests should also be given an awareness of protecting the environment. For example, the information cards placed in their rooms can prevent the excessive use of detergents and water.

The applications mentioned in general include crucial points in preventing environmental damage in the tourism sector. In addition to all these measures, there are examples of environmentally friendly activities implemented in the hospitality sector: Greenstar chain hotels in Finland are one of the first carbon-neutral businesses. This hotel chain focuses on emission-free travel and offers its customers free rental bikes and charging points for electric cars to travel around the city. In these hotels, built on small plots to save as much land as possible, Finnish wood is heavily preferred. Some places have moss walls and hotel carpets produced using recycled materials of 63%. These hotels, which are also environmentally friendly in food and beverages, offer organic tea and coffee tastes (Green Star Hotels, 2022).

Radisson Hotel Group, a highly effective business in environmentalist activities, annually determines water and energy uses and the waste amount and takes savings measures. The group has set a target of reducing carbon emissions by 30% by 2025. Furthermore, instead of disposable plastic straws and mixers, they use wood materials in their services and prevent a significant amount of plastic from dispersing in nature. It avoids cleaning products that are harmful to the environment and human health and chooses its suppliers from environmentally friendly businesses (Radission Hotels, 2022).

Seven Springs Resort in the USA contracted with the Ebara Environmental Engineering Company to have the food waste recycled by composting and have the hotel waste recovered as helpful fertilizers for the region (Lee & Park, 2009). A recycled paper left in Holiday Inn rooms includes a statement: "Can you help us help the environment? Imagine the tons of unnecessarily washed hotel linens every day globally and thus the damage of the chemicals to our waters. Take action now, and please help us stop this pollution. If you leave this card on your bed, you will get service with the same sheet. For a healthy environment..." (Çetin Gürkan et al., 2015).

Rilano Hotel in the Germany acts with the policy of "Less washing, less pollution". The hotel has warnings stating that towels can be hanged on a hanger unless a change is required for guests, thus contributing to the protection of the environment. In addition, there is a "Green Card" application to encourage guests to protect the environment. Thanks to this card, people who do not want room cleaning are offered free drinks at the hotel bar. There are also areas where people who come to the hotel with their electric vehicles can charge their vehicles free of charge. In addition, to contribute to sustainable gastronomy, there is an area in the garden of the hotel where it grows its own spices and herbs. This application of the hotel helps to reduce food waste and greenhouse gas emissions (The Rilono Hotel München, 2022).

Gaia Napa Valley Hotel in the USA is among the environmentally friendly enterprises. This hotel obtains 10% of its electricity from solar panels and employs Solatube Tubular Skylights. These large lamps illuminate the lobby, rooms, and corridors by absorbing the sunlight. This establishment, which has many environmental activities in the hotel, shares them with its guests in one corner, thanks to three computer screens called the "Energy Usage Panel" and one interactive screen. In these panels, electricity usage, carbon dioxide emission, and water usage measurements are updated every fifteen minutes and presented to the guests. Thus, while training guests about environmentalist awareness, the business gains value by highlighting its efforts in this area (Gaia Napa Valley Hotel, 2007).

CONCLUSION

With the industrial revolution, the acceleration of technology and overusing of scarce resources because of individual ambitions have brought environmental problems to dangerous dimensions. In short, this situation has accelerated the deterioration of the natural balance and the destruction of the physical environment. In the face of environmental problems, people who want to live in a cleaner and more sustainable environment have sought solutions to prevent environmental pollution. In particular, they tried to refrain from environmentally harmful businesses and products and reflected these behaviors in their purchasing decisions. In the end, businesses could not resist frequent and effective social reactions, and as a result of efforts to make the activities more environmentally friendly, the concept of green marketing emerged.

The concept of green marketing has affected the tourism sector as well as affected many others. Since touristic activities such as accommodation, eating, and drinking, entertainment increased, natural areas have been over-exploited and damaged. With the increasing number of visitors, the environmental damage has become substantial. However, the environment and the tourism sector are in an inseparable relationship because the tourism sector's existence, quality, and sustainability tightly depend on the environment. Tourism activity is often directly related to protecting the natural environment. While arranging their marketing strategies, tourism businesses aiming for more market share and competitive advantage should consider target audiences' demands, design environmentally friendly products, and highlight these activities in their marketing communications.

Hospitality businesses, perhaps the largest field in the tourism sector, must regulate their activities and develop environmentally friendly strategies to reduce their massive energy consumption and environmental damage. Previous studies revealed that hospitality businesses consumed more water and energy and caused more air pollution and waste than other sectors. These businesses can protect the environment and sustainability by taking some steps. The current study, including the activities of hospitality businesses for the environment, evaluated the sustainability of these activities.

FUTURE RESEARCH DIRECTIONS

There are many actions that individuals and businesses can take to protect the environment. First of all, individuals should always reflect their environmentally friendly behaviors to businesses and pressure them to exhibit such behaviors. Tourism businesses that always use the environment as a resource should also participate and lead this change. In this study, environmentally friendly practices are discussed only on the basis of hospitality businesses. However, adopting the green marketing approach of each tourism-related business will reduce the costs and thus provide more profit. At the same time, it will cause steps to be taken to protect the environment, which is seen as the most important source of tourism, and to ensure its sustainability. Researches on hospitality businesses show that especially the amount of water and energy consumption is quite high, waste materials pollute the environment, cause noise pollution and sound pollution. In order to disseminate and implement the green hotel management approach, businesses should prioritize environmental awareness of hotel owners and managers, determine long-term policies and be willing to plan this together with all their stakeholders. In addition, it can be said that the green products used in hospitality businesses are quite limited. It is thought that increasing and developing green product varieties will also contribute to the issue of sustainability. In addition, the necessary environmental training should be given to the personnel working closely with the environment, and incentive programs should be used to ensure that the employees always do their work with an environmentalist attitude. Finally, it is recommended that all applications be checked at regular intervals, renewed together with the developing technology and supported by various organizations.

REFERENCES

American Marketing Association. (2017). *Definitions of marketing.* https://www.ama.org/the-definition-of-marketing-what-is-marketing/

Atay, L., & Dilek, E. (2013). Konaklama işletmelerinde yeşil pazarlama uygulamaları: İbis otel örneği. *Süleyman Demirel Üniversitesi İktisadi ve İdari Bilimler Fakültesi Dergisi, 18*(1), 203–219.

Ay, C., & Ecevit, Z. (2005). Çevre bilinçli tüketiciler. *Akdeniz Üniversitesi İktisadi ve İdari Bilimler Fakültesi Dergisi, 5*(10), 238–263.

Aytekin, P. (2007). Yeşil pazarlama stratejileri. *Celal Bayar Üniversitesi Sosyal Bilimler Dergisi, 2*(2), 36–45.

Baki, B., & Cengiz, E. (2002). Toplam kalite çevre yönetimi. *Uludağ Üniversitesi İktisadi ve İdari Bilimler Dergisi, 21*(1), 153–175.

Çabuk, S., Nakıboğlu, B., & Keleş, C. (2008). Tüketicilerin yeşil ürün satın alma davranışlarının sosyo demografik değişkenler açısından incelenmesi. *Çukurova Üniversitesi Sosyal Bilimler Enstitüsü Dergisi, 17*(1), 85-102.

Çakıcı, C. A., Akoğlan Kozak, M., Azaltun, M., Sökmen, A., & Sarıışık, M. (2002). *Otel işletmeciliği.* Detay Yayıncılık.

Çetin Gürkan, G., Dönmez Polat, D., & Demiralay, T. (2015). Turistlerde çevre bilincinin çevreye duyarlı müşteri davranışı ve çevreye duyarlı konaklama işletmelerinde kalma tercihleri üzerindeki etkisi. *Ekonomi ve Yönetim Araştırmaları Dergisi, 4*(1), 114–133.

Chamorro, A., & Bañegil, T. M. (2006). Green marketing philosophy: A study of Spanish firms with ecolabels. *Corporate Social Responsibility and Environmental Management, 13*(1), 11–24. doi:10.1002/csr.83

Chen, Y. S., Lai, S. B., & Wen, C. T. (2006). The influence of green innovation performance on corporate advantage in Taiwan. *Journal of Business Ethics, 67*(4), 331–339. doi:10.100710551-006-9025-5

Clow, K. E., & Baack, D. (2007). *Integrated advertising promotion and marketing communications* (3rd ed.). Pearson Prentice Hal.

De Fran, A. L. (1996). Go green: An environmental checklist for the lodging industry. *The Cornell Hotel and Restaurant Administration Quarterly, 37*(6), 84–85. doi:10.1177/001088049603700612

Demir, C., & Çevirgen, A. (2006). *Turizm ve çevre yönetimi - Sürdürülebilir gelişme yaklaşımı*. Nobel Yayın Dağıtım.

Deng, J., King, B., & Bauer, T. (2002). Evaluating natural attractions for tourism. *Annals of Tourism Research*, 29(2), 422–438. doi:10.1016/S0160-7383(01)00068-8

Dilek, S. E. (2012). *Turizm işletmelerinde yeşil pazarlama uygulamaları: Bir alan araştırması (Yayımlanmamış Yüksek Lisans Tezi)*. Çanakkale Onsekiz Mart Üniversitesi.

Djaadi, N. (2016). *Yeşil pazarlama uygulamalarının tüketici satın alma davranışları üzerine etkisi: Türkiye ve Cezayir örneği (Yayımlanmamış Yüksek Lisans Tezi)*. Trakya Üniversitesi.

Dolmacı, N., & Bulgan, G. (2013). Turizm etiği kapsamında çevresel duyarlılık. *Journal of Yaşar University*, 29(9), 4853–4871.

Dülgeroğlu, İ., Başol, O., & Öztürk Başol, R. (2016). Genç tüketicilerin yeşil tüketim davranışı: Uluslararası algı farklılıkları. *Mehmet Akif Ersoy Üniversitesi Sosyal Bilimler Enstitüsü Dergisi*, 8(15), 1–16.

Duymaz, S. Y. (2013). Çevre örgütlerinin çevresel yönetime katılma sürecinde dayandığı haklar. *Türkiye Barolar Birliği Dergisi*, (107), 173–198.

Erdoğan, N., & Tosun, C. (2009). Environmental performance of tourism accommodations in the protected area: Case of Goreme Historical National Park. *International Journal of Hospitality Management*, 28(3), 406–414. doi:10.1016/j.ijhm.2009.01.005

Eren, D., & Yılmaz, İ. (2008). Otel işletmelerinde yeşil pazarlama uygulamaları: Nevşehir ili örneği. In 13. Ulusal pazarlama kongresi (2008): "Pazarlamada yeni yaklaşımlar" bildiriler kitabı (pp. 25-29). Nevşehir Üniversitesi İktisadi ve İdari Bilimler Fakültesi Yayınları.

Eser, Z., Öztürk, S. A., & Korkmaz, S. (2011). *Pazarlama: Kavramlar- ilkeler- kararlar*. Siyasal Kitabevi.

Gaia Napa Valley Hotel. (2007). *Example of green accommodation business*. https://www.greenlodgingnews.com/gaia-napa-valley-hotel-spa-receives-leed-gold-certification/

Giraldo, J. M., & Castro, W. A. S. (2014). Green supply chains: Conceptual bases and trends. In Green supply chains: Applications in agroindustries (pp. 13-26). Universidad Nacional de Colombia.

Green Star Hotels. (2022). *Example of green accommodation business*. https://www.greenstar.fi/hotellit/lahti/

Gryshchenko, O., Babenko, V., Bilovodska, O., Voronkova, T., Ponomarenko, I., & Shatska, Z. (2022). Green tourism business as marketing perspective in environmental management. *Global Journal of Environmental Science and Management*, 8(1), 117–132.

Günay, T. (2017). *Turizm işletmelerinde yeşil pazarlama uygulamaları: İzmir ili örneği (Yayımlanmamış Yüksek Lisans Tezi)*. Yaşar Üniversitesi.

Hacıoğlu, N. (2008). *Turizm pazarlaması* (6th ed.). Nobel Yayın Dağıtım.

İpar, M. S. (2018). *Turistlerin yeşil otel tercihlerine yönelik algıları, çevreci davranış eğilimleri ve davranışsal niyetlerle ilişkisi (Yayımlanmamış Doktora Tezi)*. Çanakkale Onsekiz Mart Üniversitesi.

İstanbullu Dinçer, F., & Muğan Ertuğral, S. (2009). Turizm işletmelerinin pazarlamasında ürün. In Turizm işletmelerinin pazarlamasında 7P ve 7C (ss. 49-74). Değişim Aktüel Yayınevi.

Kahraman, N., & Türkay, O. (2012). *Turizm ve çevre*. Detay Yayıncılık.

Karaca, S. (2013). Tüketicilerin yeşil ürünlere ilişkin tutumlarının incelenmesine yönelik bir araştırma. *Ege Akademik Bakış*, *13*(1), 99–111. doi:10.21121/eab.2013119503

Kaur, R., Mishra, S., Yadav, S., & Shaw, T. (2022). Analysing the impact of green marketing mix on consumer purchase intention. *International Journal of Indian Culture and Business Management*, 25(3), 403–425. doi:10.1504/IJICBM.2022.122729

Kaya, İ. (2009). *Pazarlama bi' tanedir* (IV. Dijital Baskı) https://docplayer.biz.tr/829585-Pazarlama-bi-tanedir.html

Khan, M. I., Khalid, S., Zaman, U., José, A. E., & Ferreira, P. (2021). Green paradox in emerging tourism supply chains: Achieving green consumption behavior through strategic green marketing orientation, brand social responsibility, and green image. *International Journal of Environmental Research and Public Health*, 18(18), 9626. doi:10.3390/ijerph18189626 PMID:34574552

Kocagöz, E. (2011). Güncel bir konu olarak değil sürekli bir yaklaşım olarak yeşil pazarlama. In Güncel Pazarlama Yaklaşımları (pp. 47-78). Alfa Aktüel.

Kozak, M. (2014). *Sürdürebilir turizm*. Detay Yayıncılık.

Kozak, N. (2010). *Turizm pazarlaması* (3rd ed.). Detay Yayıncılık.

Lee, S., & Park, S. Y. (2009). Do socially responsible activities help hotels and casinos achieve their financial goals? *International Journal of Hospitality Management*, *28*(1), 105–112. doi:10.1016/j.ijhm.2008.06.003

Leonidou, L. C., Leonidou, C. N., Fotiadis, T. A., & Zeriti, A. (2013). Resources and capabilities as drivers of hotel environmental marketing strategy: Implications for competitive advantage and performance. *Tourism Management*, *35*, 94–110. doi:10.1016/j.tourman.2012.06.003

Lim, C., & McAleer, M. (2005). Ecologically sustainable tourism management. *Environmental Modelling & Software*, *20*(11), 1431–1438. doi:10.1016/j.envsoft.2004.09.023

Lumbaraja, P., Lubis, A. N., & Hasibuan, B. K. (2019). Sustaining Lake Toba's tourism: Role of creative industry, green tourism marketing and tourism experience. *Asian Journal of Business and Accounting*, *12*(1), 257–278. doi:10.22452/ajba.vol12no1.9

Manaktola, K., & Jauhari, V. (2007). Exploring consumer attitude and behaviour towards green practices in the lodging industry in India. *International Journal of Contemporary Hospitality Management*, *19*(5), 364–377. doi:10.1108/09596110710757534

Mastny, L. (2001). *Traveling light: New paths for international tourism*. Worldwatchpaper 159.

Menon, A., Menon, A., Chowdhury, J., & Jankovich, J. (1999). Evolving paradigm for environmental sensitivity in marketing programs: A synthesis of theory and practice. *Journal of Marketing Theory and Practice*, *7*(2), 1–15. doi:10.1080/10696679.1999.11501825

Mensah, I. (2006). Environmental management practices among hotels in the greater Accra region. *International Journal of Hospitality Management*, *25*(3), 414–431. doi:10.1016/j.ijhm.2005.02.003

Mesci, Z. (2014). Otellerin çevreci uygulamalarının değerlendirmesi. *Seyahat ve Otel İşletmeciliği Dergisi*, *11*(3), 90–102.

Mosavichechaklou, S. (2017). *Türk ve İranlı tüketicilerin yeşil satın alma davranışlarına ilişkin karşılaştırmalı bir araştırma (Yayımlanmamış Yüksek Lisans Tezi)*. İstanbul Üniversitesi.

Nemli, E. (2001). Çevreye duyarlı yönetim anlayışı. *İstanbul Üniversitesi Siyasal Bilgiler Fakültesi Dergisi*, *23*(24), 211-224.

Olalı, H., & Timur, A. (1988). *Turizm ekonomisi*. Ofis Ticaret Matbaacılık.

Onurlubaş, E., & Dinçer, D. (2016). *Yeşil pazarlama tüketici algısı üzerine bir araştırma* (1st ed.). Beta Yayıncılık.

Ottman, J. (1998). *Green marketing and opportunities for the new marketing age.* NTC Business Books.

Ottman, J. A., Stafford, E. R., & Hartman, C. L. (2006). Avoiding green marketing myopia: Ways to improve consumer appeal for environmentally preferable products. *Environment, 48*(5), 22–36. doi:10.3200/ENVT.48.5.22-36

Özcan, H., & Özgül, B. (2019). Yeşil pazarlama ve tüketicilerin yeşil ürün tercihlerini etkileyen faktörler. *Türkiye Mesleki ve Sosyal Bilimler Dergisi, 1*(1), 1–18.

Papadas, K. K., Avlonitis, G. J., & Carrigan, M. (2017). Green marketing orientation: Conceptualization, scale development and validation. *Journal of Business Research, 80*, 236–246. doi:10.1016/j.jbusres.2017.05.024

Peattie, K. (1995). *Environmental marketing management: Meeting the green challenge.* Pitman Publishing.

Peattie, K. (1999). Trappings versus substance in the greening of marketing planning. *Journal of Strategic Marketing, 7*(2), 131–148. doi:10.1080/096525499346486

Peattie, K., & Crane, A. (2005). Green marketing: Legend, myth, farce or prophesy? *Qualitative Market Research, 4*(8), 357–370. doi:10.1108/13522750510619733

Polonsky, M. J. (1994). An introduction to green marketing. *Electronic Green Journal, 1*(2). Advance online publication. doi:10.5070/G31210177

Polonsky, M. J., & Rosenberger, P. J. III. (2001). Reevaluating green marketing: A strategic approach. *Business Horizons, 44*(5), 21–30. doi:10.1016/S0007-6813(01)80057-4

Porter, M. E., & Kramer, M. R. (2006). Strategy and sosciety, the link between competitive advantage and corporate social responsibility. *Harvard Business Review, 85*(12), 78–91. PMID:17183795

Prakash, A. (2002). Green marketing, public policy and managerial strategies. *Business Strategy and the Environment, 11*(5), 285–297. doi:10.1002/bse.338

Radission Hotels. (2022). *Example of green accommodation business.* https://media.radissonhotels.net/image/responsible-business--corporate-use-only/businesscenter/16256-142211-m24296998.pdf

Revilla, G., Dodd, T. H., & Hoover, L. C. (2001). Environmental tactics used by hotel companies in Mexico. *International Journal of Hospitality & Tourism Administration, 1*(3/4), 111–127. doi:10.1300/J149v01n03_07

Rivera, J. (2002). Assessing a voluntary environmental initiative in the developing world: The Costa Rican certification for sustainable tourism. *Policy Sciences, 35*(4), 333–360. doi:10.1023/A:1021371011105

Rivera, J. (2004). Institutional pressures and voluntary environmental behavior in developing countries: Evidence from the Costa Rican hotel industry. *Society & Natural Resources, 17*(9), 779–797. doi:10.1080/08941920490493783

Rushton, A., Phil, C., & Peter, B. (2006). *Handbook of logistics and distribution management* (3rd ed.). Kogan Page Limited.

Sanchez, J., Callarisa, L., Rodríguez, M. R., & Moliner, M. A. (2006). Perceived value of the purchase of a tourism product. *Tourism Management, 27*(3), 394–409. doi:10.1016/j.tourman.2004.11.007

Sarkım, M. (2007). *Sürdürülebilir turizm kapsamında turistik ürün çeşitlendirme politikaları ve Antalya örneği (Yayımlanmamış Doktora Tezi)*. Dokuz Eylül Üniversitesi.

Sert, A. N. (2017). Konaklama işletmelerinde yeşil pazarlama uygulamaları: Doğa Residence Otel örneği. *Türk Turizm Araştırmaları Dergisi, 1*(1), 1–20. doi:10.26677/tutad.2017.0

Tabak, G., & Güneren Özdemir, E. (2019). Turistlerin çevre dostu tutumlarının çevreye duyarlı turistik ürün satın alma niyeti üzerine etkisi: Nevşehir ilinde bir araştırma. *Journal of Tourism and Gastronomy Studies, 7*(3), 1753–1787.

Tavmergen, İ. P., & Meriç, P. Ö. (1999). Çevre korumasına yönelik turizm uygulamaları: Yeşil otelcilik, doğa turizmi ve ISO 14000. *Turizmde Seçme Makaleler, 33*, 19–38.

Tek, Ö. B. (1999). *Pazarlama ilkeleri-global yönetimsel yaklaşım Türkiye uygulamaları* (8th ed.). Beta Basım Yayım.

Tekeli, M., & Kırıcı Tekeli, E. (2020). Sustainable Gastronomic Tourism. In F. Türkmen (Ed.), *Selected academic studies from turkish tourism sector* (pp. 113–133). Peter Lang.

Tenekecioğlu, B. (2004). Pazarlama konusu ve pazarlama yönetimi. In B. Tenekecioğlu (Ed.), Pazarlama yönetimi (pp. 1-14). Eskişehir: Anadolu Üniversitesi.

The Rilono Hotel München. (2022). *Example of green accommodation business.* https://www.rilano-hotel-muenchen.de/info/green-room/

Türk, M., & Gök, A. (2010). Yeşil pazarlama anlayışı açısından üretici işletmelerin sosyal sorumluluğu. *Elektronik Sosyal Bilimler Dergisi, 9*(32), 199–220.

Ural, T. (2003). *İşletme ve pazarlama etiği* (1st ed.). Detay Yayıncılık.

Usta, Ö. (1992). *Turizm.* Altın Kitaplar Yayınevi.

Üstünel, B. (2000). *Ekonominin temelleri.* Dünya Yayınları.

Uydacı, M. (2016). *Yeşil pazarlama.* Türkmen Kitabevi.

Varinli, İ. (2012). *Pazarlamada Yeni Yaklaşımlar.* Detay Yayıncılık.

Yeşil Oteller Birliği. (2015). *What are green hotels?* https://www.greenhotels.com/

Yetiş, Ş. A. (2018). Sürdürülebilir turizm kapsamında küçük ölçekli konaklama işletmelerinde yeşil pazarlama uygulamaları. *Gümüşhane Üniversitesi Sosyal Bilimler Enstitüsü Elektronik Dergisi, 9*(23), 82–98.

KEY TERMS AND DEFINITIONS

Green Hotel: Businesses having solid and liquid waste management systems, giving importance to recycling and reusing, saving water and energy, and attaching importance to protecting biological diversity.

Green Marketing: Environmentally sensitive marketing activities, policies, and procedures in generating profits and achieving objectives.

Green Place: Healthy and environmentalist distribution channels in the marketing and transportation stages of the product.

Green Price: Adding all extra costs of green marketing activities to the product price.

Green Product: The products contribute to the natural environment protection by saving energy and resource.

Green Promotion: The activities carried out to provide consumers with accurate information about the environmental characteristics of the business and the product, to raise awareness of the consumers, to remind them of the green product advantages, and to generate an environmentally friendly business impression.

Green Technology: Technologies that take care of the sustainability of natural resources at every stage from production to usage processes and also support the healthy existence of natural life.

Marketing Mix: All the marketing tools of a company to pursue its objectives in the core market.

Sustainability: Meeting the needs of the present generation without destroying the ability of future generations to meet their needs.

Sustainable Tourism: An approach that aims to meet the needs of tourists, the tourism industry, and local communities without compromising the ability of future generations to meet their needs.

Chapter 4
Impacts of Tourism Development in Developing Countries:
A Namibian Perspective

Faithfull Gonzo
University of Sunderland in London, UK

ABSTRACT

Tourism development has been viewed in terms of its contribution to economic growth. Thus, most developing countries have declared tourism as an important economic sector. Tourism is also envisaged to provide economic benefits to communities through the provision of employment. Due to the increase in tourist numbers, environmental changes to the natural resources have been a cause for concern to nations. Tourism stakeholders have incorporated environmental issues in their tourism development plans to ensure that the tourism products are sustainable, and communities are benefitting. For the communities to benefit from tourism development, the analysis of socio-cultural impacts has become of paramount importance. Governments have emphasised increasing tourism numbers to influence economic growth. The local community would then benefit from the tourism increase through multiplier effects. Thus, the chapter explores the impacts of tourism development in developing countries with a focus on Namibia as a developing country.

DOI: 10.4018/978-1-6684-6796-1.ch004

INTRODUCTION

This chapter aims to firstly provide a detailed analysis of tourism development from a global and Namibian perspective. The chapter starts by providing a definition of tourism and then present an overview of tourism development highlighting its contribution to the global economy and developing countries. Namibia as a developing country devised various strategies to enhance tourism and develop rural areas, therefore these strategies are analysed. The positive and negative impacts of tourism development are also scrutinised to establish the effects that may hinder the development of tourism, particularly rural tourism.

UNWTO (2015) defines tourism as "a social, cultural and economic phenomenon which entails the movement of people to countries or places outside their usual environment for personal or business/professional purposes." The chapter adopts this definition because it encompasses a broader view of tourism which includes socio-economic, environmental, and cultural elements.

AN OVERVIEW OF TOURISM DEVELOPMENT

Tourism development should be well planned and executed in order to create attractive tourism destinations. In his seminal work, Butler (1980) indicates that destinations develop over time. Tourism planning and development is very site specific (Gunn, 1988) but also requires policy and the integration of stakeholders to make it work. Sofield (2003) highlights the important role that the community should play in tourism development by being involved in decision making for development. On the other hand, Simpson (2008) states that the government can influence the positive and negative socio-economic effects of tourism.

Honey et al., (2010) state that tourism development offers destinations with opportunities for employment creation and improvement of community services. However, tourism development regulated by the community will economically benefit the community and influence poverty alleviation (Tosun, 2006; Wondirad & Ewnetu, 2019). Bailey and Richardson (2010) also state that tourism development is recognised as an essential device for boosting economic growth and reducing poverty.

Sharpley (2000) stated that the concept of development has changed over the years, and it is closely aligned with economic growth. Development refers to a continuous increase of income per person to empower the community to distribute its yield quicker than the population growth. Among other factors, Todaro and Smith (2011) state that enhancing the quality of life of the community by improving infrastructure is an indication of economic development. It should comprise of "the reduction of poverty and greater equity to progress in education, health and nutrition and of the protection of the environment" (World Bank, 1991). Tourism development is viewed as a process of physical change, thus Dieke (2005) identified three stages for tourism development as a process where:

- The tourists ascertain a new area of interest.
- The news of the findings spread.
- And the host society respond to this new economic activity by building facilities and offering services.

Liu (1994) indicated that tourism development is a dynamic process which involves matching tourism resources to the demands and preferences of authentic or potential tourists. Therefore, tourism development can be viewed as the expansion and preservation of the tourism industry in any geographical area. It includes devising approaches, policies and plans that influence the increase and development of tourism at a destination. The tourism industry is important for the growth and development of many destinations. Due to the potential of tourism, it is envisioned as a vehicle for improving national or regional markets. The following section will provide an analysis of the contribution of tourism to the global economy and developing countries.

CONTRIBUTION OF TOURISM TO THE GLOBAL ECONOMY

Many destinations utilise tourism as a strategic approach for socio-economic improvement through job creation and export revenue earnings. The changing demographics and the decrease in long-haul travel costs have evidently influenced the growth of international tourism (Muhanna, 2007). International tourism receipts have significantly increased between 1970 and 2009, from US$17,9 billion to US$852 billion respectively (WTO, 2010). In 2012, international tourist receipts totalled US$1,075 billion (UNWTO, 2013). In 2019, the industry was reported as a leading and robust economic sector in the world, generating US$1,7 trillion in export earnings (UNWTO, 2019a).

Similarly, from 1950 to 2015 international tourist arrivals progressively increased from 25 million to an aggregate of 1,186 billion (Glaesser et al., 2017). In 2019, the internal tourist arrivals increased to 1,5 billion (UNWTO:2019b). The international tourist arrivals in 2012 were the most resilient, experiencing one per cent growth of 4,7. However, before that tourism growth substantially fluctuated, for example in 2003 the global tourism figures decreased by 0,6% whilst in 2004 the industry experienced the largest percentage growth in twenty years (10,4%) (Consultancy, 2016). In 2020, the international tourist arrivals declined by 22% due to the COVID-19 pandemic (as indicated in Figure 1) (UNWTO, 2020). Based on the previous global uncertainties such as the economic downturn, the tourism industry proved to be resilient, and it is expected to increase at a faster pace after the pandemic (Kumar, 2020).

Figure 1. International tourist numbers before and during the COVID-19 pandemic
Source: UNWTO (2020)

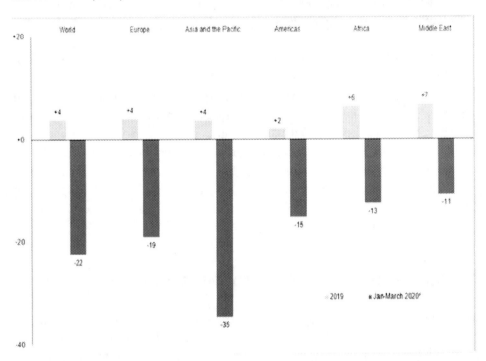

The tourism industry's direct contribution to international GDP increased by 3,3% (US$1,770 billion) in 2010 and it is anticipated to increase by 4,2% yearly (US$2,860 billion) in 2021 (Ekanayake & Long, 2012). WTTC (2017) reported that GDP in 2016 increased by 3,1% (US$2,306 billion) and it is anticipated to rise by 4,0% annually from 2017-2027. In 2020, the tourism industry contributed 10,3% GDP in total (WTTC, 2020). Given the arrival of public health emergencies such as the COVID-19 pandemic, it is yet to be established whether these projections still hold.

In 2015, tourism directly generated over 107 million jobs, it also supported (directly and indirectly) an aggregate of 284 million jobs worldwide and in 2027 the employment numbers are projected to rise to 380 million (WTTC, 2017). Furthermore, in 2016 the industry provided 109 million jobs (2 million more jobs, 1,8% increase) in the world hence 1 in 10 jobs are related to tourism (WTTC, 2017).

The tourism industry provided a total of 330 million jobs in the first quarter of 2020; however, 100 to 120 million jobs (direct) are anticipated to be at risk making it the current pandemic the worst crisis since 1950 (UNWTO, 2020). The figures above clearly indicate that tourism has the potential to grow, however, the recent pandemic may negatively impact on the industry, particularly economies such as developing countries that rely on tourism for their growth and development. It also shows the vulnerability of the industry to risks which is an even bigger challenge for developing countries. The following section review tourism development in developing countries to establish the potential of tourism in these countries.

TOURISM DEVELOPMENT IN DEVELOPING COUNTRIES

Developing countries have benefited from an expanding tourist base as far back as mid-20th century. The development of tourism, particularly international tourism, has been recognised as a priority by governments in the Southern Africa region, including the Southern Africa Development Community (SADC) (Novelli & Gebhardt, 2007). Since the 1950s, the share for the numbers of international tourist arrivals for developing countries has substantially improved from 3% in 1950 to 45% in 2001 (Muhanna, 2007). In 2013, developing countries' share of international tourist arrivals increased from 31% in 1990 to 47% in 2011 (Muchapondwa & Stage, 2013). Although there was a global increase of 52 million (4,6%) international tourists from 2014 to 2015, Africa's tourist arrivals decreased by 3% in the same year resulting in the continent experiencing the lowest figures (UNWTO, 2015). The tourist figures for Africa also declined to a total of two million. In 2018 Africa received 1,407 million international tourist arrivals earning tourism receipts of US$1,480 billion (UNCTAD, 2020). These figures clearly indicate that the tourism industry is vulnerable due to uncertainties such as the global recession and pandemics. Therefore, it is imperative to implement various strategies that encourage tourism growth.

Tourism has progressively become an important sector for governments and regions searching for socio-economic development (Kavita & Saarinen, 2016). Tourism considerably contributes to the economies of developing countries; particularly with regards to Gross Domestic Product (GDP) (Bennett et al., 1999). Africa as a developing nation rely on tourism for the growth of its economy. In 2018, tourism contributed $US42,1 billion (1,6%) to GDP whilst in 2019 it contributed 3,4% to Africa's GDP and is expected to increase to 4,1% in 2021 (African Development Bank, 2020). Least developed economies and transition economies are progressively concentrating on tourism as a pathway for development (Andrades & Dimanche, 2017). Most of the Least Developed Countries (LDCs) recognise tourism as a significant sector which has the capability for considerable economic growth (UNWTO, 2016). There are 47 countries classified as LDCs of which 33 are in Africa (United Nations, 2020). In 2015, 49 LDCs received 29 million international tourist arrivals which was a 300% increase from ten years ago (UNWTO, 2016). Tourism's GDP of LDCs contributes 9,5%, 42 out of the 47 LDCs regard tourism as an important sector of the economy (UNCTAD, 2020). These figures confirm that the contribution of tourism in LDCs has been steadily increasing. However, this trend may not continue due to the impact of the COVID-19 pandemic on travel and tourism.

Between 2011-2015, 21 million jobs were supported by tourism in Africa (UNCTAD, 2017), whilst in 2019, a total of 24,6 million jobs were supported by the travel and tourism industry (WTTC, 2019). The decline of the global tourism industry has a negative effect on the people that rely on tourism, which will ultimately have an impact on poverty and poverty alleviation efforts.

TOURISM AND INFRASTRUCTURE DEVELOPMENT

The growth of international tourism in developing countries is attributed to the development of infrastructure such as transport, the development of new source markets and the tourists' improved disposable income (Scheyvens, 2011). However, according to WTTC (2019) the sub-Saharan Africa has the least developed infrastructure in the world; therefore, tourist numbers grow at a slower pace. This indicates that infrastructure development influences tourism numbers. UNWTO (2016) elaborates that infrastructure development comprises of the provision of basic sanitation facilities, good road networks, reliable public transportation, education, and healthcare (UNWTO, 2016). Thus, it is imperative for destinations to invest in updating existing infrastructure as this improves accessibility which in turn attracts more tourism businesses. These will help alleviate poverty as more income can be realised from the tourism and related activities. Morgan and Pritchard (2006) highlight the importance of infrastructure development in alleviating poverty albeit in developed countries such as New Zealand. This sentiment was also later supported by Seetanah et al. (2009) who concluded that improved infrastructure results in reduced levels of poverty thereby confirming the existence of a positive correlation between developed infrastructures and its impact on poverty alleviation.

Nguyen and Nguyen (2013) studied the contribution of tourism to economic growth at a provincial level and found that tourism influenced economic growth in Thua Thien Hue province. Their research study also highlighted the importance of improving government policies for the economic growth to have more impact at a provincial level. Furthermore, they added that infrastructure such as transport network should be developed. Mandić et al. (2018) explored the relationship between tourism infrastructure, tourism development and recreational facilities in Croatia and conclude that the development of infrastructure and recreational facilities is determined by laws and regulations of the government. They further clarify that there is a considerable connection between the stage of the tourism development and the number of arrivals, overnights and state of the infrastructure, tourism infrastructure and recreational facilities. These conclusions agree with Seetanah et al. (2009) who studied the impact of infrastructure development on poverty alleviation. Based on the literature in this section, it is quite evident that tourism in developing, and least developed countries has the potential to contribute to economic growth and infrastructure development. It is therefore important to establish whether the growth of tourism and infrastructure development influences poverty alleviation, particularly in rural areas. The strategies implemented by Namibia to develop rural tourism will be explored in the next section.

TOURISM DEVELOPMENT IN NAMIBIA

The tourism sector in Namibia is one of the highest income earners in the country, ranking third after mining and agriculture (MET, 2016). Numerous redistributive policies aimed at bridging the gap between the rich and the poor were formulated to reduce poverty. The tourism industry in Namibia began in the 1960s, however, it was restricted to guest farms and private landowners only, who were permitted to exploit wildlife, register as game farmers and breed varied wildlife species that tourists could then pay to view or hunt (Samuelsson & Stage, 2007). In addition, wildlife in communal lands belonged to the government, clearly indicating that the local community could not benefit from tourism and therefore were not motivated to look after wildlife (Damm, 2008).

Tourist arrivals in Namibia in 1988 was estimated to be nearly 10 000, with the majority (70%) of these visitors originating from South Africa and 30% from Germany (Fourie, 1990). However, the tourist numbers declined in 1989 and 1990 due to the independence process. These figures are unreliable because tourism statistics before independence were based on assumptions. MET (1995) highlighted that the record keeping of tourists travelling to and from Namibia was conducted at South Africa's international borders only and therefore the actual figures are not available. During the same period, the tourism industry was optimistic due to several development projects that were implemented, for example the domestic airline of Namibia began to operate, and this improved tourist access to Namibia; regional markets for tourism were opened and new hotels were built whilst the old ones were upgraded.

In 1992 the white paper projected those 28 000 tourists visited Namibia, creating 20 000 jobs (direct and indirect) and the tourism activities generated $N500 million to the economy (Republic of Namibia, 1994). Five years after the independence of Namibia tourism records were still limited and not regularly published. In 1993, South Africa was still the major source market (61,8%) followed by Germany (10,6%), other European countries and regional countries like Angola, Botswana and Zambia accounting for 7,5% and less than 5% respectively (MET, 1995). The major source markets remained the same in 2001. This has now since changed, the major regional tourist source market for Namibia is Zambia (61,6%), whilst Germany continues to be the main overseas source market with 8,2% (MET, 2017).

The sector clearly indicated an upward growth, yet the Ministry of Environment and Tourism could not provide adequate proof that the industry was viable, and this led to the industry receiving a low budget which influenced a delay in decision making (MET, 2001). The number of tourists had a substantial improvement in the ten years (1993-2003) from 254 978 to 695 000 and new source markets emerged from western Europe (MET, 2004). Conversely, the war in Angola had an adverse impact on the tourism figures, particularly the north-eastern areas where several tourism enterprises closed, such that international visitors to Popa Game Park fell by approximately 10 000 (MET, 2004).

In 2004, the tourism industry in Namibia contributed N$5,242 billion (WTTC, 2006), whereas in 2006 the sector directly contributed 3,7% of GDP and 4,7% to total employment (Eita & Jordaan, 2007). As a developing country, Namibia aims to increase tourist arrivals to 8% by 2020 (Republic of Namibia, 2016). The tourism sector directly contributed N$3 billion (3%) GDP to the Namibian economy, and it also generated about 24 000 jobs in 2015 which is expected to rise to 186 000 jobs in 2025 (WTTC, 2015).

Over the years the sector has experienced an upward growth, however, the industry was impacted by the global financial crisis in 2011, experiencing a decline in the number of Namibia's tourist source markets by 10% and tourists from Europe declined by 11,2% (Namibia Tourism Board, 2013). MET (2015) indicates that the deterioration of the Angolan tourist market could have contributed to the financial crisis experienced in Namibia. During that same period, the sector also experienced a shift in demand from high-end products to low-end products, short stays and reduced spending (Namibia Tourism Board, 2013). To sustain optimistic tourism development and competitiveness of the destination in the world tourism market, it is vital to implement marketing strategies aimed at promoting the country as a quality and value-for-money destination. In Table 1, WTTC (2017) forecasted tourism growth and contribution for Namibia, displaying the possible impact on the economy.

In 2017, the tourism industry of Namibia directly contributed nearly N$5 million (2,9%) to GDP and this figure is anticipated to double (N$10,1 million) by 2028

(WTTC, 2017). In terms of employment the industry directly generated 23 000 jobs and by 2028 it is forecasted to increase to 35 000 jobs. This is a growth rate of 3,6% per year within the next ten years (WTTC, 2017), whilst in 2019, the industry contributed N$28,610 million (2,2%) to GDP and 114 600 jobs (direct and indirect) as indicated in Figure 2.

Table 1. Forecasts for tourism growth in Namibia

NAMIBIA	2017 USDmn	2017 % of total	2018 Growth	USDmn	2028 % of total	Growth
Direct contribution to GDP	369.3	2.9	8.0	756.7	3.7	6.6
Total contribution to GDP	1,778.2	13.8	5.5	3,181.9	15.6	5.4
Direct contribution to employment	23	3.2	6.5	35	3.6	3.6
Total contribution to employment	98	14.0	4.9	137	14.3	2.9
Visitor exports	326.8	6.2	10.6	645.4	6.3	6.0
Domestic spending	1,148.8	8.9	5.9	1,981.4	9.7	5.0
Leisure spending	1,206.5	2.3	7.2	2,181.0	3.1	5.4
Business spending	269.1	0.5	5.8	445.7	0.6	4.6
Capital investment	331.0	12.0	3.4	584.7	13.0	5.5

Source: WTTC (2017)

Figure 2. Key data on Namibia tourism
Source: WTTC (2020)

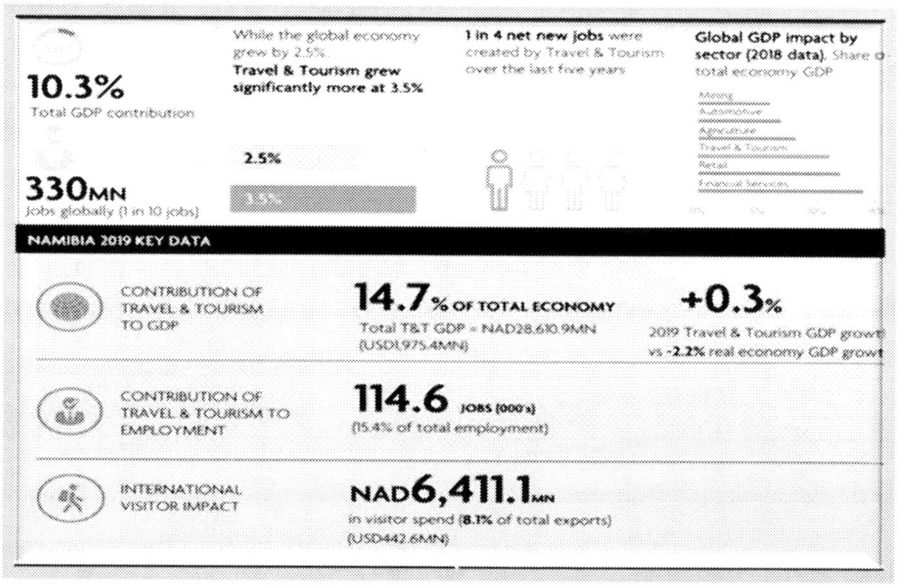

10.3% Total GDP contribution
While the global economy grew by 2.5%, Travel & Tourism grew significantly more at 3.5%
1 in 4 net new jobs were created by Travel & Tourism over the last five years
Global GDP impact by sector (2018 data). Share of total economy GDP

330MN Jobs globally (1 in 10 jobs)

NAMIBIA 2019 KEY DATA

CONTRIBUTION OF TRAVEL & TOURISM TO GDP
14.7% OF TOTAL ECONOMY
Total T&T GDP = NAD28,610.9MN (USD1,975.4MN)
+0.3%
2019 Travel & Tourism GDP growth vs -2.2% real economy GDP growth

CONTRIBUTION OF TRAVEL & TOURISM TO EMPLOYMENT
114.6 JOBS (000's)
(15.4% of total employment)

INTERNATIONAL VISITOR IMPACT
NAD6,411.1MN
in visitor spend (8.1% of total exports) (USD442.6MN)

Based on the above figures tourism in Namibia has been growing in terms of economic growth. Tourism in Namibia clearly indicates that it offers opportunities for employment. Infrastructure such as an airport promoted an increase in the number of tourist arrivals. This also offers opportunities for the rural areas to benefit from this development. The quality tourism products and activities available at a destination also influence tourism increase.

TOURISM PRODUCTS AND ACTIVITIES IN NAMIBIA

The most important component for development of rural tourism are the tourist activities, thus tourism in Namibia is customarily established on wildlife and wilderness experiences and dry topography, cultural groups and rural communities (Lapeyre, 2011). Protected areas and nature-based tourism is the most essential tourist attraction in Namibia of which 70% of the total tourism spending is accredited to these two areas (Turpie et al., 2004). Namibia has abundant wildlife with a significant number of game parks and wildlife resorts operating in the country. The Namibian national parks are utilised as a way of protecting nature and serve as tourist destinations. It emphasises the importance of local community involvement in the development and conservation of the parks to fully enjoy the benefits of the game parks (Janis, 2014).

The country offers world-renowned resources such as the Etosha National Park which is a popular international tourist destination and rich with varied wildlife species. The endangered black rhino and leopard, kori bustard (the heaviest flying bird) and elephants are popular at this park (NTB, 2020). Other popular national parks include the Dorob National Park and Coastal Namib-Naukluft park including Namib desert and Sossusvlei sand dunes and the Fish River Canyon situated in the south (MET, 2018). There are other established national parks in the Zambezi region, namely Bwabwata, Nkasa Rupara, Mudumu and Mahango. A huge amount of the tourism revenue emanates from entrance fees to national parks and tourism concessions provided for the private sector on state-owned land (Janis, 2014).

Namibia has a rich culture such as the Himba culture in the Kunene region. There are cultural and historical attractions also instituted in coastal towns like Swakopmund and in the capital city of Windhoek, adventure activities and an opportunity to explore Germany architecture and monuments showing the effect of colonialism which are presented in those areas (Moseley et al., 2007). Furthermore, Namibia is well known as a fishing and hunting destination. The hunting tourism involves guided visits for tourists who hunt trophy-quality game animals and then keep the trophies (Barnes & Novelli, 2007). Exclusive (mainly plain game species) and public hunting areas, which mainly involve high-value species, are offered in Namibia. Due to increasing anti-hunting ethics, especially from the developed world, trophy hunting is currently under growing threat. This sector holds 14% of the total tourism sector (Himavindu & Barnes, 2003). The country also offers fishing facilities in rivers and seas. This might pose threats to the sustainability of the sector. However, it is quite evident based on the figures above that the country has attractive tourism products which have influenced an upward growth in tourism numbers. The tourism attractions offer an opportunity for rural development.

NAMIBIA'S TOURISM POLICIES AND STRATEGIES

Namibia initially invested in the tourism industry with the aim of increasing the country's share in the world tourism product. The original vision of the authorities of Namibia was to change the country from an exporter of primary products and natural resources to a service economy. After independence, the Namibian government acknowledged that tourism was a priority sector (Jenkins, 2000). The White Paper on Tourism (1994) also highlighted the need to revitalise the sector to create jobs and alleviate poverty. Although policy development and implementation in Namibia is often criticised for being slow, it however developed various legislations and policies such as the National Development Plans – 1, 2, 3, 4 – all with the aim of promoting economic growth, employment and income creation and promoting rural development (National Planning Commission, 2002; Republic of Namibia, 1994, 1995a, 1995b, 2004, 2008).

The first National Biodiversity Strategy and Action Plan (NBSAP1) (2001) was launched with the purpose of managing biological resources and the environment. Thus, its key objective was to offer "a national strategic framework for natural resource management activities involving biological resources and the natural environment, including trade and economic incentives" (NBSAP1, 2001). The second NBSAP (2013-2022) focused on utilising the strategy as a driver of poverty alleviation and economic growth. Namibia's Vision 2030 (2004) predicted that by 2030 poverty will be reduced to a minimum level. Thus, its vision is to improve the quality of life of the people of Namibia and reduce poverty to a minimum. In this regard, strategies such as the National Development Plans, the 1998 Poverty Reduction Strategy and the 2001 National Poverty Reduction Action Plan programmes have been formulated with the target of reducing poverty (Namibia Planning Commission, 2002; Republic of Namibia, 2004, 2011, 2015, 2016).

The third National Development Plan's (2008) underlying vision is to reduce poverty and empower vulnerable groups. To realise the NDP 3's long term national goals, the tourism policy (2008) was formulated. Its aim is to provide a framework for the organisation of tourism resources to realise long-term national targets highlighted in the Vision 2030 such as sustained economic growth, employment creation, reduced inequalities and poverty reduction. It also provides comprehensive sections on environmental sustainability, human resource development, infrastructure and investment, planning and marketing. The policy addresses the issues of black empowerment, gender equality and partnerships with the private sector. The tourism policy of Namibia also recognises the significance of economic growth in its vision. The policy emphasised that it intends to provide a:

Mature, sustainable and responsible tourism industry contributing significantly to the economic development of Namibia and the quality of life of all her people, primarily through job creation and economic growth. (MET, 2008)

To respond to the environmental issues, policies and regulations on tourism in Namibia incorporated the environmental aspects. The tourism policy (2008) highlights that tourism in Namibia should promote environmental and ecological sustainability, and for this to be achieved the policy should collaborate with the Environment Management Act (EMA) of 2007 (MET, 2008). This regulation emphasises the importance of promoting sustainable development whilst the tourism policy underscores that the environment should be protected, and the natural resources should be economically utilised for the benefit of the current and future generations whilst ultimately satisfying the visitors profitably (MET, 2008:6). The sustainable development concept has influenced the development of alternative tourism such as green tourism and ecotourism, with the objective of reducing environmental impacts and providing benefits to the residents. Namibia's tourism industry is a leader in southern Africa when it comes to environmental sustainability (Blanke et al., 2011); it recognises the importance of using natural resources sustainably. Vision 2030 and initiatives such as eco-awards have been developed for tourism establishments.

The tourism policy is in line with the third National Development Plan which recognises tourism as a major contributor to the country's economic growth. The fourth National Development Plan also noted that economic growth should be utilised as a method to attain other goals like poverty alleviation, improved employment and industrialisation (Republic of Namibia, 2016). However, the economic growth of Namibia has not been constant due to the factors such as the global economic crisis. The economic growth of Namibia has been variable, it averaged 3,6% which was below the target of 5% (Republic of Namibia, 2012/13 to 2016/2017).

The government of Namibia is mainly involved in the drafting of these policies and aims to generate an authorising environment for both the tourism industry and foreign investors, whilst NDP 4 targets to increase income equality (NPC, 2012). Namibia's fifth Development Plan's focus is on structural transformation and modernisation; at the same time it must adhere to the four integrated pillars of sustainable development (Republic of Namibia, 2017). These include economic progression, social transformation, environmental sustainability and good governance. Therefore, the plan's goals include reduction of poverty, creating a skilled workforce and ensuring that the current and future generation sustainably appreciate the benefits of Namibia's natural resources.

Tourism is essentially an effective tool utilised to preserve natural resources and local culture (Carbone, 2005). Other tourism policies such as the communal area conservancy legislation (1996) presented rural Namibians with new opportunities and gave communities a chance to use the natural resources. To conserve their wildlife resources, the communal area residents are offered incentives. The communities were presented with an opportunity to manage and sustainably use their wildlife through live game sales, meat harvesting and trophy hunting (Damm, 2008). Also, the Nature Conservation Amendment Act (1996) allowed the community members to set up conservancies, with the purpose of supporting the government's aim of protecting natural resources and sustainably managing them. It is a community-based initiative and therefore plays an essential role in laying a strong base in the development of community tourism.

The National Tourism Growth and Development Strategy (NTGDS) was developed in 2016. Its aim was to increase the number of tourist arrivals to generate more jobs for Namibians. The strategy focuses on economic transformation and social empowerment which will be achieved by providing tangible and financial support to small- and medium-sized businesses, Black Economic Empowerment (BEE) businesses and their associates and increasing opportunities for rural tourism initiatives (MET, 2016). The National Tourism Investment Profile and Promotion Strategy (NTIPPS) (2016-2026) was also developed to provide a support framework that increases business opportunities for rural enterprises. It also aims to create a favourable environment for investors and to reduce transaction costs to allow the private sector to invest in the tourism industry (MET, 2016). Table 2 shows the government of Namibia's efforts to promote development.

IMPACTS[1] OF TOURISM DEVELOPMENT IN NAMIBIA

The tourism industry is rapidly growing, and it has been developing faster than the global economy (Perrottet & Benli, 2016). Although tourism is often viewed as an industry that present positive effects to a destination, particularly economic benefits, it is not immune to negative effects. As soon as tourism becomes a stable activity, it is important for all stakeholders involved in the tourism development of a country to be conscious of the negative effects.

Table 2. Government documents on tourism development (Namibia)

Document	Year	Main objectives
White Paper on Tourism	1994	Revitalise tourism sector to create jobs and alleviate poverty. Reduction of inequalities in income.
Namibia Tourism Development Plan	1995	Promote economic growth, reduce unemployment and create income sources. Protect wildlife.
Policy on the Promotion of Community-Based Tourism (CBT)	1995	Use of CBT in providing socio-economic development and correct previous unequal distribution of tourism ownership.
Tourism Act, Consolidated draft	1996	Ensure tourism benefits all sectors of the population. Acknowledgement of conservancies as players in tourism. Community members to run conservancies and have concessionary rights over tourism activities.
Nature Conservation Amendment Act	1996	Conservancies obtain wildlife and tourism rights to protect and manage natural resources.
First National Development Plan (NDP 1) 1995/6 -1999/2000	1996	Tourism projected to boost economic growth, reduce unemployment and promote rural development.
Second National Development Plan (NDP 2) 2001/2 -2005/2006	2002	Tourism projected to boost economic growth, reduce unemployment and promote rural development. Target set to establish 25 communal conservancies by 2005; target for tourism growth of 6% between 1999 and 2006.
Namibia Vision 2030	2004	Role of tourism in economic development, poverty alleviation and employment creation anticipated to increase.
A national tourism policy for Namibia. First draft	2005	Policy that clarifies the role of tourism in addressing objectives for NDP 2.
Third National Development Plan (NDP 3) 2007/8 -2011/12	2008	Tourism projected to boost economic growth, reduce unemployment and promote rural development.
A National Tourism Policy for Namibia.	2008	The aim is to provide a framework for the mobilisation of tourism resources to realise long-term national goals of NDP 3.
Fourth National Development Plan (NDP 4) 2012/13 - 2016/2017	2012	To create a conducive environment that helps to improve education and the health-delivery system. Tourism was identified as one of the four strategic areas.
Fifth National Development Plan (NDP5) 2017/2018- 2021/2022	2017	Reduction of poverty, creating a skilled workforce and ensuring that the current and future generation sustainably appreciate the benefits of Namibia's natural resources.

Adapted from: Nyakunu and Rogerson (2014)

Many academics analysed tourism impacts on the destination in terms of economic, environmental and socio-cultural (Deery et al. 2012) with each tourism impact highlighting positive and negative effects. However, positive economic impacts are easily identifiable than any other effects. Instead of analysing the tourism impacts from an economic perspective it is essential for destinations to critically review all aspects of tourism impacts. Weaver and Lawton (2006) stated that tourism impacts should be divided into three types; economic, environmental and socio-cultural impacts. Whilst Spenceley et al. (2009) indicated that the impact of tourism on the poor can be parted into three categories: income generation, effects of tourism on the natural and cultural environment and improvement of people's livelihood.

THE ECONOMIC IMPACTS OF TOURISM DEVELOPMENT

The tourism industry is rapidly growing, international visitors are anticipated increase to 1.8 billion by 2030 (Perrottet & Benli, 2016). Researchers and governments have documented the potential of tourism to economic growth. The impact on the economy is greater when tourists spend more in the local community. However, Weaver and Lawton, (2006) emphasised that the overall number of tourists visiting the region, their length of stay, how much they spend in the region and the circulation of expenditure throughout the economy must be analysed when deciding the economic impact of tourism. Muhanna (2007) stated that tourism development is customarily pursued for its significant impact on employment, economic growth (in GDP) and foreign exchange earnings. Cooper et al. (2008) also stated that "foreign exchange earnings, income and employment generation are the major motivations for including tourism as part of a development strategy". Whilst Scheyvens (2011) concluded that the impact of tourism on the local economies is not as much because of economic leakages in the tourism industry. The tourism policy of Namibia recognises the significance of economic growth in its vision. The policy emphasised that it intends to provide a:

Mature, sustainable and responsible tourism industry contributing significantly to the economic development of Namibia and the quality of life of all her people, primarily through job creation and economic growth. (MET, 2008)

The economic growth of Namibia has been variable, it averaged 3.6% which was below the target of 5% (Republic of Namibia, 2012/13 to 2016/2017). This influenced a negative impact on employment in 2008 where unemployment increased to 51.2% against the NDP3's unemployment target of 33.3% (Republic of Namibia, 2012/13 to 2016/2017). The contribution of tourism to foreign exchange earnings is highlighted in the tourism investment strategy of Namibia. It is emphasised as valuable to the economy of Namibia. The industry is regarded as the largest foreign exchange earner, where in 2013 foreign tourist arrivals constituted the largest number (1,374,602) which increased by 74,163 from 2012 tourist arrivals (TSR, 2013). In 2014, international tourist arrivals totalled 1,477,593 which increased by 3% in 2015 (WTTO, 2015). Thus, in 2014 the sector produced NAD7,106.8 million in visitor exports. By 2020, the foreign tourist arrivals are anticipated to increase to 1,724,000 (Pinehas, 2018). Whilst international tourist arrivals are projected to provide an aggregate of 1,947,000 by 2025 (WTTO, 2015). The foreign exchange earnings are primarily received from African countries, with Angola dominating followed by South Africa and Zambia (MET, 2016). The African market constitutes up to over one half of foreign arrivals to the country and German remains at the top for the European market (MET, 2016).

Tourism is also envisaged to provide economic benefits to a community through the development of employment and training of the poor (Scheyvens, 2011). The fact that tourism sector is a high labour-intensive industry, it is inclined to generate a high percentage of employment especially to the poor (UNCTAD, 2013:12). Tourism employment is proposed as a key instrument to poverty alleviation; however, it should not be viewed as a recipe to poverty reduction. The tourism industry is also linked with economic sectors such as agriculture, accommodation, restaurants and transport. Therefore, the tourism industry should increase demand for these sectors, and this will influence employment and circulation of currency at a local level.

The local community will however indirectly benefit from tourism if employees spend their wages locally (Spenceley et al. 2009). MET (2008:4) highlighted that tourism in Namibia is anticipated to have a wide multiplier effect, provide jobs and income outside the areas directly benefitting from tourism. Youell (1998) defined multiplier effect as an economic concept which indicates that the money spend by visitors to an area has been re-spent in the local economy. Whilst Cooper et al. (2008) indicated that the multiplier effect is when industrial sectors of an economy are interdependent for example sales from one organisation require purchases from other organisations within the local economy.

Hence, any changes in the way tourists spend at local economy will influence a change in the economy's level of production, foreign exchange flows, income and employment. In general, governments of developing countries which have substantial tourism potential should emphasise on maximising multiplier effects and reducing leakages (Scheyvens, 2011). In 2017, travel and tourism in Namibia directly supported 23 000 jobs with an overall input of 98 000 jobs (including indirect) (WTTC (Nam), 2018:1). Other positive economic impacts include the improvement of living standards of the residents through the provision of new infrastructure such as roads, airports and other amenities which benefits both the tourists and the local community. However, these benefits may not be accepted by the local community due to the differences in the residents' attitudes towards tourism development.

NEGATIVE ECONOMIC IMPACTS

The tourism industry is characterised as being highly seasonal hence this has an influence on unemployment and capacity utilisation of the tourist infrastructure. Variations in weather patterns and holiday seasons from the tourists' countries may offer job opportunities for the local community however during off peak periods the employees are faced with lack of employment and lack or low income. The tourism industry in Namibia is not immune to this, it experiences peaks and troughs.

Griffin and DeLacey (2002) suggested that organisations should have clearly defined policies that address issues of seasonality for instance offering discounted rates during off peak periods, scheduling events during off peak periods and ensuring that seasonal employees are offered work with the same employers each season. In the case of the Namibian tourism, January is the quietest month whilst the highest number of tourist arrivals is recorded in December from the African tourists (10.6%) and 9.6% in August from the European source market (MET, 2015). Thus, tourism in Namibia encounters a decline in the overseas and African markets for six to seven months per annum. To ensure that the tourism industry in Namibia receives increased revenue and creates permanent jobs, Nhongo (2018) recommended that the sector should promote domestic tourism. However, domestic tourism in Namibia has been neglected due to the culture of the residents. Moseley et al. (2007) added that the cost of travel for domestic tourists, accommodation prices and discrimination from the service providers has impacted on domestic tourism. Janis (2011) highlighted that the issue political bureaucracy impacts on the potential of domestic tourism in Namibia.

In line with seasonality, it is therefore essential for the success of an economy not to over-depend on a single economic sector. The way tourists spend their income at a tourist destination is unpredictable therefore relying on tourism alone is risky as it can lead to major economic crises. Goeldner and Ritchie (2006) highlighted that reliance on agriculture is more recommendable instead of tourism because of the need to eat. Many developing countries utilise tourism as the principal sector of economic development. The tourism industry of Namibia heavily relies on the European market (Germany and United Kingdom). Another aspect that may impact on the tourism of Namibia is the over-dependence on foreign aid, the Community Based Tourism relies on donor funding.

Honey et al. (2010) also emphasised that tourism contributes less amount to the local community due to leakages. The concept of leakages has been thoroughly explored by different researchers providing varied definitions (Janis, 2011; Mbaiwa, 2005; Mitchell and Ashley, 2010; Mowforth and Munt, 2003; Scheyvens, 2011; Wall, 2006). In essence, leakages transpire when a significant amount of the tourist spending outflows to foreign countries, this is mainly because the industry imports goods and services and develop infrastructure to meet international standards (Pearce & Butler, 2010). Hence, leakages can be viewed from a different angle, (import and export leakages) export leakages in tourism occur when profits revert back to foreign investors (Goeldner & Ritchie, 2006). Basically, only a few individuals benefit from the tourist spending because a high amount of the spending leaks back to major corporations in developed countries (Saayman, 2007 in Saayman et al. 2012). Anderson (2014) also identified three types of leakages which are evident in the Namibian tourism industry these are:

- **Internal Leakages:** The tourists pay at the destination; however, part of the payment will be utilised to purchase products to be used at the tourist destination.
- **External Leakages:** Intermediaries are involved in the packaging of the product resulting in the discrepancies between amounts paid for at the tourist destination and received in host countries.
- **Invisible Leakages:** They can be difficult to assess, these can arise from the financial sector for instance tax evasion and from the non-sustainability of environmental, cultural and historic aspects for example damage of resources like forests leading to the devaluation of a destination's value as an attraction and to the deterioration of the quality of life for local people.

Leakages is of major concern in Namibia, although it is common in the southern Africa (Janis, 2014). Due to colonialism, the tourism industry in Namibia is dominated by Germans and South Africans, they own most of the hotel chains, guest farms, tour operators and travel agencies (Lapeyre, 2009). If tourists in Namibia (European and African) use foreign airlines and the multinational hotel chains the economic benefits of tourism will be considerably reduced. Tourists from German (travelling to Namibia) can book for the whole holiday from their countries with the money not even reaching the tourist destination (All-inclusive packages), this includes flights.

The industry also buys most of the tourism products from South Africa (Janis, 2011). Although the issue of leakages in developing countries has been thoroughly explored it is regarded as a political issue thus efforts to reduce it may impact on the destination's tourism industry. In fact, efforts to address the issue of leakages in Namibia were made but had an adverse impact on the industry as thousands of tourists from South Africa were turned away resulting in loss of revenue and damage to the industry (Hartman, 2010). Chirenje et al. (2013) concluded that leakages can be minimised through the establishment of strong and sustainable linkages. Enhancing economic linkages influences a demand for local products and creation and development of employment and new opportunities for local businesses (Richardson, 2010). This, however, partly depends on the quality and consistency of the local products for the tourism market. Reinforcing inter-sectoral linkages has proved to be difficult in developing countries (UNCTAD, 2010). UNCTAD (2010) indicated that 50-60% of the tourism revenue does not leave the host country and poor people from the destination country insignificantly benefit from the tourism expenditure. Pleymarom (2012) argued that developing countries do not have reliable data on leakages.

SOCIO-CULTURAL IMPACTS OF TOURISM

Cooper et al. (2008) stated that socio-cultural impacts have a combined effect because it is difficult to differentiate sociological and cultural effects. Social impacts are the alterations in the norms and values of society that are more seeming in the short-term whilst cultural impacts can be viewed as longer-term modifications in rituals and community structures (Keiser, 2002). According to Telfer and Sharpley (2008) the socio-cultural changes are influenced by several factors, these include:

- Number and types of tourists/ tourist behaviour- the impact depends on the number of tourists (the higher the number of tourists, the higher the impact).
- Size and structure of the tourism industry-the size of the tourism industry compared to the local community.
- Importance of the tourism industry.
- Pace of the tourism industry.

Due to the local community's varied perspectives, the social and cultural impacts can be viewed as positive whilst others can be regarded as negative. Although the negative impacts attract more attention, the positive impacts include:

The Creation of Employment

The local community can significantly benefit from employment in the tourism industry, this can be achieved through community- based initiatives such as the Administrative Management Decision (ADMADE) in Zambia (Musavengane & Simatele, 2016) and the Communal Area Management Programme for Indigenous Resources (CAMPFIRE) in Zimbabwe (Mutana et al. 2013). Similarly, the National Development Plans in Namibia have promoted Community based tourism as a tool to be utilised in poverty alleviation. The National Community -Based Natural Resource Management program (CBNRM) is a conservation and a rural development initiative where the local community are given the opportunity to manage the communal natural resources (NTB, 2018). It ultimately provides the community with income through employment of the residents. Hence, this initiative's main objective is to ensure that members of the local communities have control over tourism activities so that they obtain a significant share of the benefits.

Renewal of Cultural Pride and Conservation of Cultural Heritage

The conservation of cultural heritage can be achieved through the preservation and restoration of heritage sites to keep the visitors satisfied. The infrastructure will also be upgraded for the benefit of both tourists and the local community. Also, by assisting in the maintenance of a clean and attractive environment, tourism has the potential to encourage a sense of community pride in residents (Youell, 1998). Furthermore, in Namibia (Kunene region) the government acknowledged the importance of tourism before independence and awarded tourism concessions to tour operators (Novelli & Gebhardt, 2009). Thus, tourism in that region has not only increased but the infrastructure has been upgraded to a high standard to attract local, regional, and international tourists. This has also improved the quality of life of the local community. The preservation and maintenance of cultural traditions can promote a profound sense of ownership concerning the tourism product. Cooper et al. (2008) also added that tourism facilitates ceremonies, rituals, and crafts to be improved through tourists and this stimulates pride in a destination's heritage and culture.

Promoting International Peace and Social Interaction

Tourism has the potential to encourage the local community and the tourists to socialise with each other through the local community showcasing their culture via traditional music and dance. Hence, the tourists can learn the local people's customs and traditions, thereby breaking down cultural barriers. The local community can also communicate with the tourists by educating the tourists on how to make some of the traditional items (Mason, 2008). The appreciation of the local cultures and traditions by tourists brings a sense of pride to indigenous people in their culture thus protecting cultural identity of even smaller cultural groups in a society (Inskeep, 1991:370). This type of tourism has particularly been highly promoted in the Northern region of Namibia showcasing the Ovahimba culture (Niskala, 2015). This provides both the tourists and the local community with an opportunity to communicate with different languages and cultural groups. The communication skills of the local community and tourists is improved by using official languages.

NEGATIVE SOCIO-CULTURAL IMPACTS

It is fundamentally important for tourism to be effectively planned, developed and managed for it to present the local community with positive impacts. Otherwise, the growth of tourism has been envisaged to cause an adverse impact on the local community's way of living. It may bring negative alterations on their beliefs and values. The negative socio-cultural impacts include:

Overcrowding

The influx of tourists to popular destinations can cause an immense amount of pressure on the community's amenities, the overcrowding can cause the local residents to refrain from supporting tourism activities in their area. The rights of the residents may be denied so as to make way for tourism for example they may be refused access to local beaches to facilitate tourism, thus causing frustrations to the local community (Inkeep, 1991). This is a case in point at one of the most popular destinations in Namibia (Swakopmund) where the local residents experience disruptions from tourists through noises from quad bikes, overcrowding at the beaches and lack of parking spaces (Hartman, 2015).

Demonstration Effect

Tourists have the potential to influence the behaviour of the host population. According to Telfer and Sharpley (2008) the local residents may try to vie with the behaviours and consumption habits of the tourists who visits them. However, the tourists do not necessarily have to be in contact with the local people for the demonstration effect to occur, the members of the community influenced by the tourist's behaviours will probably influence other community members through their altered attitudes (Cooper et al. 1998).

The way tourists dress may also impact on the way the local people dress especially the young people. However, Mathieson and Wall (1982) stated that the way tourists usually behave when they are on holidays is different from the way they would normally behave when they are not on vacations therefore the local people will have fallacies about the tourists. The tourists especially from developed countries will usually portray an affluent lifestyle when they are on vacations and the local people would aspire to have such a way of living, failure to meet such standards will lead to frustrations from the local people (Burns & Holden, 1995). This can also have an influence on migration, where people would migrate from rural areas to urban areas aspiring to attain the modern way of living leading to changes in the internal structure of host community (Hall & Lew, 2009). Nevertheless, demonstration effect can bring positive effects to the host community if they are inspired to get better education so as to improve their standards of living.

Moral Decline in the Community

The increase in tourism has been associated with an increase in criminal activities at a destination. Tourism has influenced a demand in prostitution in Southern Africa and other key tourist destinations in the world (Mbaiwa & Darkoh, 2009). Destinations such as Cuba and Thailand are some of the destinations which are popularly known for attracting prostitutes and sex tourism, hence, this has influenced the spread of sexually transmitted diseases such as HIV (Telfer & Sharpley, 2008). The increase of HIV/AIDS and poverty in Namibia has influenced an increase on the number of children begging for food in the streets and prostitution (Anon, 2005).

In Botswana (Okavango Delta) prostitution increased due to the increase in the number of tourists in the area (Mbaiwa, 2005), this seems to be the same scenario in the coastal areas of Namibia where the prostitutes target foreigners (Hartman, 2008). Although there is insufficient evidence available, sex tourism in Namibia has been on the increase with Windhoek being labelled as the popular location followed by Swakopmund and Walvis Bay (coastal areas) (Smit, 2016). Prostitution in Namibia is illegal and attempts to legalise it have been futile. Crime has also been on the rise Namibia particularly at the tourists' attraction areas (Nakale, 2017).

Staged Authenticity and Commodification

Culture has been condensed to a mere product for resale because most of the cultural presentations are acted (Ivanovic et al. 2009). Cooper et al. (2008) highlighted that a demand for tourism products that offer cultural authenticity is on the rise. Although destinations are equipped with this knowledge, they still choose to provide staged authenticity or to modify the products to suit the tourist's demands (George, 2008). The aim of the destination is to try and persuade the tourists that their cultural performances are authentic whilst making certain that the tourists do not see behind the stage curtains (Cooper et al. 2008). This may present the host community with challenges in trying to sustain the veracity of their culture.

Robinson (1999) defined commodification as method of imaging and changing local people's ways of life and traditions into saleable products. This can lead to the exploitation of crafts and ceremonies so as to appeal to tourists. Hence, if the host community's focus is on the monetary value of the activities there is danger of disregarding the importance of the products overtime (Mason, 2008). Crafts and tourism artefacts are made in different parts of the country and they are popular in touristic areas.

In Namibia, socio-economic challenges have forced many artists to migrate to cities like Windhoek to commercialise their skills and selling hand -made art products. Some of the artists make and sell the crafts whilst they are dressed in their traditional attire, this gives them a platform for cultural exchange and interaction with tourists as well as an opportunity to preserve their culture (Xinhua, 2018). Janis (2012) highlighted the notion of commodifying natural resources for tourism purposes, where images of tourist products and sceneries are judiciously designed to suit the customer needs. Hence, instead of the tourists enjoying the physical surrounding societies and landscapes, they would often experience pictures and products that are cautiously custom-made for them. Frent (2016) also highlighted negative socio-cultural impacts such as high rentals and imbalances on the number of holiday home owners, tourists and the local residents which may cause conflicts.

Environmental Impacts of Tourism

It is quite apparent that tourism has extensive economic benefits, yet its development presents a destination with environmental issues. The more tourists travel, the more they are likely to cause environmental changes to the natural resources. The tourists are also becoming increasingly aware about their environmental surroundings and the methods which are being used to prevent further damage. Tourism can provide an adverse effect on the natural environment locally and globally. It heavily relies on the natural environment such as the nice weather, the quality of the ecosystem and clean air and water (Gossling, 2002). Due to the dry weather conditions of Namibia, water is very scarce, and the poorest families still rely on wood fuel, it is therefore imperative for the tourism industry to consider its environmental impacts. Although the negative tourism impacts have been over-emphasised, it presents a destination with positive impacts such as the ones highlighted below by Mason (2003).

- Stimulating measures that protects the environment, wildlife and landscape.
- Assists in the promotion of the establishment of national parks and wildlife resources.
- Promotes the preservation of buildings for example world heritage sites.
- Generating income through entrance charges for the maintenance of heritage sites, historic buildings and wildlife habitats.

A framework for the study of environmental impacts was pioneered by the Organisation for Economic Co-operation and Development (OECD) in the 1970s highlighting four major environmental stressors (Cooper et al. 2008):

- Permanent environmental restructuring
- Waste product generation
- Direct environmental pressure
- Effects on the population dynamics

In line with OECD (2001) initiatives such as the Agenda 21 were adopted, it is an action plan implemented for sustainable development, it includes important principles that underpin the international and legal framework for sustainable development. Various principles include the integration of environmental protection into the development process and internalisation of environmental costs (OECD, 2001). The initiative also tackles issues of inequalities between the rich and poor countries (Cooper et al., 2008).

Namibia's tourism industry is leading in the Southern Africa on environmental sustainability (Blanke et al., 2011), it recognises the importance of using natural resources sustainably in the Vision 2030 and initiatives such as eco-awards have been developed for tourism establishments.

The tourism policy (2008) highlights the significance of environmental sustainability via environmental regulation and wildlife conservation, the policy was developed around the sustainable development notion highlighting three principles:

- Economic growth through foreign exchange
- Increasing local participation and equity
- Nature conservation and environmental sustainability

Since gaining its independence in 1990, Namibia has been promoting conservancies, in 1998 only four conservancies were registered, in 2002, 29 conservancies had been registered (MET, 2002). MET (2004) recorded that rural community members directly received N$26.1 million in financial benefits from conservancies. Currently, more than seventy conservancies have been registered with the purpose of establishing practical structures and systems of distributing benefits to rural communities and to increase the number of varied wildlife (NTB, 2018). With this regard, tourism in Namibia has been utilised as a tool that stimulates environmental conservation and improvement.

Albeit Namibia is a leader in Africa and the world in its conservation approach and community contribution in resource management, the tourism industry still faces negative environmental issues. Loss of biodiversity has a negative effect on environment for example freshwater species in Namibia have decreased due to overfishing, inadequate fishing methods and poor catchment area management (Dahlberg & Wingqvist, 2008). Furthermore, the policy makers have been criticised for being over-ambitious and setting unrealistic targets resulting in some of the objectives not being achieved, and some high-ranking decision makers do not fully appreciate the value of biodiversity (USAID, 2010).

Tourism can cause a great damage to the environment through pollution and littering (Frauman & Banks, 2011). There are different types of pollution which can destroy natural habitats and destroy natural resources, these include: water, air, noise and solid pollution. Littering is a major concern in the cities of Namibia, as it impacts on the quality of life of the residents and health of the ecosystem. Abandoned mines have also been a critical issue, where debris has been left lying around and mining structures not demolished after the closure of the mines (Nashuuta, 2018). This has considerable adverse impacts on the environment as the debris may contain chemicals that can contaminate water and soil and ultimately cause serious health issues to people and wildlife. The Ministry of Environment and Tourism is responsible for such issues yet issues of littering and illegal practises of waste disposal have been escalating.

Considering that water is a scarce commodity in the country, it vital to effectively preserve and manage it. Generally, tourists tend to over utilise resources such as water and electricity when they are on holidays than when they are at home, it is therefore to essential to enact regulations on the uses of water (especially for tourists) such as the use of swimming pools. Namibia has the Environmental Impact Assessment (EIA) in place, yet its implementation and utilisation has been viewed as being inadequate (USAID, 2010). WTTC (2006) stated that transparency concerning EIA has not been attained and government bureaucracy held back the progress in the regulation of access to resources such as the dune belt.

The Tourism Policy (2008) and the Environmental Management Act of Namibia emphasises that the development of tourism plans should be based on the carrying capacity of the area. This is when a maximum number of people who can use a site without causing any adverse impacts on the resources, plummeting visitor satisfaction or exerting negative effects on the society, economy or culture of the area (McIntyre, 1993). Although the issue of air pollution in Namibia has been considered of a less impact, some tourists attractions has been analysed for exceeding their carrying capacity.

A high number of vehicles and tourists have been congesting the roads causing a deterioration of the roads and tourist attraction sites, examples include the Sossusvlei, dolphin watching sites and fishing tourism in Walvis Bay and Caprivi Strip (RoN, 2012). However, Lea (1998) stated that measuring the impact of tourism on the environment is complex as some of the impacts can be attributed to other tourist characteristics such as their socio-economic factors. It is therefore important for the tourism industry to effectively manage the number of tourists frequenting an area and the characteristics of the destination as highlighted in the Tourism Policy of 2008.

CONCLUSION

The main purpose of this chapter is to establish the development of the global tourism industry and determine the position of the tourism sector in Africa and Namibia. This industry has been declared as a priority sector, as an economic sector, it ranks third after mining and agriculture. Thus, to clearly analyse the sector's contribution towards tourism development, this chapter started by scrutinising the development of global tourism and its contribution to the economies of developing countries especially towards employment opportunities and Gross Domestic Product. Hence, it is quite evident that tourism industry presents development prospects and has the potential to revitalise communities. The tourism numbers are continuously rising revealing that the industry is viable. In terms of Africa, tourism is envisaged to improve owing to the development of new source markets and improved source markets. However, the lack of resources in most African countries makes it difficult to calculate and provide up to date economic data. Namibia is epitomised by its dry weather; therefore, this has an influence on the type of tourism offered by the destination. Tourism in Namibia is focused on the dry geography, wildlife, and wilderness experiences. The historical background of the country plays a significant role in the development of the tourism industry. Positively, after independence the country inherited sound infrastructure, mineral wealth, and game. It is also documented as a safe country, and this offers the destination opportunities for tourism development.

REFERENCES

African Development Bank. (2020). *African economic outlook 2020: developing Africa's workforce*. African Development Bank.

Anderson, W. (2014). Cultural tourism and poverty alleviation in rural Kilimanjaro, Tanzania. *Journal of Tourism and Cultural Change*, *13*(3), 208–224. doi:10.1080/14766825.2014.935387

Andrades, L., & Dimanche, F. (2017). Destination competitiveness and tourism development in Russia: Issues and challenges. *Tourism Management*, *62*, 360–376. doi:10.1016/j.tourman.2017.05.008

Anon. (2005, Nov. 7). Teen prostitutes have few options. *Namibian*.

Bailey, E., & Richardson, R. (2010). A new economic framework for tourism decision making. *Tourism and Hospitality Research*, *10*(4), 367–376. doi:10.1057/thr.2010.14

Barnes, J. I., & Novelli, M. (2007). Trophy hunting and recreational angling in Namibia: an economy, social and environmental comparison. In B. Lovelock (Ed.), *Tourism and consumption of wildlife: hunting, shooting and sport fishing*. Routledge.

Bennett, O., Ashley, C., & Roe, D. (1999). Sustainable tourism and poverty elimination: a report to the Department for International Development. London: Deloitte and Touch: International Institute for Environment and Development: Overseas Development Institute.

Berg, B. L. (2009). *Qualitative research methods for the social sciences* (7th ed.). Pearson Education.

Blanke, J., Browne, C., Garcia, A., & Messerli, H. (2011). *Assessing Africa's travel & tourism competitiveness in the Wake of The Global Economic Crisis.* Geneva: World Economic Forum.

Bryman, A., & Bell, E. (2011). *Business research methods* (3rd ed.). Oxford University Press.

Burns, P., & Holden, A. (1995). *Tourism: a new perspective*. Prentice Hall.

Butler, R. (1980). The concept of a tourism area cycle of evolution. *The Canadian Geographer. Geographe Canadien, 24*(1), 5–12. doi:10.1111/j.1541-0064.1980.tb00970.x

Carbone, M. (2005). Sustainable tourism in developing countries: Poverty alleviation, participatory planning, and ethical issues. *European Journal of Development Research, 17*(3), 559–565. doi:10.1080/09578810500209841

Chirenje, L. I., Chitotombe, J., Gukurume, S., Chazovachii, B., & Chitongo, L. (2013). The impact of tourism leakages on local economies: A case study of Nyanga District, Zimbabwe. *Journal of Human Ecology (Delhi, India), 42*(1), 9–16. doi:10.1080/09709274.2013.11906576

Consultancy.UK. (2016). *International tourism doubles in 15 years, 1.8 billion by 2030.* Consultancy.uk.

Cooper, C., Fletcher, J., Fyall, A., Gilbert, D., & Wanhill, S. (2008). *Tourism: Principles and practice* (4th ed.). Pearson Education.

Cooper, C., Fletcher, J., Gilbert, D., Fyall, A., & Wanhill, S. (1998). *Tourism: Principles and practice* (2nd ed.). Longman.

Dahlberg, E., & Wingquist, G. O. (2008). *Namibia environmental and climate change policy brief, School of business, economics and law*. University of Gothenburg.

Damm, G. R. (2008). Recreational trophy hunting: what do we know and what should we do? In *Best practices in sustainable hunting: a guide to best practices from around the world*. CIC Technical Series Publication. International Council for Game and Wildlife Conservation.

Deery, M., Jago, L., & Fredline, L. (2012). Rethinking social impacts of tourism research: A new research agenda. *Tourism Management, 33*(1), 64–73. doi:10.1016/j.tourman.2011.01.026

Dieke, P. U. C. (2005). *The political economy of tourism development in Africa*. Cognizant Communication Corporation.

Eita, J. H., & Jordaan, A. C. (2007). Estimating the tourism potential in Namibia. Windhoek: Namibian Economic Policy Research Unit (NEPRU).

Ekanayake, E. M., & Long, A. E. (2012). Tourism development and economic growth in developing countries. *The International Journal of Business and Finance Research, 6*(1), 51–63.

Fourie, H. (1990). *Development of the tourism industry in Namibia*. Namibia University of Science and Technology.

Frauman, E., & Banks, S. (2011). Gateway community resident perceptions of tourism development: Incorporating importance-performance analysis into the limits of change framework. *Tourism Management, 13*(1), 128–140. doi:10.1016/j.tourman.2010.01.013

Frent, C. (2016). An overview on the negative impacts of tourism. *Journal of Tourism Studies and Research in Tourism, 22*, 32–37.

George, R. (2008). *Managing tourism in South Africa* (2nd ed.). Oxford University Press Southern Africa.

Glaesser, D., Kester, J., Paulose, H., Alizadeh, A., & Valentin, B. (2017). Global travel pattern: An overview. *Journal of Travel Medicine, 24*(4), 1–5. doi:10.1093/jtm/tax007 PMID:28637267

Godfrey, K., & Clarke, J. (2000). *The tourism development handbook: a practical approach to planning and marketing*. Continuum.

Goeldner, C. R., & Ritchie, J. R. B. (2006). *Tourism: principles, practices, philosophies*. Wiley.

Gossling, S. (2002). Global environmental consequences of tourism. *Global Environmental Change, 12*(4), 283–302. doi:10.1016/S0959-3780(02)00044-4

Gunn, C. A. (1988). *Tourism planning* (2nd ed.). Taylor and Francis.

Hall, C. M., & Lew, A. A. (2009). *Understanding and managing tourism impacts: an integrated approach*. Routledge. doi:10.4324/9780203875872

Hartman, A. (2008, Dec. 17). Walvis Bay prostitutes reel in the foreigners. *The Namibian*.

Hartman, A. (2010, Feb. 24). Namibia: foreign tour guide ban shocks industry. *The Namibian*.

Hartman, A. (2015, Dec.). Holiday adventures at the coast. *The Namibian*.

Himavindu, M. N., & Barnes, J. I. (2003). Trophy hunting in Namibian economy: An assessment. *South African Journal of Wildlife Research*, *33*(2), 65–70.

Honey, M., Vargas, E., & Durham, W. H. (2010). Impact of, D.C.: Center for Responsible Travel (CREST).

Inskeep, E. (1991). Tourism planning, an integrated and sustainable development approach. New York: Wiley.

Ivanovic, M. (2011). *Exploring the authenticity of the tourist experience in culture heritage tourism in South Africa.* Potchefstroom: North-West University.

Ivanovic, M., Khunou, P. S., Reynish, N., Pawson, R., Tseane, L., & Wassung, N. (2009). *Tourism development 1: Fresh perspectives*. Pearson Prentice Hall.

Janis, J. (2011). *The tourism-development nexus in Namibia: a study on national tourism policy and local tourism enterprises' policy knowledge*. University of Helsinki.

Janis, J. (2012). The role of local policy knowledge in the implementation of Namibian tourism policy. *International Journal of Tourism Policy*, *4*(4), 302–316. doi:10.1504/IJTP.2012.052547

Janis, J. (2014). Political economy of the Namibia tourism sector: Addressing post-apartheid inequality through increasing indigenous ownership. *Review of African Tourism Economy*, *41*(140), 185–200. doi:10.1080/03056244.2013.872614

Jenkins, C. (2000). The development of tourism in Namibia. In P. Dieke (Ed.), *The political economy of tourism development in Africa* (pp. 113–128). Cognizant Communication Corporation.

Kavita, E., & Saarinen, J. (2016). Tourism and community development in Namibia: Policy issues review. *Fennia*, *194*(1), 79–88. doi:10.11143/46331

Kumar, P.K. (2020, June 17). Bounce back will be faster and stronger for travel and tourism: Sanjay Datta. *Travel World*.

Lapeyre, R. (2009). Revenue sharing in community-private sector lodges in Namibia: A bargaining model. *Tourism Economics*, *15*(3), 653–669. doi:10.5367/000000009789036585

Lapeyre, R. (2011). For what stands the "B" in CBT concept: Community-based or community-biased tourism? Some insights from Namibia. *Tourism Analysis*, *16*(2), 187–202. doi:10.3727/108354211X13014081270440

Liu, J. (1994). *Pacific islands ecotourism: a public policy and planning guide*. University of Hawaii. Pacific Business Center Program.

Mandić, A., Mrnjavac, Ž., & Kordić, L. (2018). Tourism infrastructure, recreational facilities and tourism development. *Tourism and Hospitality Management*, *4*(1), 41–62. doi:10.20867/thm.24.1.12

Mason, P. (2003). *Tourism impacts, planning and management*. Butterworth-Heinemann.

Mason, P. (2008). *Tourism impacts, planning and management* (2nd ed.). Butterworth-Heinemann.

Mathieson, A., & Wall, G. (1982). *Tourism: economic, physical and social impacts*. Longman.

Mbaiwa, J. E. (2005). Enclave tourism and its social-economic impacts in the Okavango delta, Botswana. *Tourism Management*, *26*(2), 157–172. doi:10.1016/j.tourman.2003.11.005

Mbaiwa, J. E., & Darkoh, M. (2009). The socio-economic impacts of tourism in the Okavango Delta, Botswana. In J. Saarinen, F. Becker, H. Manwa, & D. Wilson (Eds.), *Sustainable tourism in Southern Africa: local communities and natural resources in transition* (pp. 210–230). Channel View Publications. doi:10.21832/9781845411107-019

McIntyre, G. (1993). *Sustainable tourism development: guide for local planners*. World Tourism Organization.

Ministry of Environment and Tourism (Namibia). (1994). *White paper on tourism*. MET.

Ministry of Environment and Tourism (Namibia). (1995). *Community-based tourism development. policy document*. MET.

Ministry of Environment and Tourism (Namibia). (1996). *Nature conservation amendment act*. MET.

Ministry of Environment and Tourism (Namibia). (2001). *Tourism statistics preliminary findings*. MET.

Ministry of Environment and Tourism (Namibia). (2002). *Tourist arrival statistics*. MET.

Ministry of Environment and Tourism (Namibia). (2004). *Namibia statistical report*. MET.

Ministry of Environment and Tourism (Namibia). (2007). *A sustainable tourism country report*. MET.

Ministry of Environment and Tourism (Namibia). (2008). *National policy on tourism for Namibia*. MET.

Ministry of Environment and Tourism (Namibia). (2016). *Tourism statistical report*. MET.

Mitchell, J., & Ashley, C. (2010). *Tourism and poverty reduction: pathways to prosperity*. Earthscan.

Morgan, N. J., & Pritchard, A. (2006). Promoting niche tourism destination brands: Case studies of New Zealand and wales. *Journal of Promotion Management, 12*(1), 17–33. doi:10.1300/J057v12n01_03

Moseley, J., Sturgis, L., & Wheeler, M. (2007). *Improving domestic tourism in Namibia*. Worcester Polythetic Institute.

Mowforth, M., & Munt, I. (2003). *Tourism and sustainability: development and new tourism in the third world* (2nd ed.). Routledge. doi:10.4324/9780203422779

Muchapondwa, E., & Stage, J. (2013). The economic impacts of tourism in Botswana, Namibia and South Africa: Is poverty subsiding? A United Nations sustainable development. *Journal, 37*(2), 80–89.

Muhanna, E. (2007). The contribution of sustainable tourism development in poverty alleviation of local communities in South Africa. *Journal of Human Resources in Hospitality & Tourism, 6*(1), 37–67. doi:10.1300/J171v06n01_03

Musavengane, R., & Simatele, D. (2016). Community-based natural resource management: The role of social capital in collaborative environmental management of tribal resources in Kwazulu-Natal, South Africa. *Journal of Southern Africa, 33*(6), 806–821. doi:10.1080/0376835X.2016.1231054

Mutana, S., Chipfuva, T., & Muchenje, B. (2013). Is tourism in Zimbabwe developing with the poor in mind? Assessing the pro-poor involvement of tourism operators located near rural areas in Zimbabwe. *Asian Social Science*, *9*(5), 154–161. doi:10.5539/ass.v9n5p154

Nakale, A. (2017, Aug. 15). Tourism ministry concerned over tourist attacks. *Newera*.

Namibia Tourism Board (NTB). (2018). *Conservation*. Namibia Tourism Board.

Namibia Tourism Board (NTB). (2020). *National parks*. Namibia Tourism Board.

Namibian Tourist Board (NTB). (2018). *Culture*. NTB. https://namibiatourism.com.na/page/culture

National Planning Commission (NPC). (2002). Second National Development Plan (NDP2), v. 1. 2001/02-2005/06. National Planning Commission.

Nguyen, T. H. M., & Nguyen, D. H. C. (2013). The contribution of tourism to economic growth in Thua Thien Hue Province (Vietnam). *International Journal of Social and Economic Research*, *3*(2), 160–168. doi:10.5958/j.2249-6270.3.2.020

Nhongo, K. (2018, Apr. 27). Locals welcome tourism incentives as domestic booms. *Windhoek Observer*.

Niskala, M. (2015). Encountering the other: The Ovahimba culture and people in Namibian tourism promotion. *Nordic Journal of African Studies*, *24*(3&4), 259–278.

Novelli, M., & Gebhardt, K. (2007). Community-based tourism in Namibia: "reality show" or "window dressing? *Current Issues in Tourism*, *10*(5), 443–479. doi:10.2167/cit332.0

Nyakunu, E., & Rogerson, C. (2014). Tourism SMMEs and policy formulation: Recent evidence from Namibia. *Mediterranean Journal of Social Sciences*, *5*(10), 244. doi:10.5901/mjss.2014.v5n10p244

OECD. (2001). The DAC guidelines: Poverty reduction: International development. Paris: OECD.

Pearce, D. G., & Butler, R. (Eds.). (2010). *Tourism research: a 20-20 vision*. Goodfellow Publishers.

Perrottet, J., & Benli, B. (2016). *Impact of tourism, how can we do this better?* World Bank.

Republic of Namibia. (1994). *White paper on tourism*. Approved by the Cabinet 29.3.1994. National Development. Office of the President.

Republic of Namibia. (1995a). *Namibia tourism development programme. Phase I - Foundation*. Ministry of Environment and Tourism.

Republic of Namibia. (1995b). *The promotion of community-based tourism. Policy Document*. Ministry of Environment and Tourism.

Republic of Namibia. (2004). *Namibia vision 2030 - policy framework for long-term*. National Development. Office of the President.

Republic of Namibia. (2008). *Third National Development Plan (NDP3) 2007/08-2011-12* (Vol. 1). National Planning Commission. Office of the President.

Republic of Namibia. (2011). *Fourth National Development Plan (NDP4) 2012/13 to 2016/17*. National Planning Commission. Office of the President.

Republic of Namibia. (2012). *Namibia poverty mapping*. National Planning Commission.

Republic of Namibia. (2015). *Poverty and deprivation in Namibia*. National Planning Commission.

Republic of Namibia. (2016). *National tourism investment profile and promotion strategy 2016-2026*. Ministry of Environment and Tourism.

Republic of Namibia. (2017). *Namibia's fifth development plan, 2017/18-2021/22*. National Planning Commission. Office of the President.

Richardson, R. B. (2010). The contribution of tourism to economic growth and food security. Michigan State University.

Robinson, M. (1999). Cultural conflicts in tourism: inevitability and inequality. In M. Robinson & P. Boniface (Eds.), *Tourism and cultural conflicts* (pp. 1–32). CABI Publishing.

Saayman, M. (2007). *En-route with tourism: an introductory text* (3rd ed.). Platinum Press.

Samuelsson, E., & Stage, J. (2007). The size and distribution of the economic impacts of Namibian hunting tourism. *South African Journal of Wildlife Research*, 37(1), 41–52. doi:10.3957/0379-4369-37.1.41

Scheyvens, R. (2011). *Tourism and poverty*. Routledge.

Seetanah, B., Ramessur, S., & Rojid, S. (2009). Does infrastructure alleviates poverty in developing countries? *International Journal of Applied Econometrics and Quantitative Studies*, 9(2), 17–36.

Sharpley, R. (2000). Rural tourism and the challenge of tourism diversification: The case of Cyprus. *Tourism Management, 23*(3), 233–244. doi:10.1016/S0261-5177(01)00078-4

Simpson, M. C. (2008). Community benefit tourism initiatives: A conceptual oxymoron. *Journal of Tourism Management, 29*(6), 1–18. doi:10.1016/j.tourman.2007.06.005

Smit, E. (2016, Dec. 6). Sex tourism a reality in Namibia. *Namibia Sun.*

Sofield, T. H. B. (2003). *Empowerment for sustainable tourism development.* Pergamon.

Spenceley, A., Ashley, C., & De Kock, M. (2009). *Tourism and local development: an introductory guide.* International Trade Centre.

Telfer, D. J., & Sharpley, R. (2008). *Tourism and development in the developing world.* Routledge.

Todaro, M. P., & Smith, S. C. (2011). Economic development (11th ed.). Pearson Education Limited.

Tosun, C. (2006). Expected nature of community participation in tourism development. *Tourism Management, 27*(3), 493–504. doi:10.1016/j.tourman.2004.12.004

Turpie, J., Lange, G., Martin, R., Davies, R., & Barnes, J. (2004). *Strengthening Namibia's system of national protected area. Subproject 1: Economic analysis and feasibility study for financing.* Ministry of Environment and Tourism.

United Nations. (2020). *About LDCs.* UN-OHRLLS. https://unohrlls.org/about-ldcs/

United Nations Conference on Trade and Development (UNCTAD). (2010). *The contribution of tourism to trade and development.* New York: United Nations. (TD/B/C. I/8.)

United Nations Conference on Trade and Development (UNCTAD). (2013). *The impact of trade on employment and poverty reduction.* Geneva: UNCTAD. (Note by the UNCTAD secretariat, 17-21 June.)

United Nations Conference on Trade and Development (UNCTAD). (2017). *Economic development in Africa report 2017.* Geneva, Switzerland: UNCTAD.

United Nations Conference on Trade and Development. (UNCTAD). (2020). *COVID-19 and tourism assessing the economic consequences.* Geneva, Switzerland: UNCTAD.

United Nations World Tourism Organisation (UNWTO). (2015). Understanding tourism: basic glossary. Madrid, Spain: UNWETO.

United Nations World Tourism Organisation (UNWTO). (2016). Tourism highlights: 2016 edition. Madrid, Spain: UNWETO.

United Nations World Tourism Organisation (UNWTO). (2019a). Exports from international tourism hit USD 1.7 trillion. Madrid, Spain: UNWETO.

United Nations World Tourism Organisation (UNWTO). (2019b). *International tourist arrivals reach 1.4 billion two years ahead of forecasts*. UNWETO.

United Nations World Tourism Organisation (UNWTO). (2020). International tourist numbers could fall 60-80% in 2020. Madrid, Spain: UNWETO.

United Nations World Tourism Organization (UNWTO). (2011). *International tourists to hit 1.8 billion by 2030*. https://www.unwto.org/archive/global/press-release/2011-10-11/international-tourists-hit-18-billion-2030#:~:text=By%20 2030%2C%20arrivals%20are%20expected,friends%20and%20family%20every%20 day

Wall, G., & Mathieson, A. (2006). *Tourism: change, impacts, and opportunities*. Pearson Education.

Weaver, D., & Lawton, L. (2007). Twenty years on: The state of contemporary ecotourism research. *Tourism Management*, 28(5), 1168–1179. doi:10.1016/j.tourman.2007.03.004

Wondirad, A., & Ewnetu, B. (2019). Community participation in tourism development as a tool to foster sustainable land and resource use practices in a national park milieu. *Land Use Policy*, 88, 104155. doi:10.1016/j.landusepol.2019.104155

World Bank. (1991). *The world development report 1991: the challenge of development*. Oxford University Press.

World Tourism Organization (WTO). (2010). *Tourism highlights*. WTO.

World Travel & Tourism Council (WTTC). (2006). *Namibia. The impact of travel & tourism on jobs and the economy*. WTTC.

World Travel and Tourism Council (WTTC). (2015). *Travel and tourism economic impact 2015 Costa Rica*. WTTC.

World Travel and Tourism Council (WTTC). (2017). *Global economic issues and impact*. WTTC.

World Travel and Tourism Council (WTTC). (2019). *Travel and tourism: economic impact 2019*. WTTC.

World Travel and Tourism Council (WTTC). (2020). *Namibia key data 2019*. WTTC.

Xinhua, N. (2018, July 8). Art gives Namibian rural nomads a new lifeline. *The Namibian*.

Xu, H., Sofield, T., & Bao, J. (2008). Community tourism in Asia: an introduction. In Tourism and community development: Asian practices. Madrid, Spain: World Tourism Organization.

Yaman, A. R., & Mohd, A. (2004). Community-based ecotourism: A new proposition for sustainable development and environmental conservation in Malaysia. *The Journal of Applied Science, 4*(4), 583–589. doi:10.3923/jas.2004.583.589

Yang, X., & Hung, K. (2014). Poverty alleviation via tourism cooperatives in China: The story of Yuhu. *International Journal of Contemporary Hospitality Management, 26*(6), 879–906. doi:10.1108/IJCHM-02-2013-0085

Youell, R. (1998). *Tourism: an introduction*. Longman.

Zambezi Population and Housing Census. (2014). *2011 population and housing census: Zambezi regional profile*. Namibian Statistics Agency.

Zapata, M. J., Hall, C. M., Lindo, P., & Vanderschaeghe, M. (2011). Can community-based tourism contribute to development and poverty alleviation? Lessons from Nicaragua. *Current Issues in Tourism, 14*(8), 725–749. doi:10.1080/13683500.2011.559200

Zeng, B., & Ryan, C. (2012). Assisting the poor in China through tourism development: A review of research. *Tourism Management, 33*(2), 239–248. doi:10.1016/j.tourman.2011.08.014

Zhao, W., & Ritchie, J. R. B. (2007). Tourism and poverty alleviation: An integrative research framework. *Current Issues in Tourism, 10*(2), 119–143. doi:10.2167/cit296.0

ENDNOTE

[1] In this study, impacts refer to the effects brought about by tourism policies, tourism-related infrastructure and tourism behaviour (Mason, 2008).

Chapter 5
Indigenous and Tribal Tourism

Amit Sharma
Shimla University, India

ABSTRACT

The interest in indigenous and tribal tourism is increasing rapidly in the new era of technologically savvy, thoughtful, and responsible travellers looking to explore less-travelled regions. This type of tourism is classified as "niche tourism," which falls under the umbrella of the sustainable tourism domain. Changed consumer behaviour has created the demand for a coherent market, which is related to the aforementioned business stream. Indigenous people are living in the natural environment in the hinterlands, which stems from inherent traditional knowledge, sustainable practices, and mystery traditions. This mysticism has led to the creation of the niche segment of indigenous and tribal tourism among the travel-savvy population around the world. Different marketing and business strategies are required to cater to different subsets of clients who may be suitable for this type of tourism.

INTRODUCTION

Indigenous peoples are diverse, rich in social and culturally destined groups and share the inheritance bonds with the natural resources of the place they live. The resonance with the land as well as with the intangible heritage, folksier, lifestyle and generation-to-generation traditions are a few uniqueness they assert even in today's modern era of globalization. Talking about the tribal peoples, they are the ones, who are "not indigenous to the region they inhabit", but that share similar characteristics with indigenous peoples, such as having socio-cultural as well as economic traditions different from other sections of the national community, identifying themselves with their ancestral territories. The word "Tribe" is taken from the Latin word "Tribus"

DOI: 10.4018/978-1-6684-6796-1.ch005

which means "one-third". Originally, the term referred to one of the three territorial groups that came together to form Rome.

According to United Nations data, about 370 million indigenous and tribal people live in 70 countries. They speak about 7,000 languages worldwide and represent 5,000 distinct cultural entities. Further, the United Nations report says: "the biggest challenge faced by these peoples and communities in relation to sustainable development is to ensure territorial security, legal recognition of ownership and control over customary land and resources, and the sustainable utilisation of lands and other renewable resources for the cultural, economic, and physical health and well-being of indigenous peoples." The maintenance of these cultural and spiritual relationships with the natural world is key to their survival as peoples or civilizations.

The mysticism and clandestine nature of indigenous and tribal people make them "very special" for the scope of tourism development and create a pull factor for tourists who would wish to experience the unique cultural heritage in tangible forms. This "extraordinary" pull factor is the driving force behind discussions about the potential of "Indigenous and tribal tourism."

As per the International Labour Organization, there is no universal definition of indigenous and tribal peoples, but ILO Convention No. 169 takes a practical approach to the issue and provides objective and subjective criteria for identifying the peoples concerned (see Article 1 of the Convention). These criteria can be summarised as in Table 1.

Table 1.

	Subjective Criteria	Objective Criteria
Indigenous peoples	Self-identification as belonging to an indigenous people	Descent from populations, who inhabited the country or geographical region at the time of conquest, colonisation or establishment of present state boundaries. They retain some or all of their own social, economic, cultural and political institutions, irrespective of their legal status.
Tribal peoples	Self-identification as belonging to a tribal people	Their social, cultural and economic conditions distinguish them from other sections of the national community. Their status is regulated wholly or partially by their own customs or traditions or by special laws or regulations.

Indigenous and tribal peoples have their own cultures, languages, customs, and institutions, which distinguish them from other parts of the societies in which they find themselves. Indigenous and tribal peoples are often known by national terms such as "native peoples," aboriginal peoples," "first nations," adivasi, janajati, hunter-gatherers, or "hill tribes. Given the diversity of peoples it aims at protecting, the Convention uses the inclusive terminology of "indigenous and tribal peoples" and ascribes the same set of rights to both groups. In Latin America, for example, the term "tribal" has been applied to certain afro-descendent communities.

INDIGENOUS AND TRIBAL TOURISM IS A PART OF NICHE TOURISM

The term "niche" has been derived from marketing management. Before the 1990s, "niche" was most commonly used to describe marketing (Robinson & Novelli, 2005). As per Toften and Hammervoll (2009), "niche marketing" can be understood as a focus on a limited market, which is generally considered to be appropriate for small or specialised businesses.

In 2005, Novelli described niche tourists as independent travellers who choose specialised activities to engage with social life and to become cosmopolitans. By considering this definition, indigenous and tribal tourism can be described as niche tourism.

Stakeholders in Indigenous and Tribal Tourism:

A "stakeholder" is a person, group, or organisation that can affect or be affected by an organization. According to Johnson, Scholes, & Whittington (2006), "stakeholders" refer to individuals or groups that depend on the organisation to fulfil their own goals and on whom, in turn, the organisation depends.

In generic terms, all must be involved in tourism planning, development, and operations in a sufficient capacity in order to ensure the longevity of the tourism industry.

The term "stakeholders in tourism development" includes, according to UNWTO (United Nations World Tourism Organization), the following players:

- National governments
- Local governments with specific competence in tourism matters
- Tourism establishments and tourism enterprises, including their associations
- Institutions engaged in financing tourism projects
- Tourism employees, tourism professionals and tourism consultants
- Trade unions of tourism employees
- Tourism education and training centers
- Travellers, including business travellers, and visitors to tourism destinations, sites and attractions

- Local populations and host communities at tourism destinations through their representatives
- Other juridical and natural persons having stakes in tourism development including non-governmental organizations specializing in tourism and directly involved in tourism projects and the supply of tourism services."

With special reference to the Indigenous and tribal tourism above players hold the sanctity, however being in nascent stage this form of tourism may not have all the relevant stakeholders covered in current scenario.

Sustainable Development Goals and Indigenous and Tribal Society

The tourism industry directly or indirectly impacts or holds the potential for all 17 sustainable development goals as defined by the United Nations Goals which are directly related to this industry are goal 8, 12, and 14 on inclusive and sustainable economic growth, sustainable consumption and production (SCP) and the sustainable use of oceans and marine resources, respectively, are considered to be directly related to tourism. As per the United Nations World Tourism Organization, the historic agreement among world leaders at the United Nations in 2015 on a universal 2030 agenda for sustainable development committed all countries to pursue a set of 17 Sustainable Development Goals (SDGs) that would lead to a better future for all. The ambitious work plan agenda sets out a global framework to end intense poverty, fight inequality and injustice, and fix climate change until 2030. In economic terms, tourism is regarded as an economic powerhouse, accounting for 10% of global GDP, 30% of service exports, and one out of every ten jobs worldwide in 2015. Tourism carries the potential to impact the Indigenous and tribal regions of the world if this form of tourism is considered as one of the mediums for tourism promotion in full throttle. There is, however, a need for more systematic policy formulation to consider the sustainable, responsible, and ethical development of tourism involving indigenous communities. The United Nations Department of Ethics, Culture, and Social Responsibility drafted a set of recommendations. The objective of these recommendations is to enhance the ability of the tourism entities to establish their operations in a responsible and sustainable manner. One point to consider is that not all indigenous and tribal communities are willing to integrate tourism into their existing social ecosystems, despite the fact that the benefits of tourism integration are enormous. Women's empowerment, youth job creation, reverse migration, economic benefits, and infrastructure development are a few to mention. Achieving sustainable development goals by the year 2030 can be fast-tracked easily with the help of tourism and the desired outcome. The framework for Indigenous tourism needs a meticulous approach, keeping eco-sensitivity and the century-old cultural inheritance in mind. Overexposure to the modern world may wreak irreversible and irreparable havoc on them. In a controlled environment, phase-wise exposure can be provided, and a few sustainable development goals can be mapped for the upliftment of such culturally rich utopias. With the gradual pace of synergy and homogeneity between both ends, more can be done in a phased manner. On the other side, initially, those tourists can be targeted who are interested in visiting indigenous communities and motivated by the desire to experience indigenous cultures and traditional lifestyles.

World Heritage and Indigenous Peoples

UNESCO (The United Nations Educational, Scientific and Cultural Organization) which is a specialized agency of the United Nations aimed at promoting world peace and security through international cooperation in education, arts, sciences and culture, is focusing on indigenous peoples along with other intangible heritage assets and have worked out operational guidelines of world heritage convention. The excerpts of the same are relevant during the discussion of indigenous and tribal tourism, as mentioned below. (https://whc.unesco.org/en/activities/496)

Many cultural and natural World Heritage sites are home to indigenous peoples. As the UNESCO policy on engaging with indigenous peoples recognizes, World Heritage sites are often located within land managed by indigenous peoples whose land use, knowledge and cultural and spiritual values and practices are related to heritage. Inspired by the United Nations Declaration on the Rights of Indigenous Peoples (UNDRIP), the UNESCO policy embraces the right of indigenous peoples to their traditional lands, territories and recognizes traditional management systems as part of new management approaches. It describes indigenous peoples as stewards of a significant part of the world's biological, cultural and linguistic diversity and as partners in site conservation and protection activities.

In line with the UNDRIP and UNESCO policy, the Operational Guidelines of the World Heritage Convention recognize the role of indigenous peoples in identifying, managing, protecting and presenting World Heritage. In this spirit, the International Indigenous Peoples Forum for World Heritage functions as a reflection platform on involving indigenous peoples in the identification, conservation and management of World Heritage properties, as noted by the World Heritage Committee at 41st session (Kraków, 2017).

In particular, the Operational Guidelines recognize:

Indigenous peoples as stakeholders and rights-holders in the identification, nomination, management and protection processes of World Heritage properties as well as in the presentation of heritage, in line with a human rights based approach. (paragraphs 12 and 211 d)

Full and effective participation of indigenous peoples in the preparation of Tentative Lists, i.e. the inventories of sites, which State Parties intend to consider for nomination. Before including sites on their Tentative List, "States Parties shall consult and cooperate in good faith with the indigenous peoples concerned through their own representative institutions in order to obtain their free, prior and informed consent." (paragraph 64)

that biological diversity and cultural diversity are closely linked and interdependent. Human activities may be consistent with the Outstanding Universal Value of the area where they are ecologically sustainable. (paragraph 90)

A thorough shared understanding of the property, its universal, national and local values and its socio-ecological context by all stakeholders, including indigenous peoples, as a possible common element of an effective management system. (paragraphs 111 and 117)

The promotion of effective, inclusive and equitable participation of communities, indigenous peoples and other stakeholders concerned with the property through legislations, policies and strategies as necessary conditions to sustainable protection, conservation, management and presentation of World Heritage properties. (paragraph 119)

Effective and inclusive participation of indigenous peoples in the nomination process to demonstrate that their free, prior and informed consent has been obtained and to enable them to have a shared responsibility with the State Party in the maintenance of the property. (paragraph 123)

Educational and capacity-building programmes that promote sustainable and inclusive economic benefits for local communities and indigenous peoples, including the promotion of local material and resource use and of local cultural and creative industries and safeguarding intangible heritage associated with World Heritage properties. (paragraph 214bis)

Traditional and indigenous knowledge held by local communities and indigenous peoples, with all necessary consent, aiming at demonstrating the contribution that the conservation and management of World Heritage properties, their buffer zones and wider setting make to sustainable development. (paragraph 215)

International Assistance requests of inclusive nature, including the involvement of local communities and indigenous peoples. (paragraph 239 j)

EXPERIENTIAL ECONOMY AND INDIGENOUS AND TRIBAL TOURISM

The concept of experiential economy in the context of indigenous and tribal tourism can be well articulated by the "Progression of Economic Value" model. As shown in the figure, the Harvard Business Review article published in July/August 1998 explained various stages of progress in economic value. In today's scenario, we are transitioning from a service economy to an experiential economy. Travelers want to have immersive experiences while travelling for leisure purposes. This meaningful travel can be attained in the experience stage of the progression of the economic value model. As per this model, "an experience is not an amorphous construct; it is as real an offering as any service, good, or commodity."

In today's service economy, many companies simply wrap experiences around their traditional offerings to sell them more effectively. To reap the full benefits of staging experiences, businesses must purposefully design immersive experience that charge a fee. This transition from selling services to selling experiences will be no easier for established companies to undertake and weather than the previous great economic shift, from the industrial to the service economy. Companies will be forced to upgrade their offerings to the next stage of economic value unless they want to be in a commoditized business.

The concept of indigenous and tribal tourism is the fourth stage of this model, where the tourist wants the core experience as well as the service delivery to be intangible. The uniqueness of the culture and social fabric of ethnic and tribal groups can be promoted as an immersive experience, and hence a symbiotic relationship can evolve between a curator (seller) and a guest (buyer).

Experiences are individualistic in nature, hence the focus on the absolutism of slow tourism, which can also be part of indigenous and tribal tourism. It is possible to easily customise the experiences by involving local communities without going beyond the resources available within the regional ecosystem.

Travelers' participation in the various components of the pre-designed activities of the experience itinerary curated for them is one of the components of a successful and memorable holiday. Another aspect is involving the travellers in an active "contribution back to society" in terms of "the *connect,*" *an* environmental relationship that unites customers with local biodiversity and creates a sense of belongingness with mother nature.

Figure 1.
Source: https://hbr.org/1998/07/welcome-to-the-experience-economy

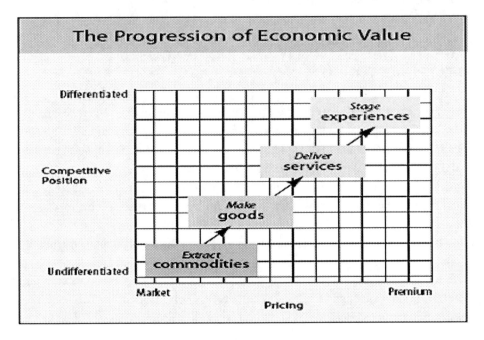

Indigenous and tribal tourism is also a form of niche tourism, which denotes how a particular tourism product can be curated to fulfil the needs of a particular clientele. Specific offerings at sought-after destinations are a few characteristics of niche tourism that are in sync with the offerings of indigenous and tribal tourism.

It is clear from the foregoing that indigenous and tribal tourism can be found in the form of experiential nature-based tourism. Mother Nature is at the heart of these communities' daily lives and is a major draw for indigenous and tribal tourism. Without modern and world-class facilities, these communities have been living happily and satisfactorily for centuries, which is quite an inquisitive and unique selling proposition to the people of the urban world. In general, travelers' industry segmentation is divided into three broad categories:

1. Uber travelers
2. Vanity driven travelers
3. Ethical travelers

This is not a formal categorization; however, travel companies strategize their business based on target customers, and hence packages are designed and sold.

Indigenous and Tribal Tourism

Business strategies are made and executed to meet the company's financial objectives. The following is a brief description of the aforementioned categories.

- **Uber Travelers:**

According to various industry experts, "a luxury trip is determined by the uniqueness and exclusivity of the experience and by the personalization of the services." Uber travellers can be considered a subset of the luxury segment. They are mature, well-traveled, and high-paying ultraluxury clients. They enjoy discovering unusual destinations and authentic experiences.

Amadeus published an interesting correlation between Maslow's hierarchy of needs and luxury travel in 2016. As per the article, "Maslow's hierarchy of needs is a psychological theory about human motivation—it shows five "needs" that as humans we feel motivated to achieve." Presented in hierarchical levels, when one level of needs is fulfilled, we begin to pursue the level above. The same theory can be applied to the luxury travel experience. The more accustomed a traveller, or a regional market of travellers, is to luxury, the higher they will need to travel up the pyramid for their expectations to be met—and for their idea of luxury to be fulfilled.

Figure 2. The Hierarchy of Luxury Travel Needs
Source: Amadeus (2016; https://amadeus.com/documents/en/travel-industry/report/shaping-the-future-of-luxury-travel-future-traveller-tribes-2030.pdf)

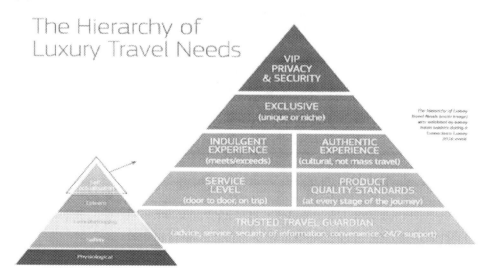

Various surveys have shown that Uber's luxury clients are generally from Generation X, which includes those born between 1965 and 1981 and part of Generation Y (born after 1981 but before 1996). They are also called Millennials. It is estimated that "when making a purchase, high-level travellers first choose the destination and then the on-site service, preferably exclusive boutique hotels, followed by international hotels." When Uber Luxury clients go on vacation, they "look for relaxation and comfort, and they also love tasting gourmet food, experiencing local culture, and going on nature excursions." This consumer behaviour is consistent with what we discussed about the inherent nature of Indigenous and tribal tourism, namely, experiencing local culture and going on nature excursions.

- **Vanity-Driven Travelers:** Those who are technologically savvy, born after 1996, well-educated, and thus concerned about climate change and sustainability, are the primary influencers of travel preferences. They use social media to decide where to travel and thereafter to showcase on social platforms their travel experiences while on the tour. This type of traveller is called an "immersive explorer" because of their interest in out-of the box ideas, gastronomy, and traditions. They also prefer exploring the world purposefully, supporting locals, and feeling immersed in the culture. They are more focused on the variety of accommodations, be they small or large, budgeted or expensive because they have varying travel budgets. A quantitative study published by the European Travel Commission (ETC) among 2,800 Gen Zers aged 18–24 in China, Germany, the United Kingdom, and the United States revealed their travel preferences and global outlook. The study confirmed that Gen Z is growing up as a globally aware generation, conscious of their own responsibility towards the environment and society. Climate change was cited by more than half of Gen Zers in Germany, the U.K., and the U.S. as the issue most important to them (52 percent). There are indicators that are in sync with the nature and scope of indigenous and tribal tourism.
- **Ethical Travelers:** The combination of Uber and vanity-driven travellers has created this new segment, which has a greater bandwidth for indigenous and tribal tourism. Having a purchasing propensity, a technological advantage, and focusing on immersive experiences Giving it back to society is one of the core motivators for holiday related travel. Various surveys have shown that more than 70% of ethical travellers need new ideas of travel, such as slow tourism, community-based tourism, and activity based tourism. We can safely say that ethical travellers are the key target customers for indigenous and tribal tourism.

However, there are numerous advantages and disadvantages to these exclusive forms of tourism that promote indigenous and tribal tourism. As a result, facilitating tourism in this unspoiled land in the lap of nature has both advantages and disadvantages for its century-old, self-sustaining ecosystem.

ADVANTAGES OF INDIGENOUS AND TRIBAL TOURISM

There are various advantages of indigenous and tribal tourism that can be broadly described under ecological, economic, and social parameters. An opportunity to capitalise on tourists' desire to contribute positively to environmental initiatives through an immersive holiday experience. It is less damaging to the environment.

- An opportunity to capitalise on tourists' desire to contribute positively to environmental initiatives through an immersive holiday experience
- It is less damaging to the environment.
- Tribal tourism will promote the development of locally generated goods and handicrafts, apart from direct and indirect jobs, and have essential multiplier effects as money is recycled into communities.
- offers substantial improvements in the tribal region development with provincial taxes and encourages local and national infrastructure growth
- A connection with the rest of the world without
- Tourists come in smaller numbers.
- Tourists are more polite and respectful.
- Niche tourists quite often pay a higher premium than mass tourists.
- There is a genuine interest in the local area, and people

DISADVANTAGE OF INDIGENOUS AND TRIBAL TOURISM

- For local communities, a lack of alternative revenue streams
- Too many visitors will be attracted in due course, and it may follow the mass tourism pathway.
- By providing similar services, niche businesses take business away from other destinations.
- Small visitor numbers mean that the economic benefits are limited.
- Activities can go in and out of vogue and popularity.
- Local beneficiaries may adopt unspurious ways and means to earn extra from travelers, such as taking the guests to restricted territories.
- Flora and fauna may be impacted due to the movement of travelers.

- Exposure to external cultures may have a negative impact on local culture.
- Local stakeholders may not get their fair share of the supply chain as it could be controlled by urban travel agents and tour operators.
- Visitors may visit the areas solely for photographic purposes rather than for an immersive experience.

MARKETING OF INDIGENOUS AND TRIBAL TOURISM

Indigenous and tribal tourism, as a part of niche tourism, needs a specialised understanding of marketing approaches. It is evident from various studies that developing niche markets in tourism is a difficult process, requiring a level of marketing expertise often not possessed by small business firms (McKercher and Robbins, 1998).

Kotler (1967) suggested that the key idea in niche marketing is specialization, and he provided the following ways by which to specialize:

- End-user specialization
- Vertical-level specialization
- Customer-size specialization
- Geographic specialization
- Product or product-line specialization
- Product-feature specialization
- Quality/price specialization
- Channel specialization

The dynamism of indigenous and tribal tourism marketing has taken centre stage, changing consumer behavior. Technological literacy, the rise in concern over ethical consumption, the maturity of the consumer market towards an experiential economy, and looking for authenticity while on vacation are a few key motivators. Such specialised products necessitate specialised marketing methods. This is also to ensure that the right facts are presented so as not to have a wide gap between customer expectations and delivery.

Tourism market mix is important for successful marketing of indigenous and tribal tourism. The 4 Ps (product, price, place, and promotion) concepts prevail very well here.

Product: As the product is a service, innovation in the service is required at each stage. The expectations of the customers are high about the mystical product of indigenous and tribal tourism. Product customization and personalised services

Indigenous and Tribal Tourism

are critical success factors for successful nice marketing, and the same is true for Indigenous and tribal tourism.

Quality assurance is another aspect of the product component. Right-fit service delivery training is the key component here.

Price: A value-based pricing strategy is one of the strategies that work for indigenous and tribal tourism. However, with the fast pace of technology and price skimming in the competitive world, new trends and pricing techniques based on demand and supply need to be considered.

Place: A place refers to "where and how" the products are to be bought. As we discussed the three types of travellers (Uber, vanity-driven, and ethical travelers), the latter, being tech-savvy and influenced by digital reviews and feedback, could be the real-time promoter, thus the emphasis on Indigenous and tribal tourism products.

Promotion: The fourth P in tourism marketing stands for promotion. Advertising, public relations, and product promotion are all aspects of publicity. The goal of promoting a service is to reveal to potential clients why they need it and why they should pay a certain price for it. Creating awareness about the target product and educating the potential customers is vital. Few fucus areas to be such as value for money, a personalsied, out of the box and memorable experience. In recent years, safety and hygiene have become equally important and key decision factors in deciding on destinations.

It is clear from the preceding discussions about niche marketing that for Indigenous and tribal tourism products.It is all about attracting more specific groups based on the experiences they're seeking.

Tourists are planning vacations that centre around their interests or passions. By tapping into those preferences through niche marketing, specific groups can be targeted.

Something to keep in mind is that these marketing tools and hub marketing expertise are more geared toward revenue generation for the intermediaries, such as travel agents and tour operators, than the actual stakeholders on the ground. This side effect of niche marketing is critical to focus on when strategizing the marketing efforts for Indigenous and tribal tourism products.

RESPONSIBILITIES OF TRAVELERS

It is a famous saying that "travel is a privilege, and with it comes a certain level of responsibility." For special interest market products like indigenous and tribal tourism, the responsibilities of the traveller increase multifold. It's now no longer enough to travel from continent to continent without an understanding of the repercussions this lifestyle may accumulate.

The Global Code of Ethics for Tourism, as published by the United Nations World Tourism Organization (UNWTO), the nodal body in the United Nations domain for tourism, The UNWTO Code of Ethics, which inspired the drafting of these tips, is a fundamental frame of reference for responsible and sustainable tourism. Adopted in 1999 by the General Assembly of the UNWTO and acknowledged by the General Assembly of the United Nations two years later, this set of principles is designed to guide key players in tourism development. The code is addressed to governments, tourism companies, destinations, local communities, and tourists alike.

A few of the excerpts:

Respect your host and your shared heritage.

Learn about local customs, traditions, and social conditions by researching your destination. It is an excellent way to learn about the local community while also getting excited about your upcoming adventure. Learn a few phrases in the local language. This can help you connect with the local community and its people in a more meaningful way. Experience and respect all that makes a tourism destination different and unique, from its history, architecture, religion, dress, and communication codes, to its music, art, and cuisine. Always ask before taking photographs of other people, as their privacy matters as much as yours. Do not offer money to get the desired picture. Pause and reflect before criticising local living conditions or customs. Learn to listen and leave your preconceptions at home. Treat with courtesy and respect staff and service providers at all tourism facilities.

Protect our planet:

Reduce your environmental impact by being a guardian of natural resources, especially forests and wetlands. Respect wildlife and their natural habitats. Animal attractions may imply cruelty. Do not purchase products made of endangered plants, animals, or non-sustainable hardwood. In protected areas, access only the places open to visitors. Do not offer money to locals to discover "no-go areas." Sleep green and go rural, as the countryside has so much to offer. Reduce waste, single-use plastic, water, and energy consumption, and plan your transport to cut carbon emissions. Leave a minimal footprint and a good impression behind.

Support the local economy:

Buy locally made crafts and products. Respect the livelihoods of local artisans by paying a fair price. Do not buy counterfeit products or items prohibited by national and international regulations. Hire local guides, spend locally, and find out about tipping practices. Support businesses that embrace diversity and equality. Slow down and spend more time in less-visited areas.

Be an informed traveler:

Research well before engaging in voluntary tourism. Choose tourism companies that have environmentally friendly policies and community projects. Some initiatives may appear to be environmentally friendly or ethical, but they do not provide adequate

Indigenous and Tribal Tourism

working conditions. Follow all applicable laws and regulations. Respect "private spaces" and follow the rules at religious sites. adhere to human rights and protect children from profiteering.

Abusing children is a serious offence. Don't give money or gifts to begging children. Instead, donate to community projects. Have fun, but keep the locals and their way of life in mind. Engage with them to learn about their culture. Take photos of protected cultural artefacts as souvenirs of your trip.

POLICIES ABOUT INDIGENOUS AND TRIBAL TOURISM:

Since 2010, global tourism arrivals have increased by nearly 50%, with an annual growth rate of more than 5%.The benefits of foreign exchange and the higher spending of international visitors have focused many governments on increasing inbound arrivals, while demand has been supported by favourable economic conditions, decreasing travel prices, continued globalisation, liberalised and more comprehensive air transport services, and the growth of digitally enabled business models and platforms that allow consumers easier access to travel products and many new destinations (UNWTO 2019a; WEF 2019; IATA 2019).

While tourism growth is projected to continue, changing demographics, improved connectivity, technological innovations, and increased recognition of the need for this growth to be more sustainable and inclusive are likely to dramatically transform the face of tourism by 2040, representing a range of opportunities and challenges for destinations (OECD, 2018). The OECD (Organisation for Economic Co-operation and Development) also mentioned that continued growth in visitor numbers raises important questions about how to best manage this growth, to benefit people, places, and businesses. The overriding priority for governments and, increasingly, society is to better look after the assets on which tourism depends. This is an issue that affects all destinations, but it is especially acute in overcrowded areas.

Various national governments are formulating specific policies to promote indigenous and tribal tourism. As tourism is an intersectoral entity, a combined approach is needed to promote local tourism globally. In the case of indigenous and tribal tourism, it is more important to focus on key areas that may make or break this form of niche tourism. Generally, it has been noticed that the lack of coordination among various government departments is a major deterrent to the upliftment of indigenous and tribal tourism.

In the United States of America, the Tribal Tourism Grant Program (TTGP) helps tribes evaluate and identify viable tourism business opportunities for their communities. aims to support tribal economic development and fulfil the mission of the NATIVE Act (Native American Tourism and Improving Visitor Experience

Act) by providing funding for tribes to conduct feasibility studies to help them make informed decisions about potential tourism projects. The act is intended to enhance and integrate Native American tourism, empower Native American communities, increase coordination and collaboration between federal tourism assets, and expand heritage and cultural tourism opportunities in the United States. The following are excerpts from the Act's purposes:

1. To enhance and integrate Native American tourism
2. To increase coordination and collaboration between Federal tourism assets to support Native American tourism and bolster recreational travel and tourism
3. To expand heritage and cultural tourism opportunities in the United States to spur economic development, create jobs, and increase tourism revenues
4. To enhance and improve self-determination and selfgovernance capabilities in the Native American community and to promote greater self-sufficiency
5. To encourage Indian tribes, tribal organizations, and Native Hawaiian organizations to engage more fully in Native American tourism activities to increase visitation to rural and remote areas in the United States that are too difficult to access or are unknown to domestic travelers and international tourists
6. To support the development of technologically innovative projects that will incorporate recreational travel and tourism information and data from federal assets to improve the visitor experience.

In other countries, too, such integrated approaches are being curated and launched; it is imperative to mention that effective coordination for diligence delivery is critical in the case of indigenous and tribal tourism.

In India, various state governments have launched tribal tourism policies. In the state of Uttar Pradesh, the excerpts of the policy are as below:

- Uttar Pradesh state government through this scheme would connect these villages inhabited by the population belonging to the Tharu tribe, mainly located on the International border of Nepal.
- The scheme would be like a Homestay scheme. The Uttar Pradesh Forest Department would be offering all the tourists who would be visiting these villages an experience of living in the natural habitat of the Tharu tribals.
- The huts where the people would get to stay would be made of grass collected from the forest.
- The Forest Department of Uttar Pradesh would also be training the tribals to communicate with the tourists.
- They tribals would also be acquainted with aspects of cleanliness and safety.

- The Tharu tribals will be allowed to charge the tourists for their home-cooked meals and accommodation provided
- The villages will be opened for both domestic and international tourists.

CONCLUSION

Indigenous and tribal tourism is a tourism activity in which indigenous people are directly involved either through control and/or by having their culture serve as the essence of the attraction. By focusing on understanding the consumer behaviors, types of travelers, and marketing strategies. this type of tourism can be flourished with great possibilities of various advantages of indigenous and tribal tourism which can be broadly described under ecological, economy and social parameters.

Stronger businesses, conservation of biodiversity, and increased participation in decision-making spaces, the empowerment of communities, women's groups, and associations, as well as the participation of women who play a significant leadership role in these community tourism activities at the local level, are a few positive outcomes of indigenous and tribal tourism. The question which needs to be focused is "what can be done to make tribal and indigenous tourism more ethical and to protect the intangible heritage from external influences exploitation". The most important aspect is to focus on ethical travelers and educate visitors on the negative effects of tribal and indigenous tourism.

REFERENCES

C169 - indigenous and tribal peoples convention, 1989 (no. 169) (n.d.). https://www.ilo.org/dyn/normlex/en/f?p=NORMLEXPUB%3A12100%3A0%3A%3ANO%3A%3AP12100_ILO_CODE%3AC169.

ETC Market Study (2020). https://etc-corporate.org/uploads/2020/07/2020_ETC-Study-Generation-Z-Travellers.pdf

Global Code of Ethics for Tourism. (2020) Available at: https://www.unwto.org/background-global-code-ethics-tourism

International Day of the World's Indigenous Peoples 9 August 2022. (2022). Available at: https://www.un.org/en/observances/indigenous-day

Johnson, G., Scholes, K., & Whittington, R. (2008). *Exploring corporate strategy: Text and cases*. Pearson education.

Kotler, P. (1967). *Marketing Management: Analysis, Planning, and Control.* Prentice Hall.

McKercher, B., & Robbins, B. (1998). Business development issues affecting nature-based tourism operators in Australia. *Journal of Sustainable Tourism, 6*(2), 36–45. doi:10.1080/09669589808667309

'Native American Tourism and Improving Visitor Experience Act. (2016). Available at: https://www.bia.gov/service/grants/ttgp/what-tribal-tourism-grant-program-ttgp

Novelli, M. (2022). Niche tourism. In *Encyclopedia of Tourism Management and Marketing* (pp. 344–347). Edward Elgar Publishing. doi:10.4337/9781800377486.niche.tourism

OECD Tourism Trends and Policies 2020. (2020). Available at: https://www.oecd.org/cfe/tourism/OECD-Tourism-Trends-Policies%202020-Highlights-ENG.pdf

Robinson, M., & Novelli, M. (2005). Niche Tourism. Contemporary issues, trends and cases. *Information and Communication Technologies in Tourism, 2001,* 294–302.

Shaping the Future of Luxury Travel Future Traveller Tribes 2030. (2016). Available at: https://amadeus.com/documents/en/travel-industry/report/shaping-the-future-of-luxury-travel-future-traveller-tribes-2030.pdf

Toften, K., & Hammervoll, T. (2009). Niche firms and marketing strategy: An exploratory study of internationally oriented niche firms. *European Journal of Marketing, 43*(11/12), 1378–1391. doi:10.1108/03090560910989948

Welcome to the Experience Economy. (2018). Available at: https://hbr.org/1998/07/welcome-to-the-experience-economy

World Heritage and Indigenous Peoples. (2019). Available at: https://whc.unesco.org/en/activities/496/

Chapter 6
Pro-Poor Tourism and Poverty Alleviation

Faithfull Cecilia Gonzo
University of Sunderland in London, UK

ABSTRACT

Tourism has been utilised as a tool for poverty alleviation globally, and its growth is envisioned to directly or indirectly impact the lives of the local communities. The dialogue on poverty alleviation led to the formulation of pro-poor tourism (PPT). PPT is defined as tourism that generates net benefits to the poor, and it should be economically, socially, environmentally, or culturally beneficial. Although PPT has the potential to benefit the poor, it is not clear how the different types of tourism impact the poor. The tourism industry is mainly driven by the private sector, particularly large international companies. Therefore, their interest in ensuring that poverty is alleviated between local communities is not guaranteed. Thus, with this view, PPT has been criticised for over-emphasising local initiatives. Similarly, the understanding of the poverty concept has been overtly debated. Hence, this chapter intends to explore the concept of PPT and its effect on poor communities.

INTRODUCTION

The concept of pro-poor tourism (PPT) has been debated by various researchers. Many academics declared that PPT can contribute to poverty alleviation, however, the opposing group have indicated that the tourism and poverty nexus is blurry. Similarly, conceptualising poverty has been debated by different scholars and policy analysts. Poverty can be defined differently by different countries therefore providing reliable comparisons amongst countries can prove to be impractical.

DOI: 10.4018/978-1-6684-6796-1.ch006

Thus, this chapter will firstly explore the poverty concept, the tourism and poverty nexus, and then the strategies implemented by the global tourism industry to tackle poverty will be discussed. The chapter will further analyse different methods used to assess the impacts of tourism on poverty. Pro-Poor Tourism Approach and effects of tourism on the poor will be discussed. The chapter will conclude by reviewing the challenges of PPT and explore how developing countries could utilise the approach to benefit the poor.

CONCEPTUALISING POVERTY

Poverty is defined differently by different countries, hence providing reliable comparisons amongst countries can prove to be impossible (Mutana et al., 2013). Mitchell and Ashley (2010) advocate that it is important to understand who the poor are first before analysing the effects of tourism on the poor and poverty alleviation. It is therefore crucial that the poverty concept and definition is notionally robust and apt to the society which it is being applied.

Originally, poverty was defined as just a lack of basic needs; it included hunger, lack of shelter and lack of medical facilities (Croes, 2014). According to the World Bank (2001) poverty is best described as "a situation where an individual lacks command over commodities that are deemed essential to realise a reasonable standard of living". It is a state of being poor, insufficiency and non-existence of resources hence it comprises of low incomes, low levels of wealth, poor environments and vulnerability (McCulloch et al., 2001). There are two types of poverty; "absolute poverty" is when the person's basic needs (such as food, shelter and clothes) are not covered, and "relative poverty" which is closely related to inequality, where the individual is regarded as poor when they are in an undoubtedly disadvantaged situation (financially or socially) in comparison to other people in the same community (Alcock, 2006). Therefore, poverty is a prescriptive concept that shows an undesirable state of affairs where individuals become deprived, excluded and disregarded. Poverty includes poor health, lack of access to water and sanitation, lack of participation in education and insecurity (World Tourism Organisation (WTO), 2004). It is therefore a mixture of illiteracy, poor health, unemployment, lack of basic infrastructure and empowerment (Croes, 2014). In this regard, it is plausible to view poverty as a multifaceted phenomenon since it consists of numerous characteristics that affect poor people (Holden, 2013; Mitchell & Ashley, 2010). The dimensions of poverty comprise of diverse characteristics of human capabilities such as the ones highlighted by the Organisation for Economic Co-operation and Development (OECD) (2001) below:

- Economic-income, livelihoods, decent work
- Human-health, education
- Political-empowerment, rights, voice
- Socio-cultural-status, dignity
- Protective-insecurity, risk, vulnerability

The political, economic, and socio-cultural impacts need to be thoroughly analysed as they may disadvantage the poor. A case in point is when some policies intended to alleviate poverty can benefit the wealthy; this can cause the gap between the poor and the rich to be widened further (Sawhill, 2003). Yet policymakers are more concerned with the growth of the tourism sector than the extent in which the tourism growth contributes to poverty alleviation (Christie, 2002). The understanding is that if the entire region gets richer, the benefits provided by the economic growth will ultimately "trickle down" to the poor through employment or public network. However, basic development of the economy cannot bring social justice and practical growth without the poverty alleviation and employment-generating opportunities for the underprivileged and marginalised segments of the society. Poverty should not be restricted to income only, but it should also be concerned with finding ways of improving quality of life (WTO, 2004). The World Summit for Social Development in Copenhagen (1995) offers that access to social services is of paramount importance for any society.

Poverty is also defined in monetary terms by means of national poverty lines; however, the definitions can vary according to geographical locations (World Vision, 2020). This notion was implemented by the World Bank (1991) to provide a context that is globally recognised, particularly for developing countries. However, defining poverty using poverty lines is debatable as there are cases of extreme poverty in some parts of developing countries. To estimate the level of poverty, most countries outline their own poverty lines, they generally base the amount on the per capita cost of some nominal consumption basket of food and other necessities (Perkins et al., 2006). The World Bank (2011:1) applies three poverty measures. Firstly, the incidence of poverty assesses the number of people living below the poverty line through income or consumption and the depth of poverty (poverty gap) intends to measure individual household distance from the stated poverty line. The poverty severity (squared poverty gap) measures the distance from the poverty line and the levels of inequality amid the poor by giving those further away from the poverty line more weight. The international poverty line considerably varies. The poverty line currently set by the World Bank is at US$1,90 which replaced the previous US$1,25 line based on the 2005 prices (Ferreira et al., 2015). It is vital to note that poverty can be construed differently by developed and developing countries, for example the US$1,90 per day implies the extreme poverty line for the world's poorest countries. Other poverty lines for developing countries typically indicates to some extent a higher standard of living, whilst higher poverty lines are more suitable for developed countries. Globally, the total number of people living in extreme poverty is still high with 10,7% (2013) surviving on less than US$1,90 a day and extreme poverty has positively reduced from affecting 1,9 billion people in 1990 to 760 million in 2013 (Weller, 2017). Sub-Saharan Africa constitutes half of the extreme poor where 389 million people still live below the poverty line of US$1,90 per day (World Bank, 2017). Mutana et al. (2013) argued that poverty is more evident in rural areas, particularly in developing countries. Hence, the measures implemented by the World Bank has been debated for its lack of impartiality, it focuses more urban environments than the authenticities of the poor people in rural areas (Chambers, 1995). Global poverty has also been increasing due to the prolonged impacts of the pandemic, the war in Ukraine, and rising inflation, with 75 million to 95 million more people anticipated to live in extreme poverty in 2022 in comparison to pre-COVID-19 predictions (World bank, 2022). It is evident, based on the analysis of the poverty concept, that the notion has been extensively explored, yet the methods of measuring it remain contentious. This creates challenges in alleviating poverty as some people might not consider themselves poor, even if they are (by definition).

Tourism and Poverty Alleviation Nexus

It is essential to analytically establish the contribution of tourism to poverty reduction as well as highlighting their connection. Tourism is envisaged to be a powerful tool to alleviate poverty. Various countries use tourism as a strategic approach for socio-economic improvement through job creation and export revenue earnings. In 2019, the industry was reported as a leading and robust economic sector in the world, generating US$1,7 trillion in export earnings (UNWTO, 2019). Correspondingly, from 1950 to 2015 international tourist arrivals progressively increased from 25 million to an aggregate of 1,186 billion (Glaesser et al., 2017). However, in 2020, the international tourist arrivals declined by 22% due to the COVID-19 pandemic (UNWTO, 2020). Globally, the tourism industry provided a total of 330 million jobs in the first quarter of 2020; however, 100 to 120 million jobs (direct) are anticipated to be at risk making the current pandemic the worst crisis since 1950 (UNWTO, 2020). The figures above clearly indicate that tourism has the potential to grow, however, the recent pandemic may negatively impact on the industry, particularly economies such as developing countries that rely on tourism for their growth and development. The tourism industry provides the local community with an opportunity for employment and most developing countries have promoted the industry as a strategic economic development tool to aid in poverty alleviation in host communities (Carbone, 2005). Developing countries have benefited from an expanding tourist base as far back as mid-20th century. The development of tourism, particularly international tourism, has been recognised as a priority by governments in the Southern Africa region, including the Southern Africa Development Community (SADC) (Novelli & Gebhardt, 2007). Since the 1950s, the share for the numbers of international tourist arrivals for developing countries has substantially improved from 3% in 1950 to 45% in 2001 (Muhanna, 2007). In 2013, developing countries' share of international tourist arrivals increased from 31% in 1990 to 47% in 2011 (Muchapondwa & Stage, 2013). In 2018 Africa received 1,407 million international tourist arrivals earning tourism receipts of US$1,480 billion (UNCTAD, 2020). Least developed economies and transition economies are progressively concentrating on tourism as a pathway for development (Andrades & Dimanche, 2017). Most of the least developed countries (LDCs) recognise tourism as a significant sector which has the capability for considerable economic growth (UNWTO, 2016). In 2015, 49 LDCs received 29 million international tourist arrivals which was a 300% increase from ten years ago (UNWTO, 2016). Between 2011-2015, 21 million jobs were supported by tourism in Africa (UNCTAD, 2017), whilst in 2019, a total of 24,6 million jobs were supported by the travel and tourism industry (WTTC, 2019). The decline of the global tourism industry has a negative effect on the people that rely on tourism, which will ultimately have an impact on poverty and poverty alleviation efforts. Considering that the industry has been growing, one would assume that its impact would only be positive.

From an economic point of view, there is limited research evidence that indicates that tourism can alleviate poverty, neither is there research that measures the connections between tourism and poverty (Blake et al., 2008). Nonetheless, Scheyvens (2007) emphasises that tourism and poverty alleviation are progressively being connected. Furthermore, Winters et al. (2013) highlight that the link between tourism and poverty exist, but the conditions under which this connection is robust is not quite clear. It is of fundamental importance for the method of measuring the poverty alleviation to be agreed on, however, this is a challenge because there is no agreed methodology on the appropriate measurement of poverty alleviation (Thomas, 2014). Tourism is regarded as a devise of economic development in emerging countries; this enables developing countries to benefit from developed countries through tourism (Cooper et al., 2008). Tourism is defined as "the world's largest voluntary transfer of resources from rich people to poor people" (Mitchell and Ashley, 2010). However, economic growth might not be beneficial to the poor, but it may profit the rich, in as much as some countries may be supporting poor families, others may be providing disproportionate gains to the rich. Therefore, it is essential to conduct an in-depth analysis of the channels through which tourism benefits are disseminated to poor households. Furthermore, for the poor to benefit from tourism it is vital for the local residents to be empowered and be involved in the decision-making process.

Yet, others (Chok et al., 2007; Harrison 2008; Scheyvens, 2007, 2011; Schilcher, 2007) argue that the barriers to poverty alleviation at an international and national level should be removed first for the potential of tourism on poverty alleviation to be realised. Luvanga and Shitundu (2003) mention that the tourism industry and poverty alleviation can be linked by recognising its merits in the development of local economies; they therefore highlight three fundamental points. Firstly, the fact that the tourists travel to the destination offers the local community including the poor an opportunity to show and sell their products, thereby reducing poverty. It is this direct link to consumers that is often emphasised in considering the poverty reduction potential of tourism because it gives the opportunity of connecting the poor directly to consumers. The tourism earnings can also be utilised to improve health and educational systems, and these will in turn lessen the impact of poverty.

Secondly, the characteristics of rural areas attract tourists and thus tourism offers them new employment prospects and providing them with income and enhanced social well-being. Snyman and Spenceley (2012) also emphasise that employment opportunities for the underprivileged is an essential element of PPT. Relying on employment on its own as a way of alleviating poverty, particularly in the tourism industry, is not a plausible strategy. This is because of most poor people are not educated and they are offered low-income jobs which do not assist in reducing poverty. Thirdly, one of tourism's characteristics is that it is labour intensive, and it employs a large number of women. Therefore, it assists in reducing poverty to vulnerable groups. Atkinson (2008) and the World Tourism Organisation (2002) echoed the same sentiments and added that tourism boosts the locally owned businesses through profits. However, this tends to enrich those who are already privileged more than reducing poverty. Similarly, another characteristic of the tourism industry is that it is highly seasonal, therefore during troughs the tourism workers will be unemployed, making it difficult to reduce the circle of poverty. Essentially, policy makers have to extend the tourism industry but neglected to thoroughly assess the extent to which the development of tourism contributes to poverty alleviation (Christie, 2002). Consequently, this happens through indirect benefits such as development of basic infrastructure, provision of clean water and improvement of communication networks (Richardson, 2010). The development of these services will influence accessibility and tourism development to and in rural areas and offer linkage opportunities with other economic sectors such as agriculture, fisheries and manufacturing. Strengthening the links between business sectors is viewed as a useful way of promoting the local economies (Mitchell & Ashley, 2010; Torres, 2003). These linkages provide the tourism sector with prospects of employing many people. As for the developing countries, inter-sectoral linkages are often viewed as weak, therefore it is crucial for the national governments of the countries to ensure that they analyse their development initiatives and poverty alleviation strategies so as to strengthen linkages (Meyer, 2007; Mitchell & Ashley, 2010). Anti-Poverty Tourism (APT) as highlighted in Figure 1 below, utilises poverty alleviation as its main focal point in any tourism development.

Figure 1. An integrated framework for anti-poverty reduction
Source: Zhao and Ritchie (2007)

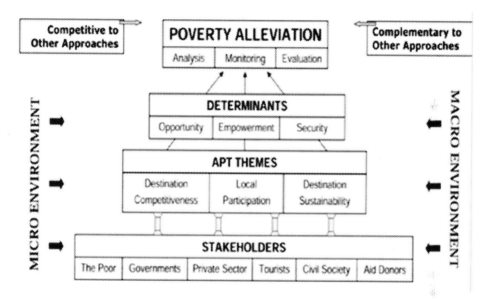

Zhao and Ritchie (2007) also identify opportunity, empowerment and security as key determinants that should be studied for the APT approach to be successful and justified. The core objectives to be considered in APT are the competitiveness of the destination, participation of the local people and sustainability of the destination (Zhao & Ritchie, 2007). However, Phi et al. (2018) argues that although the APT concept was developed to prompt change in the tourism sector that would influence the reduction of poverty, it is not quite clear how this change takes place. They add that APT interventions involved the participation of various stakeholders (The poor, governments, private sector, tourists, civil society, aid donors) who have different views and motivations on the issue of poverty, and this brings about conflicting interests and makes the APT notion complex. It is quite clear from the tourism-poverty connection analysis that tourism has the potential to reduce poverty, however, its full potential has not yet been fully scrutinised, it is therefore vital for researchers to work with all stakeholders and utilise the approach from the impact evaluation literature to recognise the effect of tourism projects on poverty (Winters et al., (2013).

Millennium Development Goals (MDGs) in Relation to Poverty

The development of MDGs influenced the rapid development of several anti-poverty tourism interventions (Saarinen & Rogerson, 2014; Manwa & Manwa, 2014:5698). The Millennium Development Goals (MDGs) were launched by 189 members of the United Nations in the year 2000, focusing on the issue of poverty, the member states established eight fundamental goals with the sole purpose of halving the number of people living on less than one dollar a day by 2015 (United Nations, 2008). Accordingly, many developing countries incorporated the MDGs strategies into their own strategies and policies. The MDGs as highlighted by UNWTO (2007:1) were expected to:

- Eradicate extreme poverty and hunger.
- Achieve universal primary education.
- Promote gender equality and empower women.
- Reduce child mortality.
- Improve maternal health.
- Combat HIV/AIDS, malaria and other diseases.
- Ensure environmental sustainability.
- Develop a global partnership for development.

Since the implementation of MDGs the tourism industry stressed the importance of linking the industry to the MDGs. As far as the tourism sector is concerned MDGs are aligned with sustainable tourism and the concept of sustainable development has been emphasised by the United Nations. The concept of sustainable development and rural development was documented in Agenda 21 (1992) which emphasises the importance of developing poor areas by devising strategies that eradicate and reduce poverty, provide jobs and generate income. The noteworthy of sustainable development in line with MDGs was also highlighted at the World Summit on sustainable development in South Africa (Johannesburg) in 2002 and at the Bali Declaration on Sustainable Tourism Development in 2005 which stressed the importance of sustainably promoting tourism (Saarinen et al., 2011). Sustainable tourism emphasises the importance of poverty alleviation which is in line with the MDG1. It is defined as "tourism that takes full responsibility of its current and future economic, social and environmental impacts whilst addressing the needs of visitors, the industry, the environment and host communities" (UNWTO, 2005:11). Therefore, from this definition, tourism can be linked to the MDG7 which ensures environmental sustainability. Similarly, as one of its characteristics, the tourism industry provides flexible labour markets and various work prospects, and this presents women and young people with an opportunity to work in the industry, thus contributing to MDG3 (Rogerson, 2012). The MDGs have been criticised for failing to fully address increasing environmental challenges such as climate change and other areas of poverty such as social exclusion and inequalities have been omitted by MDG1 (Fehling et al., 2013). Despite the critics, the UN report claimed that MDGs were successful as they managed to reduce extreme poverty, the number of children who are not in school and the percentage of the population deprived of access to safe drinking water by half (UN, 2014). The MDGs assisted the member of states in identifying areas that needed improvement. The Sustainable Development Goals (SDGs) were therefore launched in 2015 by 193 UN member states building upon the successes of the MDGs and completing the goals which were not achieved (UN, 2017).

Sustainable Development Goals (SDGs)

The member states agreed on seventeen sustainable goals with 169 targets. The SDGs takes a broader approach where it targets the basis of poverty, climate change, education and food access inequalities (UN, 2017). It aims to achieve these goals by 2030, the goals have been indicated in Table XXX. The tourism sector has embraced both the MDGs and SDGs, and as far as the SGDs are concerned the tourism industry can contribute through economic growth, social inclusion and environmental preservation (goals 8, 12, and 14). Thus, the International Year of Sustainable Tourism for Development was launched to support and promote the SDGs. It focuses on five key areas which are:

- Inclusive and sustainable economic growth.
- Social inclusiveness, employment, and poverty reduction.
- Resource efficiency, environmental protection, and climate change.
- Cultural values, diversity, and heritage.
- Mutual understanding, peace, and security (UNWTO, 2017).

UNDP, UNWTO and other agencies collaborated during the International Year of Sustainable Tourism for Development with the purpose of building knowledge, empowering, and inspiring stakeholders to take necessary action to fast-track the change towards a more sustainable tourism sector by aligning policies, business operators and investments with SDGs (UNDP and UNWTO, 2018). UNDP and UNWTO (2018) note that tourism's role to the SDGs entails both political motivation and private sector commitment. Although the success of the SDGs is yet to be realised, the framework has been criticised for being an overambitious model (169 targets) because it is too broad, whilst others highlighted that targets such as malnutrition and diseases such as malaria are incredibly optimistic and not cost effective (Aziz &

Basir, 2018). Pogge and Sengupta (2016) critically reviewed the SDGs and emphasise that the goals overlook local milieu as they take a view of "one size fits all", hence, to achieve the goals there is need for the goals to strike a balance between respecting local setting and working at the global level to restructure organisations. They also added that the goals are not binding as they fail to highlight the penalties for those who fail to abide by them. Gupta and Vegelin (2016) also critique the SDGs and state that the achievement of goals relies on the developed countries helping the developing countries (top-down approach) and this is difficult as the developed countries need to be fully committed to the concept. Thus, questions such as who will implement them and who is responsible for ensuring that it in fact will get done need to be fully addressed. The knowledgeable community and NGOs are therefore required to monitor this obligation. They also emphasised that the current global systems need to be reformed as they favour richer participants, thus it is key for the framework to be more democratic and must indicate the terms on how the rich minority should transform their own conduct and change their own interests. It is important before conducting any research that is intended to analyse the impacts of tourism on poverty, to have a clear understanding of the different methods used to assess tourism's impact on poverty.

IMPACT OF TOURISM ON POVERTY

Jamieson et al. (2004) state that the figures that indicate the impact of tourism on poverty are very limited. Thomas (2014) adds that academics seem to disagree on the appropriate measure of the impact of tourism on poverty. In fact, there is not much research focusing on local poor households; this makes it difficult for researchers to decide on the best methodology to use when conducting research on the impacts of tourism in alleviating poverty. Methods such as the Applied General Equilibrium (AGE), Input-Output models, Computable General Equilibrium (CGE), Tourism Satellite Accounts (TSA) and Social Accounting Matrices (SAMs) have been utilised to assess the impact of tourism at a macro level. The scientific tools have been criticised for failing to measure tourism impacts at a micro level for instance the TSA has been viewed as a measure of the impacts of tourism at a macro level thus it is not appropriate, particularly for a community group such as poor people. In general, Gross National Product (GNP) and the number of jobs generated have been used to determine the impact of tourism on poverty (Goodwin, 2006).

Table 1. Sustainable development goals (SDGs)

Sustainable Development Goals (SDGs)
1. End poverty in all its forms everywhere.
2. End hunger, achieve food security and improved nutrition and promote sustainable agriculture.
3. Ensure healthy lives and promote well-being for all at all ages.
4. Ensure inclusive & equitable quality education and promote lifelong learning opportunities for all.
5. Achieve gender equality and empower all women and girls.
6. Ensure availability and sustainable management of water and sanitation for all.
7. Ensure access to affordable, reliable, sustainable and modern energy for all.
8. Promote sustained, inclusive and sustainable economic growth, full and productive employment and decent work for all.
9. Build resilient infrastructure, promote inclusive and sustainable industrialization and foster innovation.
10. Reduce inequality within and among countries.
11. Make cities and human settlements inclusive, safe, resilient and sustainable.
12. Ensure sustainable consumption and production patterns.
13. Take urgent action to combat climate change and its impacts.
14. Conserve and sustainably use the oceans, seas and marine resources for sustainable development.
15. Protect, restore and promote sustainable use of terrestrial ecosystems, sustainably manage forests, combat desertification, and halt and reverse land degradation and halt biodiversity loss.
16. Promote peaceful and inclusive societies for sustainable development, provide access to justice for all and build effective, accountable and inclusive institutions at all levels.
17. Strengthen the means of implementation and revitalize the global partnership for sustainable development.

Source: United Nations Report (2018)

Tourism has been utilised as a device that will alleviate poverty; thus, it is imperative to analyse its impact at a micro level. Regularly tourism's general impact on the economy is assessed through an analysis of the effects of tourism spending through direct, indirect and induced effects utilising a multiplier effect method. The development of tourism is predominantly assessed by analysing the rising figures of international tourist arrivals, number of days the tourists spend at the destination and how much they spend (Jamieson et al., 2004). Although this approach is regarded as the most suitable way of connecting tourism and poverty alleviation, it does not provide substantial data on the degree of the impact on the poor. The PPT approach's view is that increasing economic growth enhances the benefits to "trickle down" to the poor. Thus, Pro-Poor Tourism (PPT) and the Sustainable Livelihood Approach (SLA) have been predominantly used to evaluate the impact of tourism on poverty.

Pro-Poor Tourism (PPT)

PPT was developed in the 90s and it is not a tourism product or a segment but an overall approach which aims to open up opportunities for the poor people accordingly. Developing countries have recognised PPT as an essential tool for poverty alleviation (Sharpley, 2009; Zapata et al., 2011). In most cases poor people are not included in the tourism sector and are faced with challenges of selling locally produced goods or services. This has ultimately influenced PPT to attract a lot of interest from academics, donor agencies, economists and policy makers. Economists and policy makers have utilised the term "pro-poor" largely to discern from economic developments and the types of economic development that positively impact on the lives of poor people and the ones that help them to eradicate poverty (Mahony & Van Zyl, 2002). Academics have advocated that the approach "unlocks opportunities", influences changes in government policies and tourism practices that results to a "tilting of the cake" and improved participation of the poor in tourism chains (Bennett et al., 1999; Goodwin, 2008; Roe & Urquhart, 2001).

The approach concentrates on strategies that are aimed at reducing poverty and yield benefits for poor people thus moving past the "trickle down concept" (Jamieson et al., 2004). However, Scheyvens (2007) critiqued the PPT approach for accentuating on local initiatives and failing to open up structural constraints at a national and international level. Although PPT is inadequately represented, it is an essential component of sustainable tourism, and is frequently called an "ethical cousin" of fair-trade tourism (FTT) because they both emphasise on the benefits of local people (Ravallion, 2004). However, FTT emphasises fair salaries and fair working environments in the destination. PPT is defined as "tourism that generates net benefits for the poor" (Ashley & Carney, 1999) indicating that the benefits should be more than the costs. Thus, poor people should be offered augmented access to economic benefits of tourism and the approach should also address the negative social and environmental impacts related to tourism. If tourism approaches emphasise solely on tourism growth and disregard the poor, it will fail to reduce poverty. Thus, its main aim should therefore be to place the poor and poverty at the centre. It is also important to note that PPT is not a solution but a contribution to rural development and alleviation of poverty. Bennett et al. (1999) highlights that tourism can be called pro-poor if it offers economic benefits via:

- Formation of full or part-time jobs or the growth of small, medium and micro-sized enterprises (SMMEs) opportunities.
- Investment in infrastructure inspired by tourism.
- Direct sales of goods and services to visitors by poor.
- Tax or levy on tourism income.

It is vital that the poor people obtain the net benefits even if richer people benefit more than the poor people (Ashley et al., 2001; Blake et al., 2008). Chok et al. (2007) critically analyse the ideologies of PPT and state that the approach should:

- Include poor people in decision making.
- Economically, socially, and environmentally recognise the livelihood concerns of poor people.
- Offer a balanced approach, for instance economic sectors should support pro-poor enterprises.
- Analyse the distribution of benefits and costs.
- Draw on lessons from poverty analysis and small enterprise development.

Hence, it is an approach towards tourism development and management where linkages are developed amongst tourism organisations and the poor people to influence tourism benefits to the poor (Beeton, 2005). Nonetheless, Muganda et al. (2010) researched the impact of tourism development in Tanzania and conclude that tourism development in the studied community did not improve the quality of life of the local residents and instead of the local community's household incomes to increase, their incomes were reduced, thus the gap was broadened regarding the sharing of benefits and employment access.

PPT Strategies

The main objective of PPT strategies is to open up opportunities for poor people; this could be achieved through involvement in decision making and through economic benefit and other livelihood benefits (Ashley et al., 2001; Sharpley, 2009; Zapata et al., 2011). Scheyvens (2002) highlights the PPT strategies and sectioned them into:

- Local benefits-economic benefits.
- Livelihood benefits (physical, social, and cultural developments).
- Less tangible benefits (e.g., participation).

Scheyvens (2011) expounds that the PPT strategies should concentrate on capacity building of the poor, empowering and offer support for labour rights and have more control over the tourism activities in their communities. Correspondingly, Ashley and Roe (2002) categorise the PPT strategies into three:

- **Increasing Access of the Poor to Economic Benefits:** It comprises of the development of local enterprises and job opportunities for poor people, offering them training to enhance their chances at any open opportunities and the income benefitting the whole community.
- **Dealing With Any Negative Social and Environmental Effects Which Are Linked to Tourism:** These include impacts such as lost access to land, coastal areas and social interruption.
- **Focusing on Policies, Processes, and Partnerships:** This involves formulation of policy frameworks that eliminates barriers to poor participation; to encourage involvement of poor people in tourism planning approaches and to promote partnerships between the private sector and the poor people in developing new tourism products.

Similar to Ashley and Roe (2002), Ashley et al. (2001) and the World Tourism Organisation (2002, 2004) also analyse the strategies that improve economic benefits and highlighted it as:

- Improving employment opportunities and salaries through commitments to local jobs and training the local residents.
- Developing corporate opportunities for poor communities for instance local businesses that sell inputs or tourist products; these range from food products to crafts. Thus, the strategies may be in the form of support such as financial and marketing support.
- Growth of shared community revenue. For instance, equity dividends, equal distribution of income and donations which is generally ascertained in agreement with tourism operators or government institutions.

It is quite apparent that in general the PPT strategies are interrelated, in essence, they are generally viewed as strategies that increase economic benefits, address negative effects and encourage formation of policies. The poor people should be encouraged to contribute to the decision-making procedures so that their priorities are noted and considered. It is therefore important for all the participants (government, private and public sectors, local businesses and the local community) to understand the proposed approaches and follow them. However, as indicated above, the approach encompasses a lot of stakeholders who all have different needs, hence it is essential for the strategies to be focused on poverty alleviation.

Sustainable Livelihood Approach (SLA)

Tourism has the potential to improve the livelihood of the local community; it is therefore imperative to understand how tourism impacts on the livelihood of poor people. The sustainable livelihood concept was adopted to find a way of responding to the needs of the poor people, thus various definitions of the concept emerged. Originally, Chambers and Conway (1992) state that the livelihood notion should include capabilities, assets and activities that are essential for a means of living; it should be sustainable so that it is able to cope with and recover from stresses and shocks such as a decline in tourism numbers. They also emphasised that a livelihood should contribute net benefits to other livelihoods at the local and international levels.

A Sustainable Livelihood Approach is people centred and is concerned with people's livelihoods. It therefore prioritises people's assets, their capability to endure shocks (the vulnerability context), and the policies and institutions that replicate community primacies. The livelihood framework recognises that the local community faces different impacts (positive and negative), because of the differences in family structures and wants, that are difficult to convert into monetary value for survival, hence it is vital to individually analyse them (See Figure 2).

The UK Department for International Development (DFID) (2000) then modified the definition by taking a more realistic approach of excluding the prerequisite that sustainable livelihood must contribute to net benefits of other livelihoods. DFID (2000) stresses that any sustainable livelihood approach should incorporate the ability to evade, endure and recuperate from shocks and stresses and at the same time be able to improve its capabilities and assets without deflating the natural resource base. However, both definitions emphasise the importance of going beyond defining poverty eradication by critically analysing both the positive and the negative effects of any type of tourism development on the livelihoods of the poor people (Jamieson et al., 2004).

The Institute for Environment and Development (IIED) (2000) offered that improved access to assets, enhanced income and food security, improved quality of life and reduced vulnerability are vital for the improvement of community livelihood. It is fundamental, however, to note that different homes have different access to livelihood assets (Serrat, 2017). "The Sustainable Livelihood Approach is an example of the 'multiple capital' where sustainability is dependent on the availability of capital (natural, human, social, physical and financial) and an investigation of the susceptibility milieu (trends, shocks and stresses) in which these capitals (or assets) occur (Morse & McNamara, 2013).

Figure 2. Sustainable livelihood framework
Source: Serrat (2017)

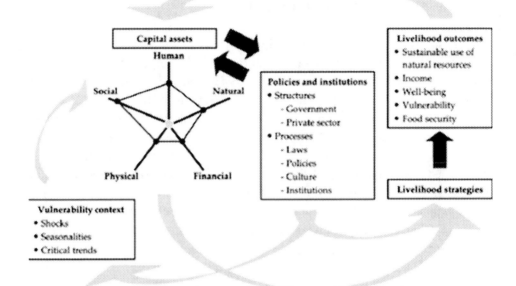

The five fundamental types of assets which are required for the livelihood of the community serve as building blocks of the framework. Ashley and Carney (1999) illustrate these capitals as:

- **Financial Capital:** These are the financial resources that people utilise to realise their livelihood objective examples include savings, pension, and access to cash. The consistent inflow of cash is an asset that is not readily available to most poor people.
- **Human Capital:** Examples include skills, ability to work, good health and knowledge of a specific group or persons. These should all allow individuals to follow different livelihood strategies and attain their livelihood objectives.
- **Natural/Cultural Capital:** They refer to the natural resources available and are useful for sustainable livelihood to be achieved. They include land, water, and wildlife.
- **Physical Capital:** These consists of the basic infrastructure and manufacturer goods required for sustainable livelihoods for instance equipment, machinery, access to affordable transport and communications.
- **Social Capital:** Comprises of the strength of groups, network, friends and how these enable each other to achieve their livelihood objectives.

The livelihood context highlights that the resources are inputs in a system where outcomes of community well-being, income, reduced vulnerability, food security and sustainable use of natural resources should be achieved. Although each of these assets are essential for the achievement of a sustainable livelihood, Morse and McNamara (2013) note that their importance revolve from household to household and over time. It is therefore imperative to acknowledge the value of livelihoods analysis to apprehend the non-financial and dynamic impacts as well as to organise assessments according to the primacies of the poor themselves (Mitchell & Ashley, 2010).

To critically review the difficulties encountered by the local community, Jamieson et al. (2004) advocates for a further examination of all the assets. They asserted that the local people's perceptions are fundamental in deciding the form of interventions needed to aid poor families to get involved in the tourism value chain and such involvement is the core of PPT (Holden, 2013). Shen, (2009) also adds the "institutional capital" notion which helps the local people to be part of the tourism value chain such as accommodation, and the issue of participation – particularly in policymaking – is also emphasised.

Ashley (2000) studied the impact of tourism on rural livelihood in Namibia and notes that for the tourism industry to capitalise on livelihood benefits, it is essential to have a clear understanding of the local people's needs. The study also highlights that the importance of locals' involvement in decision making, which could be achieved through:

- Entrusting tourism rights to community level and assisting communities with participatory planning.
- Making sure that government planning methods are participatory and responsive to local needs.
- Ensuring via government incentives, that planning by private entrepreneurs is responsive to local needs.

Serrat (2017) mentions that utilising the SLA requires a continuous analysis of the way the vulnerable people live their lives so that institutions can formulate policies and development activities which are centred on people, participatory and sustainable. Luvanga and Shitundu (2003) studied the role of tourism in poverty alleviation utilising the SLA and conclude that when tourism has strong linkages at national and local levels, it generates opportunities for the local people and alleviate poverty. Mbaiwa (2008) also used the SLA to investigate the livelihood of village people in Botswana prior to and after tourism development. The study concluded that the livelihood of the local people improved, nonetheless, external factors such as political issues in the neighbouring country of Zimbabwe and the September 11 atrocities affected the development of tourism in that area making the sustainability of global tourism for developing countries uncertain. Furthermore, a study by Cotton (2015) investigated the impact of tourism and immigration on the sustainable livelihoods of the local people determined that each of the livelihoods are interlinked and investment in education will provide the local community with more opportunities for employment and also accessibility to loans is an essential financial asset to them. However, to successfully implement the SLA it requires a significant role for local people in decision making, which can be done through delegating tourism rights to community level, offering government incentives or making certain that planning by private entrepreneurs is responsive to local needs (Ashley, 2000). Livelihood studies are essential when assessing the impacts of tourism before and after tourism development.

Sustainable Tourism-Elimination of Poverty (ST-EP) Analysis

To improve poor people's likelihood of benefiting from tourism, varied methods such as the Sustainable Tourism-Eliminating Poverty (ST-EP) and Pro-Poor Tourism (PPT) were initiated. The WTO and the United Nations Conference on Trade and Development (UNCTAD) developed the ST-EP initiative with the purpose of helping developing countries and Least Developed Countries (LDCs) to alleviate poverty via tourism. The ST-EP agenda was officiated in 2006, initially with the purpose of developing small projects by 2015. The ST-EP initiative proposed to create a basis that would promote sustained capitals for research, and it also purposed to provide a direct link between tourism and poverty alleviation, placing much emphasis on alleviating poverty through the development and creation of jobs for people living on less than one dollar a day (Ashley et al., 2007). The Tourism and Poverty Alleviation: Recommendations for Action (2004:17-30) offers more detailed guiding principles for private tourism businesses to participate in pro-poor tourism activities (WTO, 2004). The report highlights seven ways in which the poor can directly benefit from tourism:

- Provision of jobs to the poor people in tourism businesses.
- The poor people supplying goods and services to tourism organisations or giving the poor people jobs.
- The poor people directly selling goods and services to visitors through, for instance, the informal sector e.g., handcraft.
- The poor people running and starting tourism businesses like small, micro, and medium-sized enterprises (SMMEs) or CBEs (formal economy).
- The poor people benefitting from tourism proceeds, tax, and levy.

- Tourists visiting the poor people's communities and giving back to the community voluntarily. Tourism enterprises and tourists supporting the community.
- The poor people directly benefitting from tourism infrastructure or from receiving support from other sectors.

The ST-EP initiative was regarded as an effective device to provide feasible contribution to the Millennium Development Goals (MDGs) which also aspires to promote sustainable tourism (economic, social and environmental). The approach also influences different stakeholders (governments, NGOs, public society) to work together and implement strategies and policies aimed at eliminating poverty (Spenceley & Meyer, 2012). Conversely, Scheyvens (2007) contends that the ST-EP strategies mainly focus on local participation and fails to unravel structural restraints at a national and international level. The approaches utilising by ST-EP will be analysed in this research as it aims to establish the benefits of rural tourism development.

Community-Based Tourism (CBT)

Several definitions and concepts of CBT have also been offered, making it difficult to conceptualise (Ndlovu & Rogerson, 2003). CBT is within the limits of PPT because it promotes the pro-poor strategies in a community setting, therefore, it can be viewed as a form of PPT (Saayman & Giampicolli, 2015). Community-based tourism (CBT) was developed in the 1970s in response to the negative impacts of the international mass tourism development model (Cater, 1993). It was established with the purpose of supporting rural development in both developed and developing countries (George et al., 2007) although it is much prevalent in developing countries (Page et al., 2001). CBT development is also available in poor and rich countries, and it is mainly introduced in countries where inequality is high, and trust and civic participation are low (Giampiccoli et al., 2015; Lancee & Van de Werfhorst, 2011). It was established for the purpose of educating the local people so that they will be able to equip themselves and involve them in decision making (Catley, 1999). It is essential for CBT to be owned and managed by the community (George et al., 2007). Due to its profound principles, CBT has gained support from varied international organisations such as the World Tourism Organisation (2002) which also provides various aims such as community empowerment and ownership, social and economic development, conservation of natural and cultural resources, and a high-quality visitor experience. Scheyvens (2002) also advocates that CBT should economically, psychologically, socially and politically empower the host community.

It is vital that the government, non-governmental organisations (NGOs) and any other organisations collaborate with the local community to improve the social, cultural and economic conditions in communities. Thus, it should not be viewed as a profit-making initiative but aid as a way of breaking a dependency syndrome. Sin and Minca (2014) view CBT as the new way of providing a solution to bottom-up tourism development. Nonetheless, Ellis and Sheridan (2014) argue that CBT does not present solutions to a bottom-up approach, but positive results can be attained if applied effectively. Mtapuri and Giampiccoli (2013) also emphasise that CBT should be viewed as a way of promoting community development which incorporates empowerment, self-reliance, social justice, sustainability and freedom. It is quite clear that academics and different organisations agree that somehow CBT should empower its participants, however, arguments among researchers remain as to whether CBT can empower the local community (Sin & Minca, 2014). Scheyvens (2002) emphasises that the success of CBT initiatives is rarely achieved without the engagement of external sources such as NGOs, international conservation organisations or tour operators. Therefore, Guzman et al. (2011) offer that the structure of CBT should be divided into four classifications:

- Small tourist offices (may work as tour guides).
- Institutions which collaborate with the local tourism industry such as local public administrations, NGOs and universities.
- Direct service companies which can be divided into two sets: accommodation, food and beverage, and shops selling local products.
- Transport and financial businesses.

CBT provides an opportunity to alleviate poverty (Yang & Hung, 2014) since leakages are reduced at a local level (Lapeyre, 2010). Research on community-based enterprises (CBEs) by Manyara and Jones (2007) concludes that CBEs controlled by white investors or foreigners did not make a significant impact on poverty reduction at an individual household level. They also found that the CBE model heavily depends on donor funding. This notion concurs with Goodwin et al. (2009). Consequently, research by Malatji and Mtapuri (2012), observed and concluded that CBEs provide an opportunity for poverty alleviation initiatives, however, for them to be of benefit to the local community, it is vital for them to be restructured and reconstituted. Giampiccoli and Kalis (2012) indicates that external sources should provide resources such as education and infrastructure to the local community and it is vital for CBT not to be controlled by external sources in its development. They also suggested that CBT is not a panacea and should not be viewed as the only solution, but it should be incorporated in the context of strategies to promote rural development.

THE EFFECTS OF TOURISM ON THE POOR

Developing countries have promoted the tourism industry as one that promotes economic growth and aid in poverty alleviation whilst Bolwell and Weinz, (2008) argue that economic growth does not ultimately lead to the reduction of poverty. Mitchell and Ashley (2010) have advocated that tourism has the potential to offer benefits to the poor and offered three main pathways by which the benefits of tourism activity can be offered to the poor as highlighted in figure 3.

Figure 3. The impacts of tourism on poor communities
Source: Mitchell and Ashley (2010)

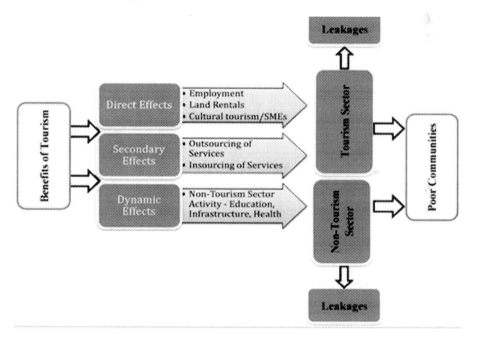

Manwa and Manwa (2014) describe the effects as pathways through which the poor can benefit from tourism. These are categorised as direct, indirect and dynamic effects of tourism. The direct effects transpire when the poor people are employed in the tourism sector and these effects should have a positive financial impact. Mitchell and Ashley (2010) section them into labour income and non-labour income. The labour income includes wages from the formal sector employment and other types of earnings such as craft selling. Direct effects may also comprise of other income earned by people from poor families in tourism value chains such as hotels, transportation and restaurants (Mitchell & Ashley, 2010). In South Africa, a study by Spenceley and Seif (2003) reveal that the local community significantly benefitted from direct employment within the tourism industry. Nonetheless, the characteristics of the tourism industry makes it difficult for the poor people to benefit from tourism; examples include seasonality influencing the employment of casual workers and low paid jobs due to lack of skills. Therefore, employment in the tourism industry on its own does not assist in poverty alleviation because of the unstable earnings (Huynh, 2011; Jolliffe & Farnsworth, 2003; Mowforth & Munt, 2003). Furthermore, Janis (2011) argues that the low position of poor people makes it difficult for them to negotiate for higher wages, thus making them more vulnerable. Consistent with the findings of Ashley et al. (2018) in Cambodia, farming is therefore the main activity for almost all rural households making up the main source of their livelihood.

The poor people can however benefit from tourism via non-labour income which comprises of the local community leasing communal land to tourism operators, starting corporate initiatives such as curio shops or craft markets and CBTs (Ashley & Roe, 2002; Hill et al., 2006). Nonetheless, the involvement of the poor in tourism and reaping the tourism benefits are restricted by competition from multinational businesses, and sometimes they are involved in the development of strategies and not rewarded the tourism benefits (Schilcher, 2007; Ashley et al., 2000). Thus, it is essential to implement a unified approach which measures the actual and perceived economic and socio-cultural impacts on poor people. Direct effects also include the non-financial livelihoods changes, for instance access to local amenities such as beaches and better-quality infrastructure (Mitchell & Ashley, 2010).

Indirect effects are secondary effects that intends to cover indirect incomes from tourism activities and these can be achieved through induced benefits from tourism employees re-spending their incomes in the local economy and through supply chains in tourism. The tourist expenses should stimulate economic activities in destinations permitting the poor people to get salaries from hotel construction and supplying goods and services (for instance food and craft products). Likewise, if the tourism sector is strongly linked with agriculture, farmers will also gain.

Lastly, dynamic effects' main purpose is to evaluate the role of tourism in poverty alleviation on the macro economy, thus it comprises of the differences in the macro economy, for example tax to support services to local people and capacity building for tourism workers. The dynamic effects are less tangible than the direct and indirect effects and it is difficult to assess their impact on the poor. They also comprise of human resource development, for example in women which upsurges their financial position and assist in dealing with gender barriers (Ashley et al., 2007). Spenceley et al. (2009) also added that tourism development and upgrading employees' skills are linked as it offers an opportunity for local people to acquire new languages and customer service skills and these skills acquired via tourism work are transferable to other sectors. Hence dynamic effects influence tourism corporate growth, natural resources base and improvement of infrastructure (Mitchell & Ashley, 2010). PPT approach has been utilised to assess the impacts of tourism on the poor, however, a lot of assessments have emphasised analysing the economic impacts indicating that economic growth provided a real measure for poverty alleviation.

RECOMMENDATIONS AND CONCLUSION

PPT aims to unlock opportunities for poor people, in particular for women (Ashley et al., 2001; Sharpley, 2009; Zapata et al., 2011), hence the approach is an important key component in solving the issue of leakages. However, PPT has been criticised for over-emphasising local initiatives. Similarly, the understanding of the poverty concept and its causes at a local level setting is limited, hence it is imperative to analyse the causes of poverty to have a clear understanding of how tourism can contribute to poverty alleviation. Debates from scholars have emerged on how to define a "poor person" and PPT fails to fully define the notion. It standardises the poor and underprivileged people in developing countries and therefore fails to consider societal differences and other factors such as economic conditions, political issues and the topographical locations.

The supporters of PPT have insisted that tourism is an essential tool for reducing poverty in comparison to other economic sectors and promotes sustainable economic growth (Ashley et al., 2001; Ashley & Mitchell, 2008; Meyer, 2007; Rogerson, 2012). Focusing on economic growth has been criticised by opponents of PPT because the approach emphasises the importance of increasing economic growth so that the poor can benefit from this growth, thus it does not sufficiently address power structures of the destination (Mowforth & Munt, 2009; Scheyvens, 2007; Mitchell & Ashley, 2010). The question remains whether most tourism businesses, especially the private organisations aiming to gain profits, will support and prioritise the view of tourism development and poverty alleviation. It is important to note that PPT should be about the needs of poor people, and they should be allowed to choose their own development primacies, yet a lot of PPT research does not include the views/ voices of the poor people (Holden et al., 2011; Pleumarom 2012; Schilcher, 2007).

Research by Wattanakuljarus and Coxhead (2008) conclude that tourism in Thailand influenced the high-income households to benefit more than the poor households and the inequality gap broadened whilst income distribution deteriorated. PPT has also been criticised for over-relying on donors, (Mowforth & Munt, 2003), the argument is that if destinations heavily rely on donor funding, it will weaken the sustainable livelihood, instead of reducing poverty, it will aggravate it. The approach advocates that poor people should participate in decision making and encourages a bottom-up approach, but Chok et al. (2007) mention that the PPT approach is driven by large organisations and governments whose emphasis is on gaining political support for tourism as a policy priority. Thus, it would normally overlook the "extreme poor" in a society (Saarinen & Rogerson, 2014). Furthermore, most of the tourism bureaucrats do not have any knowledge and training in utilising tourism as a device for poverty alleviation (Jamieson & Nadkarni). It is quite clear that PPT has been heavily criticised, yet a lot of researchers have utilised the approach to analyse the impacts of tourism on poverty alleviation and viewed the approach as significant at a local level. Other academics contended that the PPT discourse is not that analytical, consequently, the tourism sector has actively adopted pro-poor tourism to enhance its image (Butler et al., 2013; Scheyvens, 2007).

The tourism industry has also used the PPT approach to analyse the benefits offered by the tourism industry to the local community and poor people and to reduce the effects of poverty. Ashley et al. (2001) studied PPT strategies and concluded that PPT was an effective strategy when judged by the income. Yet research by Nicanor (2001) examined the practical strategies on PPT (NACOBTA) in Namibia and concludes that the poor tend to benefit from tourism in the short term (in terms of income), but livelihood impacts are difficult to quantify since the poor, donors and NGOs do not pay much attention to them. The study offered that the impacts are best measured a long period after implementation (10+ years). Similarly, Saayman et al., (2012) analysed the impact of tourism on poverty alleviation in South Africa employing the Applied General Equilibrium (AGE) model and concluded that the poor benefit very little in the short term from additional tourism inflows. In Botswana, Manwa and Manwa (2014) analysed the perceptions of stakeholders on the opportunities unlocked for the poor through the opening up of forest reserves; the research analysed the prospects tourism offered on poverty alleviation using the PPT approach. They concluded that opening up the forest reserves will provide benefits (short term and medium term), but to guarantee sustainability there is need for continuous enhancement of tourism strategies. Similarly, Truong et al. (2014) researched on tourism and poverty alleviation applying the PPT approach and concludes that the poor people's views must be valued so that the approach to alleviate poverty can be successful. In agreement with Truong et al. (2014) Phommavong (2011) studied the impacts of global tourism development on poverty reduction in Lao PDR and highlights that, in order for PPT to benefit low-income groups, it should be people centred, promote local participation and bottom-up initiatives. However, Gonzo (2022) argue that adopting a bottom-up approach would require the communities to be well educated and equipped with the right skills. Therefore, for PPT to be effective, it is imperative for destinations to develop a framework which takes a pragmatic approach and departs from the "one size fits all" approach.

It should be adaptable to different settings and focuses on the "how" than "what" the stakeholders should be doing to reduce poverty.

REFERENCES

Alcock, P. (2006). *Understanding poverty*. Palgrave Macmillan. doi:10.5040/9781350363625

Andrades, L., & Dimanche, F. (2017). Destination competitiveness and tourism development in Russia: Issues and challenges. *Tourism Management, 62*, 360–376. doi:10.1016/j.tourman.2017.05.008

Ashley, C. (2000). *The impacts of tourism on rural livelihoods: Namibia's experience*. London: Overseas Development Institute (ODI). (Working paper 128)

Ashley, C., & Carney, D. (1999). Sustainable livelihoods: lessons from early experience. London: Department for International Development (DFID).

Ashley, C., Goodwin, H., & Boyd, C. (2000). Pro-poor tourism: putting poverty at the heart of the tourism agenda. London: Overseas Development Institute (ODI). (Natural resource perspectives no. 51)

Ashley, C., & Mitchell, J. (2008). *Doing the right thing approximately not the wrong thing precisely: challenges of monitoring impacts of pro-poor interventions in tourism value chains*. London: Overseas Development Institute (ODI). (ODI working paper 291)

Ashley, C., & Roe, D. (2002). Making tourism work for the poor: Strategies and challenges in Southern Africa. *Development Southern Africa, 19*(1), 61–82. doi:10.1080/03768350220123855

Ashley, C., Roe, D., & Goodwin, H. (2001). Pro-poor tourism strategies: making tourism work for the poor: a review of experience. London: International Centre for Responsible Tourism, IIED (International Institute for Environment and Development) and ODI. (Pro-poor tourism report 1, ICRT)

Ashley, K., Harrison, H., Chan, P. H., Sothoeun, S., Young, J. R., Windsor, P. A., & Bush, R. D. (2018). Livestock and livelihoods of smallholder cattle-owning households in Cambodia: The contribution of on-farm and off-farm activities to income and food security. *Tropical Animal Health and Production, 50*(8), 1747–1761. doi:10.100711250-018-1615-6 PMID:29796792

Atkinson, D. (2008). *Creating access to economic opportunities in small and medium sized towns. Report produced for Urban Landmark*. Second Economy Strategy Project. An Initiative of the Presidency of South Africa.

Aziz, S.N.A. & Basir, S.M. (2018). Sustainable development goals: legally realistic or overambitious towards the development of the nations. *Jurnal Undang-undang dan Masyarakat, 23*, 39-47.

Beeton, S. (2005). The case study in tourism research: a multi-method case study approach. In B. W. Richter, P. Burns, & C. Palmer (Eds.), *Tourism research methods: integrating theory with practice* (pp. 37–48). CABI Publishing. doi:10.1079/9780851999968.0037

Bennett, O., Ashley, C., & Roe, D. (1999). Sustainable tourism and poverty elimination: a report to the Department for International Development. London: Deloitte and Touch: International Institute for Environment and Development: Overseas Development Institute.

Blake, A., Arbache, J. S., Sinclair, M. T., & Teles, V. (2008). Tourism and poverty relief. *Annals of Tourism Research, 35*(1), 107–126. doi:10.1016/j.annals.2007.06.013

Bolwell, D., & Weinz, W. (2008). *Reducing poverty through tourism*. Geneva: International Labor Office (ILO). Sectoral Activities Program. (Working paper 266)

Butler, R., Curran, R., & O'Gorman, K. D. (2013). Pro-poor tourism in a first world urban setting: Case study of Glasgow Govan. *International Journal of Tourism Research, 15*(5), 443–457. doi:10.1002/jtr.1888

Carbone, M. (2005). Sustainable tourism in developing countries: Poverty alleviation, participatory planning, and ethical issues. *European Journal of Development Research, 17*(3), 559–565. doi:10.1080/09578810500209841

Cater, E. A. (1993). Ecotourism in the third world: Problems for sustainable development. *Tourism Management, 14*(2), 85–90. doi:10.1016/0261-5177(93)90040-R

Catley, A. (1999). *Methods on the move: a review of veterinary uses of participatory approaches and methods focusing on experiences in dryland Africa*. International Institute for Environment and Development.

Chambers, R. (1995). *Paradigm shift and the practice of participation research perspective*. Institute of Development Studies.

Chambers, R., & Conway, G. (1992). *Sustainable rural livelihoods: practical concepts for the 21st century*. Institute of Development Studies (UK).

Chok, S., Macbeth, J., & Warren, C. (2007). Tourism as tool for poverty alleviation: A critical analysis of "pro-poor tourism" and implications for sustainability. *Current Issues in Tourism, 10*(2-3), 144–165. doi:10.2167/cit303

Christie, I. T. (2002). Tourism, growth and poverty: Framework conditions for tourism in developing countries. *Tourism Review, 57*(1/4), 35–41. doi:10.1108/eb058377

Cooper, C., Fletcher, J., Fyall, A., Gilbert, D., & Wanhill, S. (2008). *Tourism: principles and practice* (4th ed.). Pearson Education.

Cotton, F. (2015). *A case study of the conflicts women experience with tourism and immigration in Vilcabamba, Ecuador: a sustainable livelihoods perspective* [PhD thesis]. Nova Southeastern University.

Croes, R. (2014). The role of tourism in poverty reduction: An empirical assessment. *Tourism Economics, 20*(2), 207–226. doi:10.5367/te.2013.0275

Department for International Development (DFID). (2000). *Poverty elimination and the empowerment of women: strategies for achieving the international development targets*. Department for International Development.

Ellis, S., & Sheridan, L. (2014). A critical reflection on the role of stakeholders in sustainable tourism development in least-developed countries. *Tourism Planning & Development, 11*(4), 467–471. doi:10.1080/21568316.2014.894558

Fehling, M., Nelson, B. D., & Venkatapuram, S. (2013). Limitations of the millennium development goals: A literature review. *Global Public Health: An International Journal for Research, Policy and Practice, 8*(10), 1109–1122. doi:10.1080/17441692.2013.845676 PMID:24266508

Ferreira, F., Jollife, D.M., & Prydz, E.B. (2015). The international poverty line has just been raised to $1.90 a day but the global poverty is basically unchanged: How is that even possible. *World Bank Blogs*.

George, B. P., Nedelea, A., & Antony, M. (2007). The business of community-based tourism: A multi-stakeholder approach. *Tourism Issues, 3*, 1–19.

Giampiccoli, A., Jugmohan, S., & Mtapuri, O. (2015). Characteristics of community-based tourism: towards a comparison between North and South experiences. *Proceedings of the Third International Conference on Hospitality, Leisure, Sport, and Tourism*, 451-454.

Glaesser, D., Kester, J., Paulose, H., Alizadeh, A., & Valentin, B. (2017). Global travel pattern: An overview. *Journal of Travel Medicine, 24*(4), 1–5. doi:10.1093/jtm/tax007 PMID:28637267

Gonzo, F. (2022). Effects of rural tourism development on poverty alleviation: A grounded theory. *African Journal of Hospitality and Tourism Management, 3*(2), 73–95. doi:10.47963/ajhtm.v3i2.769

Goodwin, H. (2006). Measuring and reporting the impact of tourism on poverty. In J. Tribe & D. Airey (Eds.), *Developments in tourism research* (pp. 63–76). Taylor & Francis.

Goodwin, H. (2008). Pro-poor tourism: A response. *Third World Quarterly, 29*(5), 869–871. doi:10.1080/01436590802215287

Goodwin, H. (2009). Reflections on 10 years of pro-poor tourism. *Journal of Policy Research in Tourism, Leisure & Events, 1*(1), 90–94. doi:10.1080/19407960802703565

Gupta, J., & Vegelin, C. (2016). Sustainable development goals and inclusive development. *International Environmental Agreement: Politics, Law and Economics, 16*(3), 433–448. doi:10.100710784-016-9323-z

Guzman, T. L., Canizares, S. S., & Pavon, V. (2011). Community-based tourism in developing countries: A case study. *Tourismos: An International Multi-Disciplinary Journal of Tourism, 6*(1), 66–84.

Harrison, D. (2008). Pro-poor tourism: A critique. *Third World Quarterly, 29*(5), 851–868. doi:10.1080/01436590802105983

Hill, T., Nel, E., & Trotter, D. (2006). Small-scale, nature-based tourism as a pro-poor development intervention: Two examples in Kwazulu-Natal, South Africa. *Singapore Journal of Tropical Geography, 27*(2), 163–175. doi:10.1111/j.1467-9493.2006.00251.x

Holden, A. (2013). *Tourism, poverty and development in the developing world.* Taylor and Francis. doi:10.4324/9780203861547

Holden, A., Sonne, J., & Novelli, M. (2011). Tourism and poverty reduction: An interpretation by the poor of Elmina, Ghana. *Tourism Planning & Development, 8*(3), 317–334. doi:10.1080/21568316.2011.591160

Huynh, B. T. (2011). *The Cai Rang floating market, Vietnam: Towards pro-poor tourism?* [Master's dissertation]. Auckland University of Technology.

Jamieson, W., Goodwin, H., & Edmunds, C. (2004). *Contribution of tourism to poverty alleviation: Pro-poor tourism and the challenge of measuring impacts.* UNESCAP.

Jamieson, W., & Nadkarni, S. (2009). Editorial: A reality check of tourism's potential as a development tool. *Asia Pacific Journal of Tourism Research, 14*(2), 111–123. doi:10.1080/10941660902847161

Janis, J. (2011). *The tourism-development nexus in Namibia: a study on national tourism policy and local tourism enterprises' policy knowledge*. University of Helsinki.

Jolliffe, L., & Farnsworth, R. (2003). Seasonality in tourism employment: Human resources challenges. *International Journal of Contemporary Hospitality Management, 15*(6), 312–316. doi:10.1108/09596110310488140

Lancee, B., & Van de Werfhorst, H. (2011). *Income inequality and participation: a comparison of 24 European countries*. Amsterdam: Institute for Advanced Labour Studies. (GINI discussion paper 6)

Lapeyre, R. (2010). Community-based tourism as a sustainable solution to maximise impacts locally? The Tsiseb conservancy case, Namibia. *Development Southern Africa, 27*(5), 757–772. doi:10.1080/0376835X.2010.522837

Luvanga, N., & Shitundu, J. (2003). The role of tourism in poverty alleviation in Tanzania. Dar es Salaam: Mkuki na Nyota Publishers. (Research for Poverty Alleviation (REPOA). Research report 03.4)

Mahony, K. K., & Van Zyl, J. (2002). The impacts of tourism investment on rural communities: Three case studies in South Africa. *Development Southern Africa, 19*(1), 83–105. doi:10.1080/03768350220123891

Malatji, M. I., & Mtapuri, O. (2012). Can community-based tourism enterprises alleviate poverty? Toward a new organisation. *Tourism Review International, 16*(1), 1–14. doi:10.3727/154427212X13369577826825

Manwa, H., & Mwanwa, F. (2014). Poverty alleviation through pro-poor tourism: The role of Botswana forest reserves. *Sustainability, 6*(9), 5697–5713. doi:10.3390u6095697

Manyara, K., & Jones, E. (2007). Community-based tourism enterprises development in Kenya: An exploration of their potential as avenues of poverty reduction. *Journal of Sustainable Tourism, 15*(6), 628–644. doi:10.2167/jost723.0

Mbaiwa, J. E. (2008). The socio-cultural impacts of tourism development in the Okavango Delta, Botswana. *Journal of Tourism and Cultural Change, 2*(3), 163–185. doi:10.1080/14766820508668662

McCulloch, N., Winters, L. A., & Cirera, X. (2001). *Trade liberalization and poverty: a handbook*. Centre for Economic Policy Research.

Meyer, D. (2007). Pro-poor tourism: from leakages to linkages: a conceptual framework for creating linkages between the accommodation sector and 'poor' neighbouring communities. *Current Issues in Tourism, 10*(6), 558–583. doi:10.2167/cit313.0

Ming Su, M., Wall, G., & Wang, Y. (2019). Integrating tea and tourism: A sustainable livelihoods approach. *Journal of Sustainable Tourism, 27*(10), 1591–1608. doi:10.1080/09669582.2019.1648482

Mitchell, J., & Ashley, C. (2010). *Tourism and poverty reduction: pathways to prosperity*. Earthscan.

Morse, S., & McNamara, N. (2013). *Sustainable livelihood approach: a critique of theory and practice*. Springer. doi:10.1007/978-94-007-6268-8

Mowforth, M., & Munt, I. (2003). *Tourism and sustainability: development and new tourism in the third world* (2nd ed.). Routledge. doi:10.4324/9780203422779

Mtapuri, O., & Giampiccoli, A. (2013). Interrogating the role of the state and nonstate actors in community-based tourism ventures: Toward a model for spreading the benefits to the wider community. *The South African Geographical Journal, 95*(1), 1–15. doi:10.1080/03736245.2013.805078

Muchapondwa, E., & Stage, J. (2013). The economic impacts of tourism in Botswana, Namibia and South Africa: Is poverty subsiding? A United Nations sustainable development. *Journal, 37*(2), 80–89.

Muganda, M., Sahli, M., & Smith, K. (2010). Tourism's contribution to poverty alleviation: A community perspective from Tanzania. *Development Southern Africa, 27*(5), 629–646. doi:10.1080/0376835X.2010.522826

Muhanna, E. (2007). The contribution of sustainable tourism development in poverty alleviation of local communities in South Africa. *Journal of Human Resources in Hospitality & Tourism, 6*(1), 37–67. doi:10.1300/J171v06n01_03

Mutana, S., Chipfuva, T., & Muchenje, B. (2013). Is tourism in Zimbabwe developing with the poor in mind? Assessing the pro-poor involvement of tourism operators located near rural areas in Zimbabwe. *Asian Social Science, 9*(5), 154–161. doi:10.5539/ass.v9n5p154

Ndlovu, N., & Rogerson, C. M. (2003). Rural local economic development through community-based tourism: The Mehloding hiking and horse trail, Eastern cape, South Africa. *Africa Insight, 33*(1/2), 124–129.

Nicanor, N. (2001). *Practical strategies for pro-poor tourism: NACOBTA the Namibian case study*. Department for International Development.

Novelli, M., & Gebhardt, K. (2007). Community-based tourism in Namibia: "reality show" or "window dressing? *Current Issues in Tourism, 10*(5), 443–479. doi:10.2167/cit332.0

OECD. (2001). The DAC guidelines: poverty reduction: international development. Paris: OECD.

Page, S. J., Brunt, P., Busby, G., & Connell, J. (2001). *Tourism: a modern synthesis*. Thomson Learning.

Perkins, D. H., Radelet, S., & Lindauer, D. L. (Eds.). (2006). *Economics of development* (6th ed.). W.W. Norton.

Phi, G. T., Whitford, M., & Reid, S. (2018). Current issues in the method and practice, what's in the black box? Evaluating anti-poverty tourism interventions utilising theory of change. *Current Issues in Tourism, 21*(17), 1930–1945. doi:10.1080/13683500.2016.1232703

Phommavong, S. (2011). *International tourism development and poverty reduction in Lao PDR* [Dissertation]. Umeå: Umeå University. Department of Social and Economic Geography.

Pleumarom, A. (2012). *The politics of tourism, poverty reduction and sustainable development*. Third World Network.

Pogge, T., & Sengupta, M. (2016). A critique of the sustainable development goals' potential to realize the human rights of all: why being better than the MDGs is not good enough. Journal of International and Comparative Social Policy, 19(1-2), 4-20.

Ravallion, M. (2004). Pro-poor growth: a primer. World Bank. doi:10.1596/1813-9450-3242

Richardson, R. B. (2010). The contribution of tourism to economic growth and food security: Michigan State University. Department of Agricultural, Food, and Resource Economics. (Food Security collaborative working papers 97140)

Rogerson, C. M. (2012). Strengthening agriculture-tourism linkages in the developing world: Opportunities, barriers and current initiatives. *African Journal of Agricultural Research, 7*(4), 616–623.

Saarinen, J., Rogerson, C., & Manwa, H. (2011). Tourism and millennium development goals: Tourism for global development. *Current Issues in Tourism, 10*(2&3), 119–143. doi:10.1080/13683500.2011.555180

Saarinen, J., & Rogerson, C. M. (2014). Tourism and the millennium development goals: Perspectives beyond 2015. *Tourism Geographies, 16*(1), 23–30. doi:10.1080/14616688.2013.851269

Saayman, M., & Giampiccoli, A. (2016). Community-based and pro-poor tourism: Initial assessment of their relation to community development. *European Journal of Tourism Research, 12*, 145–190. doi:10.54055/ejtr.v12i.218

Saayman, M., Rossouw, R., & Krugell, W. (2012). The impact of tourism on poverty in South Africa. *Development Southern Africa, 29*(3), 462–487. doi:10.1080/0376835X.2012.706041

Sawhill, I. V. (2003). The behavioural aspects of poverty. *The Public Interest, 153*, 79–93.

Scheyvens, R. (2002). *Tourism for development: empowering communities*. Pearson Education.

Scheyvens, R. (2007). Exploring the tourism-poverty nexus. *Current Issues in Tourism, 10*(2&3), 231–254. doi:10.2167/cit318.0

Scheyvens, R. (2011). *Tourism and poverty*. Routledge.

Schilcher, D. (2007). Growth versus equity: The continuum of pro-poor tourism and neoliberal governance. *Current Issues in Tourism, 10*(2/3), 166–192. doi:10.2167/cit304.0

Serrat, O. (2017). *The sustainable livelihood approach: in knowledge solutions*. Springer. doi:10.1007/978-981-10-0983-9_5

Sharpley, R. (2009). Tourism and development challenges in the least developed countries: The case of The Gambia. *Current Issues in Tourism, 12*(4), 337–358. doi:10.1080/13683500802376240

Shen, F. (2009). *Tourism and the sustainable livelihoods approach: application within the Chinese context* [PhD thesis]. Lincoln University.

Sin, H. L., & Minca, C. (2014). Touring responsibility: The trouble with 'going local' in community-based tourism in Thailand. *Geoforum, 51*, 96–106. doi:10.1016/j.geoforum.2013.10.004

Snyman, S., & Spenceley, A. (2012). Key sustainable tourism mechanisms for poverty reduction and local socioeconomic development in Africa. *Africa Insight*, *42*(2), 76–93.

Spenceley, A., Ashley, C., & De Kock, M. (2009). *Tourism and local development: an introductory guide*. International Trade Centre.

Spenceley, A., & Meyer, D. (2012). Tourism and poverty reduction: Theory and practice in less economically developed countries. *Journal of Sustainable Tourism*, *20*(3), 297–317. doi:10.1080/09669582.2012.668909

Spenceley, A., & Seif, J. (2003). *Strategies impacts and costs of pro-poor tourism approaches in South Africa*. Overseas Development Institute.

Thomas, F. (2014). Addressing the measurement of tourism in terms of poverty reduction: Tourism value chain analysis in Lao PDR and Mali. *International Journal of Tourism Research*, *16*(4), 368–376. doi:10.1002/jtr.1930

Torres, R. (2003). Linkages between tourism and agriculture in Mexico. *Annals of Tourism Research*, *30*(3), 546–566. doi:10.1016/S0160-7383(02)00103-2

Truong, V. D., Hall, C. M., & Garry, T. (2014). Tourism and poverty alleviation: Perceptions and experiences of poor people in Sapa, Vietnam. *Journal of Sustainable Tourism*, *22*(7), 1071–1089. doi:10.1080/09669582.2013.871019

United Nations. (2014). *Millennium development goals*. United Nations.

United Nations Conference on Trade and Development (UNCTAD). (2010). *The contribution of tourism to trade and development*. New York: United Nations. (TD/B/C. I/8.)

United Nations Conference on Trade and Development (UNCTAD). (2013). *The impact of trade on employment and poverty reduction*. Geneva: UNCTAD. (Note by the UNCTAD secretariat, 17-21 June.)

United Nations Conference on Trade and Development (UNCTAD). (2017). *Economic development in Africa report 2017*. Geneva, Switzerland: UNCTAD.

United Nations Conference on Trade and Development. (UNCTAD). (2020). *COVID-19 and tourism assessing the economic consequences*. Geneva, Switzerland: UNCTAD.

United Nations Report. (2018). *Sustainable development goals*. New York: United Nations.

United Nations World Tourism Organisation (UNWTO). (2005). Making Tourism More Sustainable-A guide for Policy Makers. Madrid, Spain: UNWETO.

United Nations World Tourism Organisation (UNWTO). (2016). Tourism highlights: 2016 edition. Madrid, Spain: UNWETO.

United Nations World Tourism Organisation (UNWTO). (2017). 2017 results: The highest in seven years. Madrid, Spain: UNWETO.

United Nations World Tourism Organisation (UNWTO). (2018). Tourism and the Sustainable Development Goals - Journey to 2030. Madrid, Spain: UNWETO.

United Nations World Tourism Organisation (UNWTO). (2019). Exports from international tourism hit USD 1.7 trillion. Madrid. Spain: UNWETO.

United Nations World Tourism Organisation (UNWTO). (2020). International tourist numbers could fall 60-80% in 2020. Madrid, Spain: UNWETO.

United Nations World Tourism Organisation (WTO). (2007). *World tourism day*. WTO.

Van Zyl, C. J. (2005). *The role of tourism in the conservation of cultural heritage with particular relevance for South Africa* [PhD thesis]. University of Stellenbosch.

Wattanakuljarus, A., & Coxhead, I. (2008). Is tourism-based development good for the poor? A general equilibrium analysis for Thailand. *Journal of Policy Modeling, 30*(6), 929–955. doi:10.1016/j.jpolmod.2008.02.006

Weller, C. (2017). *The World Bank released new poverty lines: find out where your country stands*. Business Insider.

Winters, P., Corral, L., & Mora, A. M. (2013). Assessing the role of tourism in poverty alleviation: A research agenda. *Development Policy Review, 31*(2), 177–202. doi:10.1111/dpr.12002

World Bank. (1991). *The world development report 1991: the challenge of development*. Oxford University Press.

World Bank. (2001). *World Development Report 2000/2001: Attacking Poverty. World Development Report*. Oxford University Press.

World Bank. (2011). *The World Bank annual report 2011*. World Bank.

World Bank. (2017). *Economic growth for Sub-Saharan Africa looks set to pick up to a modest 2.4% earlier this year, but a big improvement on 1.3% in 2016*. World Bank.

World Bank. (2022). *Poverty*. https://www.worldbank.org/en/topic/poverty/overview

World Tourism Organisation (WTO). (2002). *Tourism and poverty alleviation*. World Tourism Organisation.

World Tourism Organisation (WTO). (2004). *Tourism and poverty alleviation: recommendation for action*. WTO.

World Travel and Tourism Council (WTTC). (2019). *Travel and tourism: economic impact 2019*. WTTC.

Zapata, M. J., Hall, C. M., Lindo, P., & Vanderschaeghe, M. (2011). Can community-based tourism contribute to development and poverty alleviation? Lessons from Nicaragua. *Current Issues in Tourism*, *14*(8), 725–749. doi:10.1080/13683500.2011.559200

Zhao, W., & Ritchie, J. R. B. (2007). Tourism and poverty alleviation: An integrative research framework. *Current Issues in Tourism*, *10*(2), 119–143. doi:10.2167/cit296.0

Chapter 7
Prospects of Tea Tourism in India:
Tea Culture With Its Influence Towards Tourists Along With the Destination

Shuvasree Banerjee
Chandigarh University, India

ABSTRACT

The social shifts in Indian society towards tea are pervasive, and they are now being seen through tourism, where local tea customs, cultures, services, and attractions are part of several tourist activities. The delightful and enjoyable experience of tea tourism might pique visitors' interests. The chance to access all knowledge and experiences linked to tea is provided by tea tourism. In the context of global tourism, tea tourism is a relatively new specialty. By generating jobs and increasing the rural economy, the development of tea tourism would assist the area and lessen insurgency and other socioeconomic issues while also protecting the environment, heritage, and culture. In order to draw tourists and increase revenue, tea farms and the government are proposing to build more amenities inside the tea garden. In the tea garden, there are various homestays where visitors may stay and enjoy all the amenities.

DOI: 10.4018/978-1-6684-6796-1.ch007

INTRODUCTION

A sensory experience that has mesmerised nature-loving travellers throughout the world for years is created by the rich perfume of tea leaves, lush green tea plantations, scenic valley filled with curling clouds, and babbling mountain streams. A cup of tea, the most popular beverage, is seen as a universal expression of hospitality, whether it is served inside a home or outside in a commercial hospitality scenario (Walton, 2001). The oldest type of tourism is around tea, and it serves as a resource with the ability to support commercial hospitality. Tea tourism is described in the literature as "the art of travelling the world in search of enjoyment that results from exposure to tracts of green tea fields." Travel agencies all over the world have seized this chance to market tea tourism packages, planning visits to tea gardens where visitors spend a few idyllic days experiencing the full immersion process from plucking, withering, rolling, and finishing teas while cherishing their moments at a charming bungalow in an exotic landscape. The emerging tea tourist hubs include India, Nepal, China, Sri Lanka, and Japan, where both customised and commercial tea tourism is practised (Joliffe and Zhuang, 2007).

Visitors to these nations have enjoyed fine infusions of fresh tea over the years, cosy stays in old bungalows, and the chance to go through the most verdant tea estates. They have also observed the tea-making process and participated in local traditional activities. They have also seen pure rivers, foggy valleys, and expansive biodiversity with a variety of flora and animals. As a "alternative type" of tourism, tea tourism is acknowledged as a tool for socioeconomic development (Su et al., 2019a, 2019b). It has enhanced rural economies through social and infrastructure advancements, improved income production, and played a crucial part in destination image creation. It has not only encouraged social connectedness and cultural heritage (Casalegno et al., 2020). Researchers contend that despite the good impact, tea tourism has failed to revitalise the local economy in the direction of sustainable development due to weak policy planning and bad administration (Bandara, 2003; Joliffe and Aslam, 2009).

As we all know, the tea plantation subsector now faces challenges in maintaining profitability and sector sustainability while managing high cost production and other particular issues specific to the sector, as well as boosting land efficiency and labour productivity. Although this business has focused on the end product's value addition and the marketing process, it might not be able to solve the issue the tea plantation sector is facing. Many tourism activities include tea, allowing visitors to experience the local tea customs, cultures, services, and attractions (Jolliffe, 2007). These circumstances make it possible for tea tourism to be a key potential for both product and service sectors to diversify and assure the long-term growth of the nation's economy, particularly in areas where tea is produced.

An method to considering the goals, scope, and priorities for development efforts is the sustainable livelihoods approach. By focusing on people's intrinsic potential in terms of their talents, social networks, access to physical and financial resources, and capacity to influence key institutions, it advances understanding about how the poor and vulnerable live and the significance of policies and institutions (Serrat, 2017). The remuneration of tea workers has not yet been impacted by the sustainability criteria, according to Raja and Mithili's study (2019). Improvements in pay or incentives are simply one measure of the sustainability of the community's livelihood on the tea plantation; other measures include increased livelihood diversity and ownership of a variety of assets (Su et al., 2019). Tourism as a sustainable livelihood strategy on a tea plantation is one of these methods. A sustainable livelihoods method may be used to investigate the connections between local community development and tourist growth and provides a path ahead (Su et al., 2019; Tao and Wall, 2009). This method may examine the economic and social benefits of tea plantations as well as their ecological and cultural aspects. Tea serves as a powerful cultural and ecological transporter. These ecological and cultural resources are two crucial ones to combine with other resources to create new means of subsistence. Tea tourism, according to Jolliffe (2007), is "driven by a curiosity in the history, customs, and use of tea." The historical, cultural, and environmental circumstances of a location are intertwined with the production and consumption of tea. These have the potential to offer diverse audiences appealing tourism experiences, such as taking in the tea landscape, visiting tea shops and museums, tasting tea, watching tea being made, taking part in tea ceremonies and cultural events, staying in accommodations with tea decor, dining on food with a tea infusion, and many other activities (Jolliffe, 2007; Jolliffe and Aslam, 2009; Cheng et al., 2010).

By drawing inspiration from this path, the current chapter seeks to comprehend the potential of tea tourism and investigate it further in order to pinpoint the problems and obstacles that remain. Thus, this chapter stresses how travelling and consuming tea may increase people's perceptions of tea plantations and their overall tea tourism experiences, which will benefit the tea industry as a whole.

BACKGROUND

The beverage of tea carries significant social and cultural significance (Joliffe and Zhuang, 2007). The production and consumption of tea have been included into tourism over the years to establish sustainable community livelihoods (Su et al., 2019a, 2019b). Tea tourism has been recognized as a specialty tourist industry that is founded on environmentally friendly and sustainable travel (Cheng et al., 2012). However, the body of research on tea tourism is still rather thin (Cheng et al., 2010).

Over the years, researchers have emphasized the necessity for more research to fully comprehend tea's function in delivering hospitality, enhancing client contentment, and offering high-quality services.

The first studies on tea tourism were conducted by Hall et al. (2003), Boniface (2017), and Joliffe and Zhuang (2007), but the study "Tea and Tourism: Tourists, Traditions, and Transformations" was deemed to be the most significant and seminal, serving as a model for subsequent studies. Tea tourism was defined as "tourism that is inspired by an interest in the history, customs, and use of tea" by Joliffe and Zhuang in 2007. Tea tourists are defined as "tourists experiencing history, culture, and customs associated to the use of tea," they continued. Their study also emphasized the variety of chances and experiences that tea can provide tourists, such as tea store tours, tea rituals, trips to tea gardens or museums, and unique stays in old bungalows on a tea estate. Joliffe and Aslam (2009) added to the body of knowledge by examining the challenges and dangers to Sri Lanka's growing tea tourist industry. According to Cheng et al. (2010), tea culture and tea tourism involve visiting lovely tea gardens, picking tea leaves, and taking part in cultural performances, all of which are activities that visitors find to be very appealing. For the first time, their study concentrated on tourists' perceptions of tea tourism in China. In their 2012 addition to the literature on tea tourism, Cheng et al. defined the main stakeholders as tea tourists, tea garden owners, local government, travel agents, and the media. They also stated that, although having significant attractions and services, tea tourism had failed in a small number of nations, which led them to the conclusion that the success of tourist development was dependent on tourism planning, marketing, and coordination among the stakeholders.

Bennike (2017) emphasized the expanding significance of Darjeeling (India) in the global tea tourist map, while researchers like Ranasinghe et al. (2017) examined product-place co-branding with Ceylon Tea (Sri Lanka). Darjeeling has drawn both local and foreign tourists throughout the years because it is the source of some of the most exclusive tea blends in the world, has gorgeous natural surroundings, and is a special site for tourism due to its colonial legacy. Tea tourism is gaining more traction and improving its reputation (Besky, 2014). Tea tourism was advocated as a marketing strategy by researchers like Fernando et al. (2017) to enhance Sri Lanka's reputation as a tourist destination. Researchers like Lin and Wen (2018) drew inspiration from earlier studies and saw tea tourism as a vehicle for social change that takes local revenue generating and poverty reduction into account. They went on to say that tea plantation tourism has a substantial influence on local cultures and tackles socioeconomic inequities in regions that produce tea. Su et al. (2019a, 2019b) claimed that integrating tea with tourism leads to the achievement of sustainable livelihood, whereas Weber (2018) came to the conclusion that tea tourism helps to preserve our national identity, enhance cultural heritage, and provide sensory experiences in tourism. The implementation of the shared economy idea in tea tourism around a few tea plantations in Darjeeling, India, was emphasized by Mondal and Samaddar (2020a). Recent studies primarily emphasize the need for more research on the social and economic disparities between visitors and hosts (Su and Zhang, 2020).

RISE OF TEA TOURISM

Tea and tourism have a long-standing link. The history of tea tourism may be traced back to the ancient trade routes that carried tea, such as the Silk Road (Hamel, 2001) and Tea Horse Road (Freeman and Ahmed, 2011), which connected the Mediterranean to China and the rest of Southeast Asia. China, Japan, the UK, and a few other South-Asian nations, including India and Sri Lanka, have all established a strong tea culture through the years. China is known for being the origin of tea as a medicinal beverage (Heiss and Heiss, 2007). Japan popularised tea ceremonies to encourage cultural tourism, despite China being credited as the pioneer in advancing tea culture with its tea markets, museums, and services relating to tea (Joliffe and Zhuang, 2007). Similarly, England has acknowledged afternoon tea as a representation of the culture and character of the country. India has taken the lead in showcasing its beautiful green tea gardens and plantations to both local and foreign tourists as tea tourism slowly carves out its own niche (Cheng et al., 2012). With three renowned tea breeds in its hands—Darjeeling, Assam, and Nilgiris teas—Indian tourism has soared and grown in popularity. Darjeeling Tea, which comes in a variety of hues and flavours, has gained notoriety for its distinctive golden-red liquor-like scent and distinctive tea-drinking experience. India is establishing itself among other kinds of alternative tourism as the heaven for tea enthusiasts thanks to its gorgeous tea farms and a wide variety of tea brands (Mondal and Samaddar, 2020a; Shah and Pate, 2016). In the same way as "English afternoon tea" and the most well-known Japanese tea, "Matcha," offer a gourmet experience with their ceremonial tea ice cream (Gupta et al., 2020). Additionally, other tea variations, such "Apple tea" in Turkey, "Floral tea" in Taiwan, and "Horse-milk tea" in Tibet, have drawn tourists' interest throughout time (Joliffe and Zhuang, 2007). Commercial tea planting has extended outside of Asia (China, India, Sri Lanka, Japan, Indonesia, and Vietnam) to nations in Africa (Kenya), South America (Argentina), and the Middle East (Iran and Turkey). Tea tourism has become a key attraction globally as a result of the increase in interest in tea drinking and engagement in tea-related activities. Tea tourism fairs and workshops are organized in a variety of forms and genres. To raise awareness and promote tea tourism among domestic and foreign visitors, the tourism ministry has been working with governing councils, marketers, and tour operators to organize a variety of festivals and seminars.

TEA AND SUSTAINABLE TOURISM

If the growth of tourism on tea plantations has the potential to employ a significant portion of the local population in tea tourist activities, it can be a sustainable method to boost the local economy. Rural green tourism is an encouraging example of business activity in rural regions [10] and may be used as a method to combat climate change (Zeppel and Beaumont, 2011). In tea-green tourism, visitors may become involved in all aspects of tea production, from picking to packaging (Chakraborty and Islam, 2020). The action on promoting hospitality is the tea tourist business where there are lots of job chances. With the main goal of drawing tourists to a specific location and satisfying their needs for pleasure, relaxation, and experience, such as the experience of picking tea, tasting tea, making a glamping tent, camping grounds, and also the lovely view of tea carpet through tea walk, hospitality can boost economic & business concerned. In the New Normal era, when people are more interested in natural tourism where they can enjoy fresh air, feel healthy, and be relaxed by viewing in beautiful natural views while strictly adhering to the COVID-19 protocol framework, these tea tourisms may enhance various financial and non-financial benefits to local communities. It also has the potential to be a sustainable tourism destination.

TEA AND ECOTOURISM

According to Mahanta (2014), ecotourism is defined as ethical travel to natural regions that helps the environment, the local community, and the social, economic, and environmental pillars of sustainable development (Devi, 2012). Due to the extensive geographic variety and different ecological diversity in the three research regions, in addition to tea eco-tours, diverse special cultivars can be developed into ecotourism objects as a genetic and in situ conservation measure (Zhouyiqi and Tao, 2012). If the government gives ecotourism development greater attention, it might become the foundation of the rural area's economy by, for example, supporting the construction of infrastructure.

TEA AND GASTRONOMY TOURISM

Currently, tea-based culinary tourism is becoming more and more well-liked and flourishing. For its simplicity in implementation and fascinating nature, gastronomy tourism is an alternative form of tourism for rural areas (Guzel and Apaydin, 2016). It includes not only food and beverages as the main objects of its attractions but also everything related to food activities, such as food ingredients, preparation, processing, and serving, as well as the cultural and local values that can affect the entire experience of tea tourism and the trip (Sukenti, 2014; Horng et al., 2012; Baran and Batman, 2013). Even though tea is the second most popular beverage after water, coffee gastronomy continues to increase in popularity. Tea tourism destination packages might be complemented with a tea house or café close to a tea plantation. In the millennial generation, tea mixology and tea blending have gained popularity as tea artisans who create distinctive tea products. The business, environment, and sustainability of the tea destination may all benefit from integrating tea scenery and cuisine based on tea foods and beverages (Guzel and Apaydin, 2016). Tourists may create customized tea servings in glamping or enjoy tea cuisine and drinks in restaurants or cafés while admiring the beauty of tea plantations. The majority of tea gastronomy tourism experiences are offered at local booths near tourist attractions and feature a variety of traditional goods made by smallholder tea farmers or by tea enterprises, including the tea beverage "teh gelang," green tea chocolates, tea chips, milk tea, etc. Building a positive reputation for promotional materials through various media, especially social media, is essential to improving tea gastronomy tourism in these two areas. These areas have a strong sense of the traditional or native tea house's authenticity, which reflects the culture of tea plantation life. Gastronomy tourism has the ability to have an influence on sustainable livelihood by educating visitors to be more receptive to tourist attractions that are environmentally friendly and include local people (Sukenti, 2014).

TOURISM AND TEA MARKETING

Significantly, tourism has the ability to improve the branding and marketing of tea-producing regions (Fernando et al., 2017a). In the upcountry region, home stay tourism in tea gardens is a significant, expanding market sector where most visitors are driven by curiosity in the history, customs, and use of tea (Kaldeen, 2020). As marketing strategies to spread the name of a tourist destination, social media marketing, electronic word-of-mouth, blogs, and printed media are used (Fernando et al., 2017b).

TOURISM AND TEA INTEGRATION AND ITS IMPACTS ON SUSTAINABLE LIVELIHOOD

The local community's economic situation is improved by tea tourism (Su et al., 2019). After the opening, recognition, and operation of the integrated tourist site in the tea plantation region, the tourism community created a range of livelihood choices. Food and drink specialty shops, agriculture shops (such strawberry farms or stores), tea and coffee specialty shops, street sellers, parking lots, places to stay at home, use the bathroom, or find other lodging options, as well as retail and transit services. Most of the time, it has had a good effect on both tourist actors and tourist visitors. Tourists benefited from natural attractions for recreation in 93% of cases, relaxation in nature in 89 percent of cases, and a pleasant setting for physical healing with family or friends in 29% of cases. Most tourists decide to stay at least one night in an area where they may camp. Their daily income also rose. Previously, they had to rely solely on wage labour on tea plantations, the care of animals, or other local jobs (gardener, housekeeper, etc.). After the epidemic, migrant employees who were laid off did not see this increase in income. The opening of new food, drink, and souvenir stalls, street sellers, parking attendants, and other lodging services that are ideal for tourist needs, such as tent services, firewood, transportation, or tea garden tours, have created a variety of new work possibilities. Living standards, local pride, and individual and group skill development for tourism services (service, communication, cookery) have all grown, with living standards increasing by 64 percent and skill development increasing by 57 percent as a whole (Sita et al., 2021). In another scenario, tea tourism would not significantly increase tea production, which is the major focus of the tea plantation industry, but it would provide tea companies with an additional source of revenue diversification. The recognition and tying together of tourism with tea production, tea history, tea culture, tea traditions, and all other aspects of tea experiences in a tea tour schema need additional work. When new arenas or attractions are opened in the tourism industry, the economic impact is taken into consideration, but the environmental impact is given top importance. This is due to the fact that the majority of tourist attractions are found upstream, where they have social and environmental obligations to the population and environment situated downstream. In tourist destinations, tea mixology and tea blending products have the potential to be incorporated as tea gastronomy tourism, similar to how coffee shops and coffee stores are already more well-known and have become a part of millennial culture. Incorporating coffee and tourism has become a sustainable livelihood strategy for development and conservation (Woyesa and Kumar, 2021). The sustainable life in the area of a tea plantation may be aided by all possible experiences that tea tourism provides, including agro-edutourism through tea tours, ecotourism of tea natural resources, tea gourmet tourism including tea products, and tea culture and its traditions. To empower and increase the accessibility of tea and tourist assets, it was necessary to emphasize better ties and increase synergy across institutional structures or levels, including the government, tea firms, and the local community (natural, physical, human, financial, and social). Therefore, the quality of life may be sustainably enhanced at all levels, including the home, local/village, and community levels, which includes the tea plantation firm. To be taken into account and predicted is that in the future, labor availability in the tea industry would be extremely competitive with other sectors, as well as with the growth of tourism, because at the moment, many of the nations that produce tea are struggling with a labor shortage. In order to create a more sustainable living that takes into account and is sensitive to local and global tea market demand, a new tea business model has to be established in the center of the tea-producing area. One of these strategies is merging tea and tourism.

Improvements in household and community livelihood diversity, supported by improved economic and human resources, are taking place at the community level in tea tourism locations. The natural environment both inside and outside the tea plantation where tea tourism is located is also being taken into consideration. Integrating tea with ecology, agriculture, cuisine, and cultural tourism in tea plantation areas may provide tourists with full tea experiences, a variety of benefits, and a significant influence on the community and businesses of tea plantations. An additional possibility for the promotion of sustainable tea tourism is provided by corporate social responsibility. One of the most crucial strategies to improve the intention to return is to increase the tea tourists' service satisfaction. The limitation of resources and skills in the development of tea and tourist integration may be overcome by forging a mutually beneficial synergy across all institutional levels. Expanding tea and tourist integration, creating partnerships, encouraging greater local engagement, and boosting local advantages as ways of life are crucial for practical consequences in the future.

FOREIGN TOURIST'S TEA PREFERENCES

The importance of the food and beverages offered to tourists for the social, economic, and ecological sustainability of a tourist destination has been recognized in a number of prior studies in the worldwide context of tourism and hospitality (Gupta & Duggal, 2020; McKercher et al., 2004). Few research have also confirmed the significant roles performed by taste, scent, color, and touch during travel and discovered that there is much more to tourism than just photographic physiognomies of the engagement (Davidson et al., 2005). Dining is increasingly being employed as a crucial activity, and local foods and drinks at the destination are now recognized as an essential component of tourism (Breakey and Breakey, 2015; Henderson, 2009). According to Quan and Wang's (2004) results, a location's food and drink may be used as a persuasive tool to enhance and shape the destination's image and brand value, but many researchers concur that it can also be a motivating factor for tourists' inclusive travel behaviors (Gupta et al., 2018; McKercher et al., 2004). Numerous studies have shown that travellers are now drawn more and more to fresh pastimes and customs that result from understanding the cultures and values of a particular location (Gupta et al., 2019, 2020; McKercher et al., 2004). Furthermore, a sizable portion of travel enjoyment is also being connected to travellers' choices and consumption of the various foods and drinks on offer at a location (Breakey and Breakey, 2015; Gee et al., 1997; Zheng et al., 1996). Therefore, understanding how international visitors' eating and drinking habits and tastes relate to the cuisine of their destination may be improved. But the focus of this study will be on how tea is preferred and how it is consumed by international visitors to India. When travelling or at home, tea and coffee are frequently recognised as two of the most popular libations (Jolliffe, 2006). The majority of studies to date have focused on tea's quality attributes (Kyung et al., 2017), drinking habits (Peck et al., 2017), its role in the hospitality sector (Jolliffe, 2006), tea tourism development, and as a component of heritage tourism, despite the fact that tea is the second-most popular beverage in the world after water (Jolliffe & Aslam, 2009). (Jolliffe & Aslam, 2009). Tea drinking is simply one aspect of numerous local cultures and customs, which are closely related to tea preparation and consumption (Jolliffe, 2007). Furthermore, prior research supports its importance and need in understanding a society's particular ethnic customs and values and establishes it as a crucial form of social expression (Peck et al., 2017). Considerable differences in the consumption and selection patterns of tea among consumers in India have been attributed to significant changes in lifestyles, family structures, psychological issues, and numerous sociocultural aspects (Urala & Lähteenmäki, 2007). Additionally, customers' diverse needs and distinct tea tastes inspire them to search for a variety of tea vending outlets that offer value for money and convenience (Byun and Han, 2004; Gupta et al., 2018). As a result, several tea cafés, kiosks, tea gardens, and Chai-points have sprouted up throughout India, giving customers a place to sample and appreciate the genuine Indian tea varietals as well as the associated cultural customs (Lee et al., 2008; Timur and Getz, 2007; Yang, 2007). Given the above-mentioned facts and the fact that India's tea culture is gradually becoming a major means for visitors to understand the ethnic Indian eating culture, tea may be seen as a means of luring international visitors and a key tourist attraction in India. In India, tea is not only regarded as a beverage but also as a method to celebrate and welcome visitors. Indians' love of tea is also evident in the abundance of tea vending machines on every street and corner in the country. From Kerala tea to the well-known Kashmiri Kahwa, several types of tea are enjoyed by both locals and visitors from abroad. One of the many subsistence methods employed by India's impoverished households to maintain and expand their revenue base amid the financial crisis is tea peddling (Timur and Getz, 2007). India has enormous potential for the growth of tea tourism since it is both the world's largest consumer and second-largest producer of tea after China (Yang, 2007). It is a particular form of niche tourist market with a large and diverse audience but a relatively small body of literature to date (Sharples, 2008), particularly in the Indian setting. This specialised tourism sector offers a variety of options to see tea production and processing facilities, giving visitors plenty of chances to get a taste of the regional tea customs and cultures. Despite the fact that the majority of recent research (Lee et al., 2008; Timur and Getz, 2007; Yang, 2007) have examined the extent of tea tourism and its impact on regional dining customs and tea consumption patterns, there have been relatively few studies that have specifically addressed India. Furthermore, only a very small number of research (Ghosh & Ghosh, 2013; Varun et al., 2009) have explored the tea preferences and purchase patterns of international visitors to India to far. Additionally, the researchers have not yet looked into the variables that influence their respective tea preferences. Due to this, there is a gap that has to be filled by this research. It could help the key players in India's tea production and vending industries to formulate strategies for adjusting and aligning tea tourism goods, improving tea cultivation methods, fostering tea tourism, and eventually improving India's image as a travel destination.

Trends in tea sales today and the potential for tea tourism in India Tea is an agricultural product with significant socio-cultural and economic ramifications, and its cultivation and consumption are intrinsically linked to the cultural, historical, and social contexts of a place, potentially offering eye-catching and alluring tourism experiences to a variety of spectators (Cheng, et al., 2010; Jolliffe & Aslam, 2009). According to Jolliffe (2007), tea tourism is motivated by a visitor's interest in history, ethnic relations, and tea drinking. It may also offer a variety of activities for tea tourists, such as going to local tea shops and museums, appreciating the tea scenery, participating in tours of the cultivation and processing of tea, attending trainings for tea connoisseurs and appreciators, and participating in programmes for tea sommeliers and tea tourism. Online classes (Asian School of Tea, 2020); participation in a range of regional ethnic celebrations and customs; lodging in places with a tea theme; eating delicacies infused with tea; participating in tea matching sessions; and many other related activities (Cheng et al., 2010; Jolliffe, 2007; Yang, 2007). By incorporating tea harvesting and related socio-cultural practises and culinary activities, it may also be used as a potent tool to create employment opportunities for locals and as a progressive measure to support and encourage the Indian tea industry, revive local ethnic culture, improve the perception of the destination, and strengthen the identities of rural areas (Kyung et al., 2017). Different types of tea served in India are now an important part of the ethnic local culture and offer a variety of opportunities, including the improvement of local tea vending business, a notable revenue source for the large Indian population, a striking way for visitors to learn about the local tea culture, the potential to launch a new business with little initial investment, and ultimately contributing to the local destination image (Calloni, 2013). This is also seen in the growth of several themed tea franchises throughout different Indian cities, such as Chaayos, Tea trails, Chai Point, Tea villas, and many more, as well as in the diversification of these businesses throughout time (The Indian Wire, 2018). Additionally, associations may be formed between the various players in the tea industry, such as tea growers, manufacturers, processing companies, retail sellers, and manufacturers of related accessories, such as saucers, tea pots, kettles, etc., with a variety of amalgamations supporting the involvement of tourism (Lee et al., 2008; Su et al., 2019). As a result, a wide range of work opportunities might be created and merged with existing living groups, thereby enhancing the sustainability of rural civilizations. According to earlier research (Kivela & Crotts, 2006; Morgan et al., 2011), a destination with a positive reputation is frequently regarded as trustworthy and dependable by foreign tourists. A few studies have also confirmed that a positive destination position influences travellers' destination loyalty and appeal (Gupta et al., 2019; Gupta & Duggal, 2020). Additionally, the availability of food and drinks, beautiful scenery, warm and friendly locals, and sincere local hospitality are some of the key elements that impact travellers' choice of location (Yuksel et al., 2010). It is crucial for the stakeholders to properly align and develop the tourism-related items given the impact of tea on the overall fulfilment and contentment of tourists. Tea tourism may be promoted in India as a key strategy for luring international visitors to experience and appreciate a wide range of Indian tea cultures. However, there is a dearth of literature on this topic, particularly in the Indian context, which creates a huge vacuum that must be filled by this chapter.

The types of Indian teas and which ones international visitors enjoy are listed below. Every country has its own unique methods for making and serving tea. This only indicates that the greatest tea in each nation is genuinely unique. For instance, tea is more than just a basic beverage in Japan, where serving tea by women dressed in kimonos follows a tradition that has been practised for more than a century. Serving tea is more important than serving any other drinks in China since it's seen as a method to interact with other people, even if the Chinese and Japanese ways are relatively comparable. There is a "British Way" of drinking tea in Western nations, particularly in the United Kingdom, known as "afternoon tea or high tea." The custom of sipping tea at four o'clock was made popular way back in 1840 by Anna Duchess of Bedford, and it is still practised today. There are over 1500 different varieties of tea. To be clear, there are only four basic types of tea: oolong tea, white tea, green tea, and black tea. Turkish tea, a black tea served in small glasses, Moroccan mint tea, a black tea with three levels of strength, Matcha tea, a Japanese green tea with vegetal flavours, Ceylon tea, a boldly flavoured tea from Sri Lanka, English breakfast tea, a Kenyan black tea known for its robust flavours, and Rooibos tea are among the most popular tea varieties and styles in the world (a sweet and nutty flavoured tea from South Africa). While on vacation, travellers like engaging in pleasurable sensuous activities such as tasting and ingesting local cuisine and beverages (Kivela & Crotts, 2006; Mill and Morrison, 2012). Drinking regional beverages while on vacation also results in stunning sensory experiences that heighten holiday enjoyment and draw travellers to a certain location (Khokhar & Magnusdottir, 2002; Morrison, 2012). A local ethnic beverage can be prepared, presented, served, consumed, and even observed, giving tourists a feeling of its distinctiveness and mystique (Gupta et al., 2019; Kivela & Crotts, 2006). Therefore, it becomes essential for every host city to take into account their local beverage preferences at the destination (Byun & Han, 2004) and supply something which is exquisite or distinctive in order to provide travellers memorable destination experiences and to improve the overall destination image. For instance, France's use of destination marketing links wine and food consumption (Gupta & Sajnani, 2019). Additionally, it is crucial for local tourism players to understand the parts of tourists' beverage preferences that contribute to more fulfilling vacations so they may develop marketing strategies that can increase overall tourist satisfaction (Gupta et al., 2019; Mill and Morrison, 2012). Therefore, taking into account tourists' beverage preferences may improve overall visitor happiness and a destination's reputation, which is important for any location that uses beverages as a primary source of tourism (Khokhar & Magnusdottir, 2002). For international visitors, India offers a wide variety of tea flavours or types. The most popular tea kinds include Darjeeling, Assam, Nilgiri, Munnar, Kangra, Sikkim, and Dooars Terai, according to provenance (Tea Board of India, 2019). Nilgiri and Sikkim types feature flowery notes, Assam, Munnar, and Darjeeling variations have strong to medium flavours, while Darjeeling and Kangra varieties have mellow flavours. Any tea variety's quality, reputation, authenticity, and features are often attributed to its place of origin. A Geographical Indication, or GI, is used to identify a crucial indication for protecting the authenticity and promoting the tea and related tourism in particular items that correspond to a certain geographical area or origin (e.g., a town, region, or nation). By using a GI, you may certify that a product has premium quality, was produced using traditional techniques, and has a particular reputation because of where it came from. As Geographical Indications in India, the names "DARJEELING," "ASSAM Orthodox," and "NILGIRI Orthodox" as well as their logos make them distinctive for international travellers (List of Geographical Indications in India, 2020). Darjeeling tea was the first item in India to be given GI classification in 2003, and the European Union officially recognised its provenance in October 2011. To the advantage of the tea producers and the Assam tea industry as a whole, the Orthodox Assam Tea was given a GI designation in 2007. In addition to these, India is proud to produce a variety of teas, including herbal, oolong, and green teas, that have medical and health advantages. Masala, Butter, and iced teas are a few variations, depending on how they are made, that international visitors really enjoy. A better application of local tea varieties/styles by local players becomes necessary in light of these tea varieties/styles by coordinating the various needs of various international visitor sections (Jolliffe, 2007; Morgan et al., 2011; Su et al., 2019).

Factors Affecting the Tea Preferences of Foreign Tourists in India

The traveler's inclusive selection of a tourism destination is significantly influenced by tea (Jolliffe, 2007; Su et al., 2019). Many nations, including China, Sri Lanka, South Korea, and Japan, have used their native ethnic tea preparation and consumption customs as tourist attractions to draw in and appeal to international visitors and promote their nations as tea tourism hotspots worldwide (Shah et al., 2015). It is crucial to investigate the factors that make up tourists' tea preferences in order to increase the inclusive tourist pleasure (Chaturvedula and Prakash, 2011; Gupta and Sajnani, 2019). This will help to make their experiences more sophisticated and enjoyable. Additionally, it could assist the parties involved in creating suitable marketing plans in accordance with the interests and needs of tourists (Breakey and Breakey, 2015). A large range of consumer behaviour studies cover a variety of topics, including tourist preferences. The definition of preference is the decision to favour one thing over another (Chang et al., 2010). In this chapter, the word "tea preference" refers to a foreign visitor's preference for a particular Indian tea variety over others offered at a place. Numerous studies have looked at the variables that affect tourists' preferences for food and drink (Gupta et al., 2018; Mak et al., 2012). Mak et al. proposed five criteria in this regard: motivational, socio-demographic, religious, and cultural, per sonal, and experience (2012). Additionally, Kim et al. (2009) divided these elements into three categories: demographic (gender, marital status, age, religion, and level of education attained); physiological - neophilia (want to try new things) and nephobia (fear of ingesting new things); and motivational (intimacy, respect, status, sensual appeal, good experience, etc.). These factors were further validated by the study conducted by Rezaee et al. (2016) who used it for evaluating the tea consumption patterns in urban consumers of Iran. Thus, for evaluating the foreign tourist's tea preferences and consumption patterns in India, a wide range of these attributes may be considered. However, for this study, foreign tourist's tea preferences in India are evaluated based only on their socio-demographics. Moreover, the relative tea preferences of the tourists are evaluated on a preferential scale using AHP model and Pairwise comparison matrix. The socio-demographic factors used for this study are: Origin country, Age, Gender, Education Attainment, Income, Religion and Marital status. Tea tastes among tourists are frequently impacted by the nation of origin. Travelers from North and South America were found to typically prefer coffee to tea. Additionally, they like iced tea over hot tea variants (Arab et al., 2009). In previous studies (Rezaee et al., 2016; Su et al., 2019) on tourists' tea preferences, it was discovered that the majority of Asian visitors (particularly those from China, Sri Lanka, Korea, Taiwan, Indonesia, and Japan) typically have a preference for tea and drink it while travelling in the host country. While travelling, it was also observed that European visitors, particularly those from the UK, Turkey, Germany, France, and Poland, preferred green tea and milk-based tea kinds (Rezaee et al., 2016). Tea use by travellers from Oceania and middle-east Asia has also been seen (Jolliffe, 2007). According to earlier surveys, the majority of European visitors like their tea with milk whereas the majority of Asian tourists choose herbal, green, or naturally flavoured tea variants that are served without milk. The visitor's taste for tea is discovered to be significantly influenced by the tourist's age (Lorenzo et al., 2003). It has been observed that travellers' tastes in tea change with age, from childhood through adolescence to maturity (Arab et al., 2009; Kim et al., 2009). It was shown that customers over 45 and in their middle years (between 35 and 45) were more likely to drink tea (Rezaee et al., 2016). However, it was discovered that young adolescents and children drank very little tea. Further research by Chaturvedula and Prakash (2011) revealed that younger consumer age groups (those under the age of 35) typically favour teas without milk as well as those flavoured with flavours, herbs, etc. or green tea, whereas their older counterparts (those over the age of 35) prefer tea served with milk. Additionally, it was shown that older customers—those 35 and older—consume tea more frequently than do younger consumers (Rezaee et al., 2016). The strong effect of gender on tourists' tea choices and consumption habits was also discovered. Rozin (2006) provided evidence of gender disparities in American consumers' nutritional consumption and beverage preferences. Yang (2007) provided additional support for this by showing that male customers are more engaged in their tea drinking habits than female consumers. Additionally, it was shown that women consume tea varietals that are often served without sugar and milk but with flavour infusions because they are more worried about their health and calorie intakes (Cao et al., 2010).

The consumer's income and level of education both influence their tea preferences and purchasing decisions (Zheng et al., 1996). The level of education a visitor has has been shown to be unwaveringly connected to the level of nutritional knowledge they have, which affects their tea choosing behaviours (O'Donnell, 1994). All of the groups were found to have comparable tea drinking habits (whether less educated or highly educated). However, it was shown that customers with higher levels of education liked tea served without milk, whereas consumers with lower levels of education preferred tea served with milk (O'Donnell, 1994). Similar results were obtained for both higher and lower income groups. Additionally, it was shown that visitors with high levels of education were apprehensive about drinking tea since they saw it as a combination of regional ethnic custom and culture (Zheng et al., 1996). Travelers' individual knowledge of local customs, traditions, and taboos grows as they visit other locations, which has a further impact on how they choose and consume food and beverages (Cao et al., 2010). Additionally, it has been discovered that religion has a major impact on consumers' preferences for and consumption patterns of tea (Grigg, 2002). Benn (2015) found that patterns of tea intake are momentarily influenced by religious ideas, customs, and beliefs. The Buddhist ethic of abstention from alcohol contributed to the rise of tea as a popular beverage in China, Taiwan, and other neighbouring south-east Asian nations. Buddhist and Taoist institutions influenced how tea was processed, grown, and sold. Around their monasteries, monks developed a variety of highly prized, erratic, and costly tea types, greatly advancing Asian tea culture (Benn, 2015). Further research revealed that prominent religious figures had a significant influence on the spread of tea use (Chieh Hsu et al., 2018; Grigg, 2002). Tea parties have become more popular as a non-alcoholic alternative to drinking alcohol on religious holidays and occasions in Islam and Hinduism. The desire for tea among customers was also found to be influenced by a person's marital status. It was shown that married persons are more likely to drink tea (Shen et al., 2019).

LIMITATIONS AND FUTURE RESEARCH AGENDAS

The study on tea tourism in the chapter was only conducted inside the boundaries of India. Future academics may investigate cross-sectional or cross-cultural studies to get in-depth understanding of the tea tourist industry. Due to its total contribution to tea tourism globally, India was chosen as a representative sample in this study's complete analysis of the industry.

Practical Implications

The tourist business operates in a dynamic environment that is always evolving. The moment has come to comprehend customer demands and preferences because travel has grown to be a vital source of self-expression. Tea tourism, along with other alternative types of travel, is slowly carving out a place for itself in the travel industry. The goal of this study is to draw attention to the important issues that require careful thought and evaluation. Every stakeholder must work together to promote tea tourism on social media and integrate it into mainstream business.

The limited geographic reach of tea tourism up to this point supports its extension through marketing strategies like tea festivals, exhibits, seminars, or cultural activities. When speaking with consumers or visitors in particular, the intersection between tea, travel, and culture must be emphasised. For tea tourism to flourish sustainably, proper oversight must be provided since environmental preservation is of the highest importance. In addition to highlighting cultural characteristics, tea tourism has a good socioeconomic aspect that has to be further investigated. In order to promote this type of tourism, it is necessary to train highly trained tea craftsmen who will not only impart superior information about tea farming but also effectively serve visitors to the tea estates. These modest actions will strengthen the community's identity while also strengthening the social capital and cultural diversity of the area. In light of this, the current study significantly links tea tourism and sustainable development. The report will help destination tourist organisations and other service providers update their approach from a socioeconomic standpoint. The current article offers a variety of opportunities for policymakers and destination marketing organisations to implement appropriate legislative guidelines for making all stakeholders socially and ecologically responsible (Mondal and Samaddar, 2020b). This chapter aspires to develop a resilient and sustainable tea tourist industry that will not only thrive and flourish on its own but also foster an environment conducive to the survival and prosperity of future generations. The current chapter will also serve as a point of reference in the field of tea tourist research, directing subsequent researchers in broadening the field and enhancing the literature with fresher discoveries.

REFERENCES

Arab, L., Liu, W., & Elashoff, D. (2009). Green and black tea consumption and risk of stroke: A meta-analysis. *Stroke*, *40*(1), 1786–1792. doi:10.1161/STROKEAHA.108.538470 PMID:19228856

Asian School of Tea. (2020, August 19). Using one tiny leaf to make one big difference. Asian School of Tea. https://asianschooloftea.org/

Aslam, M. S. M., & Joliffe, L. (2015). Repurposing colonial tea heritage through historic lodging. *Journal of Heritage Tourism*, *10*(2), 111–128. doi:10.1080/1743873X.2014.985226

Bandara, H. M. (2003). *Tourism Planning in Sri Lanka. Malawana, Stamford Lake*. PVT.

Baran, Z. and Batman, O. (2013). Destinasyon pazarlamasında mutfak kültürünün rolü: Sakarya örneği. 14 Ulus. Tur. Kongresi Bildir. *Kitabı*, 5–8.

Benn, J. (2015). *Tea in China: A religious and cultural History*. University of Hawai'i Press. www.jstor.org/stable/j.ctt13x1kn2

Bennike, R. (2017). Frontier commodification: Governing land, labour and leisure in Darjeeling, India. *South Asia, 40*(2), 256–271. doi:10.1080/00856401.2017.1289618

Besky, S. (2014). The labor of terroir and the terroir of labor: Geographical indication and Darjeeling tea plantations. *Agriculture and Human Values, 31*(1), 83–96. doi:10.100710460-013-9452-8

Boniface, P. (2017). *Tasting Tourism: Travelling for Food and Drink*. Routledge. doi:10.4324/9781315241777

Breakey, N. M., & Breakey, H. E. (2015). Tourism and Aldo Leopold's 'cultural harvest': Creating virtuous tourists as agents of sustainability. *Journal of Sustainable Tourism, 23*(1), 85–103. doi:10.1080/09669582.2014.924954

Byun, J. O., & Han, J. S. (2004). A study on perception and actual status of utilization for green tea. *Journal of the Korean Society of Food Culture, 19*(2), 184–192.

Calloni, M. (2013). Street food on the move: A socio-philosophical approach. *Journal of the Science of Food and Agriculture, 93*(14), 3406–3413. doi:10.1002/jsfa.6353 PMID:23963865

Cao, H., Qiao, L., Zhang, H., & Chen, J. (2010). Exposure and risk assessment for aluminium and heavy metals in Puerh tea. *The Science of the Total Environment, 408*(1), 2777–2784. doi:10.1016/j.scitotenv.2010.03.019 PMID:20413147

Casalegno, C., Candelo, E., Santoro, G., & Kitchen, P. (2020). The perception of tourism in coffee producing equatorial countries: An empirical analysis. *Psychology and Marketing, 37*(1), 154–166. doi:10.1002/mar.21291

Chakraborty, A. and Islam, S.S. (2020). Impact of tea tourism in Dooars, North Bengal. *An overview Mukt Shabd J. 9*, 5789–804.

Chaturvedula, V. S. P., & Prakash, I. (2011). The aroma, taste, color and bioactive constituents of tea. *Journal of Medicinal Plants Research, 5*(11), 2110–2124. doi:10.5897/JMPR

Cheng, S., Hu, J., Fox, D., & Zhang, Y. (2012). Tea-tourism development in Xinyang, China: Stakeholders' view. *Tourism Management Perspectives, 2/3*, 28–34. doi:10.1016/j.tmp.2011.12.001

Cheng, S., Xu, F., Zhang, J., & Zhang, Y. (2010). Tourists' attitudes toward tea tourism: A case study in Xinyang, China. *Journal of Travel & Tourism Marketing*, *27*(2), 211–220. doi:10.1080/10548401003590526

Cheng, S. W., Xu, F., Zhang, J., & Zhang, Y. T. (2010). Tourists' attitudes toward tea tourism: A case study in Xinyang. *Journal of Travel & Tourism Marketing*, *27*(2), 211–220. doi:10.1080/10548401003590526

Chieh, H., Richard, H., Robinson, N. S., & Scott, N. (2018). Traditional food consumption behaviour: The case of Taiwan. *Tourism Recreation Research*, *43*(4), 456–469. doi:10.1080/02508281.2018.1475879

Davidson, J., Bondi, L., & Smith, M. (2005). Emotional Geographies. Ashgate. Eric, A,F, & Asafo-Adjei, R. (2013). Traditional food preferences of tourists in Ghana. *British Food Journal*, *115*(7), 987–1002. doi:10.1108/BFJ-11-2010-0197

Devi, M. K. (2012). Ecotourism in assam: A promising opportunity for development. *South Asian J. Tour. Herit.*, *5*, 179–192.

Fernando, P. I. N., Kumari, K., & Rajapaksha, R. (2017b). Destination marketing to promote tea tourism socio-economic approach on community development. *Int. Rev. Manag. Bus. Res.*, *6*, 68–75. doi:10.2139srn.3877264

Fernando, P. I. N., Rajapaksha, R., & Kumari, K. (2017a). Tea tourism as a marketing tool: A strategy to develop the image of Sri Lanka as an attractive tourism destination Kelaniya. *Journal of Management*, *5*, 64–79.

Fernando, P., Rajapaksha, R.M. & Kumari, K. (2017). Tea-tourism as a marketing tool: a strategy to develop the image of Sri Lanka as an attractive tourism destination. *Kelaniya Journal of Management, 5*(2).

Freeman, M., & Ahmed, S. (2011). *Tea Horse Road: China's Ancient Trade Road to Tibet*. River Books.

Gee, Y. G., Maken, J. C., & Choy, D. J. (1997). *The travel industry*. Wiley.

Ghosh, M., & Ghosh, A. (2013). Consumer buying behaviour in relation to consumption of tea – A study of Pune city. *International Journal of Sales and Marketing Management Research and Development*, *3*(2), 47–54.

Grigg, D. (2002). The worlds of tea and coffee: Patterns of consumption. *GeoJournal*, *57*(1), 283–294. doi:10.1023/B:GEJO.0000007249.91153.c3

Gupta, G., Roy, H., & Promsivapallop, P. (2020). Local cuisine image dimensions and its impact on foreign tourist's perceived food contentment in Delhi. *Tourism Recreation Research*. doi:10.1080/02508281.2020.1816762

Gupta, V., & Duggal, S. (2020). How do the tourists' behavioural intentions influenced by their perceived food authenticity: A case of Delhi? *Journal of Culinary Science & Technology, 1764430*. doi:10.1080/15428052.2020

Gupta, V., Khanna, K., & Gupta, R. K. (2018). A study on the street food dimensions and its effects on consumer attitude and behavioural intentions. *Tourism Review, 73*(3), 374–388. doi:10.1108/TR-03-2018-0033

Gupta, V., Khanna, K., & Gupta, R. K. (2019). Preferential analysis of street food amongst the foreign tourists: A case of Delhi region. *International Journal of Tourism Cities, 6*(3), 511–528. doi:10.1108/IJTC-07-2018-0054

Gupta, V., & Sajnani, M. (2019). Risk and benefit perceptions related to wine consumption and how it influences consumers' attitude and behavioural intentions in India. *British Food Journal, 122*(8), 2569–2585. doi:10.1108/BFJ-06-2019-0464

Gupta, V., Sajnani, M., Dixit, S. K., & Khanna, K. (2020). Foreign tourist's tea preferences and relevance to destination attraction in India. *Tourism Recreation Research*, 1–15.

Guzel, B., & Apaydin, M. (2016). Gastronomy in Tourism Global issues and trends in tourism. University Press Cambridge.

Hall, C. M., Mitchell, R., & Sharples, L. (2003). *Consuming Places: The Role of Food, Wine and Tourism in Regional Development*. Butterworth Heinemann.

Hamel, G. (2001). Leading the revolution. Strategy & Leadership, Harvard Business School Press, Boston, MA.

Heiss, M. L., & Heiss, R. J. (2007). The Story of Tea: A Cultural History and Drinking Guide, Random House Digital, Inc. .

Joliffe, L., & Aslam, M. S. (2009). Tea heritage tourism: Evidence from Sri Lanka. *Journal of Heritage Tourism, 4*(4), 331–344.

Henderson, J. C. (2009). Food tourism reviewed. *British Food Journal, 111*(4), 317–326. doi:10.1108/00070700910951470

Horng, J. S., Liu, C. H., Chou, H. Y., & Tsai, C. Y. (2012). Understanding the impact of culinary brand equity and destination familiarity on travel intentions. *Tourism Management, 33*(4), 815–824. doi:10.1016/j.tourman.2011.09.004

Joliffe, L., & Zhuang, P. (2007). Tourism development and the tea gardens of fuding, China. In *Tea Tourism: Global Trends and Development* (pp. 133–144). Channel View Publications. doi:10.21832/9781845410582-011

Jolliffe, L. (2006). Tea and hospitality: More than a Cuppa. *International Journal of Contemporary Hospitality Management*, *18*(1), 164–168. doi:10.1108/09596110610646718

Jolliffe, L. (2007). *Tea and tourism: Tourists, traditions and transformations*. Channel View. doi:10.21832/9781845410582

Jolliffe, L. (2007). *Tea and Tourism: Tourists, Traditions and Transformations* (Vol. 11). Channel View Publications. doi:10.21832/9781845410582

Jolliffe, L., & Aslam, M. S. M. (2009). Tea heritage tourism: Evidence from Sri Lanka. *Journal of Heritage Tourism*, *4*(4), 331–344. doi:10.1080/17438730903186607

Jolliffe, L., & Aslam, M. S. M. (2009). Tea heritage tourism: Evidence from Sri Lanka. *Journal of Heritage Tourism*, *4*(4), 331–344. doi:10.1080/17438730903186607

Kaldeen, M. (2020). Marketing potentials to promote tea tourism in Sri Lanka. *The 6th International Tourism Research Conference and Tourism Leader's Summit*.

Khokhar, S., & Magnusdottir, S. G. M. (2002). Total phenol, catechin, and caffeine contents of teas commonly consumed in the United Kingdom. *Journal of Agricultural and Food Chemistry*, *50*(3), 565–570. doi:10.1021/jf0101531 PMID:11804530

Kim, Y. G., Eves, A., & Scarles, C. (2009). Building a model of local food consumption on trips and holidays: A grounded theory approach. *International Journal of Hospitality Management*, *28*(3), 423–431. doi:10.1016/j.ijhm.2008.11.005

Kivela, J., & Crotts, J. (2006). Tourism and gastronomy: Gastronomy's influence on how tourists experience a destination. *Journal of Hospitality & Tourism Research (Washington, D.C.)*, *30*(3), 354–377. doi:10.1177/1096348006286797

Kyung, H., Mark, A., & Meehee, C. (2017). Green tea quality attributes: A cross-cultural study of consumer perceptions using importance–performance analysis (IPA). *Journal of Foodservice Business Research*. doi:10.1080/15378020.2017.1368809

Lee, S. M., Chung, S. J., Lee, O. H., Lee, H. S., Kim, Y. K., & Kim, K. O. (2008). Development of sample preparation, presentation procedure and sensory descriptive analysis of green tea. *Journal of Sensory Studies*, *23*(4), 450–467. doi:10.1111/j.1745-459X.2008.00165.x

List of geographical indications in India. (2020, July, 16). Wikipedia. https://en.wikipedia.org/wiki/List_of_geographical_indications_in_India.

Lorenzo, M., Claudia, S., & Cannella, C. (2003). Eating habits and appetite control in the elderly: The anorexia of aging. *International Psychogeriatrics, 15*(1), 73–87. doi:10.1017/S1041610203008779 PMID:12834202

Magar, C. K., & Kar, B. K. (2016). Tea plantations and Socio-Cultural transformation: The case of Assam (India). *Space and Culture, India, 4*(1), 25–39. doi:10.20896aci.v4i1.188

Mahanta, M. G. D. (2014). Ecotourism and Dibru-Saikhowa National Park. *J. Agric. Life Sci., 1*, 91–94.

Mak, A. H. N., Lumbers, M., Eves, A., & Chang, R. C. Y. (2012). Factors influencing tourist food consumption. *International Journal of Hospitality Management, 31*(3), 928–936. doi:10.1016/j.ijhm.2011.10.012

Mill, R. C., & Morrison, A. M. (2012). *The tourism system* (7th ed.). Kendall/Hunt Publishing.

Mondal, S., & Samaddar, K. (2020a). Issues and challenges in implementing sharing economy in tourism: A triangulation study. *Management of Environmental Quality, 32*(1), 64–81. doi:10.1108/MEQ-03-2020-0054

Mondal, S., & Samaddar, K. (2020b). Responsible tourism towards sustainable development: Literature review and research agenda. *Asia Pacific Business Review*, 1–38.

Morgan, N., Pritchard, A., & Pride, R. (2011). *Destination brands: Managing place reputation*. Elsevier Butterworth-Heinemann.

Morrison, A. M. (2012). *Marketing and managing tourism destinations*. Routledge. Nunnally, J. C., & Bernstein, I. H. (1994). *Psychometric theory* (3rd ed.). McGraw-Hill., doi:10.1177/014662169501900308

O'Donnell, C. (1994). Food products for different age groups: Formulating for the ages. *Prepared Food, 3*(2), 39–44. doi:10.1375/jhtm.18.1.1

Peck Ting, G., Adeline, S., & Yien, T. (2017). Our tea-drinking habits: Effects of brewing cycles and infusion time on total phenol content and antioxidants of common teas. *Journal of Culinary Science & Technology*. Advance online publication. doi:10.1080/15428052.2017.1409673

Quan, S., & Wang, N. (2004). Towards a structural model of the tourist experience: An illustration from food experience in tourism. *Tourism Management, 25*(3), 297–305. doi:10.1016/S0261-5177(03)00130-4

Raja, M., & Mythili, C. (2019). Sustainable livelihood and economic status of tea labourers in the Nilgiris District. *IOSR J. Econ. Financ., 10,* 33–38.

Ranasinghe, W. T., Thaichon, P., & Ranasinghe, M. (2017). An analysis of product-place co-branding: The case of ceylon tea. *Asia Pacific Journal of Marketing and Logistics, 29*(1), 200–214. doi:10.1108/APJML-10-2015-0156

Rezaee, E., Mirlohi, M., Hassanzadeh, A., & Fallah, A. (2016). Factors affecting tea consumption pattern in an urban society in Isfahan, Iran. *Journal of Education and Health Promotion, 5,* 13. doi:. 184568 doi:10.4103/2277-9531

Rozin, P. (2006). The integration of biological, social, cultural and psychological influences on food choice. In R. Shepherd & M. Raats (Eds.), *The psychology of food choice* (pp. 19–39). CABI. doi:10.1079/9780851990323.0019

Samaddar, K., & Menon, P. (2020). Non-deceptive counterfeit products: A morphological analysis of literature and future research agenda. *Journal of Strategic Marketing*, 1–24. doi:10.1080/0965254X.2020.1772348

Serrat, O. (2017). The Sustainable Livelihoods Approach Knowledge Solutions (Singapura: Springer). pp 21–6.

Shah, S., Gani, A., Ahmad, M., Shah, A., Gani, A., & Massodi, F. A. (2015). In vitro antioxidant and antiproliferative activity of microwave-extracted green tea and black tea (Camellia sinensis): A comparative study. *NUTRAfoods : International Journal of Science and Marketing for Nutraceutical Actives, Raw Materials, Finish Products, 14*(4), 207–215. doi:10.100713749-015-0050-9

Shah, S. K., & Pate, V. A. (2016). Tea production in India: Challenges and opportunities. *Journal of Tea Science Research, 6*(5), 1–6.

Shen, K., Zhang, B., & Feng, Q. (2019). Association between tea consumption and depressive symptom among Chinese older adults. *BMC Geriatrics, 19*(1), 246–261. doi:10.118612877-019-1259-z PMID:31484503

Sita, K., Aji, T. M., & Hanim, W. (2021). Integrating tea and tourism: A potential sustainable livelihood approach for Indonesia tea producer central area. *IOP Conference Series. Earth and Environmental Science, 892*(1), 892. doi:10.1088/1755-1315/892/1/012104

Su, M. M., Wall, G., & Wang, Y. (2019). Integrating tea and tourism: A sustainable livelihoods approach. *Journal of Sustainable Tourism*, *27*(10), 1591–1608. doi:10.1080/09669582.2019.1648482

Su, M. M., Wall, G., Wang, Y., & Jin, M. (2019b). Livelihood sustainability in a rural tourism destination Hetu town, Anhui province, China. *Tourism Management*, *71*, 272–281. doi:10.1016/j.tourman.2018.10.019

Su, X., & Zhang, H. (2020). Tea drinking and the tastescapes of wellbeing in tourism. *Tourism Geographies*, 1–21. doi:10.1080/14616688.2020.1750685

Sukenti, K. (2014). Gastronomy tourism in several neighbor countries of Indonesia: A brief review. *Journal of Indonesian Tourism and Development Studies*, *2*(2), 55–63. doi:10.21776/ub.jitode.2014.002.02.03

Tao, T. C. H., & Wall, G. (2009). Tourism as a sustainable livelihood strategy. *Tourism Management*, *30*(1), 90–98. doi:10.1016/j.tourman.2008.03.009

Tea Board of India. (October, 2019). *Tea varieties in India*. Tea Board of India. http://www.teaboard.gov.in/ TEABOARDCSM/MTA=

The Indian Wire. (2018). List of top 10 start ups in India that made it big selling chai. Retrieved April 30, 2020 from https://www.theindianwire.com/startups/top-tea-selling startups-india-74220/

Timur, S., & Getz, D. (2007). A network perspective on managing stakeholders for sustainable urban tourism. *International Journal of Contemporary Hospitality Management*, *20*(4), 445–461. doi:10.1108/09596110810873543

Urala, N., & Lähteenmäki, L. (2007). Consumers' changing attitudes towards functional foods. *Food Quality and Preference*, *18*(1), 1–12. doi:10.1016/j.foodqual.2005.06.007

Varun, T. C., Kerutagi, M. G., Kunnal, L. B., Basavaraja, H., Ashalatha, K. V., & Dodamani, M. T. (2009). Consumption patterns of coffee and tea in Karnataka. *Karnataka Journal of Agricultural Sciences*, *22*(4), 824–827.

Walton, J. K. (2001). *The Hospitality Trades: A Social History*. Butterworth-Heinemann.

Weber, I. (2018). Tea for tourists: Cultural capital, representation, and borrowing in the tea culture of mainland China and Taiwan. *Academica Turistica*, *12*(2), 143–154. doi:10.26493/2335-4194.11.143-154

Woyesa, T., & Kumar, S. (2021). Potential of coffee tourism for rural development in Ethiopia: A sustainable livelihood approach. *Environment, Development and Sustainability, 23*(1), 815–832. doi:10.100710668-020-00610-7

Yang, Z. (2007). Tea culture and Sino-American Tea connections. *Chinese American Studies, 1*(2), 8–14.

Yuksel, A., Yuksel, F., & Bilim, Y. (2010). Destination attachment: Effects on customer satisfaction andcognitive, affective and conative loyalty. *Tourism Management, 31*(2), 274–284. doi:10.1016/j.tourman.2009.03.007

Zeppel, H., & Beaumont, N. (2011). *Green Tourism Futures: Climate Change Responses by Australian Government Tourism Agencies* (Vol. 2). University of Southern Queensland, Australian Centre for Sustainable.

Zheng, W., Doyle, T. J., Kushi, L. H., Sellers, T. A., Hong, C. P., & Folsom, A. R. (1996). Tea consumption and cancer incidence in a prospective cohort study of postmenopausal women. *American Journal of Epidemiology, 144*(1), 175–182. doi:10.1093/oxfordjournals.aje.a008905 PMID:8678049

Zhouyiqi, C. and Tao, W. (2012). Application of special tea cultivars in landscape design of ecotourism tea gardens. *J. Crops, 2.*

Chapter 8
Reinforcing Tourism Carrying Capacity Assessments:
Holistic Approach and Future Research Directions

Ravi Sharma
Symbiosis Institute of International Business, Symbiosis International University (Deemed), Pune, India

ABSTRACT

Carrying capacity assessment assists in estimating human intervention thresholds bearable to natural-social ecosystems, specifically in tourism. Earlier studies implemented isolated determining system combinations, namely physical-ecological, socio-cultural, political-economic, and perceptual-psychological, impacting carrying capacity assessments. Results obtained through experts' opinion and systematic literature review meta-analysis suggest a lack of policy-governance components. Imperatively, policy matters governing environmental issues are crucial; especially in tourism, policy-governance systems form holistic components for achieving resilience and enhanced thresholds. This must be well-integrated into the carrying capacity assessment framework, as proposed and outlined as an outcome of this review and in the best interest of society. Validation of the framework using accurate data from the tourism domain through further research will motivate researchers and practitioners.

DOI: 10.4018/978-1-6684-6796-1.ch008

INTRODUCTION

Three categories of "carrying capacity" assessments of an area, namely physical, environmental, and perceptual/psychological - primarily seem to focus upon the negative impacts of physical resource saturation, ecological degradation, and psychological decline of visitors' experience (Pearce, 1989; La Rocca, 2005). World Tourism Organization (WTO) proposed the definition of the term "carrying capacity" as *'the maximum number of people that may visit a tourist destination at the same time, without destroying the physical, economic, socio-cultural environment and an unacceptable decrease in the quality of visitors' satisfaction'* (PAP/RAC, 1997; UNWTO 1981; Corbau, Benedetto, Congiatu, Simeoni, & Carnoni, 2019). Similarly, other researchers and academicians have subsequently attempted to redefine 'carrying capacity' in the context of tourism, such as "...the level of human activity an area can accommodate without the area deteriorating, the resident community being adversely affected, or the quality of visitors' experience declining" (Chamberlain, 1997); while authors defined it in terms of certain threshold levels for tourism activities and presented it beyond which the damage to the bio-physical environment will occur (Clark, 1997); and, presents as the measure of the tolerance value of the destination site beyond which the impacts may become visible due to tourism activities (Middleton and Hawkins, 1998); to name a few.

The above-cited definitions pinpoint the interplay between crucial variables, such as human visitor interventions, physical resource saturation, environmental degradation, and quality of visitor experiences which impact the tourism carrying capacity of a destination. Researchers have also attempted to deconstruct the TCC concept and discuss its relationships which are found in the works of Wall (1982), O'Reilly (1986), Lindberg, McCool, & Stankey, 1997; Lindberg & McCool (1998), McCool & Lime, (2001); Castellani, Sala, & Pitea, (2007) with few studies researching upon environmental impacts of tourism (Bimonte & Punzo, 2011; Zhong, Deng, Song, & Ding, 2011; Zacarias, Williams, & Newton, 2011; Salerno, Viviano, Manfredi, Caroli, Thakuri, & Tartari, 2013; de Sousa, Pereira, da Costa, & Jiménez, 2014; Cimnaghi & Mussini, 2015; Sharma, 2016; Zhang, Li, Su, & Hu, 2017; Prokopiou, Tselentis, & Toanoglou, 2013; Han, 2018). In recent times with the expansion in tourism horizon in different applied sectors such as medical, natural, adventure, protected areas, ecotourism and several others, the associated impact of these activities are widespread and exploding in multiple dimensions. Hence, it will be more appropriate to revisit the carrying capacity assessment and its attributes to address the current tourism scenario. Further, existing assessment methodologies and frameworks are considered in an isolated or dichotomous system, which dilutes the overall effectiveness of carrying capacity assessments. In this regard, through a review of existing literature using meta-analysis approach, this study attempts to identify gaps and evolution of the tourism carrying capacity concept for proposing a more integrated and comprehensive framework for future carrying capacity assessment. The same could help practitioners, researchers, and managers better estimate decisions related to destination management and policy-making.

Background

Dimensions of Tourism Carrying Capacity Assessment

While tourism carrying capacity could be viewed as an aggregative indicator, there are multiple dimensions of theoretical and practical underpinnings to the concept and context to attain depth in decision making and strategic management. Theoretically, existing definitions portray 'carrying capacity as the tipping/threshold point at which a tourist destination experiences adverse or damaging consequence impacted by the quantum of people. Parallel to it, several dimensions accounting for the increasing burden/saturation include physical (e.g., people, infrastructure); psychological (e.g., visitors' satisfaction, perceptions); environmental (e.g., natural resource, place/space, destination type, season); time (e.g., duration of stay); economic (e.g., goods and services, tourism activities); and, socio-cultural (e.g., set of beliefs, customs, practices and behavior; culture). From a conceptual perspective, on the one hand, carrying capacity seems to be easily understood and accepted; however, in practical terms, it displays a myriad of difficulties in implementations leading to multidimensionality; while, on the other such multidimensionality also inherits complexity in management and implementation when viewed as a macro system. Therefore, a comprehensive assessment is desired to manage these, such as the physical-ecological system, socio-cultural system, political-economic system, and perceptual-psychological system.

In a similar vein using the systems perspective, few researchers have viewed tourism in numerous ways, such as a complex interlinked system and adaptive (Farrell & Twining-Ward, 2004; Lacitignola, Petrosillo, Cataldi, & Zurlini, 2007); and systems with the social-ecological phenomenon (Allison & Hobbs, 2006; Bodin, 2017; Gunderson, 2001; Schianetz & Kavanagh, 2008; Walker & Salt, 2012). In this context, economic development and environmental protection are major conflicting objectives (Smith & Eadington, 1992). In the 1960s, Carrying Capacity Assessment (CCA) was introduced as a method of quantifying calculation for defining land-use limits and imposing development regulators in a factual manner (Clark, 1997) to restrict the number of visitors to a tourist destination. O'Reilly (1986) suggests that there is no tourism form entirely without impact. One way to solve this problem is to lay down the limits of acceptable change for the interrelated carrying capacities.

Estimation of appropriateness for deciding tourism carrying capacities using frameworks and calculations has been attempted in a few notable works, namely Limits of Acceptable Change (LAC) (Stankey, Cole, Lucas, Petersen, & Frissell, 1985); Visitor Impact Management (VIM) (Graefe, Kuss, & Vaske, 1990; Farrell & Marion, 2002); and Visitor Experience and Resource Protection (VERP) (Shelby & Heberlein, 1987; National Park Service, 1997; Manning, 2001; Fefer, De Urioste-Stone, Daigle, & Silka, 2018). However, it is observed that while growth and development limits could be flexibly manipulated through regulatory and investment measures, which are usually intrinsic non-modifiable numbers, the tourism carrying capacity concept needs further refurbishment with the integration of additional components, including cultural approaches and policy needs (Salerno, Viviano, Manfredi, Caroli, Thakuri, & Tartari, 2013). From the above discussions, several challenging and intriguing issues emerge in the tourism carrying capacity context, characterizing a need to consider the multidimensionality complexities involved in identifying and relating dimensional requirements, transforming resource capacities into sustainable capabilities, and objectively harnessing the performance efficiency and effectiveness in tourism planning and management. In this study, we endeavor to evaluate critical components that influence the tourism carrying capacity along with their inter-relationships as evidenced by extensive literature review, identify gaps and propose a comprehensive conceptual framework.

This study is a way forward in terms of its presentation exploring the multidimensional relationships of carrying capacity approaches in tourism literature. The interconnectedness and linkages evolved with different environmental, socio-cultural, economic and psychological coverage dimensions. This interconnectedness and relations of evolution will aid in constructing a conceptual development and suggesting gaps via addressing through a proposed framework. Reviewing this concept through a quantitative approach of the meta-analysis will also add to the domain knowledge in sustainable tourism studies, as a thorough meta-analysis was missing in a handful of researches conducted earlier on one specific theme. The application of data analytical tools capable of scientific mining, processing and analysis of data quantitatively to study the link amongst the dimensions will assist in establishing the present gaps, future trends and value addition to the knowledge in the tourism carrying capacity domain with more authenticity. This approach will aid in describing the intellectual construct in the domain research, diffusion, and evolution of knowledge about tourism carrying capacities assessments. Over time, its emerging concepts present the conceptual and thematic dynamics with validation and confidence. The interdisciplinary interconnectedness involving the collaboration dynamics amongst the authors contributed to the tourism carrying capacity studies and will describe future research agendas. This agglomeration will provide a robust research trajectory in a holistic approach for future investigations.

Analyzing Gaps in Existing Tourism Carrying Capacity Assessment

An intrinsic need for an in-depth literature review was crucial to understand multiple dimensions of TCC assessment techniques in vogue and inform empirical research about the depth of recent literature, its application, and its state of the art. In this regard, the systematic literature review approach suggested by Tranfield, Denyer, & Smart (2003) helps develop evidence-based knowledge through a systematic review implemented in our search for knowledge. The core research questions from this quest are "What are the various dimensions/constructs that impact the tourism carrying capacity assessments?" What association linkages of study categories are covered in the tourism carrying capacity assessments? and "Can we propose an extended tourism carrying capacity framework for future assessments?"

An informal process involving experts' opinion was adopted to prepare for the review. A focused group discussion was conducted with a panel comprising eighteen domain experts from multidisciplinary streams such as environmental sciences, tourism officials, community development/social anthropologists, forest officials, not-for-profit organization representatives, researchers, and academicians. As a panel discussion outcome, the experts highlighted ecological, sociological, and behavioral carrying capacity as primary constructs in tourism carrying capacity assessments. The other constructs prominently used in the literature on tourism carrying capacity are environmental carrying capacity, economic carrying capacity and physical carrying capacity. To further validate the findings, we implemented a Scopus-based database search for analyzing existing literature and identifying gaps in carrying capacity assessment studies. A comprehensive and structured search was conducted using pre-determined keywords and search strings relating to the domain, as elaborated in the following section.

Literature Search and Data Processing

The literature search was conducted to explore the tourism carrying capacity contributions along with the trajectory development in knowledge from 1982 to April 2020. The investigation was performed using the Scopus research database, a widely used and comprehensive database used in the academic world. The retrieved results can uncover the intellectual structure over time (Santa Soriano, Álvarez, & Valdés, 2018) and permit the evaluation of the growth of a given research field (Ellegaard & Wallin, 2015). Recent trend employing co-citation analysis is a new form of meta-analytical research of the literature (Kim & McMillan, 2008). The citation and co-citation analysis help identify the zones of the most pioneering research work and further map the research output based on the previous influential work (Fetscherin & Heinrich, 2015; Fetscherin & Usunier, 2012).

For this study, by searching the terms in a combination of keywords "tourism" AND "carrying capacity*," with "framework*" OR "assessment*," as a string search to retrieve the articles in the titles, abstracts, or keywords of the Scopus database in English language articles before April 2020. The probe enables the researchers to identify the relevant to tourism carrying capacities focusing on assessments and application of frameworks. Further applying the inclusion criteria, viz., consideration of final published papers and only journal papers result in 267 articles (N=267). The bibliographic information of retrieved documents was downloaded for further quantitative meta-analyses in the *.bib* format (*Figure 1*).

Text, Topic Mining, and Citation Analysis

The *.bib* format data file is further used for the meta-analysis, including the bibliometric analysis, thematic evolution (historiograph), and factorial analysis using the R- studio package. The *.bib* file data is first used for citation and co-citation matrix using BibExcel software and further transformed into an excel sheet to sort the papers based on the selected authors having the highest citations, further normalizing the sorted data for cluster analyses. The BibExcel is open-source academic bibliographic software developed by the OllePersson (Åström, Danell, Larsen, Schneider, & Schlemmer, 2009). Using the BibExcel and the frequency counts for the citations for the publication under investigation, the processing and 'cut-off' point based on the highest cited papers were established. For selection, the top articles with minimum of three or more citations were selected, resulting in a total of 43 articles for meta-analyses. This result in the generation of a co-citation matrix, which is further exported to the statistical analysis package IBM SPSS®v.21 software.

The co-citation matrix using SPSS software was normalized, and the co-word analysis and multivariate analyses were performed to form the clusters of the highest cited publications. The advantage of this cluster would be to identify the relevant clusters and assist in exploring the evolution of research domains and future research directions through gap identification in tourism carrying capacity assessments and components used. The full- texts of these clusters of most-cited authors were also reviewed qualitatively in the traditional analysis for affective content analysis.

Figure 1. Methodology for data retrieval and meta-analysis of tourism carrying capacity research

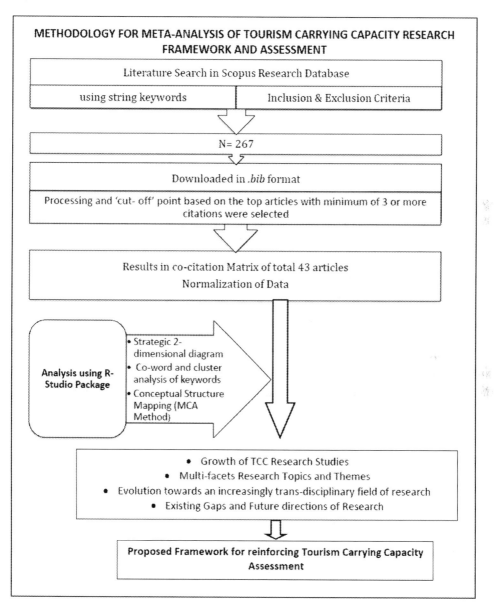

Clusters and Mapping

The R-studio package was used for the co-word analyses and clustering of keywords. The co-word analysis is used for the mapping of science and linkage associations. The mapping of co-word analysis is revealed because of the keyword interconnections, which are reflected as clusters (themes). The cluster highlights the research themes and is characterized by the parameter's 'density' and 'centrality' (Cahlik, 2000; Coulter, Monarch, & Konda, 1998). The classifying of these themes into four groups is revealed through the strategic two-dimension diagram, which is drawn from both median and mean values of centrality and density, where the x-axis represents the centrality and the y-axis as the density of keyword rank values (Cahlik, 2000; Callon, Courtial, & Laville, 1991; Courtial, 1994; He 1999). The centrality (called Callon's Centrality) measures the external strength and association to other themes using the degree of interaction of the network with other networks (Callon, Courtial, & Laville, 1991). This provides the importance of themes in the development of the entire research field in question.

On the other hand, the density (also called Callon's density) majorly focuses on measuring the internal strength of the network. This strength is based on keywords belonging to the theme and the number of keywords in the themes, thereby indicating the theme's development. The four quadrants of the two-dimensional strategic diagram can be understood as a set of research themes where each quadrant expresses the different themes.

The four quadrants of the two-dimensional strategic diagram represent the following themes and trends of the research field (Cobo, López-Herrera, Herrera-Viedma, & Herrera, 2011; Cahlik, 2000):

- The upper right quadrant represents the *motor themes* of the domain research, i.e., they are both developed and essential for the mapping and structuring of a research field as they are related externally to apply concepts and closely related conceptual themes.
- The lower-right keyword clusters in the quadrant represent the basic and transversal themes, which are essential but are not developed. They might be considered necessary for future research or trends in research.
- The upper-left quadrant keyword clusters represent the well-developed themes with internal ties but no external connections. They are peripheral and very specialized in characteristics of only marginal importance.
- The lower-left quadrant keyword clusters represent weakly developed themes having low centrality and density values but marginal importance. They generally represent either emerging or disappearing themes.

In addition to co-word conceptual mapping, the exploratory multivariate technique using multiple correspondence analysis (MCA) was applied for the numerical analysis of multivariate categorical data and conceptual structure graphical presentation of the cluster themes (Greenacre & Blasius, 2006; Lebart, Morineau, & Warwick, 1984) predominant in the field of tourism carrying capacity assessments. The graph generated by the multiple correspondence analyses (MCA) of identified topics using the *conceptual structure*-function of the R-package were clusters express the common themes (Aria & Cuccurullo, 2017). The words are plotted on a two-dimensional map. These are represented based on the relative positions of the points and the keyword distribution along the dimensions (Dim1 and Dim 2), representing the association with similar distribution (Cuccurullo, Aria, & Sarto, 2016).

The analysis and multivariate analysis will aid in understanding the knowledge development, including growth in tourism carrying capacity studies; the multi-access of the research themes and evolution depicting multidisciplinary facets of carrying capacity research. The discussion and analysis will explore the significant research gaps and lead to future research directions, including a proposal of a framework for future carrying capacity assessments based on the results revealed.

Table 1. Descriptive of relevant publications in tourism carrying capacity assessment studies (n=267)

Description	Results
Documents (Journal articles)	267
Sources (Only journals)	138
Author's Keywords	790
Period	1982 - 2020
Average citations/ documents	17.52
Authors	716
Author Appearances	798
multi-authored documents	658
Single-authored documents	58
Documents/ Author	0.373
Authors / Document	2.68
Co-Authors / Documents	2.99
Collaboration Index	3.21

FINDINGS AND FUTURE RESEARCH DIRECTIONS

A Rapidly Growing Interest in Tourism Carrying Capacity Studies

Seven relevant papers were published annually, each getting 17.52 citations per document. The average contributor per document is 2.68, having a collaboration index of 3.21 from 1982 to 2020 (**Table 1**). Those papers were published in a total of 138 source titles. The annual scientific production growth is 8.6% in tourism carrying capacity research.

The trend and change detections of annual publications show that there has been rapidly growing interest in TCC studies since year 1990s (*Figure 2a*). Most of the top contributing sources are WIT Transactions on Ecology and environment and Sustainability (Switzerland), which proceeded by the Journal of Sustainable Tourism and the Asia Pacific Journal of Tourism Research. Also, the surge in growth of keywords like 'carrying capacity and 'tourism carrying capacity' shows growth from the late 1990s. Sustainable tourism, sustainability and sustainable development show growth from 2000 (*Figure 2b*). Regarding source impact (h-Index), the 'Journal of Sustainable Tourism' (h-index= 11) contributed the highest with total citations of 474. This is followed by 'Tourism Management' (h-Index=8), 'Journal of Environmental Management (h-Index= 7) and 'Annals of Tourism Research (h-Index= 6) in terms of both research output and citations.

Multi-Facets Research Topics and Themes

As the research topics are identified through the titles, abstracts and keywords, the results reveal the thematic segregation and advances in tourism carrying capacity research. The significant issues include major components of tourism carrying capacity approaches, viz., physical carrying capacity, tourism carrying capacity, ecological carrying capacity and social carrying capacity. Towards the sustainable tourism studies, the majority of topic coverage includes ecotourism, sustainable development through nature-based tourism and other topics like impacts and over-tourism (*Figure 3*). The co-word analysis through the strategic diagram depicts the different evolution and linkages of the area in the tourism carrying capacity application field. These areas can be defined in the broad categories of essential themes, specialized (niche) themes, emerging (or disappearing) themes, and motor themes based on the mean values of the Callon's centrality and Callon's density and are represented in the lower right quadrant, upper left quadrant, lower left quadrant and upper right quadrant respectively of *Figure 3*.

Reinforcing Tourism Carrying Capacity Assessments

Figure 2. a) Source growth of top five source titles from 1982-2020 b) Keyword growth based on occurrence from 1982 to 2020
(Source: Scopus Database)

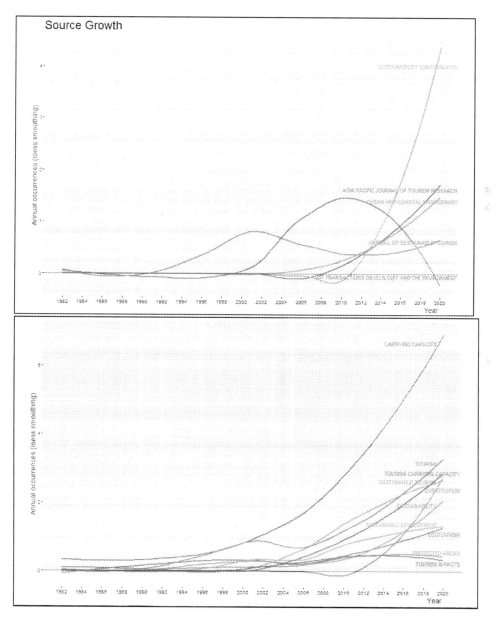

Basic Themes: The study depicts five significant groups of basic themes still relevant in tourism management. These groups involve recreation management and threshold studies, the types of tourism (e.g., nature-based tourism, rural tourism etc.) and sustainable development linkages, and the remaining groups predominantly comprising of carrying capacity types in different aspects like cultural heritage, environment, and economic development linking with sustainability in tourism studies. The different types of carrying capacities cover the tourism carrying capacity application, coastal carrying capacity and threshold values as a part of different studies.

Specialized niche themes: Under the carrying capacity applications, the physical carrying capacity and social carrying capacity have been evolved as the extension of basic themes to study the broad dimensions of environment, economic growth and understanding of the tourism area life cycle (management). The carrying capacity studies focus on protected areas and coastal studies in terms of determining ecological footprints as the key motor themes from the niche domain of carrying capacity study as having closer centrality and density co-word values.

No developed motor themes are projected from the study in the tourism carrying capacity aspect. Still, the ecological footprints and sustainability themes have provided the future of research and shown the capability of growth in the coming decade. Similarly, the study has revealed that the tourism carrying capacity and its association with other domains are still in demand. These topics and research are still pertinent in the current context. This is concluded through the strategic diagram not showing any grouping in the lower left quadrant, which generally depicts the *disappearing themes* in the research journey of the topic.

On the other hand, the key focus and predominant types of carrying capacity widely studied are physical (including ecological/environment) and social (including cultural) carrying capacity categories. The perception or psychological carrying capacities are not explored to the potential presented by the fact that these keywords' strength is fragile and therefore not shown in the thematic groups of the study. The topic explicitly related to tourism footprint, sustainability and ecotourism using the carrying capacity study seems to have experienced an extension and advancements in applications in recent times.

The results revealed by applying higher-level statistics and quantitative analysis using MCA suggest the same topics in the conceptual mapping structure of authors' keywords (Figure 4). The boundary of clusters shows the more focused themes and their interconnectedness with the other topics. The results of these factorial analyses are interpreted based on the relative positions of the points (keywords in the conceptual structure map) and their distribution along the dimensions. The keywords are more similar in distribution the closer they are represented on the map.

The major focus of tourism capacity is on social, environmental, and tourism carrying capacities, with the majority of the studies applying these approaches for the conservation, protection or destination management. The key prime focus of these applications remains protected areas and beach management. The sub domains

Figure 3. The strategic diagram of thematic groups and evolution of carrying capacity-based studies

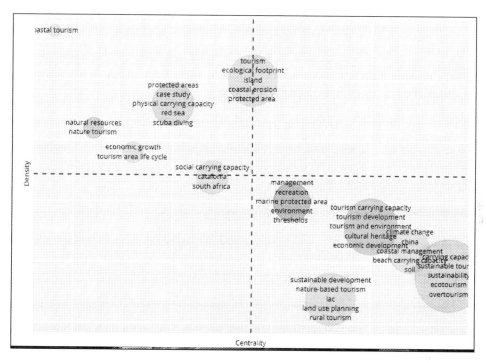

explored under the destination management by carrying capacity assessments were visitors' management, highlighting visitors' impact and overcrowding threshold, and identifying indicators for estimating destinations' carrying capacities. The same approaches have also shown higher occurrence in terms of ecotourism development and sustainable tourism planning. Determining the threshold number of visitors or the environmental component remains the core and basic foundation of carrying capacity assessment approaches in tourism studies. Sustainability, climate change and ecological footprinting studies emerged as the recent trend in the application of carrying capacity studies.

Evolution Towards an Increasingly Transdisciplinary Field of Research

To further understand the genesis of knowledge on the application of tourism carrying capacity assessments and converging literature development seems to be emerging, we employed the historiographical compilation and identified the most influential contribution in the field. This is evident by the historical direct citation network of the top thirty articles that are most cited within the N=267 retrieved, as discussed in the methodology section (*Figure 5*). The historical top-30 citation network allowed us to answer one of the most challenging questions- what are the key areas and types covered and converged during the TCC assessment as a comprehensive field of knowledge. Also, diving into the full- texts of the top-30 keystone papers helps understand how their research work has evolved. This historical network represents the total number of publications per year and citation scores like the global citation network (GCS) and local citation network (LCS). The total four interlinkages of the top papers appear to form a flow of evolution of literature knowledge growth in the TCC assessments and provide a broad spectrum of research providing the foundation backbone to the emerged studies (*Figure 5*).

Figure 4. Clustering of topics (factorial map) identified from the authors' keywords of the sampled papers from the Scopus research Database. The graph generated by the exploratory multivariate technique- MCA using the conceptual structure-function of the R-package where the resulted clusters highlight the common themes
(Aria & Cuccurullo, 2017)

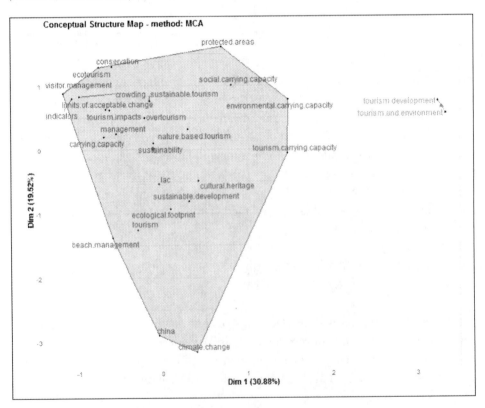

The concept of carrying capacity adopted from earlier studies was widely applied and cited in the 1990s, forming the foundation for most studies in terms of author impact presented in the form of GCS. The critical focus of the studies in this time was focused on describing the overview of the concepts of carrying capacity with the objectives of resource management (Farrell & Runyan, 1991) and the advantages of tourism impact relating tourism associated problems with the exceeding social and environmental carrying capacities predominantly (Zurick, 1992). The other approach used parallel to carrying capacity was the 'threshold' approach for the recreational activities and environment (Davis & Tisdell, 1996). These approaches threshold or environmental or sociological domains were further translated and cited by the upcoming researchers for translating environmental carrying capacity assessment to tourism development strategies (Brown, Turner, Hameed, & Bateman, 1997). Further, the environmental and sociological domain concept was enhanced by the extension of ecological and cultural carrying capacity for sustainable tourism (Brown, Turner, Hameed, & Bateman, 1997). The Papageorgiou & Brotherton (1999) contributes to the application of ecological and another concept perceptual carrying capacity for developing a management planning framework.

These concepts of physical-ecological and socio-cultural carrying capacities were extended to different recreational or natural destinations by the researchers with higher impact in the forthcoming as the application of carrying capacity approaches (Simón, Narangajavana, & Marques, 2004). Herath (2002) further advocates the use of analytical carrying capacity as crucial for the decision analysis techniques for better planning of ecotourism and natural resource management along with sociological perceptions and visitors' satisfaction. On similar themes, the management of carrying capacity for the tourist attractions was advocated by (Manning, Wang, Valliere, Lawson, & Newman, 2002). The market-driven management and factors and the political perspectives of carrying capacity assessment were addressed for the heritage sites (Doorne, 2000). The carrying capacity application is explored for various recreational coastal areas and activities like sea diving and the acceptable rate of diving on coral reefs (Zakai & Chadwick-Furman, 2002) and quantifying the acceptable levels of visitors using the carrying capacity concept (Leujak & Ormond, 2008). For the coastal areas, the social and ecological carrying capacity with perception and behavior of visitors (Leujak & Ormond, 2007) and quantifying the impacts of socio-economic characteristics (Chung, Au, & Qiu, 2013) were used as an extension of knowledge in carrying capacity concept.

Apart from coastal areas, the concept application is also well established and developed over the period of time for assessing tourism carrying capacities of natural areas for providing advantages in maintaining administrative-economic sustainability and community-based support (Lobo et al., 2013), perception carrying capacity for determining acceptability for national parks (Neuts & Nijkamp, 2012). This is presented as an application extension of the research conducted to understand the nature of limits of growth and draw a relationship between sustainable tourism development (Saarinen, 2006) and visitor's perception and experience of the environment and physical infrastructure (Sæþórsdóttir, 2010).

Recreation carrying capacity for the management of tourist destination management and practice of carrying capacity assessments by considering the different aspects of physical-ecological and socio-cultural carrying capacity variables (Zacarias, Williams, & Newton, 2011) which has resulted in the estimation of carrying capacity for the environment of different destinations like beaches and coastlines (Chen & Teng, 2016). The presentation of potential solutions from the established carrying capacity and in case of the failure of carrying capacity is advocated in a study leading to practical implementation, planning and policy implications by sustainability initiatives at destinations facing political and socio-economic challenges (Larson & Poudyal, 2012; Jurado et al., 2012). Recent studies have included climate-induced changes like sea-level rise to enhance the destinations and increase the recreational carrying capacity of the destination sites (Jiménez, 2017).

Figure 5. Historiographic representation of top-30 articles in tourism carrying capacity assessments

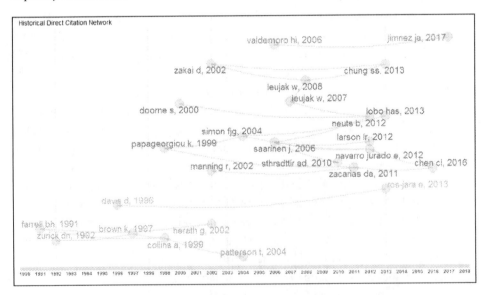

The historical citation result suggests and complements our earlier co-word analysis findings that the major groups of carrying capacity assessments used were physical-ecological and socio-cultural carrying capacities as a key aspect for exploring the objectives. The perception (psychological) and perpetual carrying capacity studies and socio-economic carrying capacity domain were widely used. The political and administrative carrying capacity still has a long way to explore. It has the potential to develop a holistic framework for carrying out a capacity assessment for sustainable tourism management and planning. There are no indications of any policy- governance-related indicator sets used as carrying capacity assessments in tourism development.

CONCLUSION

A brief review of the carrying capacity assessment method in the tourism domain is undertaken in this policy-related context. The synthesis of experts' opinions through focus group discussion presented three important constructs widely used for carrying capacity studies. This is also evidenced through the systematic review of existing literature (Scopus), wherein the three major constructs viz. physical, economic and environmental/ecological components were highly focused on carrying capacity studies. Additionally, socio-cultural and political components also got fair coverage. This review, through the research approaches, suggests that the "policy" and "governance" indicators have not been considered while carrying out global tourism carrying capacity studies. The assessment of tourism carrying capacity in absentia of a policy-governance component does not represent an integrated and robust analysis system. This gap, therefore, calls for consideration of the proposed extended framework for tourism carrying capacity.

Systems Theory and Resilience

Interdisciplinary study of systems is naturally cohesive, interrelated, interdependent parts (natural or artificial), surrounded and influenced by their environment. In this regard, Von Bertalanffy (1969) developed a 'general systems theory' that could explain all systems in all fields of Science for knowledgeable actions. Consolidating the above components, it could be logically understood that systems ecology and tourism carrying capacity should interplay in an environment conducive to all its elements and stakeholders. Resilience in carrying capacity assessment and sustainability in tourism management systems invariably will assist in timely calibration and mitigating unforeseen risks, thus quick recovering from impending crises. 'Resilience' as a concept within systems ecology was first attempted in the 1970s as an operational risk mitigation strategy and is more recently being pursued in financial, urban and environmental security discourses (Walker & Cooper, 2011). It also offers an interdisciplinary examination of governance in linked social-ecological systems, especially where minimal attention in planning theory scholarship to environmental and ecological considerations is a driving concern (Wilkinson, 2012).

Proposal for Reinforcing Tourism Carrying Capacity Assessments Through Policy and Governance Systems

Subsequent to the analysis and synthesis of results as discussed in earlier sections, a need is emphasized for effective and efficient policy implementations and succinct governance measures that could lucidly interplay among these existing systems in totality. This will enable in achieving optimum tourism carrying capacities. It is difficult to formulate policies that could guarantee sustained tourism without impacting its systems ecology. Earlier reviews on the tourism topic (Witt & Witt, 1995; Kulendran & King, 1997) use classical black-box econometric models which forecast demand for number of tourist arrivals or services as a function of income, prices, transportation costs and a few other qualitative indicators. In this regard, an extensive literature review conducted by Lim (1997) finds that these studies do not account for the environmental factor and concentrate on economic factors only.

Emphasis on Policy-Governance Systems

The government and public institutions have been prompting in policy making and instituting initiatives for tourist destinations for a long time. Few suggested policy indicators of measurement include regulatory measures, such as environmental protection and resource utilization (Farsari, Butler, & Szivas, 2011), legal sanction of policies and institutional regulatory mechanisms (Buckley, 2010; Blagescu & Young, 2006; de Oliveira, 2003), and public-private partnership to promote sustainable tourism (Pastras & Bramwell, 2013; Dredge, 2006; Hall, 1999). However, there is still a yawning gap in coordination among different stakeholder actors, institutional and administrative arrangements, structures, practices and policies that assess tourism carrying capacities and oversee the other interrelated systems. In light of this scenario, we emphasize the integration of the policy-governance system overarching all other interacting systems towards better tourism carrying capacities.

Proposed Tourism Carrying Capacity Assessment Framework

A conceptual framework is proposed for tourism carrying capacity assessment (refer to **Fig. 6**) which holistically includes multiple dimensions interconnected with different systems and managed by policy-governance systems.

Figure 6. Tourism carrying capacity assessment framework
(Source: Author)

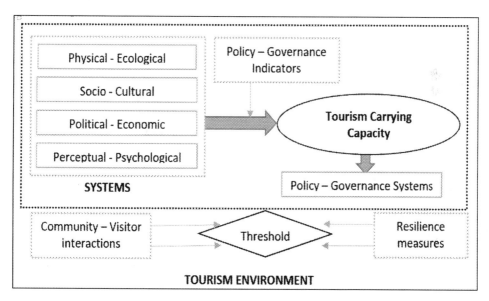

The study suggests that policy-governance systems need to be reinforced as a significant system determinant in addition to others for holistic carrying capacity assessments. It integrates crucial system determinants towards tourism carrying capacity assessment depicted through a conceptual framework that has social and system implications for several stakeholders of the society. This framework also needs further validation by analyzing and synthesizing carrying capacity data for the indicators and scale assessment. This will enhance the reliability and replicability of the carrying capacity assessment framework, which is foreseen in future research directions. However, the scale selection and reliability of indicators at the initial stages of assessment will remain a challenge.

ACKNOWLEDGMENT

The author is grateful to Prof. Venkatesh Iyengar, for his support and suggestions for draft paper structuring and proofreading of the manuscript.

REFERENCES

Allison, H. E., & Hobbs, R. J. (2006). *Science and Policy in Natural Resource Management: Understanding system complexity*. Cambridge University Press. doi:10.1017/CBO9780511618062

Aria, M., & Cuccurullo, C. (2017). bibliometrix: An R-tool for comprehensive science mapping analysis. *Journal of Informetrics, 11*(4), 959–975. doi:10.1016/j.joi.2017.08.007

Åström, F., Danell, R., Larsen, B., Schneider, J. W., & Schlemmer, B. (2009). *Celebrating Scholarly Communication Studies: A Festschrift for Olle Persson at his 60th Birthday*. Research Portal. https://portal.research.lu.se/ws/files/5902071/1458992.pdf

Bertalanffy, L. V. (1969). General system theory: Foundations, development, applications.

Bimonte, S., & Punzo, L. F. (2011). Tourism, residents' attitudes and perceived carrying capacity with an experimental study in five Tuscan destinations. *International Journal of Sustainable Development, 14*(3-4), 242–261. doi:10.1504/IJSD.2011.041964

Blagescu, M., & Young, J. (2006). *Capacity development for policy advocacy: current thinking and approaches among agencies supporting civil society organisations*. Overseas Development Institute.

Bodin, Ö. (2017). Collaborative environmental governance: Achieving collective action in social-ecological systems. *Science, 357*(6352), eaan1114. doi:10.1126cience.aan1114 PMID:28818915

Brown, K., Turner, R. K., Hameed, H., & Bateman, I. A. N. (1997). Environmental carrying capacity and tourism development in the Maldives and Nepal. *Environmental Conservation, 24*(4), 316–325. doi:10.1017/S0376892997000428

Buckley, R. (2010). *Conservation tourism*. CAB International Publishing. doi:10.1079/9781845936655.0000

Cahlik, T. (2000). Comparison of the maps of Science. *Scientometrics*, *49*(3), 373–387. doi:10.1023/A:1010581421990

Callon, M., Courtial, J. P., & Laville, F. (1991). Co-word analysis as a tool for describing the network of interactions between basic and technological research: The case of polymer chemistry. *Scientometrics*, *22*(1), 155–205. doi:10.1007/BF02019280

Castellani, V., Sala, S., & Pitea, D. (2007). A new method for tourism carrying capacity assessment. *WIT Transactions on Ecology and the Environment*, *106*, 365–374. doi:10.2495/ECO070341

Chamberlain, K. (1997). *Carrying capacity*. UNEP Industry and Environment, 8.

Chen, C. L., & Teng, N. (2016). Management priorities and carrying capacity at a high-use beach from tourists' perspectives: A way towards sustainable beach tourism. *Marine Policy*, *74*, 213–219. doi:10.1016/j.marpol.2016.09.030

Chung, S. S., Au, A., & Qiu, J. W. (2013). Understanding the underwater behaviour of scuba divers in Hong Kong. *Environmental Management*, *51*(4), 824–837. doi:10.100700267-013-0023-y PMID:23471632

Cimnaghi, E., & Mussini, P. (2015). An application of tourism carrying capacity assessment at two Italian cultural heritage sites. *Journal of Heritage Tourism*, *10*(3), 302–313. doi:10.1080/1743873X.2014.988158

Clark, J. (1997). *Coastal Zone Management Handbook*. Lewis Publishers.

Cobo, M. J., López-Herrera, A. G., Herrera-Viedma, E., & Herrera, F. (2011). An approach for detecting, quantifying, and visualizing the evolution of a research field: A practical application to the fuzzy sets theory field. *Journal of Informetrics*, *5*(1), 146–166. doi:10.1016/j.joi.2010.10.002

Corbau, C., Benedetto, G., Congiatu, P. P., Simeoni, U., & Carboni, D. (2019). Tourism analysis at Asinara Island (Italy): Carrying capacity and web evaluations in two pocket beaches. *Ocean and Coastal Management*, *169*, 27–36. doi:10.1016/j.ocecoaman.2018.12.004

Coulter, N., Monarch, I., & Konda, S. (1998). Software engineering as seen through its research literature: A study in co-word analysis. *Journal of the American Society for Information Science*, *49*(13), 1206–1223. doi:10.1002/(SICI)1097-4571(1998)49:13<1206::AID-ASI7>3.0.CO;2-F

Courtial, J. (1994). A coword analysis of scientometrics. *Scientometrics*, *31*(3), 251–260. doi:10.1007/BF02016875

Davis, D., & Tisdell, C. (1996). Economic management of recreational scuba diving and the environment. *Journal of Environmental Management, 48*(3), 229–248. doi:10.1006/jema.1996.0075

de Oliveira, J. A. P. (2003). Governmental responses to tourism development: Three Brazilian case studies. *Tourism Management, 24*(1), 97–110. doi:10.1016/S0261-5177(02)00046-8

de Sousa, R. C., Pereira, L. C., da Costa, R. M., & Jiménez, J. A. (2014). Tourism carrying capacity on estuarine beaches in the Brazilian Amazon region. *Journal of Coastal Research, 70*(sp1), 545–550. doi:10.2112/SI70-092.1

Doorne, S. (2000). Caves, cultures and crowds: Carrying capacity meets consumer sovereignty. *Journal of Sustainable Tourism, 8*(2), 116–130. doi:10.1080/09669580008667352

Dredge, D. (2006). Policy networks and the local organisation of tourism. *Tourism Management, 27*(2), 269–280. doi:10.1016/j.tourman.2004.10.003

Ellegaard, O., & Wallin, J. A. (2015). The bibliometric analysis of scholarly production: How great is the impact? *Scientometrics, 105*(3), 1809–1831. doi:10.100711192-015-1645-z PMID:26594073

Farrell, B. H., & Runyan, D. (1991). Ecology and tourism. *Annals of Tourism Research, 18*(1), 26–40. doi:10.1016/0160-7383(91)90037-C

Farrell, B. H., & Twining-Ward, L. (2004). Reconceptualizing tourism. *Annals of Tourism Research, 31*(2), 274–295. doi:10.1016/j.annals.2003.12.002

Farrell, T. A., & Marion, J. L. (2002). The protected area visitor impact management (PAVIM) framework: A simplified process for making management decisions. *Journal of Sustainable Tourism, 10*(1), 31–51. doi:10.1080/09669580208667151

Farsari, I., Butler, R. W., & Szivas, E. (2011). Complexity in tourism policies: A cognitive mapping approach. *Annals of Tourism Research, 38*(3), 1110–1134. doi:10.1016/j.annals.2011.03.007

Fefer, J., De Urioste-Stone, S. M., Daigle, J., & Silka, L. (2018). Understanding the perceived effectiveness of applying the visitor experience and resource protection (VERP) framework for recreation planning: A multi-case study in US National Parks. *Qualitative Report, 23*(7), 1561–1582. doi:10.46743/2160-3715/2018.3228

Fetscherin, M., & Heinrich, D. (2015). Consumer brand relationships research: A bibliometric citation meta-analysis. *Journal of Business Research, 68*(2), 380–390. doi:10.1016/j.jbusres.2014.06.010

Fetscherin, M., & Usunier, J. (2012). Corporate branding: An interdisciplinary literature review. *European Journal of Marketing*, 46(5), 733–753. doi:10.1108/03090561211212494

Graefe, A., Kuss, F. R., & Vaske, J. (1990). *Visitor Impact Management: A Review of Research* (Vol. 1). National Parks and Conservation Association.

Greenacre, M., & Blasius, J. (2006). *Multiple correspondence analysis and related methods*. CRC press. doi:10.1201/9781420011319

Gunderson, L. H. (2001). *Panarchy: understanding transformations in human and natural systems*. Island press.

Hall, C. M. (1999). Rethinking collaboration and partnership: A public policy perspective. *Journal of Sustainable Tourism*, 7(3-4), 274–289. doi:10.1080/09669589908667340

Han, J. (2018). Carrying capacity of low carbon tourism environment in coastal areas from the perspective of ecological efficiency. *Journal of Coastal Research*, (83), 199–203.

He, Q. (1999). Knowledge discovery through co-word analysis. *Library Trends*, 48, 133–159.

Herath, G. (2002). Research methodologies for planning ecotourism and nature conservation. *Tourism Economics*, 8(1), 77–101. doi:10.5367/000000002101298007

Jiménez, J. A., Valdemoro, H. I., Bosom, E., Sánchez-Arcilla, A., & Nicholls, R. J. (2017). Impacts of sea-level rise-induced erosion on the Catalan coast. *Regional Environmental Change*, 17(2), 593–603. doi:10.100710113-016-1052-x

Jurado, E. N., Tejada, M. T., García, F. A., González, J. C., Macías, R. C., Peña, J. D., & Gutiérrez, O. M. (2012). Carrying capacity assessment for tourist destinations. Methodology for the creation of synthetic indicators applied in a coastal area. *Tourism Management*, 33(6), 1337–1346. doi:10.1016/j.tourman.2011.12.017

Kim, J., & McMillan, S. J. (2008). Evaluation of internet advertising research: A bibliometric analysis of citations from key sources. *Journal of Advertising*, 37(1), 99–112. doi:10.2753/JOA0091-3367370108

Kulendran, N., & King, M. L. (1997). Forecasting international quarterly tourist flows using error-correction and time-series models. *International Journal of Forecasting*, 13(3), 319–327. doi:10.1016/S0169-2070(97)00020-4

La Rocca, R. A. (2005). Mass Tourism and Urban System: Some suggestions to manage the impacts on the city. [eRTR]. *Ereview of Tourism Research, 3*(1), 8–17.

Lacitignola, D., Petrosillo, I., Cataldi, M., & Zurlini, G. (2007). Modelling socio-ecological tourism-based systems for sustainability. *Ecological Modelling, 206*(1-2), 191–204. doi:10.1016/j.ecolmodel.2007.03.034

Larson, L. R., & Poudyal, N. C. (2012). Developing sustainable tourism through adaptive resource management: A case study of Machu Picchu, Peru. *Journal of Sustainable Tourism, 20*(7), 917–938. doi:10.1080/09669582.2012.667217

Lebart, L., Morineau, A., & Warwick, K. M. (1984). *Multivariate descriptive statistical analysis: Correspondence analysis and related techniques for large matrices*. Wiley., doi:10.1002/asm.3150050207

Leujak, W., & Ormond, R. F. (2007). Visitor perceptions and the shifting social carrying capacity of South Sinai's coral reefs. *Environmental Management, 39*(4), 472–489. doi:10.100700267-006-0040-1 PMID:17318694

Leujak, W., & Ormond, R. F. (2008). Quantifying acceptable levels of visitor use on Red Sea reef flats. *Aquatic Conservation, 18*(6), 930–944. doi:10.1002/aqc.870

Lim, C. (1997). Review of international tourism demand models. *Annals of Tourism Research, 24*(4), 835–849. doi:10.1016/S0160-7383(97)00049-2

Lindberg, K., McCool, S., & Stankey, G. (1997). Rethinking carrying capacity. *Annals of Tourism Research, 24*(2), 461–465. doi:10.1016/S0160-7383(97)80018-7

Lindberg, K., & McCool, S. F. (1998). A critique of environmental carrying capacity as a means of managing the effects of tourism development. *Environmental Conservation, 25*(4), 291–292. doi:10.1017/S0376892998000368

Lobo, H. A. S., Trajano, E., de Alcântara Marinho, M., Bichuette, M. E., Scaleante, J. A. B., Scaleante, O. A. F., & Laterza, F. V. (2013). Projection of tourist scenarios onto fragility maps: Framework for determination of provisional tourist carrying capacity in a Brazilian show cave. *Tourism Management, 35*, 234–243. doi:10.1016/j.tourman.2012.07.008

Manning, R. (2001). Programs that work. Visitor experience and resource protection: A framework for managing the carrying capacity of National Parks. *Journal of Park and Recreation Administration, 19*(1), 93–108.

Manning, R., Wang, B., Valliere, W., Lawson, S., & Newman, P. (2002). Research to estimate and manage carrying capacity of a tourist attraction: A study of Alcatraz Island. *Journal of Sustainable Tourism, 10*(5), 388–404. doi:10.1080/09669580208667175

McCool, S. F., & Lime, D. W. (2001). Tourism carrying capacity: Tempting fantasy or useful reality? *Journal of Sustainable Tourism*, *9*(5), 372–388. doi:10.1080/09669580108667409

Middleton, V. T., & Hawkins, R. (1998). *Sustainable tourism: A marketing perspective.* Routledge.

National Park Service. (1997). *A Summary of the Visitor Experience and Resource Protection (VERP) Framework. Publication no. NPS D-1214.* NPS Denver Service Center.

Neuts, B., & Nijkamp, P. (2012). Tourist crowding perception and acceptability in cities: An applied modelling study on Bruges. *Annals of Tourism Research*, *39*(4), 2133–2153. doi:10.1016/j.annals.2012.07.016

O'Reilly, A. M. (1986). Tourism carrying capacity: Concept and issues. *Tourism Management*, *7*(4), 254–258. doi:10.1016/0261-5177(86)90035-X

Papageorgiou, K., & Brotherton, I. (1999). A management planning framework based on ecological, perceptual and economic carrying capacity: The case study of Vikos-Aoos National Park, Greece. *Journal of Environmental Management*, *56*(4), 271–284. doi:10.1006/jema.1999.0285

PAP/RAC. (1997). Guidelines for Carrying Capacity Assessment for Tourism in Mediterranean Coastal Areas. PAP-9/1997/G.1. Split, (Priority Actions Programme Regional Activity Centre).

Pastras, P., & Bramwell, B. (2013). A strategic-relational approach to tourism policy. *Annals of Tourism Research*, *43*, 390–414. doi:10.1016/j.annals.2013.06.009

Pearce, D. C. (1989). *Tourist Development.* Longman Scientific and Technical Publishers.

Prokopiou, D. G., Tselentis, B. S., & Toanoglou, M. (2013). Carrying capacity assessment in tourism: The case of Northern Sporades islands. *WIT Transactions on Ecology and the Environment*, *169*, 115–123. doi:10.2495/CP130101

Saarinen, J. (2006). Traditions of sustainability in tourism studies. *Annals of Tourism Research*, *33*(4), 1121–1140. doi:10.1016/j.annals.2006.06.007

Sæþórsdóttir, A. D. (2010). Planning nature tourism in Iceland based on tourist attitudes. *Tourism Geographies*, *12*(1), 25–52. doi:10.1080/14616680903493639

Salerno, F., Viviano, G., Manfredi, E. C., Caroli, P., Thakuri, S., & Tartari, G. (2013). Multiple Carrying Capacities from a management-oriented perspective to operationalize sustainable tourism in protected areas. *Journal of Environmental Management, 128*, 116–125. doi:10.1016/j.jenvman.2013.04.043 PMID:23728182

Salerno, F., Viviano, G., Manfredi, E. C., Caroli, P., Thakuri, S., & Tartari, G. (2013). Multiple carrying capacities from a management-oriented perspective to operationalize sustainable tourism in protected areas. *Journal of Environmental Management, 128*, 116–125. doi:10.1016/j.jenvman.2013.04.043 PMID:23728182

Santa Soriano, A., Álvarez, C. L., & Valdés, R. M. T. (2018). Bibliometric analysis to identify an emerging research area: Public Relations Intelligence—a challenge to strengthen technological observatories in the network society. *Scientometrics, 115*(3), 1591–1614. doi:10.100711192-018-2651-8

Schianetz, K., & Kavanagh, L. (2008). Sustainability indicators for tourism destinations: A complex adaptive systems approach using systemic indicator systems. *Journal of Sustainable Tourism, 16*(6), 601–628. doi:10.1080/09669580802159651

Sharma, R. (2016). Evaluating total carrying capacity of tourism using impact indicators. *Global Journal of Environmental Science and Management, 2*(2), 187–196. doi:10.7508/gjesm.2016.02.009

Shelby, B., & Heberlein, T. A. (1987). *Carrying capacity in recreation settings*. Oregon State University Press.

Simón, F. J. G., Narangajavana, Y., & Marques, D. P. (2004). Carrying capacity in the tourism industry: A case study of Hengistbury Head. *Tourism Management, 25*(2), 275–283. doi:10.1016/S0261-5177(03)00089-X

Smith, V. L., & Eadington, W. R. (1992). *Tourism alternatives: Potentials and problems in the development of tourism*. University of Pennsylvania Press. doi:10.9783/9781512807462

Stankey, G. H., Cole, D. N., Lucas, R. C., Petersen, M. E., & Frissell, S. S. (1985). *The limits of acceptable change (LAC) system for wilderness planning*. INT-176, USDA, Forest Service, Internmountain Forest and Range Experiment Station, Ogden, Utah. doi:10.5962/bhl.title.109310

Tranfield, D., Denyer, D., & Smart, P. (2003). Towards a methodology for developing evidence-informed management knowledge by means of systematic review. *British Journal of Management, 14*(3), 207–222. doi:10.1111/1467-8551.00375

UNWTO. (1981). Saturation of Tourist Destinations. Report of the Secretary General, Madrid.

Walker, B., & Salt, D. (2012). *Resilience thinking: sustaining ecosystems and people in a changing world*. Island Press.

Walker, J., & Cooper, M. (2011). Genealogies of resilience: From systems ecology to the political economy of crisis adaptation. *Security Dialogue*, *42*(2), 143–160. doi:10.1177/0967010611399616

Wall, G. (1982). Cycles and capacity: Incipient theory or conceptual contradiction? *Tourism Management*, *3*(3), 188–192. doi:10.1016/0261-5177(82)90067-X

Wilkinson, C. (2012). Social-ecological resilience: Insights and issues for planning theory. *Planning Theory*, *11*(2), 148–169. doi:10.1177/1473095211426274

Witt, S. F., & Witt, C. A. (1995). Forecasting tourism demand: A review of empirical research. *International Journal of Forecasting*, *11*(3), 447–475. doi:10.1016/0169-2070(95)00591-7

Zacarias, D. A., Williams, A. T., & Newton, A. (2011). Recreation carrying capacity estimations to support beach management at Praia de Faro, Portugal. *Applied Geography (Sevenoaks, England)*, *31*(3), 1075–1081. doi:10.1016/j.apgeog.2011.01.020

Zacarias, D. A., Williams, A. T., & Newton, A. (2011). Recreation carrying capacity estimations to support beach management at Praia de Faro, Portugal. *Applied Geography (Sevenoaks, England)*, *31*(3), 1075–1081. doi:10.1016/j.apgeog.2011.01.020

Zakai, D., & Chadwick-Furman, N. E. (2002). Impacts of intensive recreational diving on reef corals at Eilat, northern Red Sea. *Biological Conservation*, *105*(2), 179–187. doi:10.1016/S0006-3207(01)00181-1

Zhang, Y., Li, X. R., Su, Q., & Hu, X. (2017). Exploring a theme park's tourism carrying capacity: A demand-side analysis. *Tourism Management*, *59*, 564–578. doi:10.1016/j.tourman.2016.08.019

Zhong, L., Deng, J., Song, Z., & Ding, P. (2011). Research on environmental impacts of tourism in China: Progress and prospect. *Journal of Environmental Management*, *92*(11), 2972–2983. doi:10.1016/j.jenvman.2011.07.011 PMID:21821344

Zurick, D. N. (1992). Adventure travel and sustainable tourism in the peripheral economy of Nepal. *Annals of the Association of American Geographers*, *82*(4), 608–628. doi:10.1111/j.1467-8306.1992.tb01720.x

Chapter 9
The Impact of Small Island Sports Events on Developing Sustainable Tourism

Ian Arnott
University of Westminster, UK

ABSTRACT

Small islands rely heavily on tourism as a way of an economic boost, as well as a way of growth for business development, in particular, hospitality. One of the ways that several islands around the world have excelled in this is through hosting sports events as a way of sustainable tourism and there are many examples of this such as Hawaii that have $200 million dollar source of revenue and 94% of inbound tourists coming to the island for this type of tourism. This is just one example that is discussed within the chapter along with others as such stakeholders as the International Island Games that takes place every two years on 24 small islands around the world. Key areas that will be discussed as how the community must be involved in any type of tourism development due to the number of potential tourists who may visit the island and its potential positive or negative impact that this might have.

INTRODUCTION

Small Islands a way of Community Development

Small islands project images of peace and tranquillity when it comes to the thoughts of the discerning tourist. However, when it comes to community development it must ensure that it is beneficial for all, e.g., both for the local community and businesses

DOI: 10.4018/978-1-6684-6796-1.ch009

in all areas such as tourism and hospitality and those various sectors that are linked to this. However, this comes along with political and economic adversity also, transportation and communication shortages, uncontrolled tourism development and can attribute to community displacement, social disruption issues from inbound outsiders, (Royle, 2001; Lim and Cooper, 2009). The focus of island tourism and community development through sport and sports events has mainly been on an economic, infrastructural one rather than social and community ones, resulting in several examples of the failure of sports tourism through over development and displacement of mass tourism such as Malta which has been widely written about (Kakazu, 1994; Conlin and Baum, 1995; Briguglio et al., 1996; Lockhart and Drakakis Smith,1997; Hampton and Christensen, 1999; Royle, 2001; Gayle and Apostolopoulos, 2002; Lim and Cooper, 2009; Weed and Bull, 2004).

That said the development of islands through this type of tourism can also be very beneficial in the way of an all-year-round tourism and job creation for the local community and business development through a need for more in the way of hotels, restaurants, transport in the way of taxi's, buses, railways, and general tourism in showcasing the local attractions and the provision of other leisure activities. Whatever the impact the community must acknowledge that tourism development also has an impact on their quality of lives in many ways when it comes to economic prosperity in the areas described within this chapter. There have also been studies undertaken on the improvement of quality life (Ridderstadt, Roes and Njikamp, 2015) (QoL) by exploring material and non-material benefits from tourism development. QoL refers to material and non-material dimensions that it is believed that define people's lives (Stiglitz, Sen, & Fitoussi, 2009). In this sense, a material element such as income generated from inbound tourists spending money is only one of many determinants of people's QoL. According to Sen (1999), QoL centres "on the way human life goes and not just on the resources or income that a person command gained from increased business from tourism. Non-material conditions such as health, environmental quality, security, and feelings of pride in one's own community are also important from people wanting to visit the island for whatever reason. So, what is clear and apparent that there are large benefits to small island not only as island but also as a local community in offering, delivering different types of non-traditional tourism such as sport and sports events. There are many such examples as Mallorca known as a cyclist haven and has multiple training camps for athletes such as swimming, triathlon as well as holding an annual Ironman triathlon event attracting thousands of athletes from all around the world. This is one example of many which will be discussed throughout the chapter as a way of developing what can be called sustainable tourism, and it is important to understand and assess the attitudes of the community towards tourism and in this case sports events tourism (Lee, 2013). If the community of the hosting/ delivering destination is allowed to actively participate in the event planning process and being made aware of its impact in this area that is being discussed a small island it is more likely that such ideologies and opportunities would be successful in the long term and sustainable (Byrd, Bosley, & Dronberger, 2009). The host community is the key stakeholder for any tourism event and should be the central point in the tourism planning processes (Boonsiritomachai and Phonthanukitithaworn, 2019). The community perceptions of sports tourism and sports events tourism can affect the residents' behaviour toward athletes and their spouse/ coaching team/ partners to their region and the events held locally. Thus, investigating these perceptions is vital (Getz & Page, 2016). Also has been mentioned earlier community involvement can be considered an important factor in the development of sports tourism (Lepp, 2007; Boonsiritomachai and Phonthanukitithaworn, 2019). In recognition of the diversity of reactions among residents to the development of tourism, authors of extant studies have extended the SET by integrating other enabling factors that affect people's support, such as the state of the local economy, residents' economic gain, ecocentric and environmental attitudes, use of tourism resources, and place image (Gursoy et al., 2010; Jurowski & Gursoy, 2004; Lee, 2013) as was reinforced earlier then the community are more likely to embrace in its development and the benefits it can bring.

One of the key areas that must be identified from a community's perspective is the economic prosperity it can bring from a sustainable tourism perspective and an all-year-round influx of business. The job creation in the hospitality industry by having this type of opportunity for a small island but also the potential business development and growth. However, what would be useful to understand is the type of sports tourist that would visit and island and what would be their potential expectations for a host community in forfilling these for the economic development of a destination. Deery, Jago and Fredline (2004) have attempted to categorise (figure 1) this and the sports tourist outcomes etc.

As can be seen from figure 1 the start of this understanding is the sports event itself, its attraction or sports tourist motivation. Each one as can be seen is said to have different outcomes however, for the focus of this chapter the concern is community, economic contribution, and destination image/promotion as this would be more beneficial from a small island's perspective for the development of tourism and hospitality in this case. Gammon and Robinson (1997) and Kurtzman and Zauhar (2003) have presented similar models to gain an understanding of the different types of typologies of sports tourism/ tourists however for the benefits of this section Deery, Jago and Fredline's (2004) provides the best example with regards to community development. Also, as was highlighted by Ridderstadt, Roes and Njikamp, (2015) this also attributes to the improvement of QoL (Daniels and Norman, 2003) which by far are social benefits for the community (Fredline, Jago and Deery, 2004). QoL for the community which has been mentioned is also a financial benefit from a sport tourism perspective which hopefully enhances the sense of well-being in the community and provide an increase in pride in the region as in some cases this can be reinvested in many ways as well as business gain. On the other hand, some negative effects from sports tourism can also include overcrowding of the area and an increase in the level of litter (Fredline et al, 2004) however some of these will be discussed further in the chapter as these attributes to the size and scale of the events which would needed to be considered by the planning and organising committee in the initial event concept being put forward right at the beginning.

Figure 1. Sports tourist framework
(Adapted from Deery, Jago, and Fredline, 2004)

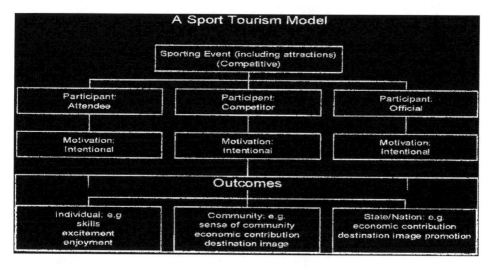

What must be acknowledged that the size and scale of events may vary on small islands so things like overcrowding, litter and some negative effects may be manageable as long as they have been considered in that initial planning stage, for example Gibson, Kapanlindou and Jang (2011) have explored these issues in smaller scaled events. They agreed that it certainly has to be an issue that needs to be considered by the planning and organising committee at that initial stage. Wilson (2006) also proposed that small-scale event sport tourism could constitute a minor issue where competitors may outnumber the spectators, they are often held annually, with little national media interest and limited economic activity compared to the large-scale events however this could be argued as other have proposed (Kakazu, 1994; Conlin and Baum,1995; Briguglio et al.,1996; Lockhart and Drakakis Smith, 1997; Hampton and Christensen, 1999; Royle, 2001; Gayle and Apostolopoulos, 2002; Lim and Cooper, 2009; Weed and Bull, 2004). Sporting events of this type held in smaller to medium sized communities tend to provide proportionately more economic benefits than if they were held in a larger city (Jurowski & Gursoy, 2004; Veltri, Miller, & Harris, 2009; Gursoy et al., 2010; Gibson et al, 2011; Lee, 2013). Examples of mega events for sports event tourism have far too many negative impacts which are well written about such as the growing critique regarding the sustainability of positive legacies from events such as the Olympic Games and the FIFA World Cup (Smith, 2009). Arguments have been put forward about the financial burdens (Lee & Taylor, 2006), the use of the facilities and management of after the event (Hiller, 2006), the environmental impacts and degradation (Chernushenko, 1996), and negative social legacies such as resident displacement and loss of their homes because of new builds and transport links (Hall & Hodges, 1996). Even the legacy of increased tourism in the post event years has been questioned (Brown, 2006). All these raise issues about the efficacy of developing national sport tourism initiatives post event and maybe questionable for a rationale for event delivery. These examples help strengthen the case for smaller islands to deliver those events that are manageable and sustainable which can in return they can continue to deliver potentially all year-round legacies. Also, the impact that this would, and will could and continue to have from a community's perspective with specific areas as the tourism and hospitality industries potentially could and will be unsurmountable in the long term socially. Therefore, the economics for the community would then take pride in this showcasing their islands such as Hawaii and others and an event held every two years around the world held called the International Annual Games (Small Island).

The discussion that has been put forward clearly states a case for sports tourism and sports events tourism for small islands and its impact on the community, however, as has been discussed like Mallorca, a haven for sport and others like Malta that at times causes displacement. It is worth exploring others and other events that bring greater tourism and hospitality to them, in the example discussed once every two years which can be said manageable. However, origins for this type of sports event began in 1985 on the Isle of Man that where an organising came together in forming the International Annual Games (IAG) or also is known as to their local communities the "Small Island International Games".

Small Island International Games

The small islands international games which were first held in 1985 on the Isle of man then was to be about creating a new recurring sporting event at that time seemed like an easier prospect than hosting a Commonwealth Games. It was during the Year of Sport that the organisers first put together a programme for an event that would become known as the Inter-Island Games (Mcdonnell, 2021). In 1985, as part of their Year of Sport, the Isle of Man set in motion an exciting and ambitious plan to bring together athletes from small islands across the world to take part in a new sporting festival — the 'Inter-Island Games'. 700 sportsmen and -women from 15 islands landed on Manx soil for what the UK national press dubbed the 'Small Islands Mini Olympics'(Iiga, 2022). Competitors hailed from the Faroe Islands and Scandinavia in the northern hemisphere, the British Isles, the Mediterranean and as far afield as St Helena in the South Atlantic—a 5,000-mile trip. After a week of events in eight different sports the festival was deemed such a success it was agreed to continue it every other year, with the second Games to be held in Guernsey in 1987 (Iiga, 2022). Over the next 12 years the Games travelled to the Faroe Islands, Åland, the Isle of Wight, Gibraltar, and Jersey, where the number of competitors reached 2,000. The islands' governments also began to realise what a positive impact sport could have on a small community, promoting a healthy lifestyle, providing a focus for young people, and strengthening a nation's cultural identity (Iiga, 2022). What can be seen from such a type of sports events tourism is one of the key drivers is sustainability and reaffirming community support. Also, as table 1 demonstrates that the games has grown greatly over the years with a peak of 2430 competitors taking part in Jersey 2015. It must be acknowledged that with these competing athlete's bring spectators, officials and other athlete support which means for the duration of the event there is the potential of 7000 + inbound sports events tourist if whether they are spectating or competing. This is nearly a tenth of the population of Jersey (BBC, 2021). There are very similar examples such as Shetland with a population 22, 870 as at 2021 (Population data, 2021) and not so well developed to cater for the 14 events and number of athletes, support teams and spectators with approximately 5000+ inbound people arriving which amounts to nearly 25% of the local population. There are also more examples such at Gotland who in 2017 played host to the small island games where approximately 7000+ people arrived on the island with a local population just shy of 59,000 (Visit Sweden, 2022), 24 events/ 14 sports which amounts to nearly 15% of the population. The statistics speak for themselves and the benefits that this type of event brings to each of the host destinations however, questions would have to raised, as these events are held every two years, that could this be sustainable for the islands due to their geographical, and demographics? Also, what would be the impact socially and environmentally if these were to happen more frequently? What is useful to note from this, table 1 provides a snapshot of some of those mentioned who have hosted this event twice since 1985 which serves as good examples on how they have developed their understanding on being prepared for hosting and delivering of the events. Also, as can be seen there would be lessons learned as those hosting destinations have also doubled (Guernsey; 1987- 1049 athletes; 2003 – 2129 athletes/ Isle of Man; 1985 -700 athletes; 2001- 2020 athletes) (see table 1) in size with the number of inbound sports tourist active or passive arrivals from holding the games for the first time and how they have developed their key resources in managing such numbers.

Table 1. The Natwest International Island Games hosting destinations (Adapted from Iiga, 2022)

Year	Venue	Number of Sports	Number of Islands	Number of Competitors
1985	Isle of Man	7	15	700
1987	Guernsey	9	18	1049
1989	Faroe Islands	11	15	800
1991	Aland	13	17	1500
1993	Isle of Wight	14	19	1448
1995	Gibraltar	14	18	1214
1997	Jersey	14	20	2000
1999	Gotland	14	22	1858
2001	Isle of Man	14	22	2020
2003	Guernsey	14	23	2129
2005	Shetland	14	24	1658
2007	Rhodes	14	25	2343
2009	Aland	14	25	2286
2011	Isle of Wight	14	24	2311
2013	Bermuda	14	24	1296
2015	Jersey	14	24	2430
2017	Gotland	14	23	2333
2019	Gibraltar	14	22	1624

What can be seen from this example of up to 24 islands coming through the organisation of one body IIGA that they have not only been able to host the event bi-annually what can be classed as a mini-Olympics (mega-event) but also now have the infrastructure, support mechanisms (hospitality) to cater for increased sports events tourists. Also, if they are not hosting the event itself, they are providing support during the event in the way of an executive management committee in dealing with the event build up once they are awarded in the games very similarly to a global event. There is also that by hosting this event for those destinations that have done so suggests that hosting small-scale sport tourism events tends for the small island provides that economic value to the community with most expenditures coming from accommodation and food (Daniels & Norman, 2003; Horne, 2000; Veltri et al., 2009; Walo, Bull, & Breen, 1996). Furthermore, with the involvement of the community in the events as volunteers; namely the small island games help build pride (Daniels & Norman, 2003; Horne, 2000; Walo et al., 1996; Wilson, 2006; Ziakas, 2010), therefore the social impact, togetherness this creates a positive experience taking part and be a supporter for the event and now for its future. Walo et al (1996) noted that the use of volunteers and the use of existing facilities are two crucial factors in maximizing the social, physical, and economic benefits associated with hosting small-scale events. Walo. et al's point is demonstrated through table 1 as that each island that has held the event twice have built on and developed their facilities enabling a community legacy in sports participation. Some reports from Island games only date back to 2015; Jersey where there has been some impact of the legacy on their facilities and participation. There was investment of 2.4 million in maintenance and upgrades of the States facilities, including at Fort Regent, Les Quennevais, Springfield and FB Fields (Jersey Legacy Report, 2016). There was also put forward a proposal for potential development in the future. A new Steering Committee was formed under the chairmanship at that time of the Assistant Minister for Economic Development Tourism, Sport, and Culture with the responsibility for Sport (Jersey Legacy report, 2016). However there have been no games held there since, so the true impact will need to be revisited again. Though it must be acknowledged the IGA do stipulate that:

- The creation of new sporting venues (or the upgrading of the existing ones), which has the potential for post-Games community/special events use (developing sports and encouraging the Host Island's population to be more physically active.
- The creation and modernisation of the (tourism) infrastructure (hotels, airport, roads etc)
- The representation of a Host Island and its culture.
- Enhancing the Host Island's international image and demonstrating that they can deliver major events on the world stage.
- Using the presence of the international media to send out various messages to the rest of the world (including the creation of a favourable tourist image for the Host Island).
- The involvement of the community as volunteers.
- The development of skills and knowledge of local people.
- Economic benefit from the Games (increased tourism and business activity).
- Using the Games to encourage a better understanding and appreciation of the rich heritage and culture of other Member Islands and developing the Host Island's international links.

- The pride, life-long memories, and feel-good factor for the local population. (IGA, 2022)

Each small island who hosts the small island games tourism and hospitality amongst some of the ten key points that a destination will gain from sports event delivery naturally benefit the community from a financial gain perspective. This is further reinforced, like others by Presnza and Sheehan (2013) that events can benefit the community well-being through increased employment, income, output, investment, extra services as well as new sources of entertainment and enhancements. Also, yet again to the quality of life (Deccio and Baloglu, 2002) which is highlighted through many examples discussed within this section as well outcomes put forward by the Jersey Legacy Report (2015). Though there positive and negative impacts influence the residents' attitudes and perceptions toward sports events, on small islands. It also must be acknowledged that social impacts of tourism development have drawn attention to the appropriate weighting of residents' wellbeing in small island destinations (Yang et al., 2010) as it is commonly recognised that Tourism through sporting events residents who are positively disposed to the development of this specific type of tourism and its related products – such as events – will enhance the tourist experience and contribute to the destination's attractiveness (Zhou, 2010). However, as discussed earlier several issues but others such as increased crime and rubbish as was as well also potential displacement as some of the islands hosting the games their population has been in some cases equating 15% equal to the general population. As well as this consideration it must be argued about will a host destination from a small island's perspective have continued tourism and hospitality post an International Island Games? As well it has been documented (Lasek and Rhiova, 2010) the positive impacts of tourism on local communities can potentially be jeopardized by degradation of the heritage resources (Aas et al., 2005) when the influx of mass sports events tourism consumption takes places. Where this is the case many contradictions between the aims of the different stakeholders can occur, especially both the potential organising committees, the IGA as well as the local community. That said when you are hosting such as Gibraltar the impacts are not so high as they have a total of 700 hotels, 200 cruise ship arrivals yearly clearly have the capacity to cater with some elements of displacement, but also like Jersey has tourism as one of its main economies. Jersey for example has over 770,000 visitors to the island every year (see table 2). What can be clearly seen from this that like Gibraltar, Jersey has the capacity for sports events delivery and yet again the influx for active or passive sports tourists as it has a vibrant island and the community embracing tourism as one of its main economies. Table 3 provides a good insight of the accommodation types on Jersey where it has over 7,000 which would be what an international game would bring in numbers as table 1 highlights. That said it could be argued this would not only impact the community but also their earning potential from an inbound tourism perspective. Therefore, further issues could arise in this example is does the government stop inbound normal inbound tourists during this time, yet again year-round tourism displacement during the event? How does this impact the community's earning potential from its normal all year around income from a hospitality perspective? Are there aftereffects on general tourism post International Games or are there peaks from this as those participating revisit the islands? And does this bring a continuation of legacies for sports events?

Though these questions are asked they serve as a good example of those islands that are developed for being a host for the IGA event and the potential longevity and sustainability of community and hospitality benefits from the event itself. As well as this the Small Island games reports that are available on the IGA's website there are a variety of examples how some of the legacies have impacted the host communities from a social perspective.

Table 2. Tourism visitors to Jersey 2019 (adapted from opendata.gov, 2022)

Type of Visitor Type	Number of visits
Total visits	770,700
Holiday visits	514,600
Business	66,100
Visits to friends and relatives	112,900
Other	77,000
Visits lasting one or more night	645,500
Day trip visits	125,100

Table 3. Registered visitor accommodation in Jersey, 2017

	Hotels	Guest-houses	Self catering	Campsites	Youth hostels	All visitor accom.
Total premises	58	35	32	6	2	133
Total bed spaces	7,589	796	~	~	146	8,531
Total bedrooms	3,724	398	~	~	33	4,155
Self-catering spaces	62	35	1,193	~	~	1,290
Self-catering units	19	9	338	~	~	366
Campsite bed spaces	~	~	~	747	40	787
Total persons accommodated	7,651	831	1,193	747	186	10,60

These benefits from a social perspective are essential as they will also welcome future tourist and then naturally ensure that their hospitality is a key factor for people returning, but what has been already identified the economic sustainability of sports events as a vehicle to also help sustain community businesses. The IGA games serve as a good example of how a bi-annual event supports a small island and those changes that can be made; however, it must be argued that with the potential displacement of tourism and the hospitality industry all year round will some islands cope with this such Malta who takes part and has a reputation for sports tourism and sports events as well as others. The numbers highlighted in table 1 and 2 highlight that such events hosted by the IGA that the number of sports tourists who would visit a small island, that all year around sports events tourism could be better managed if these numbers were spread potentially. By hopefully, say of one island coordinating their events evenly there would be less of a strain on resources from a tourism and hospitality perspective, e.g., for example a balance of seasonality of events and training events. Whatever decision an even balance from a coordinated approach for sports events tourism as there are not only athletes which has been discussed earlier but supported in various dimensions. When it comes to sports events tourism itself participants/ consumers will make an island destination a key priority within their decision-making process well in advance and base this on social context. How does the host community welcome sports tourists, what types of hospitality does the island for example offer which has been discussed earlier in this chapter? Weed (2006) shares this through Figure 2 which reflects on how early this decision-making process takes place.

The figure highlights that destination plays a high factor in the decision-making process and therefore if sports events organisers work closer with the tourism and hospitality on the island that this potentially could be managed appropriately. Such areas as restaurants, hotels and localised transport could be managed well enabling that all the stakeholder in this type of activity could work closer together and coordinate their specific sectors. This could be in many ways such as appropriate staffing, coordination of timings for transport providers, restaurant seating availability as well as hotel beds. Also, there are multiple opportunities for stakeholders such discounted opportunities to sports events participants/ teams so that both the hospitality and tourism sectors on the islands can gain a financial benefit from such opportunities and a piece of the lion's share. However, though these opportunities maybe capitalised in it is essential that those offering all year-round opportunities may also not see repeat visitation from the same sports event's tourist. Aicher, Karadkis and Eddosary (2015) identified when they explored this in running events and their motivations though it was recognised that the sports events tourist motivation was to experience a destinations culture. It did not always mean repeat visitation (Kaplanindou and Gibson, 2010). Kim and Chalip (2004) argued this in such cases that larger events sports tourists see that learning about new cultures and repeat was important to them. Also, communities hosting destinations was an important factor (Mcghee et al, 2003) and a decision maker for those wishing to participate. Therefore, it has been put forward that a destinations scenery culture, community, new places (Kaplanidou and Vogt, 2010) are directly related to a sports event's tourists choice supporting what Kim and Chalip (2004) put forward. This is further demonstrated when Snelgrove and Wood (2010) put forward that a small island, in this case, its attractiveness enhances and motivates sports events tourists to choose a specific destination. So, this reinforces figure 2 put forward by Weed (2006) that sport tourists' choices are most certainly an early part of any decision they make. It once again reinforces that an island needs to capitalise on this in the many areas that have already been discussed and some of the examples on how it can and does contribute to the host destination.

Figure 2. Sports tourism destination choices model
(Adapted from Weed 2006)

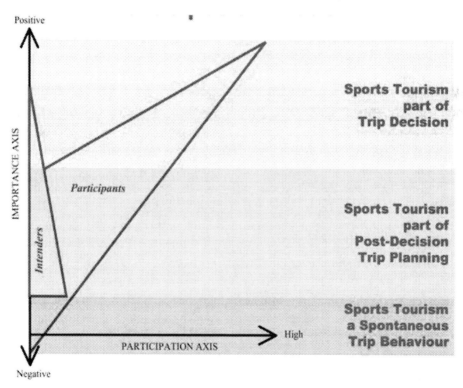

What must be further acknowledged whoever the host small island destination is the contribution to all the stakeholders from an economic, social, environmental point of view it must be a positive one as the some of the examples that have been shared provide and serve.

It is evident that this type of activity from a small islands point of view can impact the community, especially in some cases where it could maybe be dependent on this type of tourism and source of revenue for the hospitality industry. A study undertaken by Gibson, Kaplanidou and Kang (2012) a decade ago looked at six small events found that they most certainly benefited local hosting communities over an 18-month period in the areas that have been discussed throughout this chapter. Social indicators from this study showed that the hospitality sector was the most beneficial from what was classed a Senior Games (50.2%) and swimming (90.9%) was an area that was in greater demand. Where in Youth type activities shopping was important of similar sports events that were being hosted (Soccer 56.4%; Softball; 52.3: Swimming 50.9%) therefore from an economic perspective these had an impact on the local hosting community. Some arguments that could be put forward from these findings it could be suggested that a small island, if they have the infrastructure may wish to consider these types of sports events, they wish to host based on some these figures put forward from this research. Though this is so, and based on the findings presented by Gibson, Kaplanidou and Kang (2012), a small island, they may have to think about becoming niche in the sports events that they are offering that have more of an economic impact in some of the areas that have been highlighted. That said not every small island, depending on their size and scope may have the capacity to focus on a particular area of the economy from one type of sports event. One small island such like this is the island Langkawi which hosts an annual Ironman Triathlon event and focuses on its tourism having been given the status of a World Geopark and Geoforest (Marzuki, 2011). In 2007 tourism was boasted to have over 2,300,000 inbound tourists to such a small island, needless to say the islands main economy is built on this and is part of Langkawi's Development Authority Legislation (Act 423) (Marzuki, 2011). In 2019 IRONMAN Malaysia saw the biggest ever number of sports events active participant tourists with over 2,500 participants registering. Of those who registered injury and health free it had a total of over 910 triathletes which made up 35.5% of the total entries. Japanese participants were second (11%), followed by Singapore (6.5%) and Indonesia (5.1%). The 2019 IRONMAN Malaysia and IRONMAN 70.3 Langkawi would not have been possible without the help of 1,500 volunteers, who worked tirelessly throughout the course (Wires, 2019). This was prior to the pandemic and therefore these figures may change for November 5th, 2022, and it would be useful to reflect on the Ironman sports events of this nature coming up, that is now restriction free and are seeing an increase in the number of participants taking part.

These types of events bring a certain type of consumer which begin to reflect on figures 1 and 2 to put forward Deery, Jago and Fredline's, (2004) framework and Weed (2006) on destination choices and as well as their wants and needs/ outcomes as a sports event's tourist. These with a focus on destination, community, and the economic contribution. The Ironman sports events serves as a very good example such as the likes of the island like Langkawi where the average athlete comes with +1 person therefore, they are all 42% athletes/ spectators looking for accommodation, using localised transport and eating out in restaurants and staying for several nights due to its location from the mainland and accessibility. These types of events are held all over the world and lead to the Hawaii Ironman Championships which are a pinnacle of the sports event participants goals in most cases from these events therefore can be seen as a good source of revenue for an island.

Ironman Hawaii's Impact on the Island

The Hawaii Ironman is a World Championship event for those athletes wishing to aspire to compete in Kona. The event, itself not only is a major sports events playing host to a minimal of 2,000 athletes every year on the island, but also a major source of guaranteed income for mass sports events tourism and has been since 1978. Hawaii's Department of Business, Economic Development, and Tourism determine the net change in tourism for a variety of sporting events as well as the Ironman events itself. Some of the data in research (Bauman, Matheson &Mouri, 2009) isolated the impact of these sporting events, while looking at fluctuations that occur across different months and days of the week. Though the data estimated in some cases the dollar impact, which is the more relevant indicator of economic success from small island sports events tourism the Honolulu Marathon, the Ironman Triathlon, and the Pro Bowl. It was estimated that the Honolulu Marathon produces 2,183 to 6,519 in net arrivals while the Pro Bowl attracts about 5,596 to 6,726 in net arrivals and the Ironman Triathlon attracts between 1,880 and 3,583 net visitors (Bauman, Matheson & Mouri, 2009). However, the numbers have grown so it now brings 4,000 + visitors before, during and after the event takes place which forms close to like figures as the Pro Bowl on the island. This example serves as a good example where an island puts sports events tourism at the front of its strategy and the impact that this could have as an all-round year type of tourism as Hawaii has recognised. In 2007, the Hawaiian Tourism Authority budget was approximately US$70 million, the majority of which (US$37.5 million) were devoted to general marketing toward sports events visitors and associated leisure activities (Bauman, Matheson & Mouri, 2009). More than 10% of the agency's budget (US$7.7 million) was specifically focused sports events marketing. HTA is the largest state-sponsored tourism agency in the United States with a budget over 5 times that of the average state. Indeed,

Hawaii's spending on sport events marketing alone exceeds the entire marketing budgets for state tourism. (Hotel Online, 2005). The JAL ITU World Age Group Triathlon Championships is held in Honolulu, the Ford Ironman World Championships in Kona on the Big Island and the Nissan Xterra World Championships in Maui so triathlon events on a whole are clearly a great destination for Hawaii. The JAL event is held in Hawaii and the first time the three events were held in one location. Organisers estimated that the JAL world championship event will generate more than $20 million for the Honolulu economy. Actual numbers were not available at press time. The Ironman event, headquartered at King Kamehamehas Kona Beach Hotel since 1989, draws international media attention and contributes as much as 10% of the entire month's occupancy for Kailua-Kona hotels (Myre, 2005). What can be seen from this example, with HTA's spend on sports events marketing that the island gains multiple benefits from hosting triathlons and more. The total amount that has been reported that sports events bring to the island is $200 million. This coming from such Major sports events, including as those that have been mentioned as the Pro Bowl, the PGA's Sony Open and the Ford Ironman World Championships from the Hawaii Tourism Authority and the Honolulu Marathon Association of tourist spend (Yuen, 2012). In 2012 the Hawaii Tourism authority undertook research on the impact of tourism growth and participation (table 4 & 5) between 2012-2013

Table 3 identifies the average length of stay and where, for example that the average tourist stays for 7.1 days in Kona which demonstrates that potentially during this period those taking part in the Ironman sports event as well as the event Nissan Xterra World Championships in Maui (8.1 days) (Munekiyo & Hiraga, 2014) are having an impact on the economy. The economic benefactors are clearly tourism and hospitality because people having an extended stay which supports table 4 on the types of tourist participation/ consumption activities on the island.

Table 4. Average length of stay by island 2012 (Adapted Munekiyo & Hiraga, 2014)

	Average length of stay (Days)
Total	9.4
Oahu	7.3
Maui	8.1
Molokai	4.9
Lanai	3.6
Kaui	7.5
Big Island	7.3
Hilo	3.9
Kona	7.1

Table 4 highlights that 94.7% that visit the states of Hawaii are interested in the consumption of recreation which encompasses different types of activity, but most certainly sports events are part of the listing and also 2nd main source of tourism on Hilo which is 74.3% (Munekiyo and Hiraga, 2014).

Table 5. Visitor activity participation, state of Hawaii and Hilo 2012 (Adapted Munekiyo and Hiraga, 2014).

Participation Type	Types of Activities	States of Hawaii	Hilo
Sightseeing	Self-guided/Drive Around Island Helicopter/Airplane Tour Boat/Submarine Tour Whale Watching Visit Communities Limo, Van/Bus Tour Scenic Views/Natural Landmarks Movie/TV film location	93.5%	91.5%
Recreation	Beach/sunbathing/swimming Surfing/bodyboarding/paddleboarding Canoeing/kayaking Snorkelling/scuba diving Jet skiing/parasailing/windsurfing Golf Running/jogging/fitness walking Spa Backpacking/hiking/camping Agritourism Sports event/tournament State Parks/Botanical Gardens	94.7%	74.3%
Entertainment	Lunch/sunset/dinner/evening cruise Live music/stage show Nightclub/dancing/bar/karaoke Fine dining Family restaurant/diner Fast Food Cafe/Coffee House Ethnic dining Prepared own meal	98.5%	71.1%
Shopping	Mall/Department stores Designer boutiques Hotel stores Swap meet/Flea market Discount/outlet stores Supermarkets Farmers Market Convenience Stores Duty Free stores Local shops/artisans	96.6%	69.6%
Culture	Historic military site Other historic site Museum/art gallery Luau Polynesian show/hula Lessons, Hula/Canoeing Ukulele Lessons Play/concert/theatre Art/craft fair Festivals	69.4%	34.1%
Meeting		7.5%	2.2%
Convention		4.5%	1.0%

What must be also recognised from these two tables that as well as supporting the boost in tourism and hospitality that these types of tourists have another impact of the island's economy which is shopping 96.6% and 69% respectively demonstrating that it is a sustainable generally on the island's economy (Munekiyo and Hiraga, 2014). However, it must be acknowledged with the example of the Island games Hawaii is much more developed for this type of tourism the figures show in the tables that have been presented within the examples presented in the chapter. That said with $200 million worth to the island with sports events tourism it is useful to share its impact if they could develop these further.

Chapter Summary

What is clear that small island sports events tourism can have impact without a doubt for the long term in tourism and hospitality and has the long-term sustainability as an economic driver as some of the examples that have been shared of those islands highlighted within the chapter. Also, the improvement of the quality of life as was discussed by Ridderstadt, Roes and Njikamp, (2015) who discussed the material and non-material benefits from sports event tourism development as it plays an essential part when islands want to consider this type of tourism. However, as has been discussed small island sports event can bring a lot of benefits and those examples such as the small island games which is held every two years around the world is also an opportunity to celebrate the islands culture and what it has to offer to those visiting and participating.

From the examples such as the economic benefits for small island the impact and it has on the hosting community can be multiple not only from income generation from the spend as has been highlighted from examples of sports events on the Island States of Hawaii with an income of $200 million (Munekiyo and Hiraga, 2014), the volunteerism in supporting events of its nature. As Prezna and Sheyan (2013) through the economic benefits this brings higher employment of those on the island and hosting destination due to the increase of inbound tourists and increased spend on hospitality but also other areas as transportation and others such like. But what also must be acknowledged with investment of this type of tourism islands want and must see repeat visitation (Aicher, Karadkis and Eddosary 2015) in other areas as the islands culture as has been previously discussed. But as well as the positive aspects there needs to be a balance through the management and organising committees that some issues this can be also come with such types of tourism are considered so the community and the island have positive and sustainable legacies.

REFERENCES

Aas, Ch., Ladkin, A., & Fletcher, J. (2005). Stakeholder collaboration and heritage management. *Annals of Tourism Research*, *32*(1), 28–48. doi:10.1016/j.annals.2004.04.005

Aicher, T. J., Karadkis, K., & Eddosary, M. M. (2015). Comparison of sport tourists' and locals' motivation to participate in a running event. *International Journal of Event and Festival Management*, 6(3), 215–234. doi:10.1108/IJEFM-03-2015-0011

Bauman, R. W., Matheson, V. A., & Mouri, C. (2009). Bowling in Hawaii Examining the Effectiveness of Sports-Based Tourism Strategies. *Journal of Sports Economics*, 10(1), 107–123. doi:10.1177/1527002508327401

Boonsiritomachai, W and Phonthanukitithaworm, C., (2019) Residents' Support for Sports Events Tourism Development in Beach City. *The Role of Community's Participation and Tourism Impacts.*

Briguglio, L., Archer, B., Jafari, J., & Wall, G. (1996). *Sustainable Tourism in Islands and Small States.* Issues and Policies.

Brown, D. (2006). *Olympics does not mean tourism victory.* eTurbonews: eTN. www.travelwirenews.com

Byrd, E. T., Bosley, H. E., & Dronberger, M. G. (2009). Comparisons of stakeholder perceptions of tourism impacts in rural Eastern North Carolina. *Tourism Management*, 30(5), 693–703. doi:10.1016/j.tourman.2008.10.021

Chernushenko, D. (1996). Sports tourism goes sustainable: The Lillehammer experience. *Visions in Leisure and Business*, 15, 65–73.

Conlin, M. V., & Baum, T. (1995). *Island Tourism: Management Principles and Practice.* Wiley.

Daniels, M. J., & Norman, W. C. (2003). Estimating the Economic Impacts of Seven Regular Sport Tourism Events. *Journal of Sport & Tourism*, 8(4), 214–222. doi:10.1080/1477508032000161528

Deccio, C., & Baloglu, S. (2002). Nonhost community resident reactions to the 2002 Winter Olympics: The spillover impacts. *Journal of Travel Research*, 41(1), 46–56. doi:10.1177/0047287502041001006

Deery, M., Jago, L., & Fredline, L. (2004). Sport tourism or event tourism: Are they one and the same? Journal of Sport &amp. *Tourism (Zagreb)*, 9(3), 235–245.

Gammon, S., & Robertson, T. (1997). Sport Tourism: A Conceptual Framework. *Journal of Sport & Tourism*, 4(3), 5–12. doi:10.1080/10295399708718632

Gayle, D. J., & Apostolopoulos, Y. (2002). From MIRAB to TOURAB. In D. J. Gayle & Y. Apostolopoulos (Eds.), *Island Tourism and Sustainable Development: Caribbean, Pacific, and Mediterranean Experiences* (pp. 3–14). Praeger.

Getz, D., & Page, S. J. (2016). Progress and prospects for event tourism research. *Tourism Management*, *52*, 593–631. doi:10.1016/j.tourman.2015.03.007

Gibson, H., Chang, S., Kang, S., & Jun, S. (2009). Insights on running and hosting a small regional marathon. *Presented at the International Conference on Festivals and Events Research.*

Gibson, H. J., Kaplanidou, K., & Kang, S. J. (2011). Small-scale event sport tourism: A case study in sustainable tourism. *Sport Management Review*, *15*(2), 160–170. doi:10.1016/j.smr.2011.08.013

Gibson, H. J., Kaplanidou, K., & Kang, S. J. (2012). Small-scale event sport tourism: A case study in sustainable tourism. *Sport Management Review*, *15*(2), 160–170. doi:10.1016/j.smr.2011.08.013

Gursoy, D., & Rutherford, D. G. (2004). Host attitudes toward tourism: An improved structural model. *Annals of Tourism Research*, *31*(3), 495–516. doi:10.1016/j.annals.2003.08.008

Hall, C., & Hodges, J. (1996). The party's great, but what about the hangover? The housing and social impacts of mega-events with special reference to the 2000 Sydney Olympics. *Festival Management & Event Tourism*, *4*(1), 13–20. doi:10.3727/106527096792232414

Hampton, M. P., & Christensen, J. E. (1999). Treasure Island revisited. Jersey's offshore finance centre crisis: Implications for other small island economics. *Environment & Planning*, *31*(9), 1619–1637. doi:10.1068/a311619

Hiller, H. (2006). Post-event outcomes and the post-modern turn: The Olympics and urban transformation. *European Sport Management Quarterly*, *6*(4), 317–332. doi:10.1080/16184740601154458

Horne, W. (2000). Municipal economic development via hallmark events. *Journal of Tourism Studies*, *11*(1), 30–36.

International Island Games Association. (2022) *About the Games*. IIGA. www.iiga.org

Jurowski, C., Uysal, M., & Williams, D. R. (1997). A theo- retical analysis of host community resident reactions to tourism. *Journal of Travel Research*, *36*(2), 3–11. doi:10.1177/004728759703600202

Kakazu, H. (1994). *Sustainable Development of Small Islands Economics*. Waterview.

Kim, N. S., & Chalip, L. (2004). Why travel to the FIFA World Cup? Effects of motives, background, interest, and constraints. *Tourism Management, 25*(6), 695–707. doi:10.1016/j.tourman.2003.08.011

Kurtzman, J., & Zauhar, J. (2003). A Wave in Time – The Sports Tourism Phenomena. *Journal of Sport & Tourism, 1*(1), 35–47. doi:10.1080/14775080306239

Lasek, A., and Rhiova, I. (2010) The role of heritage tourism in the Shetland Islands. *International Journal Of Culture, Tourism And Hospitality Research, 4*(2), 118-129.

Lee, C., & Taylor, T. (2006). Critical reflections on the economic impact assessment of a mega-event: The case of 2002 FIFA World Cup. *Tourism Management, 26*(4), 595–603. doi:10.1016/j.tourman.2004.03.002

Lee, T. H. (2013). Influence analysis of community resident support for sustainable tourism development. *Tourism Management, 34*, 37–46. doi:10.1016/j.tourman.2012.03.007

Lepp, A. (2007). Residents' attitudes towards tourism in Bigodi village, Uganda. *Tourism Management, 28*(3), 876–885. doi:10.1016/j.tourman.2006.03.004

Lim, C., & Cooper, C. (2009). Beyond Sustainability; Optimising Island Tourism Development. *International Journal of Tourism Research, 11*(1), 89–103. doi:10.1002/jtr.688

Lockhart, D. & Smith, D.W. (1997). Island Tourism: Trends and Prospects. Pinter: London.

Marzuki, A., (2011) Resident Attitudes Towards Impacts from Tourism Development in Langkawi Islands, Malaysia. *World Applied Sciences Journal, 12*, 25-34.

Mcdowell, M. L. (2021). 'Come alive in '85¢: The Isle of Man Year of Sport, the first Island Games, and the shifting sands of sport event tourism. *Journal of Tourism History, 13*(3), 290–310. doi:10.1080/1755182X.2021.2008024

McGehee, N. G., Yoon, Y., & Cardenas, D. (2003). Involvement and travel for recreational runners in North Carolina. *Journal of Sport Management, 17*(3), 305–324. doi:10.1123/jsm.17.3.305

Munekiyo and Hiraga. (2014). *Tourism Market Study*. Banyan Drive.

Myre, M. (2005) Sports tourism a burgeoning niche market for islands. *Travel Weekly*. http://www.travelweekly.com

Online, H. (2005). Hawaii, Illinois, and Pennsylvania have biggest budgets for travel and tourism promotion; TIA Ranks all the states budgets for 2005. *Hotel Online.* http:// www.hotel-online.com

Bauman, R. W., Matheson, V. A., & Mouri, C. (2009). Bowling in Hawaii Examining the Effectiveness of Sports-Based Tourism Strategies. *Journal of Sports Economics, 10*(1), 107–123.

Presnza, A., & Sheehan, L. (2013). Planning tourism through sports events. *International Journal of Event and Festival Management, 4*(2), 125–139. doi:10.1108/17582951311325890

Jersey Legacy Report (2016). Fit for the future. *Sports Strategy.*

Ridderstaat, J., Croes, R., & Nijkamp, P. (2016). A two- way causal chain between tourism development and quality of life in a small island destination: An empirical analysis. *Journal of Sustainable Tourism, 24*(10), 1461–1479. doi:10.1080/09669 582.2015.1122016

Royle, S. A. (2001). *A Geography of Islands: Small Island Insularity.* Routledge. doi:10.4324/9780203227404

Sen, A. (1999). *Development as Freedom.* Anchor Books.

Smith, A. (2009). Theorising the relationship between major sports events and social sustainability. *Journal of Sport & Tourism, 14*(2-3), 109–120. doi:10.1080/14775080902965033

Snelgrove, R., & Wood, L. (2010). Attracting and leveraging visitors at a charity cycling event. *Journal of Sport & Tourism, 15*(4), 269–285. doi:10.1080/1477508 5.2010.533918

Stiglitz, J., Sen, A., & Fitoussi, J. (2009). *Report by the commission on the measurement of economic performance and social progress.* UN Stats. http://www.unstats.un.org

Veltri, F., Miller, J., & Harris, A. (2009). Club sport national tournament: Economic impact of a small event on a mid-size community. *Recreational Sports Journal, 33*(2), 119–128. doi:10.1123/rsj.33.2.119

Walo, M., Bull, A., & Breen, H. (1996). Achieving economic benefits for local events; a case study of local sports events. *Festival Management & Event Tourism, 4*(3), 95–106. doi:10.3727/106527096792195353

Weed, M. (2006). *Sports Tourism and the development of sports events.* Idrotts Forum. www.idrottsforum.org

Wilson, R. (2006). The economic impact of local sport events: Significant, limited or otherwise? A case study of four swimming events. *Managing Leisure*, *11*(1), 57–70. doi:10.1080/13606710500445718

Wires. (2019). Historic 2019 Ironman Malaysia Sees Biggest Ever Participation in Langkawi. *Wires.* www.asiatri.com

Yang, J., Zeng, X., & Yingkang, G. (2010). Local residents' perceptions of the impact of 2010 EXPO. *Journal of Convention & Event Tourism*, *11*(3), 161–175. doi:10.1080/15470148.2010.502030

Yuen, S. (2012) The business of sport in Hawaii. *Hawaii Business Magazine.* http://www.hawaiibusiness.com

Zhou, J. Y. (2010). Resident perceptions toward the impacts of the Macao Grand Prix. *Journal of Convention & Event Tourism*, *11*(2), 138–153. doi:10.1080/15470148.2010.485179

Ziakas, V. (2010). Understanding an event portfolio: The uncovering of interrelationships, synergies, and leveraging opportunities. *Journal of Policy Research in Tourism, Leisure & Events*, *2*(2), 144–164. doi:10.1080/19407963.2010.482274

Chapter 10
The Impact of Tourism Development on Community Quality of Life (QoL)

Latif Oztosun
University of Sunderland in London, UK

ABSTRACT

The impact of planners' development operations on host governments and residents has emerged as a growing subject of study in recent years, as it has become widely accepted that planners and entrepreneurs must consider the perspectives of the host community if the sector is to be successful in the long-term. However, there has been insufficient emphasis on local communities, their needs, and, most crucially, their assessment of the impact on their quality of life. This chapter discusses why and how tourism and hospitality planners must consider inhabitants' attitudes and opinions, particularly when it comes to legislation that may affect their way of life.

INTRODUCTION

It is commonly acknowledged among scholars and policymakers that long-term success of any tourist destination is attainable when the perspectives of the local people are considered in tourism strategy and development. (Haywood, 1988; Nunkoo & Ramkissoon, 2009a, 2010; Pearce, Moscardo, & Ross, 1996; Tosun, 2006).

The influence of development activities of planners on host governments and inhabitants has become a rising field of research in recent years, as it has become generally acknowledged that planners and entrepreneurs must consider the opinions of the host community if the sector is to be long-term viable. (Allen, Long, Perdue

DOI: 10.4018/978-1-6684-6796-1.ch010

and Kieselbach 1988; Ap and Crompton 1998; Belisle and Hoy 1980; Doxey 1975; Maddox 1985; Murphy 1983). However, little emphasis has been focused on local communities, their needs, and importantly their perception of the impact on their quality of life (Lankford, 1994). Tourism and Hospitality planners must consider the attitudes and perceptions of residents, especially in respect to policies that may impact their way of life (Ap, 1992). Thank fully for local communities, tourism development and the connection to the improvement of their quality of life (QoL) has gained much attention over recent years. It is now accepted amongst scholars that in) order for the long-term success of developments that taking local community views is the bedrock of the development process (Nunkoo & Ramkissoon, 2011).

The local community's attitude towards tourism development and their overall support in respect to their QoL depends upon the way in which is it evaluated. The literature comprises mainly of predictors of "tourism attitudes, community attachment, community life satisfaction, and quality of life by using such indicators as economic gain, personal growth (e.g., employment), and length of stay in tourism destinations" (e.g., Brunt & Courtney, 1999; Jurowski, Uysal, & Williams, 1997; McGehee & Andereck, 2004).

There is of course the conversation around the economic gain, but there is seldom any discussion and research on locals perceived value of tourism as an indicator and predictor of community life satisfaction along with QoL. This move away from the economic value, is abstract for some tourism and hospitality developers, but has featured in respect to the overall marketing and PR exercises of their product (Woo, Kim, and Uysal, 2015).

Community support for tourism is necessary to ensure the overall economic stability of the development and industry. This general change in ethos has come partly from government and the changing landscape in respect to understanding the long-term viability of destinations in respect to their commercial appeal (Jamaludin, Othman & Awang, 2009). Therefore, it is essentially that a positive perception amongst locals and the wider community will have an impact on their overall support for any such development, especially in consideration of the perceived benefit that is generate from any such development – jobs, income, status etc. (Dyer, Aberdeen & Schuler, 2007).

Therefore, we must look for ways in which to measure residents' perceptions and community attitudes to development. These could very well be objective outcomes for locals, such as understanding the perceived economic benefits brough on by employment and the trickle down effect that improves everyone in the communities standard of living (Ko & Stewart, 2002; McGehee & Andereck, 2004; Snepenger, O'Connell, & Snepenger, 2001).

Tourism development impact studies have long showcased how community conditions are influenced and impacted by both the negative and positive consequences of tourism (Andereck 1994; Belisle and Hoy 1980; Brunt and Courtney 1999; Lankford and Howard 1994; Liu, et al. 1987; Liu and Var 1986; McCool and Martin 1994; Perdue, et al. 1987, 1990; Pizam 1978).

It has widely argued that development of any given community used domain yields multiple changed to the lives of the host community. Once a destination community evolves to be a tourism destination, the living experiences of those residents inevitably become impacted both positive and negative outcomes. This is no doubt differs depending on the socio-cultural makeup of the population residing within an area in question (Yu, Cole, and Chancellor, 2016)

In respect to the history of QoL literature, many scholars have debated over the meaning since the 1960's. Andereck and Nyaupane (2011) have stated that "there are more than 100 definitions for QoL." Clearly, defining the subject area is tough as it is clearly problematic to differentiate between such terms as "well-being," "welfare," and "happiness" according to Puczkó & Smith (2011). Andrews and Withey (1976), defined QoL using a single question such as, "how do you feel about your life as a whole?"

However, in an attempt to be clear, it is important to look how QoL is defined from a multidisciplinary angle. Therefore, QoL can be considered to be an multifaceted concept that relates many aspects of a residents life, which includes including physical health, psychological well-being, and social well-being (Dolnicar, Lazarevski, & Yanamandram, 2012). Hopefully, by the end of this research residents will feel as, Meeberg (1993, p. 37) put it, that QoL "is a feeling of overall life satisfaction, as determined by the mentally alert individual whose life is being evaluated."

The very fundamentals of sustainable tourism development suggest that any form of development must meet the needs of locals. This is particularly in reference to the standard of living in which the local population are accustomed to and feel they should have. This concept therefore must consider not least of all the environmental impact, and economic outcomes, but also the experience of both visitor and guest. It is the case that the hos community will lean towards supporting tourism development endeavours by developers if their Quality of Life (QOL) is ensured. In consideration of this aspect, if tourism developers are to meet the needs of the local population and therefore receive support for their project, resident's QOL considerations must be a major consideration (McCool and Martin 1994).

Focus within studies of host perceptions on tourism development impacts have looked at three key areas of benefits and cost, essentially oriented on the social exchange theory – firstly, the economic element: income derived from great job opportunities, taxation for local government and inflation. The second element is the socio-cultural effect: increase in antisocial behaviour, including crime, overcrowding, as well as improvement of community image, pride and improvement in infrastructure. Thirdly, the environmental consequences such as pollution, loss of natural habitat, wildlife loss, to name but a few. One element missing from this section ought to be some of the enhancements that development can bring in terms of rejuvenation of brownfield sites that would otherwise have been left derelict (Andereck 1994; Andereck and Jurowski 2006; Jurowski 1994; Marcouiller 1997).

Positive tourism development impacts that greatly enhance host communities QOL are the array of job opportunities brought to the fore from tier one and two suppliers, as well as improved infrastructural benefits that locals would benefit from as well as guests (Belisle and Hoy 1980; Liu, et al. 1987; Liu and Var 1986; McCool and Martin 1994; Perdue, et al. 1990). However, these considerations are positive in the whole, the negative outcomes of development can lead to a deleterious effect on host communities QOL when overcrowding, conflicts, as in the case of Doxey's Irridex Model (1975) showcases when tourism levels reach a certain capacity over spans of time, congestion, and the resulting pollution, along with crime and the increase in the cost of living are taken into account (Andereck 1994; Belisle and Hoy 1980; Brunt and Courtney 1999; Cohen 1988; Lindberg and Johnson 1997; Liu, et al. 1987; McCool and Martin 1994; Perdue, et al. 1990; Pizam1978).

Current literature on tourism development focuses on measurement of impacts, this in turn can change residents QOL. When tourism development impacts are assessed in this manner, it should not be assumed that this measure truly understands residents true understanding of the development, and therefore their true QOL. Whilst it is true that tourism developments impacts can change residents QOL, the current measures only suffice in representing residents' perceptions on impacts, not necessarily their lived experience. Perceptions of excessive traffic, only when experienced becomes a factor in downgrading locals QOL. In this way, studies on the QOL for host communities should look to directly investigate the lived experiences of residents (Yu, Cole, and Chancellor, 2016).

Community Quality of Life and Tourism Impacts

It is argued that most communities when faced with consideration of whether to support tourism development consider the economic aspects that ultimately improve their standard of living. However, when balanced with the potentially harmful by product such as increased costs of living this may denigrate the host communities QOL (Liu and Var 1986). Additionally, the true economic upside may not be full representative and potentially skewed; especially if development deteriorates social or physical environments (Jurowski and Gursoy 2004; Roehl 1999). The consequences, whether positive or negative in consideration of the economic, socio-cultural and environmental factors, go about changing the dynamic of resident's overall experience and ultimately their QOL (Yu, Cole, and Chancellor, 2016).

Research has explored factors that influence residents QOL, within it, it notes that host communities' perceptions of life satisfaction vary with reference to the level of tourism development (Allen et al. 1988). These studies have gone on to deep dive into residents' perceptions of the importance of their satisfaction on various QOL factors by utilising seven of the key community life dimensions, such as public service, formal education, environment, recreation opportunities, economics, citizen involvement and social opportunity, and medical service (Allen and Beattie 1984; Allen, et al. 1987; Allen, et al. 1988). When the results were analysed further it suggested that resident's perception on the impact to community life directly correlated to the level and impact of tourism development. Tourism development is therefore implicated in influencing community life in respect to levels of satisfaction among residents (Yu, Cole, and Chancellor, 2016).

(Ko and Stewart 2002; Vargas-Sanchez et al. 2009) have discussed community satisfaction as a key mediation tool in mitigating negative tourism development impacts and uplifting resident support. Ko and Stewart (2002) uncovered that overall community satisfaction is related to perceived positive and perceived negative tourism impacts with the hypotheses that a relationship between personal benefits from tourism development and community satisfaction was rejected. In a study in Minas de Riotinto, Spain, Vargas- Sanchez et al. (2009) applied Ko and Stewart's hypotheses which concluded that overall community satisfaction was indeed related to resident perception of positive tourism impacts. If balanced well, overall community satisfaction, which includes satisfaction with neighbourhood conditions and community services, act as useful precursor of community support for additional tourism development (Nunkoo and Ramkissoon, 2010a, b)

Tourism-Related Community Quality of Life

The conceptualization of the emerging topic of Quality of Life (QOL) has become an emerging topic that has received broad conversation within the literature. The many studies of resident's attitudes towards tourism development have in uncovered those residents recognize tourism impacts in their community, which ultimately affects their Quality of Life (QOL). The concept of QOL has been deemed complex, and those complexities arise as we digress into the multiple aspects of resident's lives and environs (Schalock 1996). QOL has been studied in various ranges that stem from the perspective of the individual local resident to their family, the overall community, their metropolitan area, to entire countries, through either a subjective lens and objective perspectives (Sirgy et al. 1995; Sirgy et al.2000). Many definitions have arisen for the idea of QOL, Phillips (2006) stated that: happiness, life satisfaction, and subject well-being are close to the notion of quality of life, but they are not mutually exclusive, where Sirgy et al. (2000) associated individuals' QOL to their life satisfaction. However, the established theory in QOL research is the bottom-up spill over theory (Andrew and Withey 1976; Campbell et al. 1976; Diener 1984). It has been proposed that an individual's QOL is ultimately a function of other domains of satisfaction that includes factors such as community, work, family, and leisure with each a function of its subdomains (Sirgy et al. 2000). This notion has been expanded on further to community QOL models which incorporate the overall sum of satisfaction factors along with aspects of the community - community conditions such as satisfaction with conservation of local environment, pace of changes to the natural landscape, race relations, the cost of living with associated house price increase and crime (Sirgy and Cornwell 2001).

Other community focused QOL research has attempted to understand a community's well-being, feelings, and perceptions by using satisfaction measurements (Yu, Cole, and Chancellor, 2016). Community QOL can therefore be defined and measured as a representative group of socio-economic of individuals with consideration of environmental indicators that all contribute to the liveability and desirability of the region Epley and Menon, 2008).

Yu, Cole, and Chancellor (2016) propose that tourism-related community quality of life (TCQOL) is "resident perceptions of community living experiences affected by tourism development" TCQOL is modelled on two dimensions therefore, resident's satisfaction with community conditions and also satisfaction with community services. Residents' satisfaction with community conditions are in respect to residents' evaluations of the quality of various physical, social, and economic conditions and aspects of the community such as crime and safety, recreational and entertainment activities, infrastructure, traffic condition, parks, job opportunities, and taxes. These factors have been identified in explaining residents' community living experience (Grzeskowiak, et al. 2003).

TCQOL Model

Sirgy and Cornell's community QOL model (2001) evaluates the perceptions of satisfaction, importance, and tourism effects to evaluate resident support in relation to the community quality of life in the context of tourism development for the host community (Andereck and Nyaupane 2010).

The literature on tourism impacts states that development affects community services either positively or negatively (Ap 1990; Ap 1992; Ap and Crompton 1998; Belisle and Hoy 1980; Brunt and Courtney 1999; Keogh 1989; Lankford and Howard 1994; Liu and Var 1986; Milman and Pizam 1988; Pizam 1978). However, satisfaction with community services in this respect analyses resident evaluations of the various services provided locally from policing, fire/rescue, business services and non-profit services that are potentially influenced by tourism development (Grzeskowiak, et al. 2003).

Figure 1.
Yu, Cole, and Chancellor (2016)

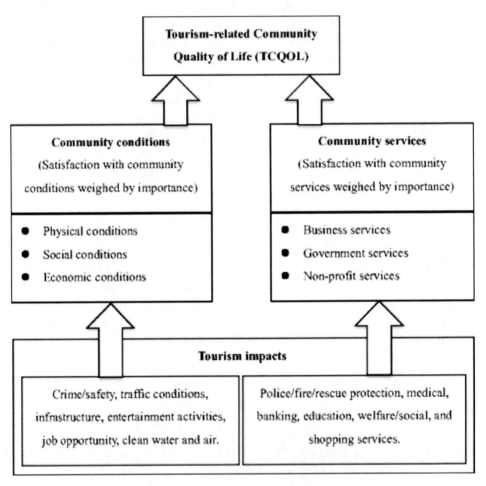

These indicators are extracted from existing and current tourism and community quality of life literature (Yu, Cole, and Chancellor, 2016). The TCQOL indicators are listed in Table 1. In a recent study in Orange County, USA questionnaires were sent to residents to rate both importance (1=not at all important to 5=extremely important) and satisfaction (1=not at all satisfied to 5=extremely satisfied) with each TCQOL indicator. The research assessed the host communities perceived effects of tourism with each TCQOL indicator (1=tourism greatly decreases to

5=tourism greatly increases) with the ultimate purpose of utilising these scales calculate and determine TCQOL scores. (Yu, Cole, and Chancellor, 2016). The TCQOL score is come to on the results derives from the importance, satisfaction, and the perceived effects of tourism development on community QOL (Andereck and Nyaupane 2010; Brown et al. 1998; Massam 2002). This TCQOL score then goes to represent the local communities' perceptions of how tourism development influences their community QOL. This approach assesses the value of community QOL indicators by enveloping: satisfaction, importance, and tourism effect scales. (Yu, Cole, and Chancellor, 2016).

Extant research has suggested that an appraisal of a residents QOL should take into account with residents' satisfactions and their values (importance) in consideration (Brown et al.1998; Massam, 2002). This in turn allows research to evaluate host communities' preferences and conclusions of those said values and satisfactions (Brown et al. 1998; Felce and Perry 1995; Massam 2002). With this format, the literature suggests a computation of the QOL scores using the below formula:

QOL score= (satisfaction*importance) ½

This formulaic representation shows the "square root of satisfaction" of residents multiplying the importance and therefore represents resident perceptions of each community QOL indicators as shown in table 1. Where the quality-of-life score ranged from 1 to 5, the square root aims to maintain consistency of the interval ratio (Yu, Cole, and Chancellor, 2016).

The calculation of TCQOL scores however, in previous studies have measured tourism development effects and the QOL (based on the indices) by multiplying QOL scores and perceptions of tourism development effects (positive and negative) (Andereck and Jurowski 2006; Andereck and Nyaupane 2010). Therefore, the TCQOL scores are calculated by utilising the host communities perceived tourism effects in connection with QOL scores.

The equation that showcases TCQOL scores is:

TCQOL = QOL*(tourism effect)

The formula results suggest that the higher the TCQOL scoring, host communities perceive there to be a greater, or more positive community QOL attributed to tourism development, and vice versa (Yu, Cole, and Chancellor, 2016).

These calculations serve the balance of scales required in measuring the complexities of everyone's (sometimes) subjective experience through the varying timescales of development. The ideas put forward have their limitations in respect to the continuum in which host communities are placed on in respect to the time each development takes to conclude. Therefore, collection of data at a single point can skew the result outcomes.

Testing the validity of the methods prescribed above have already been justified in the various elements of literature on the subject and conducted by Yu, Cole, and Chancellor, (2016).

It is evident and clear that local communities play a pivotal and important role in the success of tourism development. Support from residents is now considered essential in the process of development, especially so in the planning, operation, and sustainability of tourism (Jurowski 1994). Importantly, the host community are now recognized in the overall tourism experience of a destination. Resident involvement and support is now acknowledged for the success of any new development that relates to tourism ventures (Andereck and Vogt 2000; Ap 1992).

The tenets of sustainable tourism development and practices showcased in the literature review go on to highlight adhering to these principles in relation to how they are important to the overall quality of life of locals. To address some of the inevitable issues that occur within any form of development in relation to local communities' quality of life, this research proposal aims to assess tourism-related community quality of life (TCQOL) by way of attempting to uncover residents' community living experiences in the context of tourism development and quality of life.

REFERENCES

Allen, L. R., & Beattie, R. (1984). The role of leisure as an indicator of overall satisfaction with community life. *Journal of Leisure Research*, *16*(2), 99–109. doi:10.1080/00222216.1984.11969578

Allen, L. R., Long, P. T., & Perdue, R. R. (1987). *Satisfaction in rural communities and the role of leisure*. Leisure Today.

Allen, L. R., Long, P. T., Perdue, R. R., & Kieselbach, S. (1988). The impact of tourism development on residents' perceptions of community life. *Journal of Travel Research*, *27*(1), 16–21. doi:10.1177/004728758802700104

Andereck, K. L. (1994). *Environmental consequences of tourism: A review of recent research*. Paper presented at the Leisure Research Symposium. National Recreation and Park Association Congress.

Andereck, K. L., & Jurowski, C. (2006). Tourism and quality of life. In J. Gayle & N. Norma Polovitz (Eds.), *Quality Tourism Experiences* (pp. 136–154). Elsevier. doi:10.1016/B978-0-7506-7811-7.50016-X

Andereck, K. L., & Nyaupane, G. P. (2010). Exploring the nature of tourism and quality of life perceptions among residents. *Journal of Travel Research*.

Andereck, K. L., & Vogt, C. A. (2000). The relationship between residents' attitudes toward tourism and tourism development options. *Journal of Travel Research, 39*(1), 27–36. doi:10.1177/004728750003900104

Andrew, F. M., & Withey, S. B. (1976). *Social indicators of well-being: America's perception of life quality.* Plenum Press. doi:10.1007/978-1-4684-2253-5

Andrews, Frank & Withey, Stephen. (1976). Social Indicators of Well-Being: America's Perception of Life Quality.

Ap, J. (1990). Residents' perceptions research on the social impacts of tourism. *Annals of Tourism Research, 17*(4), 610–616. doi:10.1016/0160-7383(90)90032-M

Ap, J. (1992). Residents' perceptions on tourism impacts. *Annals of Tourism Research, 19*(4), 665–690. doi:10.1016/0160-7383(92)90060-3

Ap, J., & Crompton, J. L. (1998). Developing and testing a tourism impact scale. *Journal of Travel Research, 37*(2), 120–130. doi:10.1177/004728759803700203

BBC News. (2022). *London Resort: Swanscombe Peninsula site confirmed special status.* BBC. https://www.bbc.co.uk/news/uk-england-kent-59236138

Belisle, F. J., & Hoy, D. R. (1980). The perceived impact of tourism by residents a case study in Santa Marta, Colombia. *Annals of Tourism Research, 7*(1), 83–101. doi:10.1016/S0160-7383(80)80008-9

Brown, I., Raphael, D., & Renwick, R. (1998). *Quality of life profile, 2. Quality of Life Research Unit.* Center for Health Promotion: University of Toronto.

Brunt, P., & Courtney, P. (1999). Host perceptions of sociocultural impacts. *Annals of Tourism Research, 26*(3), 493–515. doi:10.1016/S0160-7383(99)00003-1

Brymen, A., & Bell, E. (2007). *Business Research Methods, Oxford: Oxford University Campbell, A., Converse, P. E., & Rodgers, W. L. (1976). The quality of American life: Perspectives, evaluations, and satisfactions.* Russell Sage.

Cohen, E. (1988). Tourism and AIDS in Thailand. *Annals of Tourism Research, 15*(4), 467–486. doi:10.1016/0160-7383(88)90044-8

Diener, E. (1984). Subjective well-being. *Psychological Bulletin, 95*(3), 542–575. doi:10.1037/0033-2909.95.3.542 PMID:6399758

Dolnicar, S., Lazarevski, K., & Yanamandram, V. (2012). Quality-of-life and travel motivations: integrating the two concepts in the Grevillea Model. In *Handbook of tourism and quality-of-life research* (pp. 293–308). Springer. doi:10.1007/978-94-007-2288-0_17

Dyer, P., Aberdeen, L., & Schuler, S. (2007). Tourism impacts on an Australian indigenous community. *Tourism Management*, 24(1), 83–95. doi:10.1016/S0261-5177(02)00049-3

Epley, D., & Menon, M. (2008). A method of assembling cross-sectional indicators into a community quality of life. *Social Indicators Research*, 88(2), 281–296. doi:10.100711205-007-9190-7

Felce, D., & Perry, J. (1995). Quality of life: Its definition and measurement. *Research in Developmental Disabilities*, 16(1), 51–74. doi:10.1016/0891-4222(94)00028-8 PMID:7701092

Grzeskowiak, S., Sirgy, M. J., & Widgery, R. (2003). Residents' satisfaction with community services: Predictors and outcomes. *The Journal of Regional Analysis & Policy*, 33(2), 1–36.

Hanafiah, M.H., M.F. Harun and Jamaluddin M.R., (2010). Bilateral Trade and Tourism Demand. *World Applied Sciences Journal, 10*(Special Issue of Tourism & Hospitality), 110- 114.

Harrison, D. (2001). Tourism in small islands and microstates. *Tourism Recreation Research*, 26(3), 3–8. doi:10.1080/02508281.2001.11081193

Haywood, K. M. (1988). Responsible and responsive tourism planning in the community. *Tourism Management*, 9(2), 105–118. doi:10.1016/0261-5177(88)90020-9

Jamaludin, M., Othman, N., & Awang, A. R. (2012). Community based homestay programme: A personal experience. *Procedia: Social and Behavioral Sciences, 42*, 451–459. doi:10.1016/j.sbspro.2012.04.210

Jurowski, C. (1994). *The interplay of elements affecting host community resident attitudes toward tourism: A path analytic approach.* [Doctoral dissertation, Virginia Tech University].

Jurowski, C., & Gursoy, D. (2004). Distance effects on residents' attitudes toward tourism. *Annals of Tourism Research*, 31(2), 296–312. doi:10.1016/j.annals.2003.12.005

Jurowski, C., Uysal, M., & Williams, D. R. (1997). A Theoretical Analysis of Host Community Resident Reactions to Tourism. *Journal of Travel Research*, *36*(2), 3–11. doi:10.1177/004728759703600202

Keogh, B. (1989). Social impacts. In G. Wall (Ed.), *Outdoor recreation in Canada*. Wiley.

Kim, K., Uysal, M., & Sirgy, J. (2013). How does tourism in a community impacts the quality of life of community residents? *Tourism Management*, *36*, 527–540. doi:10.1016/j.tourman.2012.09.005

Ko, D.-W., & Stewart, W. P. (2002). A structural equation model of residents' attitudes for tourism development. *Tourism Management*, *23*(5), 521–530. doi:10.1016/S0261-5177(02)00006-7

Krippendorf, J. (2010). *Holidaymakers*. Taylor & Francis. doi:10.4324/9780080939032

Lankford, S. V., & Howard, D. R. (1994). Developing a tourism impact attitude scale. *Annals of Tourism Research*, *21*(1), 121–139. doi:10.1016/0160-7383(94)90008-6

Lankford, S. V., & Howard, D. R. (1994). Developing a tourism impact attitude scale. *Annals of Tourism Research*, *21*(1), 121–139. doi:10.1016/0160-7383(94)90008-6

Lee, D. & Sirgy, M. (1995). Determinants of involvement in the consumer/marketing life domain in relation to quality of life: A theoretical model and research agenda. *Developments in Quality of Life Studies in Marketing*, 13-18.

Liang, Z. X., & Hui, T. K. (2016). Residents' quality of life and attitudes toward tourism development in China. *Tourism Management*, *57*, 56–67. doi:10.1016/j.tourman.2016.05.001

Liburd, J. J., Benckendorff, P., & Carlsen, J. (2012). Tourism and Quality of Life: How Does Tourism Measure Up? In M. Uysal, R. Perdue, & J. Sirgy (Eds.), *Handbook of Tourism and Quality-of-Life Research: Enhancing the Lives of Tourists and Residents of Host Communities*. Springer Publishers. doi:10.1007/978-94-007-2288-0_7

Lindberg, K., & Johnson, R. L. (1997). Modelling resident attitudes toward tourism. *Annals of Tourism Research*, *24*(2), 402–424. doi:10.1016/S0160-7383(97)80009-6

Liu, J. C., Sheldon, P. J., & Var, T. (1987). Resident perception of the environmental impacts of tourism. *Annals of Tourism Research*, *14*(1), 17–37. doi:10.1016/0160-7383(87)90045-4

Liu, J. C., & Var, T. (1986). Resident attitudes toward tourism impacts in Hawaii. *Annals of Tourism Research*, *13*(2), 193–214. doi:10.1016/0160-7383(86)90037-X

Marcouiller, D. W. (1997). Toward integrative tourism planning in rural America. *Journal of Planning Literature*, *11*(3), 337–357. doi:10.1177/088541229701100306

Massam, B. H. (2002). Quality of life: Public planning and private living. *Progress in Planning*, *58*(3), 141–227. doi:10.1016/S0305-9006(02)00023-5

McCool, S. F., & Martin, S. R. (1994). Community attachment and attitudes toward tourism development. *Journal of Travel Research*, *32*(3), 29–34. doi:10.1177/004728759403200305

McGehee, N. G., & Andereck, K. L. (2004). Factors predicting rural residents' support of tourism. *Journal of Travel Research*, *43*(2), 131–140. doi:10.1177/0047287504268234

Meeberg, G. A. (1993). Quality of life: A concept analysis. *Journal of Advanced Nursing*, *18*(1), 32–38. doi:10.1046/j.1365-2648.1993.18010032.x PMID:8429165

Milman, A., & Pizam, A. (1988). Social impacts of tourism on central Florida. *Annals of Tourism Research*, *15*(2), 191–204. doi:10.1016/0160-7383(88)90082-5

Nunkoo, R., & Ramkissoon, H. (2010a). Modeling community support for a proposed integrated resort project. *Journal of Sustainable Tourism*, *18*(2), 257–277. doi:10.1080/09669580903290991

Nunkoo, R., & Ramkissoon, H. (2010b). Residents' satisfaction with community attributes and support for tourism. *Journal of Hospitality & Tourism Research (Washington, D.C.)*.

Nunkoo, R., & Ramkissoon, H. (2011). Residents' satisfaction with community attributes and support for tourism. *Journal of Hospitality & Tourism Research (Washington, D.C.)*, *35*(2), 171–190. doi:10.1177/1096348010384600

Pearce, P. L., Moscardo, G., & Ross, G. F. (1996). *Tourism community relationships*. Pergamon.

Perdue, R. R., Long, P. T., & Allen, L. R. (1987). Rural resident tourism perceptions and attitudes. *Annals of Tourism Research*, *14*(3), 420–429. doi:10.1016/0160-7383(87)90112-5

Perdue, R. R., Long, P. T., & Allen, L. R. (1990). Resident support for tourism development. *Annals of Tourism Research*, *17*(4), 586–599. doi:10.1016/0160-7383(90)90029-Q

Phillips, D. (2006). *Quality of life: Concept, policy and practice*. New York. Routledge. doi:10.4324/9780203356630

Pizam, A. (1978). Tourism's impacts: The social costs to the destination community as perceived by its residents. *Journal of Travel Research, 16*(4), 8–12. doi:10.1177/004728757801600402

Puczkó, L., & Smith, M. (2011). Tourism-Specific Quality-of-Life Index: The Budapest Model. In M. Budruk & R. Phillips (Eds.), Social Indicators Research Series: Vol. 43. *Quality-of-Life Community Indicators for Parks, Recreation and Tourism Management*. Springer. doi:10.1007/978-90-481-9861-0_9

Roehl, W. S. (1999). Quality of life issues in a casino destination. *Journal of Business Research, 44*(3), 223–229. doi:10.1016/S0148-2963(97)00203-8

Saunders, M., Lewis, P., & Thornhill, A. (2009). *Research methods for business students*. Pearson education.

Schalock, R. L. (1996). *Quality of life: Conceptualization and measurement, 1*. American Association on Mental Retardation.

Sirgy, M. J., & Cornwell, T. (2001)... *Social Indicators Research, 56*(2), 125–143. doi:10.1023/A:1012254826324

Sirgy, M. J., Meadow, H. L., & Samli, A. C. (1995). Past, persent and future: An overview of quality-of-life research in marketing. In M. J. Sirgy & A. C. Samli (Eds.), *New Dimensions in marketing/quality-of-life research* (pp. 335–364). Quorum Books.

Sirgy, M. J., Rahtz, D. R., Cicic, M., & Underwood, R. (2000). A method for assessing residents' satisfaction with community-based services: A quality-of-life perspective. *Social Indicators Research, 49*(3), 279–316. doi:10.1023/A:1006990718673

Smith, G., (2008). *Does gender influence online survey participation? A record-linkage analysis of university faculty online survey response behavior*. ERIC Document Reproduction Service No. ED 501717.

Snepenger, D., O'Connell, R., & Snepenger, M. (2001). The embrace-withdraw continuum scale: Operationalizing residents' responses toward tourism development. *Journal of Travel Research, 40*(2), 155–161. doi:10.1177/004728750104000206

Telfer, D. (2002) The evolution of tourism and development theory. In R. Sharpley and D. Telfer (eds) Tourism and Development: Concepts and Issues (pp. 35 78). Clevedon: Channel View.

Tosun, C. (2006). Expected nature of community participation in tourism development. *Tourism Management, 27*(3), 493–504. doi:10.1016/j.tourman.2004.12.004

Uysal, M., Woo, E., & Singal, M. (2012). The Tourist Area Life Cycle (TALC) and Its Effect on the Quality of- Life (QOL) of Destination Community. In M. Uysal, R. Perdue, & J. Sirgy (Eds.), *Handbook of Tourism and Quality-of-Life Research* (pp. 423–443). Springer. doi:10.1007/978-94-007-2288-0_25

Vargas-Sanchez, A., Plaza-Mejia, M. A., & Porras-Bueno, N. (2009). Understanding residents' attitudes toward the development of industrial tourism in a former mining community. *Journal of Travel Research, 47*(3), 373–387. doi:10.1177/0047287508322783

Williams, J., & Lawson, R. (2001). Community issues and resident opinions of tourism. *Annals of Tourism Research, 28*(2), 269–290. doi:10.1016/S0160-7383(00)00030-X

Woo, E., Kim, H., & Uysal, M. (2015). Life satisfaction and support for tourism development. *Annals of Tourism Research, 50*, 84–97. doi:10.1016/j.annals.2014.11.001

Yu, C. P., Cole, S. T., & Chancellor, C. (2016). Assessing Community Quality of Life in the Context of Tourism Development. *Applied Research in Quality of Life, 11*(1), 147–162. doi:10.100711482-014-9359-6

The Impact of Tourism Development on Community Quality of Life (QoL)

APPENDIX

Table 1. List of TCQOL indicators

Community conditions		
	A.	Job opportunities
	B.	Property values
	C.	Prices for goods and services
	D.	Cost of living
	E.	Infrastructure (roads, bridges, utilities)
	F.	Traffic conditions
	G.	Crime level
	H.	Personal safety
	I.	Entertainment opportunities
	J.	Recreation opportunities
	K.	Clean air and water
	L.	Conditions of cultural/historical sites
	M.	Conditions of wildlife habitats
	N.	Conditions of natural areas
	O.	Overall appearance in the community
	P.	Overall community livability
	Q.	Overall community conditions
Community services		
	A.	Formal education
	B.	Medical availability and services
	C.	Fire protection services
	D.	Police protection services
	E.	Garbage collection services
	F.	Public transportation services
	G.	Banking services
	H.	Shopping facilities and services
	I.	Restaurant facilities and services
	J.	Recreational facilities and services
	K.	Family supporting services
	M.	Overall community services

Sources: Andereck and Jurowski 2006; Andereck and Nyaupane 2010; Grzeskowiak, et al. 2003; Ko and Stewart 2002; Perdue, et al. 1990; Schalock 1996; Sirgy and Cornwell 2001; Sirgy, et al. 2000

Chapter 11
The Role of Ecotourism in Sustainable Development

İrem Yıldırım
Nevşehir Hacı Bektaş Veli University, Turkey

Ezgi Kırıcı Tekeli
Karamanoğlu Mehmetbey University, Turkey

ABSTRACT

As a concept, development was evaluated only as an economic goal until the 1970s, and its physical, social, and cultural environment elements were ignored and left in the background. The concept of development has turned into a sustainable development phenomenon, which includes physical, social, and cultural factors, as people notice environmental pollution over time. Sustainable development, which integrates the mission of many industries interacting with the environment, has also gained ground in the tourism industry and has led to sustainable tourism understanding. Therefore, destinations have developed different tourism types within the sustainable tourism framework. Ecotourism has come to the forefront as a tourism type that can minimize physical, social, and cultural damage of tourism to the environment. Therefore, the current study, aiming to reveal the impact of ecotourism on sustainable development, covered the subjects of sustainability, sustainable development, sustainable tourism, ecotourism, and the relationship between sustainable development and ecotourism.

DOI: 10.4018/978-1-6684-6796-1.ch011

INTRODUCTION

Although the tourism notion has significantly changed in history, the tourism sector has always been popular and attractive. Tourism-oriented incentives of destinations revitalize tourism investments and activities and thus create a basis for increasing human mobility. While tourism activities were on a small scale in the early years, they grew gradually (Nunkoo, 2015). The continuously rising tourist numbers and the financial turnover in the world tourism sector exhibit the huge dimension that tourism has reached.

However, as mass mobility causes excessive consumption and rapid destruction of the resources available in tourism, it complicates the environmental controls on tourism activities. In other words, the ever-increasing interest in tourism may cause adverse effects, such as uncontrolled use of resources (Pickaver et al., 2010). In this context, the concept of sustainable tourism has emerged and started to gain ground in all tourism activities. Sustainable tourism has been an approach for protecting the socio-cultural structure of the local people in the region, contributing to the economic welfare of the local people, and minimizing the unfavorable environmental effects of tourism activities (Cinnioğlu, 2015).

Ecotourism, a type of tourism that minimizes the damage caused by tourism to the environment and contributes to the regional economy, is one of the most important types of tourism that ensures the sustainability of tourism activities (Cinnioğlu, 2015). Ecotourism is considered crucial for a sustainable environment and development. Unsustainable tourism and tourist activities cannot survive for a long time. Ecotourism practices should focus on nature and the environment, be accordant with the cultural structure, and be considerate and protective of ecological values. This way of thinking has led to efforts to reveal the ecotourism potential of many regions (Acott et al., 1998; Arat & Çalımlı, 2018; Blamey, 1997).

The current study, which investigated the role of ecotourism in sustainable development, first addressed the concepts of "sustainability" and "sustainable development" and the significance of sustainable development. After explaining the economic, socio-cultural, and environmental dimensions of sustainability, the authors discussed the concept and scope of sustainable tourism. Then, they mentioned the interaction between sustainable tourism and the environment. Later, this study, which touches on the interaction of sustainable tourism and the environment, explained the "concept of ecotourism" and revealed the interaction of ecotourism with the environment. Finally, the current study addressed the relationship between sustainable development and ecotourism, made some suggestions, and discussed the subject from a holistic perspective.

THE SUSTAINABILITY AND SUSTAINABLE DEVELOPMENT CONCEPTS

The concept of sustainability was first used by the German scientist Hans Carl Von Carlowitz in his economics book "Sylvicultura Oeconomica" in 1712. This concept, which aimed to protect forests and wildlife that were damaged by mining exploration, was later used in the scope of excessive fishing activities. The sustainability concept was actively involved in taking measures for proper soil cultivation and protecting soil structure in the 1930s (Vehkamäki, 2005). In this context, sustainability is *"a model that combines environmental balance and economic growth by emphasizing the effective use of natural resources and the importance of environmental quality, meeting the needs of today without compromising the needs of future generations"* (Hayta, 2009: 145). Coccossis (1996: 3) defines sustainability as *"reestablishing the balance that should exist between social, environmental and economic purposes but deteriorated by the negative effects of humans on environmental resources."* On the other hand, Middleton and Hawkins (1998: 38) define sustainability as *"a balance that provides harmony between human activities and social, cultural and natural environment."*

Sustainability is a phenomenon that has been the subject of many different fields, such as agriculture, tourism, manufacturing, and cuisine. World Commission on Environment and Development (WCED) was the chief organization that brought sustainability to the fore (WCED, 1987). WCED has identified sustainability as one of the primary deficiencies of the development phenomenon (Karadaş, 2008). The development notion had only been evaluated in economic terms until the 1970s. This approach ignored cultural, social, and environmental dimensions and thought that economic growth could overcome the situations such as natural destruction, poverty, and inequality. However, the passage of time has proven that this view was wrong. The Brundtland Report (Our Common Future), published by the WCED and the United Nations in 1987, referred to the concept of "sustainable development" and drew attention to the necessity of realizing universal strategies aiming at sustainable development. The Commission stated that the basis of sustainable development should be *"a process that takes into account the needs of both present and future generations on issues such as the use of raw material resources, the type of investments, the objectives of technological developments and institutional changes"* (Damore, 1992: 259). Based on the Commission's opinion, the concept of sustainable development is expressed by the three-circle model (Figure 1) below (Mensah & Castro, 2004).

Figure 1. Three-circle model
(Mensah & Castro, 2004)

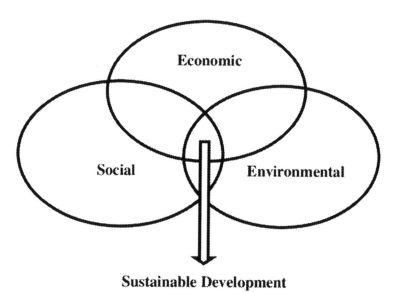

Some sustainable development principles should be determined by considering the parameters depicted in Figure 1. First, growth and development should aim for the satisfaction of the vital needs of society. Second, in order to talk about the harmony between "growth" and "environment", the continuity of natural resources should be ensured by considering the carrying capacity of natural areas. Third, it is necessary to act with the concept of justice in using natural resources for both today and future generations. Besides, the philosophy of sustainable development includes a new trend in thoughts and changes in behavior, attitudes, and value judgments. These basic principles that make up the philosophy of sustainable development are as follows (Kahraman, 1994):

- Ensuring "continuity" in all renewable and non-renewable resources (natural, cultural, ecological, biological),
- Prioritizing a "qualitative growth" that can meet the needs of society,
- Pursuing "justice" in the distribution of resources between generations,
- Determining and applying ethical rules to contribute to sustainable development by making "morality" dominant in attitudes, behaviors, and understandings in the relationship between the environment and economic life.

Continuity, qualitative growth, justice, and morality are significant concepts for sustainable development. The dimensions of economic, social, and environmental sustainability, which are the basis of sustainable development, are explained as follows:

- *Economic Sustainability:* Economic sustainability makes it possible to optimize the development alternatives of a region (Becker, 2002). Both environmental and economic sustainability should be "green" (Hatipoğlu et al., 2016). The Sustainable Development Report has indicated the "green economy" as a crucial tool for eradicating poverty and ensuring economic development. Again, the report stated that sustainable economic growth would effectively increase social participation, improve human welfare, create employment, and maintain the healthy functioning of ecosystems. Tourism assets are effective sub-dimensions in economic sustainability. For this reason, it is necessary to carefully evaluate the attractions of each destination considering the tourism development. How touristic attractions will serve tourism is crucial in terms of sustainability (Koban & Eker İşçioğlu, 2019). Besides, tourism revenues are also among the issues related to economic sustainability. In this context, establishing links among tourism-related business lines (manufacturing, construction, agriculture, etc.) appears as a method to increase economic benefit. Thus, through the strong connections established, tourism revenues flow into the national economy. Tourism revenues added to the national economy create a multiplier effect on country economies and strengthen the enterprises operating in the tourism industry. This situation reveals the importance of economic sustainability (Cernat & Gourdon, 2007).

- *Social Sustainability:* Social sustainability is a *"process that supports the healthy continuity and development of society to meet the needs of not only the current society but also future generations"* (Business Dictionary, 2019). Social sustainability is a sustainable development goal that considers the welfare of the whole society. The document titled "We Are Transforming People and Planet for Our World: 2030 Sustainable Development Summit" released 17 principles in the context of Sustainable Development Goals. The 11th principle *"making cities and human settlements inclusive, safe, strong, and sustainable"* concerns social sustainability (Özdemir, 2018: 15). The social sustainability dimension in tourism means the participation of local communities in tourism activities. The environmental aspect is also an important issue in social sustainability. There are socio-ecological sustainability activities where these two dimensions are handled together (Cernat & Gourdon, 2007). Likewise, there is a relationship between social sustainability and ecotourism. Although ecotourism is thought to be related to the environmental effects of tourism, as a matter of fact, ecotourism constitutes the social dimension of sustainability as it includes cultural and social themes. In addition, two of the five principles of ecotourism activities, namely, *"providing financial benefits and empowerment for the local people"* and *"raising sensitivity to the political, environmental, and social climate of the host country,"* are evaluated within social sustainability (Collin & Collin, 2009: 175). In terms of tourism, issues such as education of visitors and local people, increasing local people's life quality, disadvantaged social groups' participation in tourism, and local attendance in the decision-making process in destination management are also crucial to social sustainability (Hatipoğlu et al., 2016).

- ***Environmental Sustainability:*** The word "environmental" emerges from the relationship between the human and natural systems. This word differs in meaning from the word "ecology" where the elements in the system are interdependent. However, the environment concept also appears as a subset of ecology. Environmental sustainability plays an active role in protecting and managing non-renewable resources essential to life. In addition, environmental sustainability aims to minimize soil, water, and air pollution and to carry out various activities to protect biodiversity (UNWTO & UNEP, 2005). The environmental sustainability principle *"re-establishes essential services for supportive ecosystems that meet the needs of society and connects system elements with balance and resilience in case of over-utilization and biodiversity-reducing actions"* (Costanza & Patten, 1995: 194). One of the most critical sub-dimensions of environmental sustainability is the sustainability of the infrastructure, which is the life source of societies. The prominence of a destination in the tourism industry is related to the quality of its infrastructure, and accessibility to tourist attractions depends on the quality of the infrastructure (Cernat & Gourdon, 2007).

THE CONCEPT AND SCOPE OF SUSTAINABLE TOURISM

Sustainable tourism–as a part of Sustainable development–was first mentioned at the 1992 "United Nations Conference on Environment and Development" held in Rio de Janeiro. In this context, the "Agenda 21 Action Report" was created for the travel and tourism industries and associated with the concept of sustainable development (Neto, 2003). Later, with the Green Report published by the European Union in 1995, the notion of "sustainable tourism" was officially recognized and gained ground in the literature (Şen et al., 2018). Sustainable tourism is basically about adapting sustainable development to the tourism industry. It refers to the long-term use of tourism assets and the application of principles to reduce the adverse effects of tourism while increasing its positive sides (Weaver, 2006).

Although the definition of "sustainable tourism" resembles the definition of "sustainability" it is generally defined as *"an understanding that aims to meet the needs of tourists, the tourism sector, and local communities in a way that does not endanger the ability of future generations to meet their needs"* (Kuhn, 2007: 289). In this context, Güler and Tufan (2013: 357) define sustainable tourism as *"a positive approach based on the principle of protecting environmental and social values, aiming to maximize the harmony between the tourism sector, tourists, local people, and the environment."* Similarly, Demir and Çevirgen (2006) believe sustainable tourism might be possible when cultural, historical, natural, and biological diversity are perfectly available in tourism destinations. Drawing attention to the balance between economic expectations and the use of natural resources, Akış (1997: 37) defined sustainable tourism as *"initiatives to increase tourism capacity and product quality without adversely affecting the natural environment and human resources."*

While sustainable tourism provides opportunities for touristic experiences, it also ensures that this utilization does not pollute, harm, and overconsume touristic resources. Thus, it allows for the utilization of future generations and protects historical and natural beauty. In this respect, sustainable tourism appears as an economic development model. Sustainable tourism is a contract against nature. It carries the social responsibility of meeting the needs of today's tourists and local people while pursuing to develop future opportunities. Thus, it brings all resource management, obligatory ecological processes, cultural integrity, biological diversity, and economic, aesthetic, and social requirements to the fore. Therefore, sustainable tourism products are products processed in harmony between touristic development and the local environment, society, and culture (Güneş, 2008; Özgüç, 2007).

Focusing only on the economic dimension of tourism destroys the natural infrastructure in destinations, thus making it hard to transfer touristic values to future generations in a healthy way. In the 1990s, the fact that the tourists preferred an unspoiled environment enlightened the tourism industry on this issue, and they took the protection of environmental values as a mission. Thus, searches for alternative tourism types based on sustainable tourism have begun (Özbey, 2002). The close relationship between tourism and the environment has once again revealed the importance of the concept of sustainability. Therefore, the relationship between tourism and the environment must not harm both parties. Sustainability plays an active role in establishing the balance. Which and how tourism assets should be provided to tourists is a critical issue in sustainable tourism. Sustainable tourism is an approach that tries to reduce the problems among tourists, the environment, and the tourism industry which is aware that the chief sources of tourism are natural, cultural, social, historical, and environmental resources (Doğan, 2010).

The Role of Ecotourism in Sustainable Development

Tourism, among the rapidly growing industries in the world, has exhaustible and non-renewable resources and operates depending on historical, cultural, and natural resources. This industry, which rests on the preference of tourists, reveals the necessity of protecting environmental assets. Besides, natural, historical, cultural, and artificial resources (infrastructure and superstructure) should be protected for sustainable development. The understanding of sustainable tourism does not deny the necessity for growth and development but argues that growth and development should be within boundaries. This view of sustainable tourism is an understanding that considers the ecosystem, carrying capacity calculations, and the interests of the local people (Güneş, 2008).

Development in any destination without a sustainable tourism approach might bring positive opportunities such as employment and high income, but also cause some deterioration in the socio-cultural and physical structure. The most significant reason for the physical environment deterioration is ignoring the destination's carrying capacity. The excessive concentration of tourist demand in a particular area and the agglomerations beyond capacity negatively affect the destination attractiveness, the tourism industry, and other touristic employment areas. Such problems negatively influence the social structure and cause tourism to be at an undesirable size in destinations. In this context, sustainable tourism reduces all unfavorable socio-cultural, environmental, and natural effects caused by tourism (Doğan, 2010).

THE INTERACTION BETWEEN SUSTAINABLE TOURISM AND THE ENVIRONMENT

The tourism phenomenon contains many variables, including the environment. The environment where tourism activities take place consists of living entities (such as humans, vegetation, and animal communities), non-living entities (such as air, soil, water, climate, historical and natural structures, tangible and intangible cultural heritages), and physical and social ambiance (such as social, political and economic conditions) (Pekin, 2011). Therefore, the environment is among the most prominent resources of tourism. Today, resource consumption in the tourism industry increases, as in all sectors, depending on the increasing consumption rate. This situation, which develops against the environment, causes tourism to consume its own resources. In this context, a sustainable, clean, and protected environment is a must for an outstanding tourism activity (Şanlıöz Özgen et al., 2016).

A clean, protected, and orderly environment attracts tourists and allows many different tourism types to emerge. For example, nature-based ecotourism has developed based on the sustainability principle. Also, a protected and clean environment is necessary for many tourism types, such as highland tourism, agricultural tourism, bird watching, and trekking, which are among ecotourism activities. Apart from these nature-based (physical environment) tourism types, there are also social environment-based tourism types. For example, cultural tourism, one of the leading social environment-based tourism, needs a protected and orderly environment–as in ecotourism–and thus creates a power of attraction (Erdoğan, 2010).

In general, the environment and tourism have some positive and negative effects on each other. These situations are as follows:

- *__The Effects of the Environment on Tourism:__* Tourism and the environment are two interdependent phenomena. In this circle, the environment creates resources for tourism activities, and the tourism sector protects the environment that provides the resources (Demir & Çevirgen, 2006). The physical and social environment plays a critical role by diversifying tourism activities, ensuring its continuity all the year, and increasing tourism revenues. For example, Las Vegas, an artificial city built entirely with human factors, welcomes an average of 40 million tourists annually. Again, consisting of only natural elements, the Grand Canyon attracts an average of 4 million people yearly. Besides, cities such as Rome, Istanbul, Barcelona, and London, which are at the forefront with their cultural attractions, host millions of tourists annually and increase their incomes (UNWTO, 2016). These examples and numbers show how important natural, cultural, and social environments are for tourism activities. The effect of the environment on tourism also suggests the impact of tourism on the environment (Demir & Çevirgen, 2006).
- *__The Effects of Tourism on the Environment:__* Tourism creates both positive and negative effects on the environment. Boosting employment, closing the countries' current account deficits, eliminating income inequality, and increasing the gross national income ratio are positive economic effects (Olalı & Timur, 1988). In addition, tourism has many positive effects on the social and cultural environment. It provides many social influences, such as developing tolerance, instilling environmental awareness, increasing the rate of foreign language learning, developing rural areas, and providing leisure time habits (Rızaoğlu, 2004). Besides all these positive effects on the environment, tourism also has many adverse effects based on the human factor and travel dynamics. For example, airlines are the most preferred transportation mode in touristic travels. Airplanes emit a range of greenhouse gases throughout the various stages of flight. The emission of carbon dioxide and other greenhouse gases is among the most important causes of global climate change. In addition, the demands of tourists–such as accommodation, food and beverage, entertainment, and shopping in the destinations– directly affect the physical environment. These demands might proliferate

waste, increase plastic use, and destroy agricultural lands and forest areas. Furthermore, cultural degeneration, alienation, the disappearance of cultural values, and changes in beliefs and behaviors are examples of the unfavorable effects of tourism on the social environment (Olalı & Timur, 1988).

The mobility created by approximately one and a half billion people around the world, of course, could cause some negative situations in the environment. What matters is keeping negative situations at a minimum level, maximizing positive results, and ensuring sustainability (UNWTO, 2020).

THE CONCEPT AND SCOPE OF ECOTOURISM

Under this title, the concept of ecotourism has been examined in depth. In this context, first of all, the emergence and development of the concept of ecotourism are discussed, and then the characteristics and principles of ecotourism are mentioned.

The Emergence and Development of Ecotourism

The word ecology, whose origin is Greek, is the combination of the words "oikos and logos." The ecotourism concept is scientifically derived from the word ecology. Ecology is a branch of science that studies organisms and their relationships with their environment. Like all organisms, humans interact with their environment. From an ecological point of view, it is crucial to protect biological communities and respect local people. Therefore, the ecotourism concept aims to protect the local people and the features of destinations (Edmonds & Leposky, 1998).

The concept of ecotourism brings together tourism and conservation concepts. In 1976, Budowski handled the first scientific study involving these concepts. This study, named "Tourism and environmental conservation: Conflict, coexistence, or symbiosis?" contributed to the ecotourism literature by including relevant notions. The direct use of the concept of ecotourism, on the other hand, dates back to an earlier date. Some claim that Hetzer was the first person to use the conception in 1965. Hetzer has included the concept of "ecological tourism" while suggesting alternative and responsible tourism. In the 1970s, the Canadian Government used the ecotourism notion in ecotour programs. The brochures published in Canada gave information about ecotours at that time but made no definition. Furthermore, some argue that Miller used the concept in 1978 and Mathieson and Wall in 1982 (Orams, 1995; Ward, 1997).

The widespread use of the concept of ecotourism coincided with the end of the 1980s when mass tourism became widespread. The damage caused by mass tourism to the natural environment has caused a public backlash and led to the development of the nature-based tourism idea. The concept of ecotourism has developed over these years. Thus, thanks to the ecotourism concept, the importance of protecting the natural environment has been understood. In the end, "ecology" was combined with "tourism" and yielded a more popular concept (Orams, 1995).

There is no internationally accepted definition of ecotourism. Many researchers in this field state that the concept is highly controversial, and no single universal description is available (Campbell, 1999). The main reason for this confusion and uncertainty regarding ecotourism is ecotourists' poorly understood attitudes and behaviors (Diamantis, 1998). In general, ecotourists are *"people who have free time to travel, have high economic income, are well-educated, and are curious about the natural environment."* However, this definition does not help to establish a standard definition of ecotourism (Ballantine & Eagles, 1994: 210).

Ceballos-Lascuarin (1987) was the first person to define the concept of ecotourism. Ceballos-Lascuarin (1987: 13) has described the notion as *"travel to relatively unspoiled and uncontaminated natural areas for specific purposes, such as exploring, viewing landscapes, and taking care of wild plants and wildlife."* Pratiwi (2000: 8) considered ecotourism as *"a type of tourism that requires using resources without running out of or destroying them."* However, ecotourism is not only a type of tourism but also an opportunity for local people to develop socially and protect endangered natural habitats. Based on this approach, ecotourism is expressed as *"travels that contribute to the local people, take care to preserve the ecosystem integrity, provide economic opportunities and understand the structure of the natural environment"* (Khan, 1997: 989). The International Ecotourism Association, on the other hand, defined ecotourism as *"responsible travel to natural areas that conserves the environment, sustains the well-being of local people and emphasizes education"* (The International Ecotourism Society, 2015).

The definitions for the ecotourism concept show similar features to each other. On the other hand, this concept was interpreted from different perspectives in the historical process. The tourism industry has seen ecotourism as a valuable marketing tool in directing tourists toward natural and cultural destinations. Economists state that ecotourism can generate employment in economically underdeveloped destinations. Resource management experts and nature conservators regard ecotourism as an educational tool that enhances nature conservation programs and an income tool for financing these programs. Finally, people who focused on the adverse effects of tourism development held ecotourism as a necessity for the sustainability of tourism resources. Considering the concept of ecotourism from different perspectives has contributed significantly to the notion (Pratiwi, 2000).

The Features and Principles of Ecotourism

Despite various definitions of ecotourism, the concept mainly covers two features: The interests of tourists in nature and protecting the environment. Here, it is crucial to take sustainability principles as a basis; otherwise, ecotourism will not continue (Mananyi, 1998). Therefore, ecotourism should care about the local community, be sensitive to social demands, protect the ecosystem and natural environment from adverse situations, emphasize the importance of the natural environment, and provide long-term benefits to the destinations. A society and environment-based approach is the most significant feature of ecotourism (Manning & Dougherty, 1995).

It is possible to make some inferences in line with the explanations about ecotourism. At this point, the characteristics of ecotourism should be elaborated based on tourist types, location, activity, opportunity, and development approach and process. Tourists who prefer ecotourism enjoy visiting natural and cultural environments and are interested in learning about the local culture (tourist type). Ecotourists mostly prefer natural areas (location). In ecotourism, it is crucial to use resources without harming the environment and support environmental education (activity). In addition, particular care should be taken to use environmentally friendly technologies and local resources (opportunity). While ecotourism provides economic development, on the one hand, it also protects the natural environment (development approach). In addition, ecotourism minimizes the unfavorable effects on society and the environment (development process) (Pratiwi, 2000).

As understood from the characteristics of ecotourism, the concept has developed as an idea rather than a discipline. The International Ecotourism Association came together with governments, non-governmental organizations, private sector businesses, academics, and local communities and determined the principles of ecotourism after long-term discussions. The principles of ecotourism are as follows (Wood, 2002):

- Minimizing the natural and cultural effects that may harm a destination,
- Educating tourists visiting a destination about the environment,
- Emphasizing the importance of environmentally responsible businesses–to meet the needs of a destination and protect its nature and culture–that can cooperate with the community and local governments,
- Generating income for the management and protection of natural and protected areas in a destination,
- Preparing visitor management schedules for places planning to become ecotourism destinations,

- Evaluating positive and negative effects on a destination, minimizing the adverse effects, and encouraging the use of environmental and social studies besides long-term control programs,
- Striving to provide economic benefits to local communities and local businesses living in natural areas within the boundaries of a destination,
- Adopting a tourism approach that will not exceed the environmental and social change limits decided by researchers and local people in a destination,
- Providing an infrastructure minimizing fossil fuel use, protecting local plants and wildlife, and being in harmony with the natural and cultural environment.

The concept of ecotourism, in principle, attaches importance to the sustainability of economic, socio-cultural, and environmental advantages offered by tourism. Therefore, ecotourism pays attention to environmental, natural, and cultural heritage protection, providing tourists with information about heritage values, making tourists feel free, including local people in ecotourism plans, and helping local people to earn economic welfare, and considering these as principles (Marques, 2000).

THE INTERACTION BETWEEN ECOTOURISM AND THE ENVIRONMENT

In a destination, ecotourism interacts with the economic, socio-cultural, and physical environments. Although ecotourism is the best way of sustainability in tourism, it can cause both positive and negative influences on the environment. However, ecotourism, with its principles for the protection of the ecosystem, is accepted as a type of tourism that will have the minimum negative impact on the environment (Arabatzis & Grigoroudis, 2010; Çevirgen, 2003).

Because of the economic incentives, the conservation of natural areas provides economic benefits to destinations, and there are positive financial developments in the destinations where ecotourism takes place. Thanks to the changing tourism approach worldwide, ecotourism has become a type of tourism with a considerable financial return. After the national and local governments provided proper incentives for ecotourism destinations, the contribution of ecotourism to the economy has increased. Indeed, ecotourism should provide a sustainable livelihood and form an economic basis for local people. Only in this way can ecotourism achieve its purpose (Ankaya et al., 2018; Das & Chatterjee, 2015).

Ecotourism provides many benefits to businesses operating in the tourism industry, such as hotels, restaurants, souvenir shops, travel agencies, and tour operators. These benefits are rising foreign exchange-based trade in the country, direct or indirect employment, improved infrastructure facilities, boosting local production and sale, and preserving local culture. Besides the positive effects of ecotourism, there are also some unfavorable effects. The most important one is the seasonal occurrence of ecotourism activities in a destination. This situation both raises the operational costs of tourism enterprises and limits employment opportunities within a certain period. Another negative impact stems from the distance of the ecotourism centers from settlements, which causes an increase in costs for tourists (Tisdell, 1996).

Ecotourism also has some positive effects on the socio-cultural environment. Since the increasing number of ecotourists desire to discover nature, ecotourism is becoming widespread. Ecotourists establish a close relationship with the local people, and eventually, a cultural exchange occurs between the tourist and the local people. Ecotourists are very willing to learn about the culture of the local people. Local people, who are aware of this situation, attach more importance to protecting cultural values (Ankaya et al., 2018). As a result of the positive influences of ecotourism, states preserve cultural resources and attractions, traditions become prominent, local trading activities increases, and education activities develop. The socio-cultural environment also has some adverse effects, which local people might suffer. In destinations where ecotourism activities are very intense, excessive dependence on tourism can emerge, crime rates increase, family structures change, traditional practices might disappear, an over-pressure toward local activities could occur, and culture becomes commercialized (Matthews, 2002).

The effects of ecotourism on the physical environment are also crucial. Tourists attach great importance to the pristine natural areas in the destinations visited. Ecotourism protects and improves these areas, encourages individual or small group travel, and prevents the carrying capacity from being exceeded. Thus, natural resource consumption drops to a minimum level, and recyclable products are recycled. In addition, ecotourism allows for taking more efficient care of natural areas and gives importance to the preservation of local architecture (Arabatzis & Grigoroudis, 2010; Kıvılcım, 2020).

On the other hand, with the tourists' increasing demands, ecotourism has started to create adverse effects on the physical environment. Increasing demand causes mass tourism and an exceeding carrying capacity. New buildings in natural areas deteriorate the local architecture and historical texture and raise environmental pollution. Garbage and waste thrown into the environment by unconscious tourists harm the ecosystem. After all, damaged wildlife, decreased endemic plant species, endangered underwater life, expanding steppe areas, and spoiled forest areas are the primary reasons for landslides and erosion. The impacts of unorganized ecotourism activities will cause many more negative events. Essential to reducing the unfavorable effects is raising awareness of tourists with all tourism stakeholders' participation. At this point, this training should instill tourism businesses, local people, and tourists in environmental responsibility and consciousness (Arabatzis & Grigoroudis, 2010; Kıvılcım, 2020).

RELATIONSHIP BETWEEN SUSTAINABLE DEVELOPMENT AND ECOTOURISM

Sustainable development leans on equal distribution of economic and social tourism benefits among the local people and the continuity of cultural integrity and environmental resources (Yonglong, 1996). Many types of tourism have emerged because alternative tourism types are necessary for sustainable development in tourism. Ecotourism is one of these types of tourism and has significantly developed with globally accepted sustainable ecological practices. In particular, the tendency of tourists to nature-based travel has increased ecotourism activities and reduced the adverse effects of tourism on the environment (Diamantis & Ladkin, 1999).

In ecotourism destinations, tourists make some expenses to meet their accommodation, food and beverage, and entertainment needs and thus provide economic benefits to local people and businesses. In addition, socio-cultural interaction develops with local people. Ecotourism also contributes to environmental development. In ecotourism destinations, several strategies to protect flora and fauna, including pre-visit training on sustainability, are crucial. Therefore, the approach of "educate and benefit" is possible. To put it more clearly, providing pre-visit training to tourists in ecotourism destinations has positive effects on the behavior of tourists during their visit and contributes to the continuity of resources (İnan, 2007).

Tourist guidance services provided in ecotourism destinations also increase the tourists' utilization of natural resources and minimize the adverse effects. Thus, it contributes to the protection and sustainability of natural resources. Furthermore, tourist guides should specialize in a particular area. For example, ecotourism guidance appears as a field of expertise. Having sufficient knowledge about the relevant destination contributes positively to the natural environment (Erkol Bayram, 2019).

As a primary condition for sustainable development, some issues must be scheduled and practiced with the participation of all stakeholders. Some researchers suggest that ecotourism destinations will show sustainable development in terms of the economic, socio-cultural, and physical environment, with a total emphasis on five aspects: An integrated approach, a planned and slow start, education and training, local benefit, evaluation and recycling (Masberg & Morales, 1999).

Tisdell (1998) mentions the necessity of four elements by referring to the importance of sustainable development in successfully realizing ecotourism activities. The first is creating economic value. Ecotourism destinations should be profitable for tour operators, travel agencies, and tourism professionals. The second is for environmental protection. The number of tourists and carrying capacity are significant determinants in protecting ecotourism destinations. The third is social acceptability. Here, local people's economic benefit from ecotourism affects the sustainability of ecotourism. If locals gain a profit, they are satisfied with eco-tourists visiting the destination. The fourth is political sustainability. Out-of-tourism use of natural areas should be limited and meticulously controlled, but it should be kept in mind that local people react to banning the use of the relevant destination altogether.

The sustainability of ecotourism varies depending on economic, social, and environmental development. In other words, economic, social, and environmental developments are success factors separately. *Economic success factors* cover the political environment, legal systems, government policies, security, and infrastructure. While community participation or partnership, a good definition of society, improvement of social communication, poverty, and social participation are *social success factors*, the environmental quality of the destination, ecological limitations, and water availability are among the *environmental factors*. Since economic, social, and environmental developments are success factors, sector investors should consider these factors before making an ecotourism investment at a destination (Parker & Khare, 2005).

Ecotourism activities are in great demand in the world, and ecotourism provides social, environmental, and economic benefits to destinations. Vietnam, Nepal, Australia, New Zealand, USA, Costa Rica, Cambodia, Norway, Ecuador, Peru, Kenya, Tanzania, France, Italy, Spain, Germany, UK, and Türkiye are among the countries where ecotourism activities take place. Tourists frequently prefer visiting national parks, watching landscapes, being in natural areas, observing wildlife, bird watching, trekking, farm visits, highland visits, cycling tours, angling, etc., in ecotourism destinations (Kasalak, 2015). The increasing number of tourists participating in such activities ensures that ecotourism destinations generate high income. In addition, ecotourism's focus on society and the environment causes positive developments in the local people and the physical environment. On the other hand, the adverse effects of ecotourism on the economic, social, and physical environment can emerge in destinations where no sustainable tourism approach applies. As a result, ecotourism might have positive and negative effects on sustainable development.

CONCLUSION

Many underdeveloped countries implement development policies to increase their economic welfare levels. The development phenomenon was considered only as "increasing national income" before the 1970s. However, development strategies planned only according to economic factors caused countries to ignore social, cultural, and physical environmental elements. Eventually, while these countries were trying to develop economically, they overlooked the unfavorable effects on the environment. However, in time, people grew an environmental consciousness and turned the "bare" development concept into "sustainable development" including the social, cultural, and physical environment. Thanks to sustainable development, environmental damages went down, and a great sensitivity to environmental sustainability emerged (Bousrih, 2013; Cinnioğlu, 2015; Tekeli & Kırıcı Tekeli, 2020).

Besides, the sustainable development concept, which changed people's consumption habits, has affected their tourism preferences. New and unusual tourist and tourism types have emerged. Thus, the classical tourism understanding has been replaced by ecotourism intertwined with nature. Ecotourism, which adopts a sustainable tourism approach, protects the existing ecosystem, helps to increase economic and socio-cultural welfare, and ensures its development by protecting natural areas. In this respect, ecotourism contributes to economic, socio-cultural, and environmental development and supports the sustainable development of the relevant destination. Ecotourism is considered a type of tourism that causes the slightest damage to the environment (Demir, 2011; Öztürk & Mengüloğlu, 2008).

FUTURE RESEARCH DIRECTIONS

Detailed information about flora and fauna and the social structure of an ecotourism destination is essential to succeed in ecotourism activities. This basic information will make it easier to market the relevant destination by emphasizing unique ecotourism activities in the future. At the same time, learning about the socio-cultural structure of the local people, their perspectives on the natural environment, and income levels in the ecotourism destinations will help to determine the ecotourism potential correctly. Through this information, it will be possible to comprehend whether ecotourism in this place will be successful and sustainable (Demir, 2011).

Furthermore, national strategic plans and activity methods are necessary for successful and sustainable ecotourism. Local people must participate in preparing strategic plans. In other words, tourism stakeholders such as local people, tourism businesses, and non-governmental organizations should act together. In addition to national strategic programs, the state should have a tourism strategy for ecotourism in a region. Relevant policies should support the economic benefit of local people in ecotourism investments. Simply put, ecotourism policies should be sensitive towards the environment and society. Ecotourism targets, characteristics, and principles only succeed by focusing on the environment and local people (Kuter & Ünal, 2009).

REFERENCES

Akış, S. (1999). Sürdürülebilir turizm ve Türkiye. *Anatolia Turizm Araştırmaları Dergisi, 10*, 36–46.

Ankaya, F. Ü., Yazıcı, K., Balık, G., & Aslan, B. G. (2018). Dünya'da ve Türkiye'de ekoturizm, sosyal-kültürel ve ekonomik katkıları. *Ulusal Çevre Bilimleri Araştırma Dergisi, 1*(2), 69–72.

Arabatzis, G., & Grigoroudis, E. (2010). Visitors' satisfaction, perceptions and gap analysis: The case of Dadia-Lefkimi-Souflion National Park. *Forest Policy and Economics, 12*(3), 163–172. doi:10.1016/j.forpol.2009.09.008

Ballantine, J. L., & Eagles, P. F. J. (1994). Defining Canadian ecotourists. *Journal of Sustainable Tourism, 2*(4), 210–214. doi:10.1080/09669589409510698

Bayram, G. E. (2019). Turist rehberleri bakış açısıyla ekoturizm: Algı, sorumluluk ve rollerin tespitine yönelik bir araştırma. *Journal of Recreation and Tourism Research, 6*(1), 81–91. doi:10.31771/jrtr.2019.17

Becker, D. F. (2002). Sustentabilidade: Um novo (velho) paradigma de desenvolvimento regional. In D. F. Becker (Ed.), Desenvolvimento sustentável: Necessidade e ou possibilidade? (pp. 27-94). Sant Cruz do Sul: Edunisc.

Bousrih, L. (2013). Social capital, human capital and sustainable economic development. *Poznań University of Economics Review, 13*(3), 42–54.

Business Dictionary. (2019). What is sustainable? *Business Dictionary.* http://www.businessdictionary.com/definition/social-sustainability.html

Campbell, L. M. (1999). Ecotourism in rural developing communities. *Annals of Tourism Research, 26*(3), 534–553. doi:10.1016/S0160-7383(99)00005-5

Ceballos-Lascurain, H. (1987). The future of 'ecotourism'. *Mexico Journal,* 13-14.

Cernat, L., & Gourdon, J. (2007). *Is the concept of sustainable tourism sustainable?* United Nations Publication.

Çevirgen, A. (2003). *Sürdürülebilir turizm kapsamında ekoturizm ve Edremit yöresi için bir model önerisi* [Yayımlanmamış doktora tezi]. Dokuz Eylül Üniversitesi.

Cinnioğlu, H. (2015). Sürdürülebilir ekonomik kalkınma kapsamında ekoturizmin çevre üzerindeki etkilerinin eleştirel bir bakış açısıyla incelenmesi. *Sosyal Bilimler Metinleri, 1*, 1–22.

Coccossis, H. (1996). Tourism and sustainability: Perspectives and implications. *European Experiences*, 1-21.

Collin, R. B., & Collin, R. W. (2009). *Encyclopedia of sustainability*. Greenwood Press.

Costanza, R., & Bernard, C. P. (1995). Defining and predicting sustainability. *Ecological Economics*, *15*(3), 193–196. doi:10.1016/0921-8009(95)00048-8

D'amore, L. J. (1992). Sürdürülebilir turizmin desteklenmesi. *Tourism Management*, *9*, 258–262. doi:10.1016/0261-5177(92)90096-P

Das, M., & Chatterjee, B. (2015). Ecotourism: A panacea or a predicament? *Tourism Management Perspectives*, *14*, 3–16. doi:10.1016/j.tmp.2015.01.002

Demir, C., & Çevirgen, A. (2006). *Turizm ve çevre yönetimi: Sürdürülebilir gelişme yaklaşımı*. Nobel Yayıncılık.

Demir, S. (2011). *İğneada'nın ekoturizm potansiyelinin saptanması* [Yayımlanmamış yüksek lisans tezi]. İstanbul Teknik Üniversitesi.

Diamantis, D. (1998). Consumer behavior and ecotourism products [Editorial]. *Annals of Tourism Research*, *25*(2), 515–528. doi:10.1016/S0160-7383(97)00076-5

Diamantis, D., & Ladkin, A. (1999). The links between sustainable tourism and ecotourism: A definitional and operational perspective. *Journal of Tourism Studies*, *10*(2), 35–46.

Doğan, M. (2010). *Ekomüze odaklı sürdürülebilir destinasyon ve Gökçeada üzerine bir uygulama* [Yayımlanmamış yüksek lisans tezi]. Çanakkale Onsekiz Mart Üniversitesi.

Edmonds, J., & Leposky, G. (1998, June). Ecotourism and sustainable tourism development in Southeast Asia [Conference presentation]. *Third International Conference of the Asia Pacific Tourism Association*, Hong Kong.

Erdoğan, N. (2010). *Ekoturizmin ve doğa temelli turizmin geldikleri noktadaki kavramsal çerçeve*. TOD-EG Türkiye Ormancılar Derneği Ekoturizm Çalıştayı.

Güler, O., & Tufan, E. (2013). Sürdürülebilir bir yatırım örneği olarak yeşil otelcilik. İçinde Ş. Aydın Tükeltürk & M. Boz (Eds.), *Turizmde güncel konu ve eğilimler* (pp. 357-374). Detay Yayıncılık.

Güneş, G. (2008). Turizmin sürdürülebilirliği için ekoturizm. *Popüler Bilim*, *15*(177), 28–30.

Hayta, A. B. (2009). Sürdürülebilir tüketim davranışının kazanılmasında tüketici eğitiminin rolü. *Journal of Ahi Evran University Kırşehir Faculty of Education*, *10*(3), 143–151.

İnan, Ç. (2007). *Yıldız (Istranca) Dağları ve çevresindeki floradan sürdürülebilir kırsal kalkınma ve ekoturizm amacıyla yararlanma olanakları* [Yayımlanmamış yüksek lisans tezi]. Namık Kemal Üniversitesi.

Kahraman, N. (1994). *Sürdürülebilir kalkınma ve turizm*. I. Turizm Sempozyumu.

Karadaş, F. (2008). *Sürdürülebilir kalkınma çerçevesinde Türkiye'de enerji sektörü ve politikaları* [Yayımlanmamış yüksek lisans tezi]. Gaziantep Üniversitesi.

Kasalak, M. A. (2015). Dünya'da ekoturizm pazarı ve ekoturizmin ülke gelirlerine katkıları. *Journal of Recreation and Tourism Research*, *2*(2), 20–26.

Khan, M. M. (1997). Tourism development and dependency theory: Mass tourism vs. ecotourism. *Annals of Tourism Research*, *24*(4), 988–991. doi:10.1016/S0160-7383(97)00033-9

Kıvılcım, B. (2020). *Sürdürülebilir turizm kapsamında seyahat acentelerinin ekoturizm faaliyetleri: Doğu Karadeniz Bölgesinde bir araştırma* [Yayımlanmamış doktora tezi]. Atatürk Üniversitesi.

Koban, E., & Eker İşçioğlu, T. (2019). *Turizm pazarlaması rekabet yaklaşımıyla*. Ekin Publishing.

Kuhn, L. (2007). Sustainable tourism as emergent discourse. *World Futures*, *63*(3-4), 286–297. doi:10.1080/02604020601174950

Kuter, N., & Ünal, H. E. (2009). Sürdürülebilirlik kapsamında ekoturizmin çevresel, ekonomik ve sosyo-kültürel etkileri. *Kastamonu Üniversitesi Orman Fakültesi Dergisi*, *9*(2), 146–156.

Mananyi, A. (1998). Optimal management of ecotourism. *Tourism Economics*, *4*(2), 147–169. doi:10.1177/135481669800400203

Manning, E. W., & Dougherty, T. D. (1995). Sustainable tourism: Preserving the golden goose. *The Cornell Hotel and Restaurant Administration Quarterly*, *36*(2), 4–42. doi:10.1016/0010-8804(95)93841-H

Marques, L. C. (2000, July). *An evaluation of ecolodges in the Brazilian Amazon* [Conference presentation]. Ecotourism Conference, Dominican Republic.

Masberg, B. A., & Morales, N. (1999). A case analysis of strategies in ecotourism development. *Aquatic Ecosystem Health & Management, 2*(3), 289–300. doi:10.1080/14634989908656965

Matthews, E. J. (2002). *Ecotourism: Are current practices delivering desired outcomes? A comparative case study analysis* [Unpublished master's thesis, State University].

Mensah, A. M., & Castro, L. C. (2004). Sustainable resource use & sustainable development: A contradiction. Center for Development Research, University of Bonn, 1-22.

Middleton, V., & Hawkins, R. (1998). *Sustainable tourism: A marketing perspective.* Butterworth and Heinemann.

Neto, F. (2003). A new approach to sustainable tourism development: Moving beyond environmental protection. *Natural Resources Forum, 27*(3), 212–222. doi:10.1111/1477-8947.00056

Olalı, H., & Timur, A. (1988). *Turizm ekonomisi.* Ofset Matbaacılık.

Orams, M. B. (1995). Towards a more desirable form of ecotourism. *Tourism Management, 16*(1), 3–8. doi:10.1016/0261-5177(94)00001-Q

Özbey, R. F. (2002). Sustainable tourism development in globalization progress, globalization and sustainable development. *International Scientific Conference, Bulgaria.*

Özdemir, G. (2018). *Food waste management within sustainability perspective: A study on five star chain hotels* [Yayımlanmamış doktora tezi]. Gazi Üniversitesi.

Özgüç, N. (2007). *Turizm coğrafyası.* Çantay Kitabevi.

Öztürk, T., & Mengüloğlu, M. (2008). Sürdürülebilir kalkınmada fiziksel kırsal alan planlaması. *Anadolu Tarım Bilimleri Dergisi, 23*(3), 209–215.

Parker, S., & Khare, A. (2005). Understanding, success factors for ensuring sustainability in ecotourism development in Southern Africa. *Journal of Ecotourism, 4*(1), 32–46. doi:10.1080/14724040508668436

Pekin, F. (2011). *Çözüm: Kültür turizmi.* İletişim Yayınları.

Pratiwi, S. (2000). *Understanding local community participation in ecotourism development: A critical analysis of select published literature* [Unpublished master's thesis, Michigan State University].

Rızaoğlu, B. (2004). *Turizmin sosyo-kültürel temelleri*. Detay yayıncılık.

Şanlıöz Özgen, H. K., Dilek, S. E., Türksoy, S. S., & Kaygalak Çelebi, S. (2016). Turizm ve çevre: Kavramsal çerçeve. İçinde N. Koçak (Ed.), Sürdürülebilir turizm yönetimi (pp. 1-22). Detay Yayıncılık.

Şen, H., Kaya, A., & Alpaslan, B. (2018). Sürdürülebilirlik üzerine tarihsel ve güncel bir perspektif. *Ekonomik Yaklaşım Derneği, 20*(107), 1–47.

Tekeli, M., & Kırıcı Tekeli, E. (2020). Sustainable gastronomic tourism. In F. Türkmen (Ed.), *Selected academic studies from Turkish tourism sector* (pp. 113–133). Peter Lang.

The International Ecotourism Society. (2015). *What is ecotourism?* TIES. https://ecotourism.org/what-is-ecotourism/

Tisdell, C. (1996). Ecotourism, economics, and the environment: Observations from China. *Journal of Travel Research, 34*(4), 11–19. doi:10.1177/004728759603400402

Tisdell, C. (1998). Ecotourism: Aspect of its sustainability and compatibility with conservation, social and other objectives. *Australian Journal of Hospitality Management, 5*(2), 11–21.

UNWTO & UNEP. (2005). *Making tourism more sustainable: A guide for policymakers*. UNWTO, Madrid and UNEP, Paris. http://www.unep.fr/shared/publications/pdf/dtix0592xpa-tourismpolicyen.pdf

Vehkamäki, S. (2005). The concept of sustainability in modern times. In A. Jalkanen & P. Nygren (Eds.), *Sustainable use of renewable natural resources from principles to practices* (pp. 23–35). University of Helsinki Department of Forest Ecology Publications.

Ward, N. K. (1997). *Ecotourism: Reality or rhetoric. Ecotourism development in the state of Quintana Roo, Mexico* [Unpublished master's thesis, University of Portsmouth].

WCED. (1987). Our common future, report of world commission on environment and development. UN. http://www.un-documents.net/our-common-future.pdf

Weaver, D. (2006). *Sustainable tourism*. Butterworth and Heinemann.

Wood, M. E. (2002). *Ecotourism: Principles, practices & policies for sustainability*. United Nations Publication.

Yonglong, L. (1996). Eco-tourism industry development-an alternative to sustainable use of landscape resources. *Journal of Environmental Sciences (China), 8*(3), 298–307.

KEY TERMS AND DEFINITIONS

Ecology: A branch of science that studies organisms and their environmental relationships.

Ecotourism: Educational, environmental, folkloric, nature-sensitive ecological travels.

Ecotourists: People who have free time to travel, have high economic income, are well-educated, and are interested in the natural environment.

Environment: The ambience in which an organism lives.

Sustainability: A balance that ensures harmony between human activities and the social, cultural, and natural environment.

Sustainable Development: A development type that considers both present and future generation needs while using raw material resources, making investments, determining the goals of technological developments, and institutional changes.

Sustainable Tourism: An understanding that aims to meet the needs of the tourism industry and local communities without endangering future generations' ability to meet their needs.

Chapter 12
Using Indigenous Sport and Games for Sustainable Community Tourism in Barbados

Wendy Cynthia Sealy
Institute of Psychology, Business, and Human Sciences, University of Chichester, UK

Paul Wheeler
Institute of Sports, University of Chichester, UK

ABSTRACT

Sustainable tourism development in the Caribbean is inhibited by several challenges, such as diseconomies of scale and scope and other structural and resource constraints. These challenges are further exacerbated by the heavy prominence of transnational conglomerates. As a result, many Caribbean islands do not appropriate the full value from tourism with the majority of the revenues and profits accruing to companies based outside the region. Many tourists who visit these islands do not venture into the local communities as they are encouraged to stay in the all-inclusive enclaves. Researchers have long recognised that indigenous sports tourism can be a tool that would allow marginalised communities to achieve greater control of their livelihoods. This chapter will focus on sports and games that are deeply rooted in Barbadian culture and history. Using a case study approach, the authors will show how they can be monetised and fused with other aspects of community culture to attract a different type of tourists who will venture into the local communities and spend their money there.

DOI: 10.4018/978-1-6684-6796-1.ch012

INTRODUCTION/BACKGROUND

Barbados is located at the southern end of the archipelago that makes up the islands of the eastern Caribbean. Since the island's independence in 1966, the economy of Barbados has been transformed from a low-income economy dependent upon sugar production into an upper middle-income economy based on tourism and the offshore sector. With an estimated population of 287,375 individuals in 2020, Barbados traditionally promotes itself as an upmarket tourist destination with a 'snob appeal' which demands a premium price. Its comparative advantage is derived from the 3-Ss of Sea, Sun and Sand but the island's distinctiveness is enhanced by an array of attractions including several historical sites, cultural activities, beautiful beaches, friendly citizens, special events and a vibrant folk culture. However, over the years the character and appeal of the destination has changed with all-inclusive resorts making up a significant portion of hotel rooms.

Tourism has been the major earner of foreign exchange for Barbados but, Covid-19 has generated the worst tourism demand shock in history. Real GDP grew by just 1.4% in 2021 following a 14.0% decline in 2020. Tourism GDP shrank further in 2021 and accounted for 73% of lost output relative to 2019 levels (https://crisis24.garda.com/insights-intelligence/intelligence/country-reports/barbados).bn. As of 2017, the national debt of Barbados stood at US$7.92 billion (Chase 2019. Chase (2019) attributes this to Barbados' neo-colonial economy. The Covid-19 crisis has exposed these economic weaknesses, vulnerabilities and lack of diversity. This has certainly forced policy makers into crisis management about the recovery of tourism in the short and long term. There is urgent need for a more sustainable model of tourism development for Barbados. However, Barbados' problems started long before the Covid-19 pandemic and will continue thereafter if the structure of ownership, management and control of the tourism industry does not change. Barbados suffers from a lack of coordination of indigenous driven policies, and the habit of short-term, rather than long-term tourism planning (Sealy, 2017). Successive governments favour foreign investment for tourism development and would grant generous tax concessions to foreign companies to set up tourism businesses. According to Chase (2019), these transnational corporations have benefited greatly from tax breaks and contracts but claims that 'the government's frivolous actions of giving away money to many non-Bajan private and corporate investors ……has ultimately hurt the economy and the citizens of Barbados'.

Many tourist destinations in the Caribbean are not receiving their fair share of the value generated by tourism. Transnational ownership of Caribbean hotels, attractions and tour operators ensure that consumer behaviour, product development and price is controlled by entities outside the region. Foreign entities have contributed to substantial leakage of foreign exchange revenues, social polarization, social exclusion, structural social inequalities, and environmental degradation (Bhola-Paul, 2015). 37 to 90% of tourism expenditure generated by Caribbean tourism accrues to the foreign countries where the transnationals are based (Pattullo, 2006; Sealy, 2017). In Cuba, only 30-38% of tourist expenditure remain on the island (Simpson, 2014). This neo-colonial economic structure has resulted in many indigenous tourism businesses closing or significantly reducing their business activity. Barbadian historian, Hilary Beckles, once referred to tourism as the 'new plantocracy' (Beckles, 1990); likewise, Weaver (1989), called it 'plantation tourism' or 'apartheid tourism' as it was recently called by Elliott & Neitotti, (2008). This rhetoric is due to tourism's structural similarities to the plantation economies of the 17th and 18th centuries (Beckles, 1990; Brohman, 1996; Chase, 2019; Lewis, 2002; Pattullo, 2006; Strachan, 2002; Weaver, 1989). These similarities include the dominant role of expatriate capital, management, control, profit repatriation, labor exploitation and social inequalities.

While the sugar cane, tobacco and cotton industries appropriated much of 17th and 18th century profits to the metropole, the 21st century culprit is 'tourism'. The tour operators, all-inclusive hotels and the foreign based international chain hotels and resorts all have stakes in Barbados' tourism. The tour operator operates in a very capitalistic and liberalized oligopolistic system where they control their own transportation companies (charter airlines), travel agencies, and hotels at the destination through vertical and horizontal integration which facilitates their dominance of the market (Dale, 2000; Inkson & Minnaert, 2012; Klemm & Parkinson, 2001; Mohammad & Ammar, 2015). Alarmingly, over 90% of all tourism bookings into Barbados is through tour operators (Sealy, 2017).

The other culprit is the all-inclusive resort. All-inclusive visitors are discouraged from venturing outside the resorts to spend money in locally owned enterprises which decreases the opportunities for local restaurants, taxi drivers, craftsmen, vendors and farmers to earn a living from tourism as the money becomes exclusively concentrated within the hands of the foreign conglomerates that own these hotels (Williams, 2012). All-inclusive resorts offer accommodation, meals, tours and recreational activities for one price (Turner and Troiano (1987). These services are then offered within the hotel 'enclaved' as several resorts own and operate their own boutiques, gifts shops, watersports operations, tour busses and mini-marts. As 'enclaved' economies they marginalise and polarise local traders. Consequently, the average per capita spending of visitors is minimised (Pattullo, 2006). Although all-inclusives attract high volumes of visitors the expenditure, per capita, is low resulting in a 'zero-dollar' tourism economy (King *et al*, 2006) Because of their ability to produce large volumes of visitors' local authorities tend to grant foreign investors major concessions and tax breaks that are not given to local tourism business owners. Even when local entrepreneurs work with international hotels, they are exploited by them. Reports of delays on payments for goods and services are common and they impose their foreign business ethics on local businesses which work in the hotel's favour (Jonnson, 2018). Only recently the Guardian published a research report, from UK Charity Tourism Concern regarding how all-inclusive resorts are hurting the local people in resort areas in Tenerife, Kenya and Barbados (McVeigh, 2014). They found that hotel staff had worse working conditions and labour rights and were subjected to more stress and longer hours than those in other types of hotels (McVeigh, 2014). Unfortunately, these resorts promote socio-cultural aversions and forms of tourists racism and xenophobia (Kock et al., 2019). So notorious is the social and economic impact on local environments that ScottDunn (2023) has urged travellers to do more research and to take more sustainable and ethical holidays.

Over the last 20 years all-inclusive tourism enclaves have grown in Barbados, with the most recent being Marriott International's acquisition of seven (7) hotels of the Elegant Hotels chain and the newly opened 450 room Wyndham Sam Lords Castle. As this Barbadian hotel owner explained:

A number of the resorts (non all-inclusive) and restaurants are closing and turning into condominiums because the all-inclusive product has killed the restaurant trade, and it is killing the smaller, independently run hotels. All-inclusive don't provide any business to Barbados, except for the resort the people stay in. They don't provide any business to the restaurants, taxis, shops, supermarkets, gas stations, because people go to the resorts and stay there. It's not good for Barbados; it's not good for tourism" (Sealy, 2020).

Seventy-five to eighty percent of the vacation expenses of all-inclusive package tours are allocated to tour operators, airlines, hotels and other global corporations headquartered in a foreign country (Kondo, 2008). All-inclusive resorts take advantage of bulk buying and they depend on the reliability of suppliers, the quantity and quality of supplies to cater to the taste of international visitors (Kock, 2016). If these resorts used local supply chains, the economic benefits for the destination would be enormous but regretfully, this is not the case. Only 16% of fruit and 20% of fish consumed in Caribbean hotels are sourced locally (Caribbean Development Bank, 2017). While large scale hotel investment generates mainly low pay jobs the current structure of the industry has not resulted in any cascading, long-term wealth for locals and consequently the island remains stagnant and under developed. In all fairness, a recent study into the impacts of foreign hotel investment into Barbados did reveal that although resort hotel managers wanted their hotels to create positive local impacts, the structure of their organisations and their operating models did not readily facilitate this (Jonnson, 2018). The structure of tourism has not served the island well and has, in fact, hindered the sustainable development of indigenous business and exacerbated economic problems. Consequently, Barbados remains unprogressive. Only structural change and the targeting of different markets with a more allocentric type of tourists can reverse the situation.

This research revolves around questions about the extent to which traditional games and sport in Barbados could be used to stimulated local community engagement to minimise the oligopolistic powers that appropriate the majority of the wealth made from tourism. These questions are answered through the analysis of three case studies of successful indigenous sport event tourism ventures. The authors also draw on their knowledge of community sport, tourism management and the sport history of Barbados. The discussion proposes the transformation and utilization of indigenous sports and games into systematic but authentic sport products that would inspire economic and socially marginalised indigenous groups in Barbados to adopt entrepreneurial behaviours in sport tourism that would create a new tourism and engage visitors and locals in a cultural exchange to foster local wealth generation and sustainable development.

Community and Indigenous Based Tourism and Sport Tourism

In places like Barbados with a history of slavery, oppression and exploitation, anything associated with the plantation such as cultural rituals and practices are rejected because they historically represent hardship. However, the United Nations development goals for 2015-2030 has set "Sustainable Development Goals" (SDGs) which specifically cite sports as the vehicle for Development & Peace" in developing countries (Ruhanen & Whitford, 2016). Sports tourism can contribute to economic, social, psychological and political empowerment among residents with positive commercial benefits for indigenous communities. As will be demonstrated from the case studies, indigenous sports are a form of niche tourism and nostalgia tourism that can attract media attention and serve as destination marketing tools and image formation due to their uniqueness (Herstein & Berger, 2013; Pyo, Cook & Howell, 1988). One of the major benefits of indigenous sports tourism is that it is an authentic and differentiated type of tourism product, which although can be copied by other organisations and groups, the authenticity of the sport cannot be perfectly imitated. Such sports can get tourists out of the all-inclusive enclaves for more meaningful experiences of the island culture in 'purer' and 'simpler' surroundings (Ruhanen & Whitford, 2016).

In Australia indigenous experiences earned an estimated A$570 million. Researchers found that tourists who participated in indigenous experiences spent an average of A$3,800 in Australia, or 39% more than the average for all travellers. The academic literature contains several examples of successful indigenous sports tourism. For instance, Muchtar *et al*. (2021) argues that indigenous sports create a tourist attraction. They claim that sports tourism increases destination competitiveness and can earn foreign exchange which is exactly what Barbados needs. They cite the Marathon Championship in Jakarta as an example of a successful sport event managed by community leaders. Indigenous sport events can also be fused with other cultural products to provide an enhanced and vibrant experience for participants, spectators and visitors. Such fusion can include arts and crafts shows, cultural entertainment and displays of visual and creative arts. Similarly, Gibson, Kaplanidou & Kang (2012) concluded that small-scale events were a viable alternative to large scale events which are normally associated with negative results due to the needs for expensive, one-off infrastructure. They found that small events promote a consistent annual flow of visitors, use existing facilities, and are of a size that is compatible with the host community.

Case Studies in Indigenous Sports

Indigenous events, however, are staged across the globe and many have a long and significant history. Three such events are analysed here.

The Braemar Gathering

The Braemar Gathering is an annual event that channels a celebration of Scottishness through displays of tartan, bagpipes, dancing, and brute strength. They evoke a particular representation of Scotland and its sporting and cultural history and portray a popular image of the country for tourists to associate with (Jarvie 2003). The specific competitions include tossing the caber and the other heavyweight contests, such as 'throwing the weight over the bar', together with multiple running races, music and dancing events, totalling over 80 competitions that are contested over one day.

The Gathering draws tens of thousands of visitors from all over the world to the small Scottish village (population of the town in 2011 stood at 808) to witness these Highland Games (The Scotsman 2016). The Braemer Gathering is one of around a hundred Highland Games that take place in Scotland every year and its origins stretch back over 1,000 years.

The Gathering started as a type of war game in 1064 during the reign of King Malcolm III (1057-1093). The modern incarnation of the Braemar Gathering began in 1815 and subsequently, they were first attended by Queen Victoria in 1838 with royal support continuing ever since. Jarvie (2004) argues that her endorsement of the games, has been the biggest single factor in the event's growth.

Almost one hundred different Highland Games of various scales are held in Scotland annually and the majority are overseen by the Scottish Games Association which was formed in 1946 to formalise the events and to regulate the rules (Brewster *et a*l, 2009) However, each event is organised separately and today, the Braemar Royal Highland Charity organises the Gathering.

Higham and Hinch (2009) have recognised the importance of the celebration of identity in defining societies and cultures. The symbolism of the Highland Games certainly portrays and promotes Scotland and its heritage with a bold and confident voice. Furthermore, sports events boost local pride through the exhibition of the local heritage and traditions (Brewster *et al* 2009). Whereas, Weed & Bull (2004) have acknowledged the key economic value of events for local income generation and community benefit through the opportunities for attendees to spend.

A 2006 economic impact identified the total revenues received through admissions alone were £460,759 (Brewster *et al.* 2009). This does not include; catering and merchandising income spend at the games or secondary spend for transport and accommodation generated locally or within the country. Estimates vary, but Scotland's Highland Games generated approximately £25m in 2020 for the nation's economy (The Scotsman 2020).

The Braemar Gathering attracts around 16,000 spectators and in the Brewster *et al.* (2009) survey it was estimated that 94% of all attendees were classified as visitors from across the UK or from overseas. Direct marketing and promotion are through the comprehensive website (https://www.braemargathering.org/) which includes details of the history of the Gathering, and all the information a visitor requires when looking to attend. In 2022 a trial live stream was available with over four hours of material broadcast.

The Gathering is organised by community volunteers, and as Shone & Parry (2004) identify, most not-for-profit charitable bodies aim to at least break even. Yet without the support of sponsors, the cost of maintaining the facilities and holding the event would not be possible to achieve this target. The events are sponsored by (mainly) local organisations and again reflect the heritage and culture that helps to maintain the Scottish brand.

In support of the annual Gathering is the Braemar Highland Games Centre, which is a new tourists attraction linked to the games, and was opened in 2018. The centre is another source of income which incorporates an exhibition hall, gallery, archive, café and shop. It enables visitors to discover the history of the Highland Games and view the associated displays of images, documents and artefacts. Online merchandising is also available including clothing, toys and of course, whisky.

The Cooper's Hill Cheese-Rolling and Wake

The Cooper's Hill Cheese-Rolling and Wake is an annual event held on the Spring Bank Holiday at Cooper's Hill, near Gloucester in England. Participants race down the 1:2 gradient, 200-yard (180m) long hill after a round of Double Gloucester cheese is sent rolling down it. Aquilino *et al.* (2020) suggest not all events require substantial funds to deliver interest and excitement. They add that many niche, alternative or even 'wacky' events have become established that deliver tangible outcomes for the host. Thus, the cheese rolling festival is an example of a cultural celebration created by and for the public.

Today people from around the globe come to chase the weighty 8lb round of cheese down the hill. It has been recorded that the cheeses can reach speeds of up to 70mph, contestants run down the hill and the first runner to the bottom wins and the cheese is the prize.

The cheese rolling contest is believed to have been around for centuries with the first recorded evidence attributed to a message given by the Gloucester town crier in 1826, yet its true origins are alleged to be over six hundred years ago (Visitgloucester 2022). Bowdin (2005) reminds us that the UK has a rich tradition of events stretching back thousands of years. Some propose that it concerned the staking of grazing rights on the common and land around Cooper's Hill (Clifford 1944). A second story is that it evolved from pagan rituals, linked to the custom of rolling objects down the hill.

The event is covered in the UK and global media including television and tourism guidebooks including the Lonely Plant and Rough Guide. This worldwide exposure created significant interest. This supports Sharply and Stones (2011) research on the importance of maintaining the heritage of local events for local people. Bradley (2014) writes that threats that constitute significant changes to long-established events, the perceived lack of ownership and the overly commercialisation can have a negative impact on the local community's ideas of the event's identity and tradition.

Some minor changes have been accepted, as traditionally whoever caught the cheese was declared the winner, but today, the person who crosses the finish line first is declared the winner (Bingham 2009). Furthermore, the real cheese wheel has been replaced with a foam replica since 2013 after fears the real round could endanger the crowd. The winner, however, still gets a real cheese round as the prize.

In 2022 the event was promoted on the official tourism website 'Visit Cheltenham' (visitcheltenham.com 2022) and a break with tradition was witnessed when it was held on a Sunday rather than the usual Bank Holiday Monday due to the Queen's Platinum Jubilee. These two developments demonstrate its survival and how it is now accepted as an officially recognised event and secondly its ability to temporarily adapt one of its core traditions. This case study demonstrates the socio-economic and cultural opportunities that indigenous events can deliver, but also highlights several lessons that organisers need to consider to ensure that they do not alienate the local community by corrupting identity and tradition.

Indigenous Multi-Sport Events in North America

For the indigenous peoples of North America, the dream of celebrating their sporting heritage commenced in the 1971 when the first modern Native Summer Games were held in Enoch, Alberta, Canada. Over 3,000 participants took part in 13 sports and significantly, several cultural events were included. Further games were organised across the next few years and in 1975 at a meeting of the National Indian Athletic Association in Nevada, USA, it was decided to hold a large-scale game for indigenous peoples (NAIG Council, 2003).

The first North American Indigenous Games (NAIG) were held in Edmonton, Alberta in Canada in July 1990 and today the governance of the Games is in the hands of North American Indigenous Games Council which was formed across 1992 and 1993. It is governed by a board of directors and supported by its member regions from Canada and the USA. The NAIG Council is a registered non-profit organisation in Maysville, Washington, USA with a similar status in Canada. It represents 13 provinces and territories in Canada and 13 regions in the United States (Fabian 2022).

The Council's vision is:

'To improve the quality of life for indigenous peoples by supporting self-determined sports and cultural activities which encourage equal access to participation in the social / cultural / spiritual fabric of the community in which they reside and which respects indigenous distinctiveness' (NAIG Council, 2023).

Since the first edition of NAIG in 1990, a further nine Games have been held across Canada and the United States with a record 8,500 participants in 17 sports at Blaine, Minnesota in 1995. The next Games will be held in Kjipuktuk (Halifax), Dartmouth and Millbrook First Nation, Nova Scotia, Canada from 15-23 July 2023. The Games will have athletes competing in 16 different sports with three traditional Indigenous sports including Canoe/Kayak, Lacrosse, and 3D Archery. The three traditional games have been sportified to suit modern sport models and each one will have a special opening ceremony to begin each event. Indeed, celebrating culture is a central part of the NAIG and they unite local values, customs and traditions into the games.

History recalls that games played by the Mi'kmaq and First Nation people, who were native to what is now Nova Scotia, tested the participant's dexterity or were a game of chance. The links between the games and religious ceremonies which go back to the dawn of time and involve a mix of myth, hero worshiping and cult hero.

The organisation of the Games and the playing of sport, as a social driver, has been recognised as a way of overcoming many of the negative factors that impact on aboriginal communities and in particular the youth (Winther, Nazer-Bloom, & Petch 1995). Sport Canada is committed to contributing, through sport, to the health, wellness, cultural identity and quality of life of aboriginal peoples (Sport Canada's Policy on Aboriginal Peoples' Participation in Sport 2005).

A 1998 report 'Sport in Canada: Everybody's Business' identify a series of issues including high levels of poverty and unemployment, poor level of education and high levels of suicide in 10-19-year olds within the aboriginal people. It also found high levels of alcohol and drug abuse contributing to disparity in their health status compared with the general population of Canada. The report highlighted the key role sport plays in improving the emotional, physical and spiritual aspects of aboriginal life (Mills, 1998).

One of the barriers to participation in sport for the aboriginal peoples is around cultural insensitivity and so sport needs to have a positive and welcoming environment to attract participants. There are a host of historic reasons that have impacted on indigenous sports participation. This included polices that deliberately 'sough to extinguish those experiences and behaviours (including sports) that were traditionally 'Indian'. This was combined with the widespread teaching of 'Western' sporting cultures as a 'sport for colonisation' project (Fabian 2022).

The hosting of the NAIG helps to overcome this by featuring indigenous sports, showcasing indigenous athletes and respecting the local values, customs and traditions (Sport Canada's Policy on Aboriginal Peoples' Participation in Sport, 2005). Sport Canada is therefore committed to involve the aboriginal people in sport at all levels and recognise that the NAIG provide opportunities for aboriginal athletes to perform in environments that reflect their culture, values and lifestyles and to share them with the wider Canadian public and internationally. Whereas modern sports are associated with the commercial interests of modern society, whereas the indigenous games are seen as 'traditional and cultural museum pieces' more suited for rituals and tourism (Fabian, 2022).

An estimated 5,000 visitors along with the athletes, coaches, officials, partners and over 3,000 volunteers from Nova Scotia will experience a cultural celebration which includes dance, songs, music, games, art and teachings. The combined total of visitor, capital, and operational spending as a result of hosting the 2023 North American Indigenous Games is expected to be $18,837,724 and the Games will support $25,500,000 of economic activity in the province of Nova Scotia.

Indigenous Sport Summary and Conclusions

At their core each of the case studies are a celebration of sporting and cultural history that promote their respective heritage with bold and confident voices. Often the origins of the sporting festivals are associated with myths and legends and the sporting activities played include niche, unique and traditional forms of sport. These elements enhance the appeal adding another dimension that contrasts with modernism.

They portray a popular image of the peoples and the destination for tourists to associate with, drawing in thousands of visitors and providing a key economic dividend for local income generation and community benefit through the opportunities for visitors to spend. The importance of promotional activities to raise awareness is recognised. This includes the traditional written and TV press coverage, but increasingly through online streaming too. Some events are actively promoted in association with the local tourism associations which broaden their appeal and increase the reach of the marketing.

Each case study has its own local organising committee to oversee the actual delivery of the games, whereas in Scotland and Canada the committees are supported by pseudo-governing bodies; the Scottish Games Association and the NAIG Council who's role is to formalise the events and regulate the rules.

Critically, the organisation of the games and the playing of sport, as a social driver are recognised as a way of overcoming several of the negative factors that impact on local indigenous communities in terms of their social and economic circumstances and challenge the public's adverse stereotypical opinions and beliefs.

Barbadian Indigenous Sport and Traditions

Barbados is in an advantageous position to develop indigenous sport tourism products. The all year-round good weather and the multitude of sports facilities across all communities, including school football and cricket playing fields, the national stadium, Sir Garfield Sobers gymnasium, the Usain bolt arena and an Olympic sized swimming pool and much more provide opportunities for a variety of different sports products to be developed.

This section explores how indigenous games and sport on the island of Barbados could be used to bring tourism development back into the hands of the locals, stimulated economic development, wealth and prosperity and bring a sense of belonging, ownership, community and sovereignty into the hands of otherwise marginalised communities on the island of Barbados. Just like the case studies above, the sports and games that are deeply rooted in Barbadian culture and history are identified. These include pitching marbles, road tennis, dominoes, hop-scotch, rounders, warri, tug-a-war, jacks, stick licking (stick fighting), beach cricket, soft ball cricket, water volleyball, beach volleyball, body surfing and surfboarding will be the focus of this section. Beach Olympics will be added here to include goat racing, sack racing, three-legged races, egg and spoon races. Many of these games are played in rural communities as a form of recreation by children and adults because they need little to no infrastructure. The authors will show how some of them can be monetised and fused with other aspects of community culture such as the Land-ship, Tuk-band and steelpan to attract a more allocentric type of tourists who will venture into the local communities for a more authentic tourism experience and to induce direct spending. Due to the word count limitations of this chapter it is not possible to include all of the sports in the below description. However, a few are presented in table 1. Notably many of these sports do not feature in the tourism brochure which is unfortunate:

Table 1. Selected Barbadian traditional sport

Name of Sport	Description	Suggested tournament Format	Infrastructure needed
Stick Licking (Stick fighting)	Bought to Barbados by African slaves. Stick licking involves a straight, fire hardened stick made from hardwood from trees such as the guava tree.	Head to Head knockout	Gymnasium
Jacks Tournament	Played sitting down, competitors bounce a small ball, pickup games pieces and catch the ball after the first bounce.	Team or individual group-finals	Tables and chairs. Set of Jacks
Dominos Tournament	Played in pairs (two against two) and is played as a series of "ends". In each "end", players attach a domino from their hand to one end of those already played so that the sum of the end tiles is divisible by five or three (Wikipedia, 2023).	Head to Head Knockout	Tables and chairs and a set of dominoes
Road Tennis	This was invented in Barbados in the 1930s. It is very similar to lawn tennis, but played on a smaller court, usually marked on the road, and with smaller rackets (the rackets are wooden paddles, slightly larger than a table tennis racket). This game is basically a blend of table and lawn tennis. It is played with a tennis ball.	Head to Head Knockout	Hard concrete surface Racquets carved out of wood and a lawn tennis ball and a slap of wood as a net.
Warri	Warri is based on counting skills, with the two contestants facing each other on an elongated wooden board with each of the twelve hollows or pits containing four "horse-nicker" seeds as they are most commonly known. The object of the game is simply to capture more than twenty-four of the opponent's seeds. The game's simplicity is very deceptive with skill and strategic decision-making needed to win.	Knockout to find the winners	Warri board. Seeds, table and chairs
Lagging/Corking	As the name implies, the objective of this game is to "cork" a player. An individual throws a softball ball high in the air and then as it falls, everyone scrambles to retrieve it. The person who retrieves the ball must then attempt to cork a person with it -try to strike the person who is the easiest target. .	One mass game with points. Last one standing is winner	Football field and a soft tennis ball.
Rounders	Rounders was a game of fun for many. Hit the ball and run fast, fast, quick, quick to home base.	Team group Knockout, semi-finals and finals	Beach/ football field, tennis ball
Beach Cricket	This a team sport. The team that's cores the most runs in 2 innings is declared the winner.	Round Robin	Beach with a carved wooden bat, tennis ball and bear boxes for stumps.

Using Indigenous Sport and Games for Sustainable Community Tourism in Barbados

The indigenous sports presented above demonstrate the scope and potential for product development in sports tourism but we wish to stress that the opportunities are limitless and do not end here.

Commercialising Indigenous Sports

There are several opportunities to generate income from indigenous sport tourism. However, while some ideas are presented below, it is recognised that income generation in any business, including sport, requires levels of creativity, innovation, a positive mind-set and sales skills. The ideas below are common in sports management but are not exhaustive:

Table 2. Sources of revenue and finance

Revenue type	Description
Internal Funding	
Ticket sales/entrance/gate fees	Ticket sales to spectators can be sold based on stadium/arena capacity. Depending on the infrastructure tickets can be sold at a higher price for areas with the most desirable views and most comfortable infrastructure. The tickets for the least desirable space or comfort would be sold at lower prices.
On-site Space Sales	Depending on the infrastructure of the arena, selling advertising billboards to companies can be a lucrative revenue stream.
Participant Fees/Team Fees	Depending on the nature of the event, participants or teams in the tournament or competition would ordinarily pay an entrance fee
Internet Broadcasting	Internet webcasting involves the live streaming of the event. Common platforms are Ustream, YouTube,4 Facebook Live Instagram Live, StreamShart, DaCast, Vimeo and others. Viewers would pay a small fee to view the webcast. In some circumstances the webcast can be free to viewers for promotional purposes.
Radio/TV Rights	Established and very popular events of a national or international interest can sell the broadcasting rights to media outlets for broadcast on live radio or television. Giving of media rights for free can also be a good strategic decision to obtain extensive exposure to promote the event at little to no cost to large audiences.
Corporate Hospitality	Corporate hospitality involves companies paying for access to exclusive spaces around the event arena for the purposes of entertaining clients and special guests. Corporate hospitality packages would normally include access to primary views, gourmet food and drink, entertainment, comfortable seating and much more,
Advertising Fees	Companies can buy advertising space in the event programme book or on the website.
Website income	Income can be earned from companies purchasing banner advertising or pop up ads on the events website. Income can be earned all year from the sale of the event's branded merchandising. Edited coverage containing highlights of the event can also be sold to media outlets for delayed broadcast on special sports programmes in the regional and international arena.

continued on following page

Table 2. Continued

Revenue type	Description
Merchandising	Involves the sale of event branded clothing and other sporting goods and souvenirs. Event literature like scorecards or programme books are also a source of income.
Catering and Craft Concessions	All events benefit from side attractions. Food and craft outlets can enhance the visitor experience and provide a source of revenue for event owners and craft outlets. The cost of the space would be based on the size. Event owners can also negotiate a small commission on catering outlet sales.
External Funding	
Sponsorship	This involves the art of packaging event assets into sellable bundles. Usually the elements have no cost and thus is a lucrative source of income. Caveats is that sponsorship bundling and sales is a skill and sponsors need to be properly managed in order to build lasting relationships. Sponsorship can be sold at tiered levels with each level generating different levels of income.
Grants	Grants and government subsidies are a useful source of funding because they usually do not need to be paid back. Grands do come with conditions that the event must demonstrate that it can meet through the submission of a bid. Bid writing is a skill that should be including in sports education programmes.
Loans	Loans can be obtained from most financial institutions but they usually require a bond or some form of physical asset. Events usually do not have tangible assets in form of physical assets. Loans come with risks as they have to be repaid weather or not the event is successful.
Fundraising	Special fundraising efforts such as dinner/dance, raffles, sponsored walks, auctions, quiz nights and auctions can generate significant funding that can be invested into the sport event.
Membership Fees	Clubs with facilities, equipment or special infrastructure can demand membership fees for their use. Membership fees can be at tiered levels such as single, couples, family, daily, monthly or yearly. Membership fees can provide a steady and reliable source of income.
Coaching & workshops	Local promoter can offer coaching services and workshops to overseas and local teams for a fee

Sources: Masterman, 2014; Lund & Nicortra, 2019.

The key to a successful revenue generation scheme is that the event first has to established what it has that it can sell. Some of the most common areas of income generation in sport is gate/entrance fees. However, much money can be made from catering concessions, billboard advertising sales and space sales. One of the major funding schemes for any sport is sponsorship. However, sponsorship is a business agreement and sports planners would need to exercise skill and sound business acumen and savvy when selling sponsorship. Training in sponsorship sales would be essential to developing innovative sponsorship packages, selling those packages and managing sponsorship agreements.

GOVERNMENT POLICY FOR INDIGENOUS SPORTS TOURISM

Government sports policy in Barbados should be predicated on the ideology of reformism which is mainly concerned with social justice and equity (Hoye, Smith, Nicholson & Westerbeek, 2008). As we have seen with the North American Native Games, the staging of native sport competitions was a way of overcoming many of the negative issues that impact the aboriginal communities. The Barbados government must approach any indigenous sporting competition with the same view in mind. He government must activate and accelerate an indigenous sports tourism programme that ensures that licensing for indigenous sport events is granted only to local enterprises so that complete ownership of indigenous sport events remain in the hands of Barbadians, in perpetuity. Government policy and its legal apparatus need to acquire the licencing and copyright protection required to protect local investors, the image of the product, any merchandising, logos and symbols from *infringer*s making a profit off the event name (Kelley, 2012). A licensing programme should ensure that locals maintain the right to control, protect and develop their cultural and social capital, traditional knowledge, cultural expressions, heritage capital, such as flora, fauna, generic resources, oral traditions, literature, sports, traditional games and visual and performing arts (Ruhanen & Whitford, 2016). A licensing programme will also protect customers from deception. Creating a safe legal environment for local sport entrepreneurs is essential to build the confidence and trust of local investors. Government needs to treat all local tourism investors as they would foreign investors by creating the same concessions, incentives and investment climate as they would for foreign investors. Outlets for start-up capital and finance would need to be a priority. Government should facilitate the availability of financial subsidies but should also work with financial institutions to eliminate the financial barriers that are traditionally imposed by banks on indigenous people in Barbados. Private sector development and access to finance remain key challenges in Barbados in respect to the costs and availability of financing for the local private sector (Alvarez & Mooney, 2020). The government must implement an indigenous financial inclusion strategy to act as a catalyst for the identification of specific barriers across crucial sectors. However, the sports events that we are suggesting do not require any major financial investment. It is up to the investor to decide how grand or sophisticated they would like their tournaments to be and this would determine the cost. Nevertheless, government needs to ensure inclusiveness so that no one is excluded due to low income or facilities. Policy formation should ensure the provision of low-cost facilities and targeted programmes directed at disadvantage communities.

One of the major roles of government would be to develop programmes and funding to encourage mass participation at the grass roots level. They must work with national and community sports bodies to develop modified games and to develop youth participation programmes (Stewart et al, 2004). Opportunities for women, LGBTQ groups and disabled persons should be part of government's remit for indigenous sports. As with several other indigenous sporting bodies, one of the major challenges of government would be to overcome the power relations between government and local stakeholders which has been a hindrance for decades in Barbados. Lack of enthusiasm, lack of trust between stakeholders, poor coordination among role players and lack of information are other hindrances that stakeholder management would have to guard against (Ngwetjana & Sifolo, 2022). Collaboration and the embedding of indigenous values into the governance of indigenous sport events will be necessary to effect positive long-term cascading outcomes as seen with the Braemar Gathering, the Cheese Rolling and Wake and the North American Native Games. It is therefore recommended that the National Sports Council take the lead in propelling such a programme forward.

It is essential that a national lottery be developed to specifically fund indigenous sport tourism initiatives in Barbados; from the staging of the games, marketing, promotion and education. This would certainly ease the pressure on public funds and reduce financial risk. Such initiatives have been very successful in countries like the United Kingdom where the National Lottery is used to fund sports at all level and is particularly used to fund special events (Masterman, 2014). In 2007 alone revenue reached was £5, 514 million (*ibid*).

Education Programmes & Financing

The lack of training in core business skills is an inhibiting factor for indigenous business. The major priority of government should be to ensure that community leaders have the skills sets to run profitable tournaments at world standards. Operators will need high levels of literacy, communication skills and personal savvy to effectively engage with visitors and sports team leaders. Financing and capital management should also be factored into educational programmes through government funding agencies like the Inter-American Development Bank and the Caribbean Development Bank. Completing the educational programme could be a condition of drawing down a grant. Along with business training it is expected that continuous hands on, practical support from government will be needed for some time to help new sport entrepreneurs get off the ground. Sustainable business management must be part of the education remit. Training in green practices and green alternatives is essential as well as in event management, sport management and environmental management. Training in strategic sport management and experience management for tournament leaders is essential (Thu & Toan, 2022). Sponsorship management and design should be part of the course outline. The university of the West Indies,

Using Indigenous Sport and Games for Sustainable Community Tourism in Barbados

Cave Hill, already offers a tourism and sports management masters degree that could be modified for community leaders and sport event planners.

Education programmes should start in the primary schools but should also aim at the wider community to educate citizens on the commercial value and benefits of cultural products, especially indigenous sports. Government education programmes should promote creativity and innovation by reforming the structure of the otherwise oppressive cultural activities of the country.

Table 3. Education programme to support indigenous sport tourism

Key Concepts for Training & Development	Content
Event design and conceptualisation	• Understand indigenous issues in sport management and the tourism industry • What is sport and its role in economic development • Identifying the 3Ws of the event; setting and achieving sport event objectives, venue analysis, assessment and identification • Event programming • Start-up workforce planning and job analysis, The role of the event manager • Event feasibility study – the operations screen, the financial screen, the human resources screening, the marketing screening. • SWOT & TOWS analysis, PEST analysis, Impacts and legacies • Stakeholder identification and management
Venue Design	• Location and accessibility - parking cars, busses, coaches, disable access, external signage, Egress & Ingress design, capacity, customer service, layout, merchandising areas, screens, press box, VIP lounge, • Design and layout – size, colon, shape, light, audience comfort, spectator sitting and general arena layout, internal signage, weather protection, air circulation, hygiene and sanitation, toilets (male-female- disable), corporate hospitality, food and drink areas, Wireless access, queuing, waiting areas • Venue safety – PA systems, emergency routes/exits, spectator control, security zones, surveillance, barriers • Players, participant areas and dressing rooms, facilities for food and drink, players comforts, Staff areas, wellbeing and comfort, Lost and found
Indigenous Sport Event Sponsorship and Revenue Generation	• What is sponsorship and what it is not? • How to conduct an event generic inventory assessment • Designing and pricing sponsorship bundles • Sponsorship sales, managing sponsors and building relationships • Communicating with sponsors and stakeholders • Revenue generation and maximization; tiered pricing, bid writing, selling space and advertising sales. • Professionalism and savviness
Event Operations	• Supplier management and contracting; event operations planning, writing an events operations plan. Health and safety and risk assessments, insurance, recruiting staff, job design & recruiting volunteers. Critical path & logistics management; programming, managing entertainers and traders, crowd management and control; load in/load out. • Evaluation and measurement. • Budgeting & financial control
Sport Event Marketing and Promotion	• Marketing planning, situation analysis; objectives setting, strategy formation. feasibility and selection. • Public relations planning and selection, media planning, distribution channels, event PR tools & techniques, sales promotions, internet & digital marketing, blogging, SEO, social media marketing. Measurement and evaluation.

Promoting Indigenous Sports Tourism

The Barbados Tourism Authority has traditionally been very successful in marketing sports tourism in Barbados. Indigenous sports tourism should be no exception and should be included in all promotional materials produced by the Barbados Tourism Authority including guides books, brochures, the 'Ins and Outs' of Barbados and similar materials. The indigenous sport events should be promoted during the annual programme of overseas international trade shows that are attended by the authority such as World Travel Market.

One of the key decisions to be made that would affect the marketing would be whether to host all indigenous sport events under a single umbrella similar to the NAIG as a festival of indigenous sports or as separate events at different times during the year. These decisions would need to consider the seasonal patterns of tourist arrivals and market forces. There are numerous opportunities for the marketing of such sports through media channels, sports writers and influencers. The internet has become a powerful tool for reaching a vast audience and several opportunities can be explored.

Key sports tour operators and other tour operators who sell cultural products should be involved as major partners for the distribution of sport tourism products. These niche tour operators attract the attention of the more adventurous tourists who are more inclined to consume cultural products than mass tourists. The international sports media (ESPN, Sky Sports) including online broadcast media, print media including newspapers and sports magazines should be invited to these events and to become partners in marketing and promotion. The international media is always looking for quirky and unusual stories designed to attract attention. A media and other partners engagement programme should be part of the overall PR strategy and could include the following.

- Joint promotions with airlines and cruise companies
- Joint promotions with hotels, adventure and sports tour operators
- A visiting regional and international journalists programme
- Fam visits for cultural and sports tour operators during the events
- Working with internet bloggers and influencers, sports publishers and lifestyle and fitness magazines to create enticing and interesting stories for their readers and viewers about indigenous sports, key tourist attractions and Barbadian culture.
- Promotion directed at the diaspora

The focus should be on high yielding tourists markets such as cultural tourists adventure tourists, wellness and active tourists and sport tourists who will spend money directly into the economy. This should also include tourists from neighbouring islands and visitors from the diaspora. Indigenous sports tourism should also be used as a catalyst to promote Barbadian art, indigenous entertainment, food and other products such as locally made arts and crafts, rum & liqueurs, local spices, leather goods, food, clothes and other handmade Barbadian products for tourist's consumption.

CONCLUSION

In recent years, tourism has not resulted in any significant or cascading benefits for many local people. Sustainable tourism has been mainly lip-service. The promise of economic growth has failed to enhance the social wellbeing and quality of life and income for the majority of Barbadians. Indigenous sport tourism is not a panacea for the eradication of inequalities in Barbados and so there will be challenges that can only be solved through active participation, patience, reflection and government policy that protects local interests. Those who are young enough would know that the annual Barbados Crop Over Festival did not immediately lead to a significant economic impact but through persistence and perseverance, 40 years later, the festival attracts visitors from around the globe and is worth US$100 million annually to the Barbados economy. The festival provides an opportunity for musicians, singers, song writers, DJs, choreographers, dancers, kadooment bands, costume designers and make-up artists to earn significant income. This event is organised by the government arm of National Cultural Foundation of Barbados.

However, in order for the indigenous populations to derive benefits from tourism they must be a willingness by the authorities to make the initiative work and locals should be the primary active, rather than passive, agents in driving the direction of indigenous sports tourism forward (Jonsson, 2018). As we saw from the above case studies, the government should make optimal use of local talent, creativity, cultural and human resources to develop a 'new tourism', of the people for the people. Long term success is also not guaranteed. Each event/sport will have to be put on trial and tested to see which ones are the most viable. It is possible that some sport events will be successful and others will not. There will be need for constant review, feedback and improvements over time.

Government should represent the entire country and not just the interests of one group. The cultural tourism market is estimated to grow at a rate of 20.77% between 2022 and 2027. The size of the market is forecast to increase by US$6600.71 million (Technavio, 2022). The above case studies show that culture can be packaged and sold to generate wealth. The Barbados government should consider how they can synergise culture and heritage with the needs of local residents, local investors and tour operators to produce a more sustainable tourism product that benefits marginalised communities - economically, socially and psychologically. Authorities can utilise historical traditions and local creativity to build on natural resources and cultural capital to provide alternative sources of income and foreign exchange which will create less dependency on mass international tourism.

REFERENCES

Alvarez, L. G., & Mooney, H. (2020). *Barriers to financial access in Barbados—Key challenges and focal areas for reform.* IADB. https://blogs.iadb.org/caribbean-dev-trends/en/barriers-to-financial-access-in-barbados-key-challenges-and-focal-areas-for-reform/

Beckles, H. (1990). *A history of Barbados: From Amerindian settlement to nation-state.* Cambridge University Press.

Bhola-Paul, H. (2015). Tourism challenges and the opportunities for sustainability: A case study of Grenada, Barbados, and Tobago. *Journal of Tourism and Hospitality Management, 3*(9-10), 204–213.

Bingham, J. (2009). *The Cotswolds: A cultural history.* Oxford University Press.

Brewster, M., Connell, J., & Page, S. (2009). The Scottish Highland Games: Evolution, development and role as a community event. *Current Issues in Tourism, 12*(3), 271–293. doi:10.1080/13683500802389730

Brohman, J. (1996). New directions in tourism for third world development. *Annals of Tourism Research, 23*(I), 48–70. doi:10.1016/0160-7383(95)00043-7

Caribbean Development Bank. (2017). *Tourism industry reform: Strategies for enhanced economic impact.* Cari Bank. https://www.caribank.org/publications/featuredpublications/tourism-industry-reform-strategies-for-enhanced-economic-impact, accessed on 09-04-2018.

Chase, N. (2019). *Barbados' debt crisis: The effects of colonialism and neoliberalism.* Scholar's Archive. https://scholarsarchive.library.albany.edu/cgi/viewcontent.cgi?article=1003&context=lacs_honors

Clifford, E. M. (1944). Cooper's Hill Wake. *Folklore, 55*(3), 125–126. doi:10.1080/0015587X.1944.9717734

Dale, C. (2002). The UK tour operator industry: A competitive analysis. *Journal of Vacation Marketing, 6*(4), 357–367. doi:10.1177/135676670000600406

Elliott, S. M., & Neirotti, L. D. (2008). Challenges of tourism in a dynamic island destination: The case of Cuba. *Tourism Geographies*, *10*(3), 375–402. doi:10.1080/14616680802236386

Fabian, T. (2022). Games within games. *The International Journal of Sport and Society*, *13*(2), 111–124. doi:10.18848/2152-7857/CGP/v13i02/111-124

Gibson, H., Kaplanidou, K., & Kang, S. J. (2012). Small-scale event sport tourism: A case study in sustainable tourism. *Sport Management Review*, *15*(2), 160–170. doi:10.1016/j.smr.2011.08.013

Gratton, C., Dobson, N., & Shibli, S. (2000). The economic importance of major sports events: A case-study of six events. *Managing Leisure*, *5*(1), 17–28. doi:10.1080/136067100375713

Gratton, C., Dobson, N., & Shibli, S. (2000). The economic importance of major sports events: A case-study of six events. *Managing Leisure*, *5*(1), 17–28. doi:10.1080/136067100375713

Herstein, R. (2012). The thin line between country, city and region branding. *Journal of Vacation Marketing*, *18*(2), 147–155. doi:10.1177/1356766711435976

Herstein, R. (2012). The thin line between country, city and region branding. *Journal of Vacation Marketing*, *18*(2), 147–155. doi:10.1177/1356766711435976

Herstein, R., & Berger, R. (2013). Much more than sports: Sports events as stimuli for city re-branding. *The Journal of Business Strategy*, *34*(2), 38–44. https://crisis24.garda.com/insights-intelligence/intelligence/country-reports/barbados . doi:10.1108/02756661311310440

Higham, J., & Hinch, T. (2009). *Sport and tourism: Globalisation, mobility and identity*. Elsevier.

Hoye, R., Nicholson, M., Westerbeek, H., Smith, A., & Stewart, B. (2008). *Sport management* (2nd ed.). Routledge., doi:10.4324/9780080943206

Inkson, C., & Minnaert, L. (2012). *Tourism management: An introduction*. Sage.

Jarvie, G. (2003). Highland games, ancient sporting traditions and social capital in modern international communities. *Studies in the Physical Culture and Tourism*, *10*(1), 27–37.

Jarvie, G. (2004). Lonach, Highland games and Scottish sports history. *Journal of Sport History*, *31*(2), 161–175.

Jonsson, C. (2018). *Impacts of tourism-related foreign direct investment in Barbados: Local experienced 'realities'*. [Thesis, Hallam University]

Kelley, D. (2012). *Sports fundraising: Dynamic methods for schools, universities and youth sport organizations*. Routledge. doi:10.4324/9780203126479

King, B., Dwyer, L., & Prideaux, B. (2006). An evaluation of ethical business practices in Australia's China inbound tourism market. *International Journal of Tourism Research, 8*(2), 127–142. doi:10.1002/jtr.563

Klemm, M., & Parkinson, L. (2001). UK tour operator strategies: Causes and consequences. *International Journal of Tourism Research, 3*(5), 367–375. doi:10.1002/jtr.351

KockF. (2016). https://www.linkedin.com/pulse/all-inclusive-resorts-potentially-negative-effects-local-richie-kock

Kock, F., Josiassen, A., & Assaf, A. G. (2019). The xenophobic tourist. *Annals of Tourism Research, 74*, 155–166. doi:10.1016/j.annals.2018.11.005

Kondo, M. (2008). The economic impact of all-inclusive resorts in Jamaica. *City Tech Writer,* (8). http://www.citytech.cuny.edu/english/docs/ctw_v3_2008.pdf.

Lewis, A. (2002). *A case study of tourism curriculum development in the Caribbean: A stakeholder perspective* [Unpublished PhD Doctoral dissertation, Buckinghamshire Chilterns University College, Brunel University].

Lunt, T., & Nicotra, E. (2019). *Event sponsorship and fundraising: An advanced guide*. Kogan Page.

Masterman, G. (2014). *Strategic sport event management* (3rd ed.). Routledge. doi:10.4324/9780203114674

McVeigh, T. (2014). All-inclusive boom leaves local workers and tour operators out in the cold. *The Guardian*. https://www.theguardian.com/travel/2014/mar/08/all-inclusive-holidays-travel-ethical-tourism

Melacon, C. (1974). *Indian Legends of Canada*. Gage.

Mills, D. (1998). Sport in Canada: Leadership, partnership and accountability—everybody's business, *6th Report of the Standing Committee on Canadian Heritage*.

Mitki, Y., Herstein, R., & Jaffe, E. (2011). Repositioning a destination in a time of crisis: the case of Jerusalem. In N. Morgan, A. Pritchard, & R. Pride (Eds.), *Destination Brands. Managing Place Reputation* (3rd ed.). Elsevier. doi:10.1016/B978-0-08-096930-5.10024-2

Mitki, Y., Herstein, R., & Jaffe, E. (2011). Repositioning a destination in a time of crisis: the case of Jerusalem. In N. Morgan, A. Pritchard, & R. Pride (Eds.), *Destination Brands. Managing Place Reputation* (3rd ed.). Elsevier. doi:10.1016/B978-0-08-096930-5.10024-2

Mohammaad, A. A., & Ammar, S. A. M. (2015). Critical success factors for the interorganizational relationship between hotels and tour operators/travel agents. *Journal of Tourism Research & Hospitality*, *4*(2), 1–9. doi:10.4172/2324-8807.1000151

Mohammaad, A. A., & Ammar, S. A. M. (2015). Critical success factors for the inter-organizational relationship between hotels and tour operators/travel agents. *Journal of Tourism Research & Hospitality*, *4*(2), 1–9. doi:10.4172/2324-8807.1000151

Muchtar, B., Evanita, S., Aimon, H., Azhar, Z., & Alhadi, Z. (2021). Mapping analysis of potential tourism products in Mandeh integrated tourism region-Indonesia. *Academy of Strategic Management Journal*, *20*, 1–6.

NAIG Council. (2002). *Home*. NAIG Council. http://www.naigcouncil.com/

Ngwetjana, S., & Sifolo, P. P. S. (2022). Sustainable Community Participation: A Reality Or A Fallacy? *Journal On Tourism &Amp; Sustainability*, *6*(1). https://ontourism.academy/journal/index.php/jots/article/view/118

Pattullo, P. (2006). Last resort: The cost of tourism in the Caribbean. Wellington

Pyo, S. S., Cook, R., & Howell, R. L. (1988). Summer Olympic tourist market: Learning from the past. *Tourism Management*, *9*(2), 137–144. doi:10.1016/0261-5177(88)90023-4

Reza, H., Keshtidar, K., Ramkissoon, H., Esfahani, M., & Asadollahi, E. (2022). Adoption of entrepreneurial behaviours in sports tourism in developing countries. *Highlights of Sustainability*, *1*(2), 41–53. doi:10.54175/hsustain1020004

Ruhanen, L., & Whitford, M. (2011). Indigenous sporting events: More than just a game. [IJEMR]. *International Journal of Event Management Research*, *6*(1), 33–49.

Sealy, W. (2017). From colonialism to transnationalism: The neo-colonial structure of Caribbean Tourism. *Journal on Tourism and Sustainability*, *1*(2), 81–92.

Sealy, W., & Seraphin, H. (2020). Hoteliers' sources of bargaining power with British tour operators: A Barbados case study. *Journal on Tourism & Sustainability*, *3*(2), 41–56.

Sharpley, R., & Stone, P. (2011). Socio-cultural impacts of events. In S. Page & J. Connell (Eds.), *Routledge Handbook of Events* (pp. 347–361). London Routledge.

Shone, A., & Parry, B. (2004). *Successful event management A practical handbook* (2nd ed.). Thomson.

Simpson, D. (2014). *Poor pay and conditions at all-inclusive resorts.* CABI. https://www.cabi.org/leisuretourism/news/23741

Sport Canada. (2005). *Policy on Aboriginal Peoples' Participation in Sport.* Sport Canada. https://citeseerx.ist.psu.edu/document?repid=rep1&type=pdf&doi=6f573ac537ecc6488954e4916f7fc27ae81d3383

Stewart, B., Nicholson, M., Smith, A., & Westerbeek, H. (2004). *Australian sport: Better by design? The evolution of Australian sport policy.* Routledge. doi:10.4324/9780203462928

Strachan, G. (2002). *Paradise and plantation: Tourism and culture in the Anglophone Caribbean.* Virginia: University of Virginia Press.

Technavio (2022). *Cultural tourism market by type, service, and geography - forecast and analysis 2023-2027.* Technavio. https://www.technavio.com/report/cultural-tourism-market-industry-analysis#:~:text=The%20cultural%20tourism%20market%20is,increase%20by%20USD%206600.71%20million

Thu, T. T., & Toan, D. T. (2022). Sport event tourism and sustainable development perspectives in Danang City. *Journal on Tourism & Amp; Sustainability, 6* (1). https://ontourism.academy/journal/index.php/jots/article/view/120

Turner, S. M., & Troiano, C. S. (1987). Notes. *The Cornell Hotel and Restaurant Administration Quarterly, 28*(3), 25–27. doi:10.1177/001088048702800311 PMID:29583616

Walo, M., Bull, A., & Breen, H. (1996). Achieving economic benefits at local events: A case study of a local sports event. *Festival Management & Event Tourism, 4*(1), 95–106. doi:10.3727/106527096792195353

Weaver, D. B. (1989). The evolution of a 'plantation' tourism landscape on the Caribbean island of Antigua. *Tijdschrift voor Economische en Sociale Geografie, 79*(5), 319–331. doi:10.1111/j.1467-9663.1988.tb01318.x

Weed, M., & Bull, A. (2005). *Sports tourism: participants, policy and providers.* Butterworth Heinemann.

Williams, T. (2012). Tourism as a neo-colonial phenomenon: Examining the works of Pattullo & Mullings. *Caribbean Quilt*, 2, 191–200. doi:10.33137/caribbeanquilt.v2i0.19313

Winther, N., Nazer-Bloom, L., & Petch, V. (1995). *A comprehensive overview of development, the North American Indigenous Games and provincial/territorial.* Aboriginal Sport Bodies.

Compilation of References

Aas, Ch., Ladkin, A., & Fletcher, J. (2005). Stakeholder collaboration and heritage management. *Annals of Tourism Research*, *32*(1), 28–48. doi:10.1016/j.annals.2004.04.005

Adom, D. (2019). The place and voice of local people, culture, and traditions: A catalyst for ecotourism development in rural communities in Ghana. *Scientific American*, *6*, e00184.

African Development Bank. (2020). *African economic outlook 2020: developing Africa's workforce*. African Development Bank.

Aicher, T. J., Karadkis, K., & Eddosary, M. M. (2015). Comparison of sport tourists' and locals' motivation to participate in a running event. *International Journal of Event and Festival Management*, *6*(3), 215–234. doi:10.1108/IJEFM-03-2015-0011

Akış, S. (1999). Sürdürülebilir turizm ve Türkiye. *Anatolia Turizm Araştırmaları Dergisi*, *10*, 36–46.

Alarcón, D. (2018). *Cómo elaborar un diagnóstico de género y turismo en un contexto rural*. Alba Sud.

Alcock, P. (2006). *Understanding poverty*. Palgrave Macmillan. doi:10.5040/9781350363625

Allen, L. R., & Beattie, R. (1984). The role of leisure as an indicator of overall satisfaction with community life. *Journal of Leisure Research*, *16*(2), 99–109. doi:10.1080/00222216.1984.11969578

Allen, L. R., Long, P. T., & Perdue, R. R. (1987). *Satisfaction in rural communities and the role of leisure*. Leisure Today.

Allen, L. R., Long, P. T., Perdue, R. R., & Kieselbach, S. (1988). The impact of tourism development on residents' perceptions of community life. *Journal of Travel Research*, *27*(1), 16–21. doi:10.1177/004728758802700104

Allison, H. E., & Hobbs, R. J. (2006). *Science and Policy in Natural Resource Management: Understanding system complexity*. Cambridge University Press. doi:10.1017/CBO9780511618062

Almeida, T., & Emmendoerfer, M. (2022). Turismo de base comunitária e desenvolvimento local sustentável: Conexões e reflexões. *Revista De Turismo Contemporâneo*, *11*(1). Advance online publication. doi:10.21680/2357-8211.2023v11n1ID29163

Compilation of References

Alvarez, L. G., & Mooney, H. (2020). *Barriers to financial access in Barbados—Key challenges and focal areas for reform.* IADB. https://blogs.iadb.org/caribbean-dev-trends/en/barriers-to-financial-access-in-barbados-key-challenges-and-focal-areas-for-reform/

American Marketing Association. (2017). *Definitions of marketing.* https://www.ama.org/the-definition-of-marketing-what-is-marketing/

Andereck, K. L. (1994). *Environmental consequences of tourism: A review of recent research.* Paper presented at the Leisure Research Symposium. National Recreation and Park Association Congress.

Andereck, K. L., & Jurowski, C. (2006). Tourism and quality of life. In J. Gayle & N. Norma Polovitz (Eds.), *Quality Tourism Experiences* (pp. 136–154). Elsevier. doi:10.1016/B978-0-7506-7811-7.50016-X

Andereck, K. L., & Nyaupane, G. P. (2010). Exploring the nature of tourism and quality of life perceptions among residents. *Journal of Travel Research.*

Andereck, K. L., & Vogt, C. A. (2000). The relationship between residents' attitudes toward tourism and tourism development options. *Journal of Travel Research, 39*(1), 27–36. doi:10.1177/004728750003900104

Anderson, W. (2014). Cultural tourism and poverty alleviation in rural Kilimanjaro, Tanzania. *Journal of Tourism and Cultural Change, 13*(3), 208–224. doi:10.1080/14766825.2014.935387

Andrades, L., & Dimanche, F. (2017). Destination competitiveness and tourism development in Russia: Issues and challenges. *Tourism Management, 62*, 360–376. doi:10.1016/j.tourman.2017.05.008

Andrew, F. M., & Withey, S. B. (1976). *Social indicators of well-being: America's perception of life quality.* Plenum Press. doi:10.1007/978-1-4684-2253-5

Andrews, Frank & Withey, Stephen. (1976). Social Indicators of Well-Being: America's Perception of Life Quality.

Ankaya, F. Ü., Yazıcı, K., Balık, G., & Aslan, B. G. (2018). Dünya'da ve Türkiye'de ekoturizm, sosyal-kültürel ve ekonomik katkıları. *Ulusal Çevre Bilimleri Araştırma Dergisi, 1*(2), 69–72.

Anon. (2005, Nov. 7). Teen prostitutes have few options. *Namibian.*

Ap, J. (1990). Residents' perceptions research on the social impacts of tourism. *Annals of Tourism Research, 17*(4), 610–616. doi:10.1016/0160-7383(90)90032-M

Ap, J. (1992). Residents' perceptions on tourism impacts. *Annals of Tourism Research, 19*(4), 665–690. doi:10.1016/0160-7383(92)90060-3

Ap, J., & Crompton, J. L. (1998). Developing and testing a tourism impact scale. *Journal of Travel Research, 37*(2), 120–130. doi:10.1177/004728759803700203

Arabatzis, G., & Grigoroudis, E. (2010). Visitors' satisfaction, perceptions and gap analysis: The case of Dadia-Lefkimi-Souflion National Park. *Forest Policy and Economics*, *12*(3), 163–172. doi:10.1016/j.forpol.2009.09.008

Arab, L., Liu, W., & Elashoff, D. (2009). Green and black tea consumption and risk of stroke: A meta-analysis. *Stroke*, *40*(1), 1786–1792. doi:10.1161/STROKEAHA.108.538470 PMID:19228856

Aria, M., & Cuccurullo, C. (2017). bibliometrix: An R-tool for comprehensive science mapping analysis. *Journal of Informetrics*, *11*(4), 959–975. doi:10.1016/j.joi.2017.08.007

Ashley, C. (2000). *The impacts of tourism on rural livelihoods: Namibia's experience*. London: Overseas Development Institute (ODI). (Working paper 128)

Ashley, C., & Carney, D. (1999). Sustainable livelihoods: lessons from early experience. London: Department for International Development (DFID).

Ashley, C., & Mitchell, J. (2008). *Doing the right thing approximately not the wrong thing precisely: challenges of monitoring impacts of pro-poor interventions in tourism value chains*. London: Overseas Development Institute (ODI). (ODI working paper 291)

Ashley, C., Goodwin, H., & Boyd, C. (2000). Pro-poor tourism: putting poverty at the heart of the tourism agenda. London: Overseas Development Institute (ODI). (Natural resource perspectives no. 51)

Ashley, C., Roe, D., & Goodwin, H. (2001). Pro-poor tourism strategies: making tourism work for the poor: a review of experience. London: International Centre for Responsible Tourism, IIED (International Institute for Environment and Development) and ODI. (Pro-poor tourism report 1, ICRT)

Ashley, C., & Roe, D. (2002). Making tourism work for the poor: Strategies and challenges in Southern Africa. *Development Southern Africa*, *19*(1), 61–82. doi:10.1080/03768350220123855

Ashley, K., Harrison, H., Chan, P. H., Sothoeun, S., Young, J. R., Windsor, P. A., & Bush, R. D. (2018). Livestock and livelihoods of smallholder cattle-owning households in Cambodia: The contribution of on-farm and off-farm activities to income and food security. *Tropical Animal Health and Production*, *50*(8), 1747–1761. doi:10.100711250-018-1615-6 PMID:29796792

Asian School of Tea. (2020, August 19). Using one tiny leaf to make one big difference. Asian School of Tea. https://asianschooloftea.org/

Aslam, M. S. M., & Joliffe, L. (2015). Repurposing colonial tea heritage through historic lodging. *Journal of Heritage Tourism*, *10*(2), 111–128. doi:10.1080/1743873X.2014.985226

Åström, F., Danell, R., Larsen, B., Schneider, J. W., & Schlemmer, B. (2009). *Celebrating Scholarly Communication Studies: A Festschrift for Olle Persson at his 60th Birthday*. Research Portal. https://portal.research.lu.se/ws/files/5902071/1458992.pdf

Compilation of References

Atay, L., & Dilek, E. (2013). Konaklama işletmelerinde yeşil pazarlama uygulamaları: İbis otel örneği. *Süleyman Demirel Üniversitesi İktisadi ve İdari Bilimler Fakültesi Dergisi, 18*(1), 203–219.

Atkinson, D. (2008). *Creating access to economic opportunities in small and medium sized towns. Report produced for Urban Landmark.* Second Economy Strategy Project. An Initiative of the Presidency of South Africa.

Ay, C., & Ecevit, Z. (2005). Çevre bilinçli tüketiciler. *Akdeniz Üniversitesi İktisadi ve İdari Bilimler Fakültesi Dergisi, 5*(10), 238–263.

Aytekin, P. (2007). Yeşil pazarlama stratejileri. *Celal Bayar Üniversitesi Sosyal Bilimler Dergisi, 2*(2), 36–45.

Aziz, S.N.A. & Basir, S.M. (2018). Sustainable development goals: legally realistic or overambitious towards the development of the nations. *Jurnal Undang-undang dan Masyarakat, 23,* 39-47.

Bailey, E., & Richardson, R. (2010). A new economic framework for tourism decision making. *Tourism and Hospitality Research, 10*(4), 367–376. doi:10.1057/thr.2010.14

Baki, B., & Cengiz, E. (2002). Toplam kalite çevre yönetimi. *Uludağ Üniversitesi İktisadi ve İdari Bilimler Dergisi, 21*(1), 153–175.

Ballantine, J. L., & Eagles, P. F. J. (1994). Defining Canadian ecotourists. *Journal of Sustainable Tourism, 2*(4), 210–214. doi:10.1080/09669589409510698

Bandara, H. M. (2003). *Tourism Planning in Sri Lanka. Malawana, Stamford Lake.* PVT.

Baran, Z. and Batman, O. (2013). Destinasyon pazarlamasında mutfak kültürünün rolü: Sakarya örneği. 14 Ulus. Tur. Kongresi Bildir. *Kitabı,* 5–8.

Barnes, J. I., & Novelli, M. (2007). Trophy hunting and recreational angling in Namibia: an economy, social and environmental comparison. In B. Lovelock (Ed.), *Tourism and consumption of wildlife: hunting, shooting and sport fishing.* Routledge.

Bastian, B. L., Metcalfe, B. D., & Zali, M. R. (2019). Gender inequality: Entrepreneurship development in the MENA Region. *Sustainability, 11*(22), 64–72. doi:10.3390u11226472

Bauman, R. W., Matheson, V. A., & Mouri, C. (2009). Bowling in Hawaii Examining the Effectiveness of Sports-Based Tourism Strategies. *Journal of Sports Economics, 10*(1), 107–123. doi:10.1177/1527002508327401

Bayram, G. E. (2019). Turist rehberleri bakış açısıyla ekoturizm: Algı, sorumluluk ve rollerin tespitine yönelik bir araştırma. *Journal of Recreation and Tourism Research, 6*(1), 81–91. doi:10.31771/jrtr.2019.17

BBC News. (2022). *London Resort: Swanscombe Peninsula site confirmed special status.* BBC. https://www.bbc.co.uk/news/uk-england-kent-59236138

Becker, D. F. (2002). Sustentabilidade: Um novo (velho) paradigma de desenvolvimento regional. In D. F. Becker (Ed.), Desenvolvimento sustentável: Necessidade e ou possibilidade? (pp. 27-94). Sant Cruz do Sul: Edunisc.

Beckles, H. (1990). *A history of Barbados: From Amerindian settlement to nation-state*. Cambridge University Press.

Beeton, S. (2005). The case study in tourism research: a multi-method case study approach. In B. W. Richter, P. Burns, & C. Palmer (Eds.), *Tourism research methods: integrating theory with practice* (pp. 37–48). CABI Publishing. doi:10.1079/9780851999968.0037

Belisle, F. J., & Hoy, D. R. (1980). The perceived impact of tourism by residents a case study in Santa Marta, Colombia. *Annals of Tourism Research*, *7*(1), 83–101. doi:10.1016/S0160-7383(80)80008-9

Benn, J. (2015). *Tea in China: A religious and cultural History*. University of Hawai'i Press. www.jstor.org/stable/j.ctt13x1kn2

Bennett, O., Ashley, C., & Roe, D. (1999). Sustainable tourism and poverty elimination: a report to the Department for International Development. London: Deloitte and Touch: International Institute for Environment and Development: Overseas Development Institute.

Bennike, R. (2017). Frontier commodification: Governing land, labour and leisure in Darjeeling, India. *South Asia*, *40*(2), 256–271. doi:10.1080/00856401.2017.1289618

Berg, B. L. (2009). *Qualitative research methods for the social sciences* (7th ed.). Pearson Education.

Bertalanffy, L. V. (1969). General system theory: Foundations, development, applications.

Besky, S. (2014). The labor of terroir and the terroir of labor: Geographical indication and Darjeeling tea plantations. *Agriculture and Human Values*, *31*(1), 83–96. doi:10.100710460-013-9452-8

Bhola-Paul, H. (2015). Tourism challenges and the opportunities for sustainability: A case study of Grenada, Barbados, and Tobago. *Journal of Tourism and Hospitality Management*, *3*(9-10), 204–213.

Bimonte, S., & Punzo, L. F. (2011). Tourism, residents' attitudes and perceived carrying capacity with an experimental study in five Tuscan destinations. *International Journal of Sustainable Development*, *14*(3-4), 242–261. doi:10.1504/IJSD.2011.041964

Bingham, J. (2009). *The Cotswolds: A cultural history*. Oxford University Press.

Blagescu, M., & Young, J. (2006). *Capacity development for policy advocacy: current thinking and approaches among agencies supporting civil society organisations*. Overseas Development Institute.

Blake, A., Arbache, J. S., Sinclair, M. T., & Teles, V. (2008). Tourism and poverty relief. *Annals of Tourism Research*, *35*(1), 107–126. doi:10.1016/j.annals.2007.06.013

Compilation of References

Blanke, J., Browne, C., Garcia, A., & Messerli, H. (2011). *Assessing Africa's travel & tourism competitiveness in the Wake of The Global Economic Crisis.* Geneva: World Economic Forum.

Bodin, Ö. (2017). Collaborative environmental governance: Achieving collective action in social-ecological systems. *Science, 357*(6352), eaan1114. doi:10.1126cience.aan1114 PMID:28818915

Bolwell, D., & Weinz, W. (2008). *Reducing poverty through tourism.* Geneva: International Labor Office (ILO). Sectoral Activities Program. (Working paper 266)

Boniface, P. (2017). *Tasting Tourism: Travelling for Food and Drink.* Routledge. doi:10.4324/9781315241777

Boonsiritomachai, W and Phonthanukitithaworm, C., (2019) Residents' Support for Sports Events Tourism Development in Beach City. *The Role of Community's Participation and Tourism Impacts.*

Bousrih, L. (2013). Social capital, human capital and sustainable economic development. *Poznań University of Economics Review, 13*(3), 42–54.

Breakey, N. M., & Breakey, H. E. (2015). Tourism and Aldo Leopold's 'cultural harvest': Creating virtuous tourists as agents of sustainability. *Journal of Sustainable Tourism, 23*(1), 85–103. doi:10.1080/09669582.2014.924954

Brewster, M., Connell, J., & Page, S. (2009). The Scottish Highland Games: Evolution, development and role as a community event. *Current Issues in Tourism, 12*(3), 271–293. doi:10.1080/13683500802389730

Briedenhann, J., & Wickens, E. (2004). Tourism routes as a tool for the economic development of rural areas—Vibrant hope or impossible dream? *Tourism Management, 25*(1), 71–79. doi:10.1016/S0261-5177(03)00063-3

Briguglio, L., Archer, B., Jafari, J., & Wall, G. (1996). *Sustainable Tourism in Islands and Small States.* Issues and Policies.

Brito, K. (2021, May 15). *PNC e OMCV promovem projeto ambiental e de microempreendedorismo feminino para beneficiar 400 pessoas.* Mindel Insite. https://mindelinsite.com/social/pnc-e-omcv-promovem-projeto-ambiental-e-de-microempreendedorismo-feminino-para-beneficiar-400-pessoas/

Brohman, J. (1996). New directions in tourism for third world development. *Annals of Tourism Research, 23*(I), 48–70. doi:10.1016/0160-7383(95)00043-7

Brown, D. (2006). *Olympics does not mean tourism victory.* eTurbonews: eTN. www.travelwirenews.com

Brown, I., Raphael, D., & Renwick, R. (1998). *Quality of life profile, 2. Quality of Life Research Unit.* Center for Health Promotion: University of Toronto.

Brown, K., Turner, R. K., Hameed, H., & Bateman, I. A. N. (1997). Environmental carrying capacity and tourism development in the Maldives and Nepal. *Environmental Conservation, 24*(4), 316–325. doi:10.1017/S0376892997000428

Brunt, P., & Courtney, P. (1999). Host perceptions of sociocultural impacts. *Annals of Tourism Research, 26*(3), 493–515. doi:10.1016/S0160-7383(99)00003-1

Bryman, A., & Bell, E. (2011). *Business research methods* (3rd ed.). Oxford University Press.

Brymen, A., & Bell, E. (2007). *Business Research Methods, Oxford: Oxford University Campbell, A., Converse, P. E., & Rodgers, W. L. (1976). The quality of American life: Perspectives, evaluations, and satisfactions.* Russell Sage.

Buckley, R. (2010). *Conservation tourism.* CAB International Publishing. doi:10.1079/9781845936655.0000

Buckley, R. (2020). Pandemic Travel Restrictions Provide a Test of Net Ecological Effects of Ecotourism and New Research Opportunities. *Journal of Travel Research.*

Burns, P., & Holden, A. (1995). *Tourism: a new perspective.* Prentice Hall.

Business Dictionary. (2019). What is sustainable? *Business Dictionary.* http://www.businessdictionary.com/definition/social-sustainability.html

Butler, J. R. (1992). *Ecotourism: Its changing face and evolving philosophy.* Paper presented to the IVth World Congress on National Parks and Protected Areas, Caracas, Venezuela.

Butler, R. (1980). The concept of a tourism area cycle of evolution. *The Canadian Geographer. Geographe Canadien, 24*(1), 5–12. doi:10.1111/j.1541-0064.1980.tb00970.x

Butler, R., Curran, R., & O'Gorman, K. D. (2013). Pro-poor tourism in a first world urban setting: Case study of Glasgow Govan. *International Journal of Tourism Research, 15*(5), 443–457. doi:10.1002/jtr.1888

Byrd, E. T., Bosley, H. E., & Dronberger, M. G. (2009). Comparisons of stakeholder perceptions of tourism impacts in rural Eastern North Carolina. *Tourism Management, 30*(5), 693–703. doi:10.1016/j.tourman.2008.10.021

Byun, J. O., & Han, J. S. (2004). A study on perception and actual status of utilization for green tea. *Journal of the Korean Society of Food Culture, 19*(2), 184–192.

C169 - indigenous and tribal peoples convention, 1989 (no. 169) (n.d.). https://www.ilo.org/dyn/normlex/en/f?p=NORMLEXPUB%3A12100%3A0%3A%3ANO%3A%3AP12100_ILO_CODE%3AC169.

Çabuk, S., Nakıboğlu, B., & Keleş, C. (2008). Tüketicilerin yeşil ürün satın alma davranışlarının sosyo demografik değişkenler açısından incelenmesi. *Çukurova Üniversitesi Sosyal Bilimler Enstitüsü Dergisi, 17*(1), 85-102.

Cahlik, T. (2000). Comparison of the maps of Science. *Scientometrics*, *49*(3), 373–387. doi:10.1023/A:1010581421990

Çakıcı, C. A., Akoğlan Kozak, M., Azaltun, M., Sökmen, A., & Sarıışık, M. (2002). *Otel işletmeciliği*. Detay Yayıncılık.

Calloni, M. (2013). Street food on the move: A socio-philosophical approach. *Journal of the Science of Food and Agriculture*, *93*(14), 3406–3413. doi:10.1002/jsfa.6353 PMID:23963865

Callon, M., Courtial, J. P., & Laville, F. (1991). Co-word analysis as a tool for describing the network of interactions between basic and technological research: The case of polymer chemistry. *Scientometrics*, *22*(1), 155–205. doi:10.1007/BF02019280

Campbell, L. M. (1999). Ecotourism in rural developing communities. *Annals of Tourism Research*, *26*(3), 534–553. doi:10.1016/S0160-7383(99)00005-5

Cao, H., Qiao, L., Zhang, H., & Chen, J. (2010). Exposure and risk assessment for aluminium and heavy metals in Puerh tea. *The Science of the Total Environment*, *408*(1), 2777–2784. doi:10.1016/j.scitotenv.2010.03.019 PMID:20413147

Carbone, M. (2005). Sustainable tourism in developing countries: Poverty alleviation, participatory planning, and ethical issues. *European Journal of Development Research*, *17*(3), 559–565. doi:10.1080/09578810500209841

Caribbean Development Bank. (2017). *Tourism industry reform: Strategies for enhanced economic impact*. Cari Bank. https://www.caribank.org/publications/featuredpublications/tourism-industry-reform-strategies-for-enhanced-economic-impact, accessed on 09-04-2018.

Casalegno, C., Candelo, E., Santoro, G., & Kitchen, P. (2020). The perception of tourism in coffee producing equatorial countries: An empirical analysis. *Psychology and Marketing*, *37*(1), 154–166. doi:10.1002/mar.21291

Castellani, V., Sala, S., & Pitea, D. (2007). A new method for tourism carrying capacity assessment. *WIT Transactions on Ecology and the Environment*, *106*, 365–374. doi:10.2495/ECO070341

Cater, E. A. (1993). Ecotourism in the third world: Problems for sustainable development. *Tourism Management*, *14*(2), 85–90. doi:10.1016/0261-5177(93)90040-R

Catley, A. (1999). *Methods on the move: a review of veterinary uses of participatory approaches and methods focusing on experiences in dryland Africa*. International Institute for Environment and Development.

Ceballos-Lascurain, H. (1987). The future of 'ecotourism'. *Mexico Journal*, 13-14.

Ceballos-Lascurain, H. (1987). The future of ecotourism. *Mexico Journal*. Available at:https://booksite.elsevier.com/samplechapters/9780750668781/9780750668781.pdf

Ceballos-Lascurain. (1996). *Tourism, Ecotourism and Protected Areas.* IUCN. Available at www.iucn.org/content/tourism-ecotourism-and-protected-areas-state-nature-based-tourism-around-world-and-guidelines-its-development

Cengiz, T., & Çalışkan, E. (2009). Ecological approach in sustainable tourism: Şavşat district example. *Scientific Research and Essays, 4*(5), 509–520.

Cernat, L., & Gourdon, J. (2007). *Is the concept of sustainable tourism sustainable?* United Nations Publication.

Çetin Gürkan, G., Dönmez Polat, D., & Demiralay, T. (2015). Turistlerde çevre bilincinin çevreye duyarlı müşteri davranışı ve çevreye duyarlı konaklama işletmelerinde kalma tercihleri üzerindeki etkisi. *Ekonomi ve Yönetim Araştırmaları Dergisi, 4*(1), 114–133.

Çevirgen, A. (2003). *Sürdürülebilir turizm kapsamında ekoturizm ve Edremit yöresi için bir model önerisi* [Yayımlanmamış doktora tezi]. Dokuz Eylül Üniversitesi.

Chakraborty, A. and Islam, S.S. (2020). Impact of tea tourism in Dooars, North Bengal. *An overview Mukt Shabd J. 9*, 5789–804.

Chamberlain, K. (1997). *Carrying capacity.* UNEP Industry and Environment, 8.

Chambers, R. (1995). *Paradigm shift and the practice of participation research perspective.* Institute of Development Studies.

Chambers, R., & Conway, G. (1992). *Sustainable rural livelihoods: practical concepts for the 21st century.* Institute of Development Studies (UK).

Chamorro, A., & Bañegil, T. M. (2006). Green marketing philosophy: A study of Spanish firms with ecolabels. *Corporate Social Responsibility and Environmental Management, 13*(1), 11–24. doi:10.1002/csr.83

Chase, N. (2019). *Barbados' debt crisis: The effects of colonialism and neoliberalism.* Scholar's Archive. https://scholarsarchive.library.albany.edu/cgi/viewcontent.cgi?article=1003&context=lacs_honors

Chaturvedula, V. S. P., & Prakash, I. (2011). The aroma, taste, color and bioactive constituents of tea. *Journal of Medicinal Plants Research, 5*(11), 2110–2124. doi:10.5897/JMPR

Chen, C. L., & Teng, N. (2016). Management priorities and carrying capacity at a high-use beach from tourists' perspectives: A way towards sustainable beach tourism. *Marine Policy, 74*, 213–219. doi:10.1016/j.marpol.2016.09.030

Cheng, S., Hu, J., Fox, D., & Zhang, Y. (2012). Tea-tourism development in Xinyang, China: Stakeholders' view. *Tourism Management Perspectives, 2/3*, 28–34. doi:10.1016/j.tmp.2011.12.001

Cheng, S., Xu, F., Zhang, J., & Zhang, Y. (2010). Tourists' attitudes toward tea tourism: A case study in Xinyang, China. *Journal of Travel & Tourism Marketing, 27*(2), 211–220. doi:10.1080/10548401003590526

Chen, Y. S., Lai, S. B., & Wen, C. T. (2006). The influence of green innovation performance on corporate advantage in Taiwan. *Journal of Business Ethics*, *67*(4), 331–339. doi:10.100710551-006-9025-5

Cherkaoui, S., Boukherouk, M., Lakhal, T., Aghzar, A., & El Youssfi, L. (2020). Conservation Amid COVID-19 Pandemic: Ecotourism Collapse Threatens Communities and Wildlife in Morocco. *E3S Web of Conferences, 183*.

Chernushenko, D. (1996). Sports tourism goes sustainable: The Lillehammer experience. *Visions in Leisure and Business*, *15*, 65–73.

Chieh, H., Richard, H., Robinson, N. S., & Scott, N. (2018). Traditional food consumption behaviour: The case of Taiwan. *Tourism Recreation Research*, *43*(4), 456–469. doi:10.1080/02508281.2018.1475879

Chirenje, L. I., Chitotombe, J., Gukurume, S., Chazovachii, B., & Chitongo, L. (2013). The impact of tourism leakages on local economies: A case study of Nyanga District, Zimbabwe. *Journal of Human Ecology (Delhi, India)*, *42*(1), 9–16. doi:10.1080/09709274.2013.11906576

Chok, S., Macbeth, J., & Warren, C. (2007). Tourism as tool for poverty alleviation: A critical analysis of "pro-poor tourism" and implications for sustainability. *Current Issues in Tourism*, *10*(2-3), 144–165. doi:10.2167/cit303

Christie, I. T. (2002). Tourism, growth and poverty: Framework conditions for tourism in developing countries. *Tourism Review*, *57*(1/4), 35–41. doi:10.1108/eb058377

Chryssoula, C., Ioanna, S., & Apostolos, T. (2015). *Bird Watching and Ecotourism: An Innovative Monitoring System to Project the Species of Lesvos Island to Potential Ecotourists*. Available at: https://ceur-ws.org/Vol-1498/HAICTA_2015_paper54.pdf

Chung, S. S., Au, A., & Qiu, J. W. (2013). Understanding the underwater behaviour of scuba divers in Hong Kong. *Environmental Management*, *51*(4), 824–837. doi:10.100700267-013-0023-y PMID:23471632

Churchill, G. A., & Peter, J. P. (1995). *Marketing: creating value for customers*. Irwin McGraw Hill.

Cimnaghi, E., & Mussini, P. (2015). An application of tourism carrying capacity assessment at two Italian cultural heritage sites. *Journal of Heritage Tourism*, *10*(3), 302–313. doi:10.1080/1743873X.2014.988158

Cinnioğlu, H. (2015). Sürdürülebilir ekonomik kalkınma kapsamında ekoturizmin çevre üzerindeki etkilerinin eleştirel bir bakış açısıyla incelenmesi. *Sosyal Bilimler Metinleri*, *1*, 1–22.

Clark, J. (1997). *Coastal Zone Management Handbook*. Lewis Publishers.

Clifford, E. M. (1944). Cooper's Hill Wake. *Folklore*, *55*(3), 125–126. doi:10.1080/0015587X.1944.9717734

Clow, K. E., & Baack, D. (2007). *Integrated advertising promotion and marketing communications* (3rd ed.). Pearson Prentice Hal.

Cobo, M. J., López-Herrera, A. G., Herrera-Viedma, E., & Herrera, F. (2011). An approach for detecting, quantifying, and visualizing the evolution of a research field: A practical application to the fuzzy sets theory field. *Journal of Informetrics*, *5*(1), 146–166. doi:10.1016/j.joi.2010.10.002

Coccossis, H. (1996). Tourism and sustainability: Perspectives and implications. *European Experiences*, 1-21.

Cohen, E. (1988). Tourism and AIDS in Thailand. *Annals of Tourism Research*, *15*(4), 467–486. doi:10.1016/0160-7383(88)90044-8

Collin, R. B., & Collin, R. W. (2009). *Encyclopedia of sustainability*. Greenwood Press.

Community Homestay Network. (2021). *Community Homestay Network Nepal*. https://www.communityhomestay.com/about

Conlin, M. V., & Baum, T. (1995). *Island Tourism: Management Principles and Practice*. Wiley.

Consultancy.UK. (2016). *International tourism doubles in 15 years, 1.8 billion by 2030*. Consultancy.uk.

Cooke, H., & Tate, K. (2011). *Project management*. Mcgraw-Hill.

Cooper, C., Fletcher, J., Fyall, A., Gilbert, D., & Wanhill, S. (2008). *Tourism: principles and practice* (4th ed.). Pearson Education.

Cooper, C., Fletcher, J., Fyall, A., Gilbert, D., & Wanhill, S. (2008). *Tourism: Principles and practice* (4th ed.). Pearson Education.

Corbau, C., Benedetto, G., Congiatu, P. P., Simeoni, U., & Carboni, D. (2019). Tourism analysis at Asinara Island (Italy): Carrying capacity and web evaluations in two pocket beaches. *Ocean and Coastal Management*, *169*, 27–36. doi:10.1016/j.ocecoaman.2018.12.004

Costanza, R., & Bernard, C. P. (1995). Defining and predicting sustainability. *Ecological Economics*, *15*(3), 193–196. doi:10.1016/0921-8009(95)00048-8

Cotton, F. (2015). *A case study of the conflicts women experience with tourism and immigration in Vilcabamba, Ecuador: a sustainable livelihoods perspective* [PhD thesis]. Nova Southeastern University.

Coulter, N., Monarch, I., & Konda, S. (1998). Software engineering as seen through its research literature: A study in co-word analysis. *Journal of the American Society for Information Science*, *49*(13), 1206–1223. doi:10.1002/(SICI)1097-4571(1998)49:13<1206::AID-ASI7>3.0.CO;2-F

Courtial, J. (1994). A coword analysis of scientometrics. *Scientometrics*, *31*(3), 251–260. doi:10.1007/BF02016875

Cox, J. R. (2009). *Turismo indígena y comunitario en Bolivia: Un instrumento para el desarrollo socio-económico e intercultural*. Plural Editores.

Croes, R. (2014). The role of tourism in poverty reduction: An empirical assessment. *Tourism Economics*, 20(2), 207–226. doi:10.5367/te.2013.0275

D'amore, L. J. (1992). Sürdürülebilir turizmin desteklenmesi. *Tourism Management*, 9, 258–262. doi:10.1016/0261-5177(92)90096-P

Dahlberg, E., & Wingquist, G. O. (2008). *Namibia environmental and climate change policy brief, School of business, economics and law*. University of Gothenburg.

Dale, C. (2002). The UK tour operator industry: A competitive analysis. *Journal of Vacation Marketing*, 6(4), 357–367. doi:10.1177/135676670000600406

Damm, G. R. (2008). Recreational trophy hunting: what do we know and what should we do? In *Best practices in sustainable hunting: a guide to best practices from around the world*. CIC Technical Series Publication. International Council for Game and Wildlife Conservation.

Daniels, M. J., & Norman, W. C. (2003). Estimating the Economic Impacts of Seven Regular Sport Tourism Events. *Journal of Sport & Tourism*, 8(4), 214–222. doi:10.1080/1477508032000161528

Das, M., & Chatterjee, B. (2015). Ecotourism: A panacea or a predicament? *Tourism Management Perspectives*, 14, 3–16. doi:10.1016/j.tmp.2015.01.002

Davidson, J., Bondi, L., & Smith, M. (2005). Emotional Geographies. Ashgate. Eric, A,F, & Asafo-Adjei, R. (2013). Traditional food preferences of tourists in Ghana. *British Food Journal*, 115(7), 987–1002. doi:10.1108/BFJ-11-2010-0197

Davis, D., & Tisdell, C. (1996). Economic management of recreational scuba diving and the environment. *Journal of Environmental Management*, 48(3), 229–248. doi:10.1006/jema.1996.0075

De Fran, A. L. (1996). Go green: An environmental checklist for the lodging industry. *The Cornell Hotel and Restaurant Administration Quarterly*, 37(6), 84–85. doi:10.1177/001088049603700612

de Oliveira, J. A. P. (2003). Governmental responses to tourism development: Three Brazilian case studies. *Tourism Management*, 24(1), 97–110. doi:10.1016/S0261-5177(02)00046-8

de Sousa, R. C., Pereira, L. C., da Costa, R. M., & Jiménez, J. A. (2014). Tourism carrying capacity on estuarine beaches in the Brazilian Amazon region. *Journal of Coastal Research*, 70(sp1), 545–550. doi:10.2112/SI70-092.1

Deccio, C., & Baloglu, S. (2002). Nonhost community resident reactions to the 2002 Winter Olympics: The spillover impacts. *Journal of Travel Research*, 41(1), 46–56. doi:10.1177/0047287502041001006

Deery, M., Jago, L., & Fredline, L. (2004). Sport tourism or event tourism: Are they one and the same? Journal of Sport &amp. *Tourism (Zagreb)*, 9(3), 235–245.

Deery, M., Jago, L., & Fredline, L. (2012). Rethinking social impacts of tourism research: A new research agenda. *Tourism Management*, *33*(1), 64–73. doi:10.1016/j.tourman.2011.01.026

Demir, C., & Çevirgen, A. (2006). *Turizm ve çevre yönetimi - Sürdürülebilir gelişme yaklaşımı*. Nobel Yayın Dağıtım.

Demir, C., & Çevirgen, A. (2006). *Turizm ve çevre yönetimi: Sürdürülebilir gelişme yaklaşımı*. Nobel Yayıncılık.

Demir, S. (2011). *İğneada'nın ekoturizm potansiyelinin saptanması* [Yayımlanmamış yüksek lisans tezi]. İstanbul Teknik Üniversitesi.

Deng, J., King, B., & Bauer, T. (2002). Evaluating natural attractions for tourism. *Annals of Tourism Research*, *29*(2), 422–438. doi:10.1016/S0160-7383(01)00068-8

Department for International Development (DFID). (2000). *Poverty elimination and the empowerment of women: strategies for achieving the international development targets*. Department for International Development.

Devi, M. K. (2012). Ecotourism in assam: A promising opportunity for development. *South Asian J. Tour. Herit.*, *5*, 179–192.

Diamantis, D. (1998). Consumer behavior and ecotourism products [Editorial]. *Annals of Tourism Research*, *25*(2), 515–528. doi:10.1016/S0160-7383(97)00076-5

Diamantis, D., & Ladkin, A. (1999). The links between sustainable tourism and ecotourism: A definitional and operational perspective. *Journal of Tourism Studies*, *10*(2), 35–46.

Dieke, P. U. C. (2005). *The political economy of tourism development in Africa*. Cognizant Communication Corporation.

Diener, E. (1984). Subjective well-being. *Psychological Bulletin*, *95*(3), 542–575. doi:10.1037/0033-2909.95.3.542 PMID:6399758

Dilek, S. E. (2012). *Turizm işletmelerinde yeşil pazarlama uygulamaları: Bir alan araştırması (Yayımlanmamış Yüksek Lisans Tezi)*. Çanakkale Onsekiz Mart Üniversitesi.

Djaadi, N. (2016). *Yeşil pazarlama uygulamalarının tüketici satın alma davranışları üzerine etkisi: Türkiye ve Cezayir örneği (Yayımlanmamış Yüksek Lisans Tezi)*. Trakya Üniversitesi.

Doğan, M. (2010). *Ekomüze odaklı sürdürülebilir destinasyon ve Gökçeada üzerine bir uygulama* [Yayımlanmamış yüksek lisans tezi]. Çanakkale Onsekiz Mart Üniversitesi.

Dolmacı, N., & Bulgan, G. (2013). Turizm etiği kapsamında çevresel duyarlılık. *Journal of Yaşar University*, *29*(9), 4853–4871.

Dolnicar, S., Lazarevski, K., & Yanamandram, V. (2012). Quality-of-life and travel motivations: integrating the two concepts in the Grevillea Model. In *Handbook of tourism and quality-of-life research* (pp. 293–308). Springer. doi:10.1007/978-94-007-2288-0_17

Compilation of References

Doorne, S. (2000). Caves, cultures and crowds: Carrying capacity meets consumer sovereignty. *Journal of Sustainable Tourism*, *8*(2), 116–130. doi:10.1080/09669580008667352

Dredge, D. (2006). Policy networks and the local organisation of tourism. *Tourism Management*, *27*(2), 269–280. doi:10.1016/j.tourman.2004.10.003

Dülgeroğlu, İ., Başol, O., & Öztürk Başol, R. (2016). Genç tüketicilerin yeşil tüketim davranışı: Uluslararası algı farklılıkları. *Mehmet Akif Ersoy Üniversitesi Sosyal Bilimler Enstitüsü Dergisi*, *8*(15), 1–16.

Duymaz, S. Y. (2013). Çevre örgütlerinin çevresel yönetime katılma sürecinde dayandığı haklar. *Türkiye Barolar Birliği Dergisi*, (107), 173–198.

Dyer, P., Aberdeen, L., & Schuler, S. (2007). Tourism impacts on an Australian indigenous community. *Tourism Management*, *24*(1), 83–95. doi:10.1016/S0261-5177(02)00049-3

Economics, O. (2020). *Global city travel: 2019 to 2025*. Oxford Economics. Available at: www.oxfordeconomics.com/recent-releases/global-city-travel-2019-to-2025

Edmonds, J., & Leposky, G. (1998, June). Ecotourism and sustainable tourism development in Southeast Asia [Conference presentation]. *Third International Conference of the Asia Pacific Tourism Association*, Hong Kong.

EIGE. (2018). *Tourism: Relevance of gender in the policy area*. European Institute for Gender Equality. https://eige.europa.eu/gender-mainstreaming/policy-areas/tourism

Eita, J. H., & Jordaan, A. C. (2007). Estimating the tourism potential in Namibia. Windhoek: Namibian Economic Policy Research Unit (NEPRU).

Ekanayake, E. M., & Long, A. E. (2012). Tourism development and economic growth in developing countries. *The International Journal of Business and Finance Research*, *6*(1), 51–63.

Ellegaard, O., & Wallin, J. A. (2015). The bibliometric analysis of scholarly production: How great is the impact? *Scientometrics*, *105*(3), 1809–1831. doi:10.100711192-015-1645-z PMID:26594073

Elliott, S. M., & Neirotti, L. D. (2008). Challenges of tourism in a dynamic island destination: The case of Cuba. *Tourism Geographies*, *10*(3), 375–402. doi:10.1080/14616680802236386

Ellis, S., & Sheridan, L. (2014). A critical reflection on the role of stakeholders in sustainable tourism development in least-developed countries. *Tourism Planning & Development*, *11*(4), 467–471. doi:10.1080/21568316.2014.894558

Epley, D., & Menon, M. (2008). A method of assembling cross-sectional indicators into a community quality of life. *Social Indicators Research*, *88*(2), 281–296. doi:10.100711205-007-9190-7

Erdoğan, N. (2010). *Ekoturizmin ve doğa temelli turizmin geldikleri noktadaki kavramsal çerçeve*. TOD-EG Türkiye Ormancılar Derneği Ekoturizm Çalıştayı.

Erdoğan, N., & Tosun, C. (2009). Environmental performance of tourism accommodations in the protected area: Case of Goreme Historical National Park. *International Journal of Hospitality Management, 28*(3), 406–414. doi:10.1016/j.ijhm.2009.01.005

Eren, D., & Yılmaz, İ. (2008). Otel işletmelerinde yeşil pazarlama uygulamaları: Nevşehir ili örneği. In 13. Ulusal pazarlama kongresi (2008): "Pazarlamada yeni yaklaşımlar" bildiriler kitabı (pp. 25-29). Nevşehir Üniversitesi İktisadi ve İdari Bilimler Fakültesi Yayınları.

Eser, Z., Öztürk, S. A., & Korkmaz, S. (2011). *Pazarlama: Kavramlar- ilkeler- kararlar*. Siyasal Kitabevi.

ETC Market Study (2020). https://etc-corporate.org/uploads/2020/07/2020_ETC-Study-Generation-Z-Travellers.pdf

EURLex. (n.d.). *Sustainable development*. https://eur-lex.europa.eu/EN/legal-content/glossary/sustainable-development.html

European Union Tourism Trends. (2020). Available at: https://www.e-unwto.org/doi/pdf/10.18111/9789284419470

Eusébio, C., Kastenholz, E., & Breda, Z. (2014). Turismo e desenvolvimento sustentável de destinos rurais: Uma visão dos stakeholders. *Revista Portuguesa de Estudos Regionais, 36*(36), 13–21. doi:10.59072/rper.vi36.418

Evans, N., Campbell, D., & Stonehouse, G. (2003). *Strategic Management for Travel and Tourism*. Butterworth-Heinemann.

Fabian, T. (2022). Games within games. *The International Journal of Sport and Society, 13*(2), 111–124. doi:10.18848/2152-7857/CGP/v13i02/111-124

Farrell, B. H., & Runyan, D. (1991). Ecology and tourism. *Annals of Tourism Research, 18*(1), 26–40. doi:10.1016/0160-7383(91)90037-C

Farrell, B. H., & Twining-Ward, L. (2004). Reconceptualizing tourism. *Annals of Tourism Research, 31*(2), 274–295. doi:10.1016/j.annals.2003.12.002

Farrell, T. A., & Marion, J. L. (2002). The protected area visitor impact management (PAVIM) framework: A simplified process for making management decisions. *Journal of Sustainable Tourism, 10*(1), 31–51. doi:10.1080/09669580208667151

Farsari, I., Butler, R. W., & Szivas, E. (2011). Complexity in tourism policies: A cognitive mapping approach. *Annals of Tourism Research, 38*(3), 1110–1134. doi:10.1016/j.annals.2011.03.007

Fefer, J., De Urioste-Stone, S. M., Daigle, J., & Silka, L. (2018). Understanding the perceived effectiveness of applying the visitor experience and resource protection (VERP) framework for recreation planning: A multi-case study in US National Parks. *Qualitative Report, 23*(7), 1561–1582. doi:10.46743/2160-3715/2018.3228

Compilation of References

Fehling, M., Nelson, B. D., & Venkatapuram, S. (2013). Limitations of the millennium development goals: A literature review. *Global Public Health: An International Journal for Research, Policy and Practice, 8*(10), 1109–1122. doi:10.1080/17441692.2013.845676 PMID:24266508

Felce, D., & Perry, J. (1995). Quality of life: Its definition and measurement. *Research in Developmental Disabilities, 16*(1), 51–74. doi:10.1016/0891-4222(94)00028-8 PMID:7701092

Fernando, P., Rajapaksha, R.M. & Kumari, K. (2017). Tea-tourism as a marketing tool: a strategy to develop the image of Sri Lanka as an attractive tourism destination. *Kelaniya Journal of Management, 5*(2).

Fernando, P. I. N., Kumari, K., & Rajapaksha, R. (2017b). Destination marketing to promote tea tourism socio-economic approach on community development. *Int. Rev. Manag. Bus. Res., 6*, 68–75. doi:10.2139srn.3877264

Fernando, P. I. N., Rajapaksha, R., & Kumari, K. (2017a). Tea tourism as a marketing tool: A strategy to develop the image of Sri Lanka as an attractive tourism destination Kelaniya. *Journal of Management, 5*, 64–79.

Ferreira, F., Jollife, D.M., & Prydz, E.B. (2015). The international poverty line has just been raised to $1.90 a day but the global poverty is basically unchanged: How is that even possible. *World Bank Blogs.*

Fetscherin, M., & Heinrich, D. (2015). Consumer brand relationships research: A bibliometric citation meta-analysis. *Journal of Business Research, 68*(2), 380–390. doi:10.1016/j.jbusres.2014.06.010

Fetscherin, M., & Usunier, J. (2012). Corporate branding: An interdisciplinary literature review. *European Journal of Marketing, 46*(5), 733–753. doi:10.1108/03090561211212494

Figueroa-Domecq, C., de Jong, A., & Williams, A. M. (2020). Gender, tourism & entrepreneurship: A critical review. *Annals of Tourism Research, 84*, 102980. doi:10.1016/j.annals.2020.102980

Forgues-Puccio, G. F., & Lauw, E. (2021). Gender inequality, corruption, and economic development. *Review of Development Economics, 25*(4), 2133–2156. doi:10.1111/rode.12793

Fotiadis, A. (2009). *The role of tourism in rural development through a comparative analysis of a Greek and a Hungarian rural tourism area.* Available at: https://pea.lib.pte.hu/bitstream/handle/pea/14945/fotiadis-anestis-phd-2009.pdf?sequence=1&isAllowed=y

Fourie, H. (1990). *Development of the tourism industry in Namibia.* Namibia University of Science and Technology.

Frauman, E., & Banks, S. (2011). Gateway community resident perceptions of tourism development: Incorporating importance-performance analysis into the limits of change framework. *Tourism Management, 13*(1), 128–140. doi:10.1016/j.tourman.2010.01.013

Freeman, M., & Ahmed, S. (2011). *Tea Horse Road: China's Ancient Trade Road to Tibet*. River Books.

Frent, C. (2016). An overview on the negative impacts of tourism. *Journal of Tourism Studies and Research in Tourism*, 22, 32–37.

Freund, D., & Hernandez-Maskivker, G. (2021). Women managers in tourism: Associations for building a sustainable world. *Tourism Management Perspectives*, 38, 100820. doi:10.1016/j.tmp.2021.100820

Gaia Napa Valley Hotel. (2007). *Example of green accommodation business*. https://www.greenlodgingnews.com/gaia-napa-valley-hotel-spa-receives-leed-gold-certification/

Gammon, S., & Robertson, T. (1997). Sport Tourism: A Conceptual Framework. *Journal of Sport & Tourism*, 4(3), 5–12. doi:10.1080/10295399708718632

Gayle, D. J., & Apostolopoulos, Y. (2002). From MIRAB to TOURAB. In D. J. Gayle & Y. Apostolopoulos (Eds.), *Island Tourism and Sustainable Development: Caribbean, Pacific, and Mediterranean Experiences* (pp. 3–14). Praeger.

Gee, Y. G., Maken, J. C., & Choy, D. J. (1997). *The travel industry*. Wiley.

George, B. P., Nedelea, A., & Antony, M. (2007). The business of community-based tourism: A multi-stakeholder approach. *Tourism Issues*, 3, 1–19.

George, R. (2008). *Managing tourism in South Africa* (2nd ed.). Oxford University Press Southern Africa.

Getz, D. (1986). Models in tourism planning: Towards integration of theory and practice. *Tourism Management*, 17(1), 21–32. doi:10.1016/0261-5177(86)90054-3

Getz, D., & Page, S. J. (2016). Progress and prospects for event tourism research. *Tourism Management*, 52, 593–631. doi:10.1016/j.tourman.2015.03.007

Ghosh, M., & Ghosh, A. (2013). Consumer buying behaviour in relation to consumption of tea – A study of Pune city. *International Journal of Sales and Marketing Management Research and Development*, 3(2), 47–54.

Giampiccoli, A., Jugmohan, S., & Mtapuri, O. (2015). Characteristics of community-based tourism: towards a comparison between North and South experiences. *Proceedings of the Third International Conference on Hospitality, Leisure, Sport, and Tourism*, 451-454.

Gibson, H. J., Kaplanidou, K., & Kang, S. J. (2011). Small-scale event sport tourism: A case study in sustainable tourism. *Sport Management Review*, 15(2), 160–170. doi:10.1016/j.smr.2011.08.013

Gibson, H., Chang, S., Kang, S., & Jun, S. (2009). Insights on running and hosting a small regional marathon. *Presented at the International Conference on Festivals and Events Research*.

Compilation of References

Giraldo, J. M., & Castro, W. A. S. (2014). Green supply chains: Conceptual bases and trends. In *Green supply chains: Applications in agroindustries* (pp. 13-26). Universidad Nacional de Colombia.

Glaesser, D., Kester, J., Paulose, H., Alizadeh, A., & Valentin, B. (2017). Global travel pattern: An overview. *Journal of Travel Medicine*, 24(4), 1–5. doi:10.1093/jtm/tax007 PMID:28637267

Global Code of Ethics for Tourism . (2020) Available at: https://www.unwto.org/background-global-code-ethics-tourism

Goddard, W., & Melville, S. (2017). *Research methodology*. Juta & Co., Repr.

Godfrey, K., & Clarke, J. (2000). *The tourism development handbook: a practical approach to planning and marketing*. Continuum.

Goeldner, Ch. R., & Ritchie, B. J. R. (2009). *Tourism: Principles, Practices, Philosophies* (11th ed.). John Wiley & Sons Inc.

Goeldner, C. R., & Ritchie, J. R. B. (2006). *Tourism: principles, practices, philosophies.* Wiley.

Goldblatt, B. (2019). Social and economic rights to challenge violence against women – examining and extending strategies. *South African Journal on Human Rights*, 35(2), 169–193. doi:10.1080/02587203.2019.1615351

Gonzo, F. (2022). Effects of rural tourism development on poverty alleviation: A grounded theory. *African Journal of Hospitality and Tourism Management*, 3(2), 73–95. doi:10.47963/ajhtm.v3i2.769

Goodwin, H. (2006). Measuring and reporting the impact of tourism on poverty. In J. Tribe & D. Airey (Eds.), *Developments in tourism research* (pp. 63–76). Taylor & Francis.

Goodwin, H. (2008). Pro-poor tourism: A response. *Third World Quarterly*, 29(5), 869–871. doi:10.1080/01436590802215287

Goodwin, H. (2009). Reflections on 10 years of pro-poor tourism. *Journal of Policy Research in Tourism, Leisure & Events*, 1(1), 90–94. doi:10.1080/19407960802703565

Gossling, S. (2002). Global environmental consequences of tourism. *Global Environmental Change*, 12(4), 283–302. doi:10.1016/S0959-3780(02)00044-4

Government of Bulgaria. (2021). *Analysis and assessment of the risk and vulnerability of sectors in the Bulgarian economy to climate change*. Available at: https://www.moew.government.bg/bg/analiz-i-ocenka-na-riska-i-uyazvimostta-na-sektorite-v-bulgarskata-ikonomika-ot-klimatichni-promeni/

Graefe, A., Kuss, F. R., & Vaske, J. (1990). *Visitor Impact Management: A Review of Research* (Vol. 1). National Parks and Conservation Association.

Gratton, C., Dobson, N., & Shibli, S. (2000). The economic importance of major sports events: A case-study of six events. *Managing Leisure*, 5(1), 17–28. doi:10.1080/136067100375713

Green Star Hotels. (2022). *Example of green accommodation business*. https://www.greenstar.fi/hotellit/lahti/

Greenacre, M., & Blasius, J. (2006). *Multiple correspondence analysis and related methods*. CRC press. doi:10.1201/9781420011319

Grigg, D. (2002). The worlds of tea and coffee: Patterns of consumption. *GeoJournal*, *57*(1), 283–294. doi:10.1023/B:GEJO.0000007249.91153.c3

Gryshchenko, O., Babenko, V., Bilovodska, O., Voronkova, T., Ponomarenko, I., & Shatska, Z. (2022). Green tourism business as marketing perspective in environmental management. *Global Journal of Environmental Science and Management*, *8*(1), 117–132.

Grzeskowiak, S., Sirgy, M. J., & Widgery, R. (2003). Residents' satisfaction with community services: Predictors and outcomes. *The Journal of Regional Analysis & Policy*, *33*(2), 1–36.

Güler, O., & Tufan, E. (2013). Sürdürülebilir bir yatırım örneği olarak yeşil otelcilik. İçinde Ş. Aydın Tükeltürk & M. Boz (Eds.), Turizmde güncel konu ve eğilimler (pp. 357-374). Detay Yayıncılık.

Günay, T. (2017). *Turizm işletmelerinde yeşil pazarlama uygulamaları: İzmir ili örneği (Yayımlanmamış Yüksek Lisans Tezi)*. Yaşar Üniversitesi.

Gunderson, L. H. (2001). *Panarchy: understanding transformations in human and natural systems*. Island press.

Güneş, G. (2008). Turizmin sürdürülebilirliği için ekoturizm. *Popüler Bilim*, *15*(177), 28–30.

Gunn, C. A. (1988). *Tourism Planning* (2nd ed.). Taylor & Francis.

Gunn, C. A. (1988). *Tourism planning* (2nd ed.). Taylor and Francis.

Gupta, G., Roy, H., & Promsivapallop, P. (2020). Local cuisine image dimensions and its impact on foreign tourist's perceived food contentment in Delhi. *Tourism Recreation Research*. doi:10.1080/02508281.2020.1816762

Gupta, J., & Vegelin, C. (2016). Sustainable development goals and inclusive development. *International Environmental Agreement: Politics, Law and Economics*, *16*(3), 433–448. doi:10.100710784-016-9323-z

Gupta, V., & Duggal, S. (2020). How do the tourists' behavioural intentions influenced by their perceived food authenticity: A case of Delhi? *Journal of Culinary Science & Technology*, *1764430*. doi:10.1080/15428052.2020

Gupta, V., Khanna, K., & Gupta, R. K. (2018). A study on the street food dimensions and its effects on consumer attitude and behavioural intentions. *Tourism Review*, *73*(3), 374–388. doi:10.1108/TR-03-2018-0033

Gupta, V., Khanna, K., & Gupta, R. K. (2019). Preferential analysis of street food amongst the foreign tourists: A case of Delhi region. *International Journal of Tourism Cities*, *6*(3), 511–528. doi:10.1108/IJTC-07-2018-0054

Gupta, V., & Sajnani, M. (2019). Risk and benefit perceptions related to wine consumption and how it influences consumers' attitude and behavioural intentions in India. *British Food Journal*, *122*(8), 2569–2585. doi:10.1108/BFJ-06-2019-0464

Gupta, V., Sajnani, M., Dixit, S. K., & Khanna, K. (2020). Foreign tourist's tea preferences and relevance to destination attraction in India. *Tourism Recreation Research*, 1–15.

Gursoy, D., & Rutherford, D. G. (2004). Host attitudes toward tourism: An improved structural model. *Annals of Tourism Research*, *31*(3), 495–516. doi:10.1016/j.annals.2003.08.008

Guzel, B., & Apaydin, M. (2016). Gastronomy in Tourism Global issues and trends in tourism. University Press Cambridge.

Guzman, T. L., Canizares, S. S., & Pavon, V. (2011). Community-based tourism in developing countries: A case study. *Tourismos: An International Multi-Disciplinary Journal of Tourism*, *6*(1), 66–84.

Hacıoğlu, N. (2008). *Turizm pazarlaması* (6th ed.). Nobel Yayın Dağıtım.

Hakim, L., Siswanto, D., & Makagoshi, N. (2017). Mangrove Conservation in East Java: The Ecotourism Development Perspectives. *Journal of Tropical Life Science*, *7*(3), 277–285. doi:10.11594/jtls.07.03.14

Hall, C. M. (1999). Rethinking collaboration and partnership: A public policy perspective. *Journal of Sustainable Tourism*, *7*(3-4), 274–289. doi:10.1080/09669589908667340

Hall, C. M., & Lew, A. A. (2009). *Understanding and managing tourism impacts: an integrated approach*. Routledge. doi:10.4324/9780203875872

Hall, C. M., Mitchell, R., & Sharples, L. (2003). *Consuming Places: The Role of Food, Wine and Tourism in Regional Development*. Butterworth Heinemann.

Hall, C., & Hodges, J. (1996). The party's great, but what about the hangover? The housing and social impacts of mega-events with special reference to the 2000 Sydney Olympics. *Festival Management & Event Tourism*, *4*(1), 13–20. doi:10.3727/106527096792232414

Hall, J. K., Daneke, G. A., & Lenox, M. J. (2010). Sustainable development and entrepreneurship: Past contributions and future directions. *Journal of Business Venturing*, *25*(5), 439–448. doi:10.1016/j.jbusvent.2010.01.002

Hamel, G. (2001). Leading the revolution. Strategy & Leadership, Harvard Business School Press, Boston, MA.

Hampton, M. P., & Christensen, J. E. (1999). Treasure Island revisited. Jersey's offshore finance centre crisis: Implications for other small island economics. *Environment & Planning, 31*(9), 1619–1637. doi:10.1068/a311619

Hanafiah, M.H., M.F. Harun and Jamaluddin M.R., (2010). Bilateral Trade and Tourism Demand. *World Applied Sciences Journal, 10*(Special Issue of Tourism & Hospitality), 110- 114.

Han, J. (2018). Carrying capacity of low carbon tourism environment in coastal areas from the perspective of ecological efficiency. *Journal of Coastal Research*, (83), 199–203.

Harrison, D. (2001). Tourism in small islands and microstates. *Tourism Recreation Research, 26*(3), 3–8. doi:10.1080/02508281.2001.11081193

Harrison, D. (2008). Pro-poor tourism: A critique. *Third World Quarterly, 29*(5), 851–868. doi:10.1080/01436590802105983

Hartman, A. (2008, Dec. 17). Walvis Bay prostitutes reel in the foreigners. *The Namibian*.

Hartman, A. (2010, Feb. 24). Namibia: foreign tour guide ban shocks industry. *The Namibian*.

Hartman, A. (2015, Dec.). Holiday adventures at the coast. *The Namibian*.

Hayta, A. B. (2009). Sürdürülebilir tüketim davranışının kazanılmasında tüketici eğitiminin rolü. *Journal of Ahi Evran University Kırşehir Faculty of Education, 10*(3), 143–151.

Haywood, K. M. (1988). Responsible and responsive tourism planning in the community. *Tourism Management, 9*(2), 105–118. doi:10.1016/0261-5177(88)90020-9

Heiss, M. L., & Heiss, R. J. (2007). *The Story of Tea: A Cultural History and Drinking Guide*, Random House Digital, Inc. .

Henderson, J. C. (2009). Food tourism reviewed. *British Food Journal, 111*(4), 317–326. doi:10.1108/00070700910951470

He, Q. (1999). Knowledge discovery through co-word analysis. *Library Trends, 48*, 133–159.

Herath, G. (2002). Research methodologies for planning ecotourism and nature conservation. *Tourism Economics, 8*(1), 77–101. doi:10.5367/000000002101298007

Herstein, R. (2012). The thin line between country, city and region branding. *Journal of Vacation Marketing, 18*(2), 147–155. doi:10.1177/1356766711435976

Herstein, R., & Berger, R. (2013). Much more than sports: Sports events as stimuli for city re-branding. *The Journal of Business Strategy, 34*(2), 38–44. https://crisis24.garda.com/insights-intelligence/intelligence/country-reports/barbados . doi:10.1108/02756661311310440

Higham, J. (2007). *Ecotourism: Competing and conflicting schools of thought*. Available at: www.researchgate.net/publication/283378699

Higham, J., & Hinch, T. (2009). *Sport and tourism: Globalisation, mobility and identity*. Elsevier.

Hiller, H. (2006). Post-event outcomes and the post-modern turn: The Olympics and urban transformation. *European Sport Management Quarterly*, 6(4), 317–332. doi:10.1080/16184740601154458

Hill, T., Nel, E., & Trotter, D. (2006). Small-scale, nature-based tourism as a pro-poor development intervention: Two examples in Kwazulu-Natal, South Africa. *Singapore Journal of Tropical Geography*, 27(2), 163–175. doi:10.1111/j.1467-9493.2006.00251.x

Himavindu, M. N., & Barnes, J. I. (2003). Trophy hunting in Namibian economy: An assessment. *South African Journal of Wildlife Research*, 33(2), 65–70.

Holden, A. (2013). *Tourism, poverty and development in the developing world*. Taylor and Francis. doi:10.4324/9780203861547

Holden, A., Sonne, J., & Novelli, M. (2011). Tourism and poverty reduction: An interpretation by the poor of Elmina, Ghana. *Tourism Planning & Development*, 8(3), 317–334. doi:10.1080/21568316.2011.591160

Holloway, J. Ch. (2012). *The business of tourism* (9th ed.). Pearson.

Honey, M., Vargas, E., & Durham, W. H. (2010). Impact of, D.C.: Center for Responsible Travel (CREST).

Horne, W. (2000). Municipal economic development via hallmark events. *Journal of Tourism Studies*, 11(1), 30–36.

Horng, J. S., Liu, C. H., Chou, H. Y., & Tsai, C. Y. (2012). Understanding the impact of culinary brand equity and destination familiarity on travel intentions. *Tourism Management*, 33(4), 815–824. doi:10.1016/j.tourman.2011.09.004

Hoye, R., Nicholson, M., Westerbeek, H., Smith, A., & Stewart, B. (2008). *Sport management* (2nd ed.). Routledge., doi:10.4324/9780080943206

Huynh, B. T. (2011). *The Cai Rang floating market, Vietnam: Towards pro-poor tourism?* [Master's dissertation]. Auckland University of Technology.

Ihtimanski, I., Nedkov, S., & Semerdzhieva, L. (2019). *Mapping the natural heritage as a source of recreation services at national scale in Bulgaria*. I.K. International Pub. House.

İnan, Ç. (2007). *Yıldız (Istranca) Dağları ve çevresindeki floradan sürdürülebilir kırsal kalkınma ve ekoturizm amacıyla yararlanma olanakları* [Yayımlanmamış yüksek lisans tezi]. Namık Kemal Üniversitesi.

Inkson, C., & Minnaert, L. (2012). *Tourism management: An introduction*. Sage.

Inskeep, E. (1991). Tourism planning, an integrated and sustainable development approach. New York: Wiley.

International Day of the World's Indigenous Peoples 9 August 2022. (2022). Available at: https://www.un.org/en/observances/indigenous-day

International Island Games Association. (2022) *About the Games.* IIGA. www.iiga.org

İpar, M. S. (2018). *Turistlerin yeşil otel tercihlerine yönelik algıları, çevreci davranış eğilimleri ve davranışsal niyetlerle ilişkisi (Yayımlanmamış Doktora Tezi).* Çanakkale Onsekiz Mart Üniversitesi.

İstanbullu Dinçer, F., & Muğan Ertuğral, S. (2009). Turizm işletmelerinin pazarlamasında ürün. In Turizm işletmelerinin pazarlamasında 7P ve 7C (ss. 49-74). Değişim Aktüel Yayınevi.

Ivanovic, M. (2011). *Exploring the authenticity of the tourist experience in culture heritage tourism in South Africa.* Potchefstroom: North-West University.

Ivanovic, M., Khunou, P. S., Reynish, N., Pawson, R., Tseane, L., & Wassung, N. (2009). *Tourism development 1: Fresh perspectives.* Pearson Prentice Hall.

Jamaludin, M., Othman, N., & Awang, A. R. (2012). Community based homestay programme: A personal experience. *Procedia: Social and Behavioral Sciences, 42,* 451–459. doi:10.1016/j.sbspro.2012.04.210

Jamieson, W., Goodwin, H., & Edmunds, C. (2004). *Contribution of tourism to poverty alleviation: Pro-poor tourism and the challenge of measuring impacts.* UNESCAP.

Jamieson, W., & Nadkarni, S. (2009). Editorial: A reality check of tourism's potential as a development tool. *Asia Pacific Journal of Tourism Research, 14*(2), 111–123. doi:10.1080/10941660902847161

Janis, J. (2011). *The tourism-development nexus in Namibia: a study on national tourism policy and local tourism enterprises' policy knowledge.* University of Helsinki.

Janis, J. (2012). The role of local policy knowledge in the implementation of Namibian tourism policy. *International Journal of Tourism Policy, 4*(4), 302–316. doi:10.1504/IJTP.2012.052547

Janis, J. (2014). Political economy of the Namibia tourism sector: Addressing post-apartheid inequality through increasing indigenous ownership. *Review of African Tourism Economy, 41*(140), 185–200. doi:10.1080/03056244.2013.872614

Jarvie, G. (2003). Highland games, ancient sporting traditions and social capital in modern international communities. *Studies in the Physical Culture and Tourism, 10*(1), 27–37.

Jarvie, G. (2004). Lonach, Highland games and Scottish sports history. *Journal of Sport History, 31*(2), 161–175.

Jayachandran, S. (2015). The roots of gender inequality in developing countries. *Annual Review of Economics, 7*(1), 63–88. doi:10.1146/annurev-economics-080614-115404

Jenkins, C. (2000). The development of tourism in Namibia. In P. Dieke (Ed.), *The political economy of tourism development in Africa* (pp. 113–128). Cognizant Communication Corporation.

Jersey Legacy Report (2016). Fit for the future. *Sports Strategy.*

Jiménez, J. A., Valdemoro, H. I., Bosom, E., Sánchez-Arcilla, A., & Nicholls, R. J. (2017). Impacts of sea-level rise-induced erosion on the Catalan coast. *Regional Environmental Change*, *17*(2), 593–603. doi:10.100710113-016-1052-x

Jing, Y., & Fucai, H. (2011). Research on Management of Ecotourism Based on Economic Models. *Energy Procedia*, *5*, 1563–1567. doi:10.1016/j.egypro.2011.03.267

Johnson, G., Scholes, K., & Whittington, R. (2008). *Exploring corporate strategy: Text and cases*. Pearson education.

Johnston, K. (2018). Women in public policy and public administration? *Public Money & Management*, *39*(3), 155–165. doi:10.1080/09540962.2018.1534421

Joliffe, L., & Aslam, M. S. (2009). Tea heritage tourism: Evidence from Sri Lanka. *Journal of Heritage Tourism*, *4*(4), 331–344.

Joliffe, L., & Zhuang, P. (2007). Tourism development and the tea gardens of fuding, China. In *Tea Tourism: Global Trends and Development* (pp. 133–144). Channel View Publications. doi:10.21832/9781845410582-011

Jolliffe, L. (2006). Tea and hospitality: More than a Cuppa. *International Journal of Contemporary Hospitality Management*, *18*(1), 164–168. doi:10.1108/09596110610646718

Jolliffe, L. (2007). *Tea and tourism: Tourists, traditions and transformations*. Channel View. doi:10.21832/9781845410582

Jolliffe, L., & Farnsworth, R. (2003). Seasonality in tourism employment: Human resources challenges. *International Journal of Contemporary Hospitality Management*, *15*(6), 312–316. doi:10.1108/09596110310488140

Jones, S. (2005). Community-Based Ecotourism: The Significance of Social Capital. *Annals of Tourism Research*, *32*(2), 303–324. doi:10.1016/j.annals.2004.06.007

Jonsson, C. (2018). *Impacts of tourism-related foreign direct investment in Barbados: Local experienced 'realities'*. [Thesis, Hallam University]

Jurado, E. N., Tejada, M. T., García, F. A., González, J. C., Macías, R. C., Peña, J. D., & Gutiérrez, O. M. (2012). Carrying capacity assessment for tourist destinations. Methodology for the creation of synthetic indicators applied in a coastal area. *Tourism Management*, *33*(6), 1337–1346. doi:10.1016/j.tourman.2011.12.017

Jurowski, C. (1994). *The interplay of elements affecting host community resident attitudes toward tourism: A path analytic approach*. [Doctoral dissertation, Virginia Tech University].

Jurowski, C., & Gursoy, D. (2004). Distance effects on residents' attitudes toward tourism. *Annals of Tourism Research*, *31*(2), 296–312. doi:10.1016/j.annals.2003.12.005

Jurowski, C., Uysal, M., & Williams, D. R. (1997). A theo-retical analysis of host community resident reactions to tourism. *Journal of Travel Research*, *36*(2), 3–11. doi:10.1177/004728759703600202

Kadt, E. (1979). *Tourism: Passport to Development?* Oxford University Press. European Charter for Sustainable and Responsible Tourism. Available at https://www.ceeweb.org/wp-content/uploads/2011/12/Commented_Tourism_Charter_CEEweb.pdf

Kahraman, N. (1994). *Sürdürülebilir kalkınma ve turizm*. I. Turizm Sempozyumu.

Kahraman, N., & Türkay, O. (2012). *Turizm ve çevre*. Detay Yayıncılık.

Kakar, N. (2018). Success Story: Ecotourism in South Africa. *Borgen Magazine*. Available at:www.borgenmagazine.com/ecotourism-in-south-africa

Kakazu, H. (1994). *Sustainable Development of Small Islands Economics*. Waterview.

Kaldeen, M. (2020). Marketing potentials to promote tea tourism in Sri Lanka. *The 6th International Tourism Research Conference and Tourism Leader's Summit.*

Karaca, S. (2013). Tüketicilerin yeşil ürünlere ilişkin tutumlarının incelenmesine yönelik bir araştırma. *Ege Akademik Bakış, 13*(1), 99–111. doi:10.21121/eab.2013119503

Karadaş, F. (2008). *Sürdürülebilir kalkınma çerçevesinde Türkiye'de enerji sektörü ve politikaları* [Yayımlanmamış yüksek lisans tezi]. Gaziantep Üniversitesi.

Kardos, M.Research on European Union Countries. (2012). The relationship between entrepreneurship, innovation and sustainable development. Research on European Union countries. *Procedia Economics and Finance, 3*, 1030–1035. doi:10.1016/S2212-5671(12)00269-9

Kasalak, M. A. (2015). Dünya'da ekoturizm pazarı ve ekoturizmin ülke gelirlerine katkıları. *Journal of Recreation and Tourism Research, 2*(2), 20–26.

Kaur, R., Mishra, S., Yadav, S., & Shaw, T. (2022). Analysing the impact of green marketing mix on consumer purchase intention. *International Journal of Indian Culture and Business Management, 25*(3), 403–425. doi:10.1504/IJICBM.2022.122729

Kavita, E., & Saarinen, J. (2016). Tourism and community development in Namibia: Policy issues review. *Fennia, 194*(1), 79–88. doi:10.11143/46331

Kaya, İ. (2009). *Pazarlama bi' tanedir* (IV. Dijital Baskı) https://docplayer.biz.tr/829585-Pazarlama-bi-tanedir.html

Kelley, D. (2012). *Sports fundraising: Dynamic methods for schools, universities and youth sport organizations*. Routledge. doi:10.4324/9780203126479

Keogh, B. (1989). Social impacts. In G. Wall (Ed.), *Outdoor recreation in Canada*. Wiley.

Khan, M. I., Khalid, S., Zaman, U., José, A. E., & Ferreira, P. (2021). Green paradox in emerging tourism supply chains: Achieving green consumption behavior through strategic green marketing orientation, brand social responsibility, and green image. *International Journal of Environmental Research and Public Health, 18*(18), 9626. doi:10.3390/ijerph18189626 PMID:34574552

Compilation of References

Khan, M. M. (1997). Tourism development and dependency theory: Mass tourism vs. ecotourism. *Annals of Tourism Research*, 24(4), 988–991. doi:10.1016/S0160-7383(97)00033-9

Khokhar, S., & Magnusdottir, S. G. M. (2002). Total phenol, catechin, and caffeine contents of teas commonly consumed in the United Kingdom. *Journal of Agricultural and Food Chemistry*, 50(3), 565–570. doi:10.1021/jf010153l PMID:11804530

Kim, J., & McMillan, S. J. (2008). Evaluation of internet advertising research: A bibliometric analysis of citations from key sources. *Journal of Advertising*, 37(1), 99–112. doi:10.2753/JOA0091-3367370108

Kim, K., Uysal, M., & Sirgy, J. (2013). How does tourism in a community impacts the quality of life of community residents? *Tourism Management*, 36, 527–540. doi:10.1016/j.tourman.2012.09.005

Kim, N. S., & Chalip, L. (2004). Why travel to the FIFA World Cup? Effects of motives, background, interest, and constraints. *Tourism Management*, 25(6), 695–707. doi:10.1016/j.tourman.2003.08.011

Kim, Y. G., Eves, A., & Scarles, C. (2009). Building a model of local food consumption on trips and holidays: A grounded theory approach. *International Journal of Hospitality Management*, 28(3), 423–431. doi:10.1016/j.ijhm.2008.11.005

King, B., Dwyer, L., & Prideaux, B. (2006). An evaluation of ethical business practices in Australia's China inbound tourism market. *International Journal of Tourism Research*, 8(2), 127–142. doi:10.1002/jtr.563

Kiper, T. (2012). *Role of Ecotourism in Sustainable Development*. Available at: https://www.intechopen.com/chapters/45414

Kivela, J., & Crotts, J. (2006). Tourism and gastronomy: Gastronomy's influence on how tourists experience a destination. *Journal of Hospitality & Tourism Research (Washington, D.C.)*, 30(3), 354–377. doi:10.1177/1096348006286797

Kıvılcım, B. (2020). *Sürdürülebilir turizm kapsamında seyahat acentelerinin ekoturizm faaliyetleri: Doğu Karadeniz Bölgesinde bir araştırma* [Yayımlanmamış doktora tezi]. Atatürk Üniversitesi.

Klemm, M., & Parkinson, L. (2001). UK tour operator strategies: Causes and consequences. *International Journal of Tourism Research*, 3(5), 367–375. doi:10.1002/jtr.351

Koban, E., & Eker İşçioğlu, T. (2019). *Turizm pazarlaması rekabet yaklaşımıyla*. Ekin Publishing.

Kocagöz, E. (2011). Güncel bir konu olarak değil sürekli bir yaklaşım olarak yeşil pazarlama. In Güncel Pazarlama Yaklaşımları (pp. 47-78). Alfa Aktüel.

Kock F. (2016). https://www.linkedin.com/pulse/all-inclusive-resorts-potentially-negative-effects-local-richie-kock

Kock, F., Josiassen, A., & Assaf, A. G. (2019). The xenophobic tourist. *Annals of Tourism Research*, 74, 155–166. doi:10.1016/j.annals.2018.11.005

Ko, D.-W., & Stewart, W. P. (2002). A structural equation model of residents' attitudes for tourism development. *Tourism Management*, *23*(5), 521–530. doi:10.1016/S0261-5177(02)00006-7

Konda, I., Starc, J., & Rodica, B. (2015). Social challenges are opportunities for sustainable development: Tracing Impacts of Social Entrepreneurship Through Innovations and Value Creation. *Economic Themes*, *53*(2), 211–229. doi:10.1515/ethemes-2015-0012

Kondo, M. (2008). The economic impact of all-inclusive resorts in Jamaica. *City Tech Writer*, (8). http://www.citytech.cuny.edu/english/docs/ctw_v3_2008.pdf.

Kotler, P. (1967). *Marketing Management: Analysis, Planning, and Control*. Prentice Hall.

Koutsou, S., Notta, O., Samathrakis, V., & Partalidou, M. (2009). Women's entrepreneurship and rural tourism in Greece: Private enterprises and cooperatives. *South European Society & Politics*, *14*(2), 191–209. doi:10.1080/13608740903037968

Kozak, M. (2014). *Sürdürebilir turizm*. Detay Yayıncılık.

Krippendorf, J. (2010). *Holiday makers*. Taylor & Francis. doi:10.4324/9780080939032

Kuhn, L. (2007). Sustainable tourism as emergent discourse. *World Futures*, *63*(3-4), 286–297. doi:10.1080/02604020601174950

Kulendran, N., & King, M. L. (1997). Forecasting international quarterly tourist flows using error-correction and time-series models. *International Journal of Forecasting*, *13*(3), 319–327. doi:10.1016/S0169-2070(97)00020-4

Kumar, P.K. (2020, June 17). Bounce back will be faster and stronger for travel and tourism: Sanjay Datta. *Travel World*.

Kurtzman, J., & Zauhar, J. (2003). A Wave in Time – The Sports Tourism Phenomena. *Journal of Sport & Tourism*, *1*(1), 35–47. doi:10.1080/14775080306239

Kuter, N., & Ünal, H. E. (2009). Sürdürülebilirlik kapsamında ekoturizmin çevresel, ekonomik ve sosyo-kültürel etkileri. *Kastamonu Üniversitesi Orman Fakültesi Dergisi*, *9*(2), 146–156.

Kyung, H., Mark, A., & Meehee, C. (2017). Green tea quality attributes: A cross-cultural study of consumer perceptions using importance–performance analysis (IPA). *Journal of Foodservice Business Research*. doi:10.1080/15378020.2017.1368809

La Rocca, R. A. (2005). Mass Tourism and Urban System: Some suggestions to manage the impacts on the city. [eRTR]. *Ereview of Tourism Research*, *3*(1), 8–17.

Lacitignola, D., Petrosillo, I., Cataldi, M., & Zurlini, G. (2007). Modelling socio-ecological tourism-based systems for sustainability. *Ecological Modelling*, *206*(1-2), 191–204. doi:10.1016/j.ecolmodel.2007.03.034

Lancee, B., & Van de Werfhorst, H. (2011). *Income inequality and participation: a comparison of 24 European countries*. Amsterdam: Institute for Advanced Labour Studies. (GINI discussion paper 6)

Lankford, S. V., & Howard, D. R. (1994). Developing a tourism impact attitude scale. *Annals of Tourism Research, 21*(1), 121–139. doi:10.1016/0160-7383(94)90008-6

Lapeyre, R. (2009). Revenue sharing in community-private sector lodges in Namibia: A bargaining model. *Tourism Economics, 15*(3), 653–669. doi:10.5367/000000009789036585

Lapeyre, R. (2010). Community-based tourism as a sustainable solution to maximise impacts locally? The Tsiseb conservancy case, Namibia. *Development Southern Africa, 27*(5), 757–772. doi:10.1080/0376835X.2010.522837

Lapeyre, R. (2011). For what stands the "B" in CBT concept: Community-based or community-biased tourism? Some insights from Namibia. *Tourism Analysis, 16*(2), 187–202. doi:10.3727/108354211X13014081270440

Larson, L. R., & Poudyal, N. C. (2012). Developing sustainable tourism through adaptive resource management: A case study of Machu Picchu, Peru. *Journal of Sustainable Tourism, 20*(7), 917–938. doi:10.1080/09669582.2012.667217

Lasek, A., and Rhiova, I. (2010) The role of heritage tourism in the Shetland Islands. *International Journal Of Culture, Tourism And Hospitality Research, 4*(2), 118-129.

Lebart, L., Morineau, A., & Warwick, K. M. (1984). *Multivariate descriptive statistical analysis: Correspondence analysis and related techniques for large matrices*. Wiley., doi:10.1002/asm.3150050207

Lee, D. & Sirgy, M. (1995). Determinants of involvement in the consumer/marketing life domain in relation to quality of life: A theoretical model and research agenda. *Developments in Quality of Life Studies in Marketing*, 13-18.

Lee, C., & Taylor, T. (2006). Critical reflections on the economic impact assessment of a mega-event: The case of 2002 FIFA World Cup. *Tourism Management, 26*(4), 595–603. doi:10.1016/j.tourman.2004.03.002

Lee, S. M., Chung, S. J., Lee, O. H., Lee, H. S., Kim, Y. K., & Kim, K. O. (2008). Development of sample preparation, presentation procedure and sensory descriptive analysis of green tea. *Journal of Sensory Studies, 23*(4), 450–467. doi:10.1111/j.1745-459X.2008.00165.x

Lee, S., & Park, S. Y. (2009). Do socially responsible activities help hotels and casinos achieve their financial goals? *International Journal of Hospitality Management, 28*(1), 105–112. doi:10.1016/j.ijhm.2008.06.003

Lee, T. H. (2013). Influence analysis of community resident support for sustainable tourism development. *Tourism Management, 34*, 37–46. doi:10.1016/j.tourman.2012.03.007

Leonidou, L. C., Leonidou, C. N., Fotiadis, T. A., & Zeriti, A. (2013). Resources and capabilities as drivers of hotel environmental marketing strategy: Implications for competitive advantage and performance. *Tourism Management, 35*, 94–110. doi:10.1016/j.tourman.2012.06.003

Lepp, A. (2007). Residents' attitudes towards tourism in Bigodi village, Uganda. *Tourism Management*, *28*(3), 876–885. doi:10.1016/j.tourman.2006.03.004

Leujak, W., & Ormond, R. F. (2007). Visitor perceptions and the shifting social carrying capacity of South Sinai's coral reefs. *Environmental Management*, *39*(4), 472–489. doi:10.100700267-006-0040-1 PMID:17318694

Leujak, W., & Ormond, R. F. (2008). Quantifying acceptable levels of visitor use on Red Sea reef flats. *Aquatic Conservation*, *18*(6), 930–944. doi:10.1002/aqc.870

Lewis, A. (2002). *A case study of tourism curriculum development in the Caribbean: A stakeholder perspective* [Unpublished PhD Doctoral dissertation, Buckinghamshire Chilterns University College, Brunel University].

Liang, Z. X., & Hui, T. K. (2016). Residents' quality of life and attitudes toward tourism development in China. *Tourism Management*, *57*, 56–67. doi:10.1016/j.tourman.2016.05.001

Liburd, J. J., Benckendorff, P., & Carlsen, J. (2012). Tourism and Quality of Life: How Does Tourism Measure Up? In M. Uysal, R. Perdue, & J. Sirgy (Eds.), *Handbook of Tourism and Quality-of-Life Research: Enhancing the Lives of Tourists and Residents of Host Communities*. Springer Publishers. doi:10.1007/978-94-007-2288-0_7

Liguori, E., & Bendickson, J. S. (2020). Rising to the challenge: Entrepreneurship ecosystems and SDG success. *Journal of the International Council for Small Business*, *1*(3–4), 118–125. doi:10.1080/26437015.2020.1827900

Lim, C. (1997). Review of international tourism demand models. *Annals of Tourism Research*, *24*(4), 835–849. doi:10.1016/S0160-7383(97)00049-2

Lim, C., & Cooper, C. (2009). Beyond Sustainability; Optimising Island Tourism Development. *International Journal of Tourism Research*, *11*(1), 89–103. doi:10.1002/jtr.688

Lim, C., & McAleer, M. (2005). Ecologically sustainable tourism management. *Environmental Modelling & Software*, *20*(11), 1431–1438. doi:10.1016/j.envsoft.2004.09.023

Lindberg, K., & Johnson, R. L. (1997). Modelling resident attitudes toward tourism. *Annals of Tourism Research*, *24*(2), 402–424. doi:10.1016/S0160-7383(97)80009-6

Lindberg, K., & McCool, S. F. (1998). A critique of environmental carrying capacity as a means of managing the effects of tourism development. *Environmental Conservation*, *25*(4), 291–292. doi:10.1017/S0376892998000368

Lindberg, K., McCool, S., & Stankey, G. (1997). Rethinking carrying capacity. *Annals of Tourism Research*, *24*(2), 461–465. doi:10.1016/S0160-7383(97)80018-7

List of geographical indications in India . (2020, July, 16). Wikipedia. https://en.wikipedia.org/wiki/List_of_geographical_ indications_in_India.

Liu, J. (1994). *Pacific islands ecotourism: a public policy and planning guide.* University of Hawaii. Pacific Business Center Program.

Liu, J. C., Sheldon, P. J., & Var, T. (1987). Resident perception of the environmental impacts of tourism. *Annals of Tourism Research, 14*(1), 17–37. doi:10.1016/0160-7383(87)90045-4

Liu, J. C., & Var, T. (1986). Resident attitudes toward tourism impacts in Hawaii. *Annals of Tourism Research, 13*(2), 193–214. doi:10.1016/0160-7383(86)90037-X

Lobo, H. A. S., Trajano, E., de Alcântara Marinho, M., Bichuette, M. E., Scaleante, J. A. B., Scaleante, O. A. F., & Laterza, F. V. (2013). Projection of tourist scenarios onto fragility maps: Framework for determination of provisional tourist carrying capacity in a Brazilian show cave. *Tourism Management, 35*, 234–243. doi:10.1016/j.tourman.2012.07.008

Lockhart, D. & Smith, D.W. (1997). Island Tourism: Trends and Prospects. Pinter: London.

Lorenzo, M., Claudia, S., & Cannella, C. (2003). Eating habits and appetite control in the elderly: The anorexia of aging. *International Psychogeriatrics, 15*(1), 73–87. doi:10.1017/S1041610203008779 PMID:12834202

Lumbaraja, P., Lubis, A. N., & Hasibuan, B. K. (2019). Sustaining Lake Toba's tourism: Role of creative industry, green tourism marketing and tourism experience. *Asian Journal of Business and Accounting, 12*(1), 257–278. doi:10.22452/ajba.vol12no1.9

Lunt, T., & Nicotra, E. (2019). *Event sponsorship and fundraising: An advanced guide.* Kogan Page.

Luvanga, N., & Shitundu, J. (2003). The role of tourism in poverty alleviation in Tanzania. Dar es Salaam: Mkuki na Nyota Publishers. (Research for Poverty Alleviation (REPOA). Research report 03.4)

Magar, C. K., & Kar, B. K. (2016). Tea plantations and Socio-Cultural transformation: The case of Assam (India). *Space and Culture, India, 4*(1), 25–39. doi:10.20896aci.v4i1.188

Maggie's Tour Company. (2021). *Meet Maggie.* https://maggiestourcompany.com/introducing-maggies-tour-company/meet-maggie/

Mahanta, M. G. D. (2014). Ecotourism and Dibru-Saikhowa National Park. *J. Agric. Life Sci., 1*, 91–94.

Mahony, K. K., & Van Zyl, J. (2002). The impacts of tourism investment on rural communities: Three case studies in South Africa. *Development Southern Africa, 19*(1), 83–105. doi:10.1080/03768350220123891

Mak, A. H. N., Lumbers, M., Eves, A., & Chang, R. C. Y. (2012). Factors influencing tourist food consumption. *International Journal of Hospitality Management, 31*(3), 928–936. doi:10.1016/j.ijhm.2011.10.012

Malatji, M. I., & Mtapuri, O. (2012). Can community-based tourism enterprises alleviate poverty? Toward a new organisation. *Tourism Review International*, *16*(1), 1–14. doi:10.3727/154427212X13369577826825

Maliti, E. (2018). Inequality in education and wealth in Tanzania: A 25-year perspective. *Social Indicators Research*, *145*(3), 901–921. doi:10.100711205-018-1838-y

Manaktola, K., & Jauhari, V. (2007). Exploring consumer attitude and behaviour towards green practices in the lodging industry in India. *International Journal of Contemporary Hospitality Management*, *19*(5), 364–377. doi:10.1108/09596110710757534

Mananyi, A. (1998). Optimal management of ecotourism. *Tourism Economics*, *4*(2), 147–169. doi:10.1177/135481669800400203

Mandić, A., Mrnjavac, Ž., & Kordić, L. (2018). Tourism infrastructure, recreational facilities and tourism development. *Tourism and Hospitality Management*, *4*(1), 41–62. doi:10.20867/thm.24.1.12

Manning, E. W., & Dougherty, T. D. (1995). Sustainable tourism: Preserving the golden goose. *The Cornell Hotel and Restaurant Administration Quarterly*, *36*(2), 4–42. doi:10.1016/0010-8804(95)93841-H

Manning, R. (2001). Programs that work. Visitor experience and resource protection: A framework for managing the carrying capacity of National Parks. *Journal of Park and Recreation Administration*, *19*(1), 93–108.

Manning, R., Wang, B., Valliere, W., Lawson, S., & Newman, P. (2002). Research to estimate and manage carrying capacity of a tourist attraction: A study of Alcatraz Island. *Journal of Sustainable Tourism*, *10*(5), 388–404. doi:10.1080/09669580208667175

Manwa, H., & Mwanwa, F. (2014). Poverty alleviation through pro-poor tourism: The role of Botswana forest reserves. *Sustainability*, *6*(9), 5697–5713. doi:10.3390u6095697

Manyara, K., & Jones, E. (2007). Community-based tourism enterprises development in Kenya: An exploration of their potential as avenues of poverty reduction. *Journal of Sustainable Tourism*, *15*(6), 628–644. doi:10.2167/jost723.0

Marcouiller, D. W. (1997). Toward integrative tourism planning in rural America. *Journal of Planning Literature*, *11*(3), 337–357. doi:10.1177/088541229701100306

Marques, L. C. (2000, July). *An evaluation of ecolodges in the Brazilian Amazon* [Conference presentation]. Ecotourism Conference, Dominican Republic.

Marzuki, A., (2011) Resident Attitudes Towards Impacts from Tourism Development in Langkawi Islands, Malaysia. *World Applied Sciences Journal*, *12*, 25-34.

Masberg, B. A., & Morales, N. (1999). A case analysis of strategies in ecotourism development. *Aquatic Ecosystem Health & Management*, *2*(3), 289–300. doi:10.1080/14634989908656965

Compilation of References

Mason, P. (2003). *Tourism impacts, planning and management*. Butterworth-Heinemann.

Massam, B. H. (2002). Quality of life: Public planning and private living. *Progress in Planning*, *58*(3), 141–227. doi:10.1016/S0305-9006(02)00023-5

Masterman, G. (2014). *Strategic sport event management* (3rd ed.). Routledge. doi:10.4324/9780203114674

Mastny, L. (2001). *Traveling light: New paths for international tourism*. Worldwatchpaper 159.

Mathieson, A., & Wall, G. (1982). *Tourism: economic, physical and social impacts*. Longman.

Matthews, E. J. (2002). *Ecotourism: Are current practices delivering desired outcomes? A comparative case study analysis* [Unpublished master's thesis, State University].

Mbaiwa, J. E. (2005). Enclave tourism and its social-economic impacts in the Okavango delta, Botswana. *Tourism Management*, *26*(2), 157–172. doi:10.1016/j.tourman.2003.11.005

Mbaiwa, J. E. (2008). The socio-cultural impacts of tourism development in the Okavango Delta, Botswana. *Journal of Tourism and Cultural Change*, *2*(3), 163–185. doi:10.1080/14766820508668662

Mbaiwa, J. E., & Darkoh, M. (2009). The socio-economic impacts of tourism in the Okavango Delta, Botswana. In J. Saarinen, F. Becker, H. Manwa, & D. Wilson (Eds.), *Sustainable tourism in Southern Africa: local communities and natural resources in transition* (pp. 210–230). Channel View Publications. doi:10.21832/9781845411107-019

McCall, C. E., & Mearns, K. F. (2021). Empowering women through community-based tourism in the Western Cape, South Africa. *Tourism Review International*, *25*(2), 157–171. doi:10.3727/154427221X16098837279967

McCool, S. F., & Lime, D. W. (2001). Tourism carrying capacity: Tempting fantasy or useful reality? *Journal of Sustainable Tourism*, *9*(5), 372–388. doi:10.1080/09669580108667409

McCool, S. F., & Martin, S. R. (1994). Community attachment and attitudes toward tourism development. *Journal of Travel Research*, *32*(3), 29–34. doi:10.1177/004728759403200305

McCulloch, N., Winters, L. A., & Cirera, X. (2001). *Trade liberalization and poverty: a handbook*. Centre for Economic Policy Research.

Mcdowell, M. L. (2021). 'Come alive in '85¢: The Isle of Man Year of Sport, the first Island Games, and the shifting sands of sport event tourism. *Journal of Tourism History*, *13*(3), 290–310. doi:10.1080/1755182X.2021.2008024

McGehee, N. G., & Andereck, K. L. (2004). Factors predicting rural residents' support of tourism. *Journal of Travel Research*, *43*(2), 131–140. doi:10.1177/0047287504268234

McGehee, N. G., Yoon, Y., & Cardenas, D. (2003). Involvement and travel for recreational runners in North Carolina. *Journal of Sport Management*, *17*(3), 305–324. doi:10.1123/jsm.17.3.305

McIntyre, G. (1993). *Sustainable tourism development: guide for local planners*. World Tourism Organization.

McKercher, B., & Robbins, B. (1998). Business development issues affecting nature-based tourism operators in Australia. *Journal of Sustainable Tourism*, 6(2), 36–45. doi:10.1080/09669589808667309

McVeigh, T. (2014). All-inclusive boom leaves local workers and tour operators out in the cold. *The Guardian*. https://www.theguardian.com/travel/2014/mar/08/all-inclusive-holidays-travel-ethical-tourism

Meeberg, G. A. (1993). Quality of life: A concept analysis. *Journal of Advanced Nursing*, 18(1), 32–38. doi:10.1046/j.1365-2648.1993.18010032.x PMID:8429165

Melacon, C. (1974). *Indian Legends of Canada*. Gage.

Menon, A., Menon, A., Chowdhury, J., & Jankovich, J. (1999). Evolving paradigm for environmental sensitivity in marketing programs: A synthesis of theory and practice. *Journal of Marketing Theory and Practice*, 7(2), 1–15. doi:10.1080/10696679.1999.11501825

Mensah, A. M., & Castro, L. C. (2004). Sustainable resource use & sustainable development: A contradiction. Center for Development Research, University of Bonn, 1-22.

Mensah, I. (2006). Environmental management practices among hotels in the greater Accra region. *International Journal of Hospitality Management*, 25(3), 414–431. doi:10.1016/j.ijhm.2005.02.003

Mesci, Z. (2014). Otellerin çevreci uygulamalarının değerlendirmesi. *Seyahat ve Otel İşletmeciliği Dergisi*, 11(3), 90–102.

Meyer, D. (2007). Pro-poor tourism: from leakages to linkages: a conceptual framework for creating linkages between the accommodation sector and 'poor' neighbouring communities. *Current Issues in Tourism*, 10(6), 558–583. doi:10.2167/cit313.0

Middleton, V. T., & Hawkins, R. (1998). *Sustainable tourism: A marketing perspective*. Routledge.

Mielke, E. J. C., & Pegas, F. V. (2013). Turismo de base comunitária no Brasil. Insustentabilidade é uma questão de gestão. *Revista Turismo Em Análise*, 24(1), 170–189. doi:10.11606/issn.1984-4867.v24i1p170-189

Mill, R. C., & Morrison, A. M. (2012). *The tourism system* (7th ed.). Kendall/Hunt Publishing.

Mills, D. (1998). Sport in Canada: Leadership, partnership and accountability—everybody's business, *6th Report of the Standing Committee on Canadian Heritage*.

Milman, A., & Pizam, A. (1988). Social impacts of tourism on central Florida. *Annals of Tourism Research*, 15(2), 191–204. doi:10.1016/0160-7383(88)90082-5

Ming Su, M., Wall, G., & Wang, Y. (2019). Integrating tea and tourism: A sustainable livelihoods approach. *Journal of Sustainable Tourism*, 27(10), 1591–1608. doi:10.1080/09669582.2019.1648482

Compilation of References

Ministry of Environment and Tourism (Namibia). (1994). *White paper on tourism.* MET.

Ministry of Environment and Tourism (Namibia). (1995). *Community-based tourism development. policy document.* MET.

Ministry of Environment and Tourism (Namibia). (1996). *Nature conservation amendment act.* MET.

Ministry of Environment and Tourism (Namibia). (2001). *Tourism statistics preliminary findings.* MET.

Ministry of Environment and Tourism (Namibia). (2002). *Tourist arrival statistics.* MET.

Ministry of Environment and Tourism (Namibia). (2004). *Namibia statistical report.* MET.

Ministry of Environment and Tourism (Namibia). (2007). *A sustainable tourism country report.* MET.

Ministry of Environment and Tourism (Namibia). (2008). *National policy on tourism for Namibia.* MET.

Ministry of Environment and Tourism (Namibia). (2016). *Tourism statistical report.* MET.

Mitchell, J., & Ashley, C. (2010). *Tourism and poverty reduction: pathways to prosperity.* Earthscan.

Mitki, Y., Herstein, R., & Jaffe, E. (2011). Repositioning a destination in a time of crisis: the case of Jerusalem. In N. Morgan, A. Pritchard, & R. Pride (Eds.), *Destination Brands. Managing Place Reputation* (3rd ed.). Elsevier. doi:10.1016/B978-0-08-096930-5.10024-2

Mitova, R., Borisova, B., & Koulov, B. (2021). Digital Marketing of Bulgarian Natural Heritage for Tourism and Recreation. *Sustainability, 13*, 13071. Available at:https://www.mrrb.bg/static/media/ups/articles/attachments/838602eca62db5f279ff6321a7a55608.pdf

Mohammaad, A. A., & Ammar, S. A. M. (2015). Critical success factors for the interorganizational relationship between hotels and tour operators/travel agents. *Journal of Tourism Research & Hospitality, 4*(2), 1–9. doi:10.4172/2324-8807.1000151

Mondal, S., & Samaddar, K. (2020a). Issues and challenges in implementing sharing economy in tourism: A triangulation study. *Management of Environmental Quality, 32*(1), 64–81. doi:10.1108/MEQ-03-2020-0054

Mondal, S., & Samaddar, K. (2020b). Responsible tourism towards sustainable development: Literature review and research agenda. *Asia Pacific Business Review*, 1–38.

Mooney, S. (2018) *Ecotourism can benefit Rural communities.* Available at www.sustainablecitynetwork.com/topic_channels/community/article_c7a6f70a- ccb0-11e8-bf4e-efa2f0cbd95b.html

Morgan, N. J., & Pritchard, A. (2006). Promoting niche tourism destination brands: Case studies of New Zealand and wales. *Journal of Promotion Management*, *12*(1), 17–33. doi:10.1300/J057v12n01_03

Morgan, N., Pritchard, A., & Pride, R. (2011). *Destination brands: Managing place reputation*. Elsevier Butterworth-Heinemann.

Morozova, I. A., Popkova, E. G., & Litvinova, T. N. (2018). Sustainable development of global entrepreneurship: Infrastructure and perspectives. *The International Entrepreneurship and Management Journal*, *15*(2), 589–597. doi:10.100711365-018-0522-7

Morrison, A. M. (2012). *Marketing and managing tourism destinations*. Routledge. Nunnally, J. C., & Bernstein, I. H. (1994). *Psychometric theory* (3rd ed.). McGraw-Hill., doi:10.1177/014662169501900308

Morse, S., & McNamara, N. (2013). *Sustainable livelihood approach: a critique of theory and practice*. Springer. doi:10.1007/978-94-007-6268-8

Mosavichechaklou, S. (2017). *Türk ve İranlı tüketicilerin yeşil satın alma davranışlarına ilişkin karşılaştırmalı bir araştırma (Yayımlanmamış Yüksek Lisans Tezi)*. İstanbul Üniversitesi.

Moseley, J., Sturgis, L., & Wheeler, M. (2007). *Improving domestic tourism in Namibia*. Worcester Polythetic Institute.

Mowforth, M., & Munt, I. (2003). *Tourism and sustainability: development and new tourism in the third world* (2nd ed.). Routledge. doi:10.4324/9780203422779

Mtapuri, O., & Giampiccoli, A. (2013). Interrogating the role of the state and nonstate actors in community-based tourism ventures: Toward a model for spreading the benefits to the wider community. *The South African Geographical Journal*, *95*(1), 1–15. doi:10.1080/03736245.2013.805078

Muchapondwa, E., & Stage, J. (2013). The economic impacts of tourism in Botswana, Namibia and South Africa: Is poverty subsiding? A United Nations sustainable development. *Journal*, *37*(2), 80–89.

Muchtar, B., Evanita, S., Aimon, H., Azhar, Z., & Alhadi, Z. (2021). Mapping analysis of potential tourism products in Mandeh integrated tourism region-Indonesia. *Academy of Strategic Management Journal*, *20*, 1–6.

Muganda, M., Sahli, M., & Smith, K. (2010). Tourism's contribution to poverty alleviation: A community perspective from Tanzania. *Development Southern Africa*, *27*(5), 629–646. doi:10.1080/0376835X.2010.522826

Muhanna, E. (2007). The contribution of sustainable tourism development in poverty alleviation of local communities in South Africa. *Journal of Human Resources in Hospitality & Tourism*, *6*(1), 37–67. doi:10.1300/J171v06n01_03

Munekiyo and Hiraga. (2014). *Tourism Market Study*. Banyan Drive.

Compilation of References

Musavengane, R., & Simatele, D. (2016). Community-based natural resource management: The role of social capital in collaborative environmental management of tribal resources in Kwazulu-Natal, South Africa. *Journal of Southern Africa*, *33*(6), 806–821. doi:10.1080/0376835X.2016.1231054

Mutana, S., Chipfuva, T., & Muchenje, B. (2013). Is tourism in Zimbabwe developing with the poor in mind? Assessing the pro-poor involvement of tourism operators located near rural areas in Zimbabwe. *Asian Social Science*, *9*(5), 154–161. doi:10.5539/ass.v9n5p154

Myre, M. (2005) Sports tourism a burgeoning niche market for islands. *Travel Weekly*. http://www.travelweekly.com

NAIG Council. (2002). *Home*. NAIG Council. http://www.naigcouncil.com/

Nakale, A. (2017, Aug. 15). Tourism ministry concerned over tourist attacks. *Newera*.

Namibia Tourism Board (NTB). (2018). *Conservation*. Namibia Tourism Board.

Namibia Tourism Board (NTB). (2020). *National parks*. Namibia Tourism Board.

Namibian Tourist Board (NTB). (2018). *Culture*. NTB. https://namibiatourism.com.na/page/culture

Nassani, A. A., Aldakhil, A. M., Abro, M. M. Q., Islam, T., & Zaman, K. (2019). The impact of tourism and finance on women empowerment. *Journal of Policy Modeling*, *41*(2), 234–254. doi:10.1016/j.jpolmod.2018.12.001

National Park Service. (1997). *A Summary of the Visitor Experience and Resource Protection (VERP) Framework. Publication no. NPS D-1214*. NPS Denver Service Center.

National Planning Commission (NPC). (2002). Second National Development Plan (NDP2), v. 1. 2001/02-2005/06. National Planning Commission.

Ndlovu, N., & Rogerson, C. M. (2003). Rural local economic development through community-based tourism: The Mehloding hiking and horse trail, Eastern cape, South Africa. *Africa Insight*, *33*(1/2), 124–129.

Nemli, E. (2001). Çevreye duyarlı yönetim anlayışı. *İstanbul Üniversitesi Siyasal Bilgiler Fakültesi Dergisi, 23*(24), 211-224.

Neto, F. (2003). A new approach to sustainable tourism development: Moving beyond environmental protection. *Natural Resources Forum*, *27*(3), 212–222. doi:10.1111/1477-8947.00056

Neuts, B., & Nijkamp, P. (2012). Tourist crowding perception and acceptability in cities: An applied modelling study on Bruges. *Annals of Tourism Research*, *39*(4), 2133–2153. doi:10.1016/j.annals.2012.07.016

Nguyen, T. H. M., & Nguyen, D. H. C. (2013). The contribution of tourism to economic growth in Thua Thien Hue Province (Vietnam). *International Journal of Social and Economic Research*, *3*(2), 160–168. doi:10.5958/j.2249-6270.3.2.020

Ngwetjana, S., & Sifolo, P. P. S. (2022). Sustainable Community Participation: A Reality Or A Fallacy? *Journal On Tourism &Amp; Sustainability, 6*(1). https://ontourism.academy/journal/index.php/jots/article/view/118

Nhongo, K. (2018, Apr. 27). Locals welcome tourism incentives as domestic booms. *Windhoek Observer*.

Nicanor, N. (2001). *Practical strategies for pro-poor tourism: NACOBTA the Namibian case study*. Department for International Development.

Niskala, M. (2015). Encountering the other: The Ovahimba culture and people in Namibian tourism promotion. *Nordic Journal of African Studies, 24*(3&4), 259–278.

Novelli, M. (2022). Niche tourism. In *Encyclopedia of Tourism Management and Marketing* (pp. 344–347). Edward Elgar Publishing. doi:10.4337/9781800377486.niche.tourism

Novelli, M., & Gebhardt, K. (2007). Community-based tourism in Namibia: "reality show" or "window dressing? *Current Issues in Tourism, 10*(5), 443–479. doi:10.2167/cit332.0

Nunkoo, R., & Ramkissoon, H. (2010a). Modeling community support for a proposed integrated resort project. *Journal of Sustainable Tourism, 18*(2), 257–277. doi:10.1080/09669580903290991

Nunkoo, R., & Ramkissoon, H. (2010b). Residents' satisfaction with community attributes and support for tourism. *Journal of Hospitality & Tourism Research (Washington, D.C.)*.

Nyakunu, E., & Rogerson, C. (2014). Tourism SMMEs and policy formulation: Recent evidence from Namibia. *Mediterranean Journal of Social Sciences, 5*(10), 244. doi:10.5901/mjss.2014.v5n10p244

O'Donnell, C. (1994). Food products for different age groups: Formulating for the ages. *Prepared Food, 3*(2), 39–44. doi:10.1375/jhtm.18.1.1

O'Reilly, A. M. (1986). Tourism carrying capacity: Concept and issues. *Tourism Management, 7*(4), 254–258. doi:10.1016/0261-5177(86)90035-X

OECD Tourism Trends and Policies 2020. (2020). Available at: https://www.oecd.org/cfe/tourism/OECD-Tourism-Trends-Policies%202020-Highlights-ENG.pdf

OECD. (2001). The DAC guidelines: poverty reduction: international development. Paris: OECD.

OECD. (2001). The DAC guidelines: Poverty reduction: International development. Paris: OECD.

Ogamba, I. K. (2018). Millennials empowerment: Youth entrepreneurship for sustainable development. *World Journal of Entrepreneurship, Management and Sustainable Development, 15*(3), 267–278. doi:10.1108/WJEMSD-05-2018-0048

Olalı, H., & Timur, A. (1988). *Turizm ekonomisi*. Ofis Ticaret Matbaacılık.

Online, H. (2005). Hawaii, Illinois, and Pennsylvania have biggest budgets for travel and tourism promotion; TIA Ranks all the states budgets for 2005. *Hotel Online*. http:// www.hotel-online.com

Compilation of References

Onurlubaş, E., & Dinçer, D. (2016). *Yeşil pazarlama tüketici algısı üzerine bir araştırma* (1st ed.). Beta Yayıncılık.

Orams, M. B. (1995). Towards a more desirable form of ecotourism. *Tourism Management*, *16*(1), 3–8. doi:10.1016/0261-5177(94)00001-Q

Osland, G., & Mackoy, R. (2012). *Education and Ecotourism. Scholarship and Professional Work - Business*. Available at: https://digitalcommons.butler.edu/cob_papers/236

Osmani, S., & Sen, A. (2003). The hidden penalties of gender inequality: Fetal origins of ill-health. *Economics and Human Biology*, *1*(1), 105–121. doi:10.1016/S1570-677X(02)00006-0 PMID:15463967

Ottman, J. (1998). *Green marketing and opportunities for the new marketing age*. NTC Business Books.

Ottman, J. A., Stafford, E. R., & Hartman, C. L. (2006). Avoiding green marketing myopia: Ways to improve consumer appeal for environmentally preferable products. *Environment*, *48*(5), 22–36. doi:10.3200/ENVT.48.5.22-36

Özbey, R. F. (2002). Sustainable tourism development in globalization progress, globalization and sustainable development. *International Scientific Conference, Bulgaria*.

Özcan, H., & Özgül, B. (2019). Yeşil pazarlama ve tüketicilerin yeşil ürün tercihlerini etkileyen faktörler. *Türkiye Mesleki ve Sosyal Bilimler Dergisi*, *1*(1), 1–18.

Özdemir, G. (2018). *Food waste management within sustainability perspective: A study on five star chain hotels* [Yayımlanmamış doktora tezi]. Gazi Üniversitesi.

Özgüç, N. (2007). *Turizm coğrafyası*. Çantay Kitabevi.

Öztürk, T., & Mengüloğlu, M. (2008). Sürdürülebilir kalkınmada fiziksel kırsal alan planlaması. *Anadolu Tarım Bilimleri Dergisi*, *23*(3), 209–215.

Page, S. J., Brunt, P., Busby, G., & Connell, J. (2001). *Tourism: a modern synthesis*. Thomson Learning.

Page, S., & Dowling, R. K. (2002). *Ecotourism*. Prentice Hall.

PAP/RAC. (1997). Guidelines for Carrying Capacity Assessment for Tourism in Mediterranean Coastal Areas. PAP-9/1997/G.1. Split, (Priority Actions Programme Regional Activity Centre).

Papadas, K. K., Avlonitis, G. J., & Carrigan, M. (2017). Green marketing orientation: Conceptualization, scale development and validation. *Journal of Business Research*, *80*, 236–246. doi:10.1016/j.jbusres.2017.05.024

Papageorgiou, K., & Brotherton, I. (1999). A management planning framework based on ecological, perceptual and economic carrying capacity: The case study of Vikos-Aoos National Park, Greece. *Journal of Environmental Management*, *56*(4), 271–284. doi:10.1006/jema.1999.0285

Parker, S., & Khare, A. (2005). Understanding, success factors for ensuring sustainability in ecoturism development in Southern Africa. *Journal of Ecotourism*, *4*(1), 32–46. doi:10.1080/14724040508668436

Pastras, P., & Bramwell, B. (2013). A strategic-relational approach to tourism policy. *Annals of Tourism Research*, *43*, 390–414. doi:10.1016/j.annals.2013.06.009

Pattullo, P. (2006). Last resort: The cost of tourism in the Caribbean. Wellington

PCN. (2021). *Who We Are - Persone Come Noi*. https://www.personecomenoi.org/who-we-are-pcn-busca

Pearce, D. C. (1989). *Tourist Development*. Longman Scientific and Technical Publishers.

Pearce, D. G., & Butler, R. (Eds.). (2010). *Tourism research: a 20-20 vision*. Goodfellow Publishers.

Pearce, P. L., Moscardo, G., & Ross, G. F. (1996). *Tourism community relationships*. Pergamon.

Peattie, K. (1995). *Environmental marketing management: Meeting the green challenge*. Pitman Publishing.

Peattie, K. (1999). Trappings versus substance in the greening of marketing planning. *Journal of Strategic Marketing*, *7*(2), 131–148. doi:10.1080/096525499346486

Peattie, K., & Crane, A. (2005). Green marketing: Legend, myth, farce or prophesy? *Qualitative Market Research*, *4*(8), 357–370. doi:10.1108/13522750510619733

Peck Ting, G., Adeline, S., & Yien, T. (2017). Our tea-drinking habits: Effects of brewing cycles and infusion time on total phenol content and antioxidants of common teas. *Journal of Culinary Science & Technology*. Advance online publication. doi:10.1080/15428052.2017.1409673

Pekin, F. (2011). *Çözüm: Kültür turizmi*. İletişim Yayınları.

Peña-Sánchez, A. R., Ruiz-Chico, J., Jiménez-García, M., & López-Sánchez, J. A. (2020). Tourism and the SDGs: An analysis of economic growth, decent employment, and gender equality in the European Union (2009–2018). *Sustainability*, *12*(13), 54–80. doi:10.3390u12135480

Perdue, R. R., Long, P. T., & Allen, L. R. (1987). Rural resident tourism perceptions and attitudes. *Annals of Tourism Research*, *14*(3), 420–429. doi:10.1016/0160-7383(87)90112-5

Perdue, R. R., Long, P. T., & Allen, L. R. (1990). Resident support for tourism development. *Annals of Tourism Research*, *17*(4), 586–599. doi:10.1016/0160-7383(90)90029-Q

Perkins, D. H., Radelet, S., & Lindauer, D. L. (Eds.). (2006). *Economics of development* (6th ed.). W.W. Norton.

Perrottet, J., & Benli, B. (2016). *Impact of tourism, how can we do this better?* World Bank.

Phi, G. T., Whitford, M., & Reid, S. (2018). Current issues in the method and practice, what's in the black box? Evaluating anti-poverty tourism interventions utilising theory of change. *Current Issues in Tourism*, *21*(17), 1930–1945. doi:10.1080/13683500.2016.1232703

Compilation of References

Phillips, D. (2006). *Quality of life: Concept, policy and practice*. New York. Routledge. doi:10.4324/9780203356630

Phommavong, S. (2011). *International tourism development and poverty reduction in Lao PDR* [Dissertation]. Umeå: Umeå University. Department of Social and Economic Geography.

Pizam, A. (1978). Tourism's impacts: The social costs to the destination community as perceived by its residents. *Journal of Travel Research*, *16*(4), 8–12. doi:10.1177/004728757801600402

Pleumarom, A. (2012). *The politics of tourism, poverty reduction and sustainable development*. Third World Network.

Pogge, T., & Sengupta, M. (2016). A critique of the sustainable development goals' potential to realize the human rights of all: why being better than the MDGs is not good enough. Journal of International and Comparative Social Policy, 19(1-2), 4-20.

Polonsky, M. J. (1994). An introduction to green marketing. *Electronic Green Journal*, *1*(2). Advance online publication. doi:10.5070/G31210177

Polonsky, M. J., & Rosenberger, P. J. III. (2001). Reevaluating green marketing: A strategic approach. *Business Horizons*, *44*(5), 21–30. doi:10.1016/S0007-6813(01)80057-4

Portales, L. (2019). Alignment of social innovation with Sustainable Development Goals. *Social Innovation and Social Entrepreneurship*, 193–204. doi:10.1007/978-3-030-13456-3_13

Porter, M. E., & Kramer, M. R. (2006). Strategy and sosciety, the link between competitive advantage and corporate social responsibility. *Harvard Business Review*, *85*(12), 78–91. PMID:17183795

Prakash, A. (2002). Green marketing, public policy and managerial strategies. *Business Strategy and the Environment*, *11*(5), 285–297. doi:10.1002/bse.338

Pratiwi, S. (2000). *Understanding local community participation in ecotourism development: A critical analysis of select published literature* [Unpublished master's thesis, Michigan State University].

Presnza, A., & Sheehan, L. (2013). Planning tourism through sports events. *International Journal of Event and Festival Management*, *4*(2), 125–139. doi:10.1108/17582951311325890

Prokopiou, D. G., Tselentis, B. S., & Toanoglou, M. (2013). Carrying capacity assessment in tourism: The case of Northern Sporades islands. *WIT Transactions on Ecology and the Environment*, *169*, 115–123. doi:10.2495/CP130101

Puczkó, L., & Smith, M. (2011). Tourism-Specific Quality-of-Life Index: The Budapest Model. In M. Budruk & R. Phillips (Eds.), Social Indicators Research Series: Vol. 43. *Quality-of-Life Community Indicators for Parks, Recreation and Tourism Management*. Springer. doi:10.1007/978-90-481-9861-0_9

Pyo, S. S., Cook, R., & Howell, R. L. (1988). Summer Olympic tourist market: Learning from the past. *Tourism Management*, *9*(2), 137–144. doi:10.1016/0261-5177(88)90023-4

Quan, S., & Wang, N. (2004). Towards a structural model of the tourist experience: An illustration from food experience in tourism. *Tourism Management*, *25*(3), 297–305. doi:10.1016/S0261-5177(03)00130-4

Radisson Hotels. (2022). *Example of green accommodation business.* https://media.radissonhotels.net/image/responsible-business--corporate-use-only/businesscenter/16256-142211-m24296998.pdf

Raja, M., & Mythili, C. (2019). Sustainable livelihood and economic status of tea labourers in the Nilgiris District. *IOSR J. Econ. Financ.*, *10*, 33–38.

Ramos, D., Malta, A., & Costa, C. (2021). Uma perspetiva teórica sobre o turismo, género e objetivos de desenvolvimento sustentável. *Revista Turismo e Desenvolvimento*, *2*(36), 619–629. doi:10.34624/rtd.v36i2.26034

Ranasinghe, W. T., Thaichon, P., & Ranasinghe, M. (2017). An analysis of product-place co-branding: The case of ceylon tea. *Asia Pacific Journal of Marketing and Logistics*, *29*(1), 200–214. doi:10.1108/APJML-10-2015-0156

Ravallion, M. (2004). Pro-poor growth: a primer. World Bank. doi:10.1596/1813-9450-3242

Republic of Namibia. (1994). *White paper on tourism.* Approved by the Cabinet 29.3.1994. National Development. Office of the President.

Republic of Namibia. (1995a). *Namibia tourism development programme. Phase I - Foundation.* Ministry of Environment and Tourism.

Republic of Namibia. (1995b). *The promotion of community-based tourism. Policy Document.* Ministry of Environment and Tourism.

Republic of Namibia. (2004). *Namibia vision 2030 - policy framework for long-term.* National Development. Office of the President.

Republic of Namibia. (2008). *Third National Development Plan (NDP3) 2007/08- 2011-12* (Vol. 1). National Planning Commission. Office of the President.

Republic of Namibia. (2011). *Fourth National Development Plan (NDP4) 2012/13 to 2016/17.* National Planning Commission. Office of the President.

Republic of Namibia. (2012). *Namibia poverty mapping.* National Planning Commission.

Republic of Namibia. (2015). *Poverty and deprivation in Namibia.* National Planning Commission.

Republic of Namibia. (2016). *National tourism investment profile and promotion strategy 2016-2026.* Ministry of Environment and Tourism.

Republic of Namibia. (2017). *Namibia's fifth development plan, 2017/18-2021/22.* National Planning Commission. Office of the President.

Compilation of References

Revilla, G., Dodd, T. H., & Hoover, L. C. (2001). Environmental tactics used by hotel companies in Mexico. *International Journal of Hospitality & Tourism Administration*, *1*(3/4), 111–127. doi:10.1300/J149v01n03_07

Rezaee, E., Mirlohi, M., Hassanzadeh, A., & Fallah, A. (2016). Factors affecting tea consumption pattern in an urban society in Isfahan, Iran. *Journal of Education and Health Promotion*, *5*, 13. doi:. 184568 doi:10.4103/2277-9531

Reza, H., Keshtidar, K., Ramkissoon, H., Esfahani, M., & Asadollahi, E. (2022). Adoption of entrepreneurial behaviours in sports tourism in developing countries. *Highlights of Sustainability*, *1*(2), 41–53. doi:10.54175/hsustain1020004

Ribeiro, M.F., Ferreira, J., & Silva, C. (2011). The Sustainable Carrying Capacity as a Tool for Environmental Beach Management. *Journal of Coastal Research*, 1411–1414.

Richardson, R. B. (2010). The contribution of tourism to economic growth and food security. Michigan State University.

Richardson, R. B. (2010). The contribution of tourism to economic growth and food security: Michigan State University. Department of Agricultural, Food, and Resource Economics. (Food Security collaborative working papers 97140)

Ridderstaat, J., Croes, R., & Nijkamp, P. (2016). A two- way causal chain between tourism development and quality of life in a small island destination: An empirical analysis. *Journal of Sustainable Tourism*, *24*(10), 1461–1479. doi:10.1080/09669582.2015.1122016

Rivera, J. (2002). Assessing a voluntary environmental initiative in the developing world: The Costa Rican certification for sustainable tourism. *Policy Sciences*, *35*(4), 333–360. doi:10.1023/A:1021371011105

Rivera, J. (2004). Institutional pressures and voluntary environmental behavior in developing countries: Evidence from the Costa Rican hotel industry. *Society & Natural Resources*, *17*(9), 779–797. doi:10.1080/08941920490493783

Rızaoğlu, B. (2004). *Turizmin sosyo-kültürel temelleri*. Detay yayıncılık.

rKrasnokutskiy, E. (2016). The Main Trends and Prospects of Development of International Tourism. *International Journal of Economics and Financial Issues*, *6*(S8), 257-262.

Robinson, M. (1999). Cultural conflicts in tourism: inevitability and inequality. In M. Robinson & P. Boniface (Eds.), *Tourism and cultural conflicts* (pp. 1–32). CABI Publishing.

Robinson, M., & Novelli, M. (2005). Niche Tourism. Contemporary issues, trends and cases. *Information and Communication Technologies in Tourism*, *2001*, 294–302.

Roehl, W. S. (1999). Quality of life issues in a casino destination. *Journal of Business Research*, *44*(3), 223–229. doi:10.1016/S0148-2963(97)00203-8

Rogerson, C. M. (2012). Strengthening agriculture-tourism linkages in the developing world: Opportunities, barriers and current initiatives. *African Journal of Agricultural Research*, *7*(4), 616–623.

Roveri, I. (2019). *Desenvolvimento do turismo de base comunitária no assentamento Ipanema – Iperó/SP* [Degree dissertation, Universidade Federal de São Carlos, Campus Sorocaba]. Repositório Institucional.

Royle, S. A. (2001). *A Geography of Islands: Small Island Insularity*. Routledge. doi:10.4324/9780203227404

Rozin, P. (2006). The integration of biological, social, cultural and psychological influences on food choice. In R. Shepherd & M. Raats (Eds.), *The psychology of food choice* (pp. 19–39). CABI. doi:10.1079/9780851990323.0019

Ruhanen, L., & Whitford, M. (2011). Indigenous sporting events: More than just a game. [IJEMR]. *International Journal of Event Management Research*, *6*(1), 33–49.

Rushton, A., Phil, C., & Peter, B. (2006). *Handbook of logistics and distribution management* (3rd ed.). Kogan Page Limited.

Saarinen, J. (2006). Traditions of sustainability in tourism studies. *Annals of Tourism Research*, *33*(4), 1121–1140. doi:10.1016/j.annals.2006.06.007

Saarinen, J., & Rogerson, C. M. (2014). Tourism and the millennium development goals: Perspectives beyond 2015. *Tourism Geographies*, *16*(1), 23–30. doi:10.1080/14616688.2013.851269

Saarinen, J., Rogerson, C., & Manwa, H. (2011). Tourism and millennium development goals: Tourism for global development. *Current Issues in Tourism*, *10*(2&3), 119–143. doi:10.1080/13683500.2011.555180

Saayman, M. (2007). *En-route with tourism: an introductory text* (3rd ed.). Platinum Press.

Saayman, M., & Giampiccoli, A. (2016). Community-based and pro-poor tourism: Initial assessment of their relation to community development. *European Journal of Tourism Research*, *12*, 145–190. doi:10.54055/ejtr.v12i.218

Saayman, M., Rossouw, R., & Krugell, W. (2012). The impact of tourism on poverty in South Africa. *Development Southern Africa*, *29*(3), 462–487. doi:10.1080/0376835X.2012.706041

Sæþórsdóttir, A. D. (2010). Planning nature tourism in Iceland based on tourist attitudes. *Tourism Geographies*, *12*(1), 25–52. doi:10.1080/14616680903493639

Salerno, F., Viviano, G., Manfredi, E. C., Caroli, P., Thakuri, S., & Tartari, G. (2013). Multiple Carrying Capacities from a management-oriented perspective to operationalize sustainable tourism in protected areas. *Journal of Environmental Management*, *128*, 116–125. doi:10.1016/j.jenvman.2013.04.043 PMID:23728182

Samaddar, K., & Menon, P. (2020). Non-deceptive counterfeit products: A morphological analysis of literature and future research agenda. *Journal of Strategic Marketing*, 1–24. doi:10.1080/0965254X.2020.1772348

Samad, S., & Alharthi, A. (2022). Untangling factors influencing women entrepreneurs' involvement in tourism and its impact on sustainable tourism development. *Administrative Sciences*, *12*(2), 52. doi:10.3390/admsci12020052

Samuelsson, E., & Stage, J. (2007). The size and distribution of the economic impacts of Namibian hunting tourism. *South African Journal of Wildlife Research*, *37*(1), 41–52. doi:10.3957/0379-4369-37.1.41

Sanchez, J., Callarisa, L., Rodríguez, M. R., & Moliner, M. A. (2006). Perceived value of the purchase of a tourism product. *Tourism Management*, *27*(3), 394–409. doi:10.1016/j.tourman.2004.11.007

Şanlıöz Özgen, H. K., Dilek, S. E., Türksoy, S. S., & Kaygalak Çelebi, S. (2016). Turizm ve çevre: Kavramsal çerçeve. İçinde N. Koçak (Ed.), Sürdürülebilir turizm yönetimi (pp. 1-22). Detay Yayıncılık.

Santa Soriano, A., Álvarez, C. L., & Valdés, R. M. T. (2018). Bibliometric analysis to identify an emerging research area: Public Relations Intelligence—a challenge to strengthen technological observatories in the network society. *Scientometrics*, *115*(3), 1591–1614. doi:10.100711192-018-2651-8

Sarkım, M. (2007). *Sürdürülebilir turizm kapsamında turistik ürün çeşitlendirme politikaları ve Antalya örneği (Yayımlanmamış Doktora Tezi)*. Dokuz Eylül Üniversitesi.

Saunders, M., Lewis, P., & Thornhill, A. (2009). *Research methods for business students*. Pearson education.

Sawhill, I. V. (2003). The behavioural aspects of poverty. *The Public Interest*, *153*, 79–93.

Schalock, R. L. (1996). *Quality of life: Conceptualization and measurement, 1*. American Association on Mental Retardation.

Scheyvens, R. (2002). *Tourism for development: empowering communities*. Pearson Education.

Scheyvens, R. (2007). Exploring the tourism-poverty nexus. *Current Issues in Tourism*, *10*(2&3), 231–254. doi:10.2167/cit318.0

Scheyvens, R. (2011). *Tourism and poverty*. Routledge.

Schianetz, K., & Kavanagh, L. (2008). Sustainability indicators for tourism destinations: A complex adaptive systems approach using systemic indicator systems. *Journal of Sustainable Tourism*, *16*(6), 601–628. doi:10.1080/09669580802159651

Schilcher, D. (2007). Growth versus equity: The continuum of pro-poor tourism and neoliberal governance. *Current Issues in Tourism*, *10*(2/3), 166–192. doi:10.2167/cit304.0

Sealy, W. (2017). From colonialism to transnationalism: The neo-colonial structure of Caribbean Tourism. *Journal on Tourism and Sustainability, 1*(2), 81–92.

Sealy, W., & Seraphin, H. (2020). Hoteliers' sources of bargaining power with British tour operators: A Barbados case study. *Journal on Tourism & Sustainability, 3*(2), 41–56.

Seetanah, B., Ramessur, S., & Rojid, S. (2009). Does infrastructure alleviates poverty in developing countries? *International Journal of Applied Econometrics and Quantitative Studies, 9*(2), 17–36.

Sen, A. (2001). The many faces of gender inequality. *New Republic*, 35–40.

Sen, A. (1999). *Development as Freedom*. Anchor Books.

Şen, H., Kaya, A., & Alpaslan, B. (2018). Sürdürülebilirlik üzerine tarihsel ve güncel bir perspektif. *Ekonomik Yaklaşım Derneği, 20*(107), 1–47.

Serrat, O. (2017). The Sustainable Livelihoods Approach Knowledge Solutions (Singapura: Springer). pp 21–6.

Serrat, O. (2017). *The sustainable livelihood approach: in knowledge solutions*. Springer. doi:10.1007/978-981-10-0983-9_5

Sert, A. N. (2017). Konaklama işletmelerinde yeşil pazarlama uygulamaları: Doğa Residence Otel örneği. *Türk Turizm Araştırmaları Dergisi, 1*(1), 1–20. doi:10.26677/tutad.2017.0

Shah, S. K., & Pate, V. A. (2016). Tea production in India: Challenges and opportunities. *Journal of Tea Science Research, 6*(5), 1–6.

Shah, S., Gani, A., Ahmad, M., Shah, A., Gani, A., & Massodi, F. A. (2015). In vitro antioxidant and antiproliferative activity of microwave-extracted green tea and black tea (Camellia sinensis): A comparative study. *NUTRAfoods: International Journal of Science and Marketing for Nutraceutical Actives, Raw Materials, Finish Products, 14*(4), 207–215. doi:10.100713749-015-0050-9

Shaping the Future of Luxury Travel Future Traveller Tribes 2030. (2016). Available at: https://amadeus.com/documents/en/travel-industry/report/shaping-the-future-of-luxury-travel-future-traveller-tribes-2030.pdf

Sharma, R. (2016). Evaluating total carrying capacity of tourism using impact indicators. *Global Journal of Environmental Science and Management, 2*(2), 187–196. doi:10.7508/gjesm.2016.02.009

Sharpley, R. (2000). Rural tourism and the challenge of tourism diversification: The case of Cyprus. *Tourism Management, 23*(3), 233–244. doi:10.1016/S0261-5177(01)00078-4

Sharpley, R. (2009). Tourism and development challenges in the least developed countries: The case of The Gambia. *Current Issues in Tourism, 12*(4), 337–358. doi:10.1080/13683500802376240

Sharpley, R., & Stone, P. (2011). Socio-cultural impacts of events. In S. Page & J. Connell (Eds.), *Routledge Handbook of Events* (pp. 347–361). London Routledge.

Compilation of References

Shelby, B., & Heberlein, T. A. (1987). *Carrying capacity in recreation settings*. Oregon State University Press.

Shen, F. (2009). *Tourism and the sustainable livelihoods approach: application within the Chinese context* [PhD thesis]. Lincoln University.

Shen, K., Zhang, B., & Feng, Q. (2019). Association between tea consumption and depressive symptom among Chinese older adults. *BMC Geriatrics*, *19*(1), 246–261. doi:10.118612877-019-1259-z PMID:31484503

Shone, A., & Parry, B. (2004). *Successful event management A practical handbook* (2nd ed.). Thomson.

Simón, F. J. G., Narangajavana, Y., & Marques, D. P. (2004). Carrying capacity in the tourism industry: A case study of Hengistbury Head. *Tourism Management*, *25*(2), 275–283. doi:10.1016/S0261-5177(03)00089-X

Simpson, D. (2014). *Poor pay and conditions at all-inclusive resorts*. CABI. https://www.cabi.org/leisuretourism/news/23741

Simpson, M. C. (2008). Community benefit tourism initiatives: A conceptual oxymoron. *Journal of Tourism Management*, *29*(6), 1–18. doi:10.1016/j.tourman.2007.06.005

Sin, H. L., & Minca, C. (2014). Touring responsibility: The trouble with 'going local' in community-based tourism in Thailand. *Geoforum*, *51*, 96–106. doi:10.1016/j.geoforum.2013.10.004

Sirgy, M. J., & Cornwell, T. (2001).. . *Social Indicators Research*, *56*(2), 125–143. doi:10.1023/A:1012254826324

Sirgy, M. J., Meadow, H. L., & Samli, A. C. (1995). Past, persent and future: An overview of quality-of-life research in marketing. In M. J. Sirgy & A. C. Samli (Eds.), *New Dimensions in marketing/quality-of-life research* (pp. 335–364). Quorum Books.

Sirgy, M. J., Rahtz, D. R., Cicic, M., & Underwood, R. (2000). A method for assessing residents' satisfaction with community-based services: A quality-of-life perspective. *Social Indicators Research*, *49*(3), 279–316. doi:10.1023/A:1006990718673

Sita, K., Aji, T. M., & Hanim, W. (2021). Integrating tea and tourism: A potential sustainable livelihood approach for Indonesia tea producer central area. *IOP Conference Series. Earth and Environmental Science*, *892*(1), 892. doi:10.1088/1755-1315/892/1/012104

Smit, E. (2016, Dec. 6). Sex tourism a reality in Namibia. *Namibia Sun*.

Smith, G., (2008). *Does gender influence online survey participation? A record-linkage analysis of university faculty online survey response behavior*. ERIC Document Reproduction Service No. ED 501717.

Smith, A. (2009). Theorising the relationship between major sports events and social sustainability. *Journal of Sport & Tourism*, *14*(2-3), 109–120. doi:10.1080/14775080902965033

Smith, V. L., & Eadington, W. R. (1992). *Tourism alternatives: Potentials and problems in the development of tourism*. University of Pennsylvania Press. doi:10.9783/9781512807462

Snelgrove, R., & Wood, L. (2010). Attracting and leveraging visitors at a charity cycling event. *Journal of Sport & Tourism*, *15*(4), 269–285. doi:10.1080/14775085.2010.533918

Snepenger, D., O'Connell, R., & Snepenger, M. (2001). The embrace-withdraw continuum scale: Operationalizing residents' responses toward tourism development. *Journal of Travel Research*, *40*(2), 155–161. doi:10.1177/004728750104000206

Snyman, S., & Spenceley, A. (2012). Key sustainable tourism mechanisms for poverty reduction and local socioeconomic development in Africa. *Africa Insight*, *42*(2), 76–93.

Sofield, T. H. B. (2003). *Empowerment for sustainable tourism development*. Pergamon.

Sowicz, T. J. (2017). Mixed methods designs. *Pain*, *158*(4), 760. doi:10.1097/j.pain.0000000000000806 PMID:28301401

Spenceley, A., Ashley, C., & De Kock, M. (2009). *Tourism and local development: an introductory guide*. International Trade Centre.

Spenceley, A., & Meyer, D. (2012). Tourism and poverty reduction: Theory and practice in less economically developed countries. *Journal of Sustainable Tourism*, *20*(3), 297–317. doi:10.1080/09669582.2012.668909

Spenceley, A., & Seif, J. (2003). *Strategies impacts and costs of pro-poor tourism approaches in South Africa*. Overseas Development Institute.

Sport Canada. (2005). *Policy on Aboriginal Peoples' Participation in Sport*. Sport Canada. https://citeseerx.ist.psu.edu/document?repid=rep1&type=pdf&doi=6f573ac537ecc6488954e4916f7fc27ae81d3383

Stankey, G. H., Cole, D. N., Lucas, R. C., Petersen, M. E., & Frissell, S. S. (1985). *The limits of acceptable change (LAC) system for wilderness planning*. INT-176, USDA, Forest Service, Internmountain Forest and Range Experiment Station, Ogden, Utah. doi:10.5962/bhl.title.109310

Stefanov, N., Petrov, G., & Alexova, D. (2018). *Factors and opportunities for development of ecotourism at Botevgrad Miunicipality, Bulgaria*. Available at: www.researchgate.net

Stewart, B., Nicholson, M., Smith, A., & Westerbeek, H. (2004). *Australian sport: Better by design? The evolution of Australian sport policy*. Routledge. doi:10.4324/9780203462928

Stiglitz, J., Sen, A., & Fitoussi, J. (2009). *Report by the commission on the measurement of economic performance and social progress*. UN Stats. http://www.unstats.un.org

Strachan, G. (2002). *Paradise and plantation: Tourism and culture in the Anglophone Caribbean*. Virginia: University of Virginia Press.

Compilation of References

Sukenti, K. (2014). Gastronomy tourism in several neighbor countries of Indonesia: A brief review. *Journal of Indonesian Tourism and Development Studies*, 2(2), 55–63. doi:10.21776/ub.jitode.2014.002.02.03

Su, M. M., Wall, G., Wang, Y., & Jin, M. (2019b). Livelihood sustainability in a rural tourism destination Hetu town, Anhui province, China. *Tourism Management*, 71, 272–281. doi:10.1016/j.tourman.2018.10.019

Su, X., & Zhang, H. (2020). Tea drinking and the tastescapes of wellbeing in tourism. *Tourism Geographies*, 1–21. doi:10.1080/14616688.2020.1750685

Tabak, G., & Güneren Özdemir, E. (2019). Turistlerin çevre dostu tutumlarının çevreye duyarlı turistik ürün satın alma niyeti üzerine etkisi: Nevşehir ilinde bir araştırma. *Journal of Tourism and Gastronomy Studies*, 7(3), 1753–1787.

Tao, T. C. H., & Wall, G. (2009). Tourism as a sustainable livelihood strategy. *Tourism Management*, 30(1), 90–98. doi:10.1016/j.tourman.2008.03.009

Tavmergen, İ. P., & Meriç, P. Ö. (1999). Çevre korumasına yönelik turizm uygulamaları: Yeşil otelcilik, doğa turizmi ve ISO 14000. *Turizmde Seçme Makaleler*, 33, 19–38.

Tea Board of India. (October, 2019). *Tea varieties in India*. Tea Board of India. http://www.teaboard.gov.in/ TEABOARDCSM/MTA=

Technavio (2022). *Cultural tourism market by type, service, and geography - forecast and analysis 2023-2027*. Technavio. https://www.technavio.com/report/cultural-tourism-market-industry-analysis#:~:text=The%20cultural%20tourism%20market%20is,increase%20by%20USD%206600.71%20million

Tekeli, M., & Kırıcı Tekeli, E. (2020). Sustainable gastronomic tourism. In F. Türkmen (Ed.), *Selected academic studies from Turkish tourism sector* (pp. 113–133). Peter Lang.

Tekeli, M., & Kırıcı Tekeli, E. (2020). Sustainable Gastronomic Tourism. In F. Türkmen (Ed.), *Selected academic studies from turkish tourism sector* (pp. 113–133). Peter Lang.

Tek, Ö. B. (1999). *Pazarlama ilkeleri-global yönetimsel yaklaşım Türkiye uygulamaları* (8th ed.). Beta Basım Yayım.

Telfer, D. (2002) The evolution of tourism and development theory. In R. Sharpley and D. Telfer (eds) Tourism and Development: Concepts and Issues (pp. 35 78). Clevedon: Channel View.

Telfer, D. J., & Sharpley, R. (2008). *Tourism and development in the developing world*. Routledge.

Tenekecioğlu, B. (2004). Pazarlama konusu ve pazarlama yönetimi. In B. Tenekecioğlu (Ed.), Pazarlama yönetimi (pp. 1-14). Eskişehir: Anadolu Üniversitesi.

The Indian Wire. (2018). List of top 10 start ups in India that made it big selling chai. Retrieved April 30, 2020 from https://www.theindianwire.com/startups/top-tea-selling startups-india-74220/

The International Ecotourism Society. (2015). *What is ecotourism?* TIES. https://ecotourism.org/what-is-ecotourism/

The International Ecotourism Society. (2019). Available at: www.bsc.smebg.net/ecotourguide/best_practices/articles/files/TIES.pdf

The Rilono Hotel München. (2022). *Example of green accommodation business*. https://www.rilano-hotel-muenchen.de/info/green-room/

Thomas, F. (2014). Addressing the measurement of tourism in terms of poverty reduction: Tourism value chain analysis in Lao PDR and Mali. *International Journal of Tourism Research*, *16*(4), 368–376. doi:10.1002/jtr.1930

Thu, T. T., & Toan, D. T. (2022). Sport event tourism and sustainable development perspectives in Danang City. *Journal on Tourism & Amp; Sustainability, 6* (1). https://ontourism.academy/journal/index.php/jots/article/view/120

Timur, S., & Getz, D. (2007). A network perspective on managing stakeholders for sustainable urban tourism. *International Journal of Contemporary Hospitality Management*, *20*(4), 445–461. doi:10.1108/09596110810873543

Tisdell, C. (1996). Ecotourism, economics, and the environment: Observations from China. *Journal of Travel Research*, *34*(4), 11–19. doi:10.1177/004728759603400402

Tisdell, C. (1998). Ecotourism: Aspect of its sustainability and compatibility with conservation, social and other objectives. *Australian Journal of Hospitality Management*, *5*(2), 11–21.

Todaro, M. P., & Smith, S. C. (2011). Economic development (11th ed.). Pearson Education Limited.

Toften, K., & Hammervoll, T. (2009). Niche firms and marketing strategy: An exploratory study of internationally oriented niche firms. *European Journal of Marketing*, *43*(11/12), 1378–1391. doi:10.1108/03090560910989948

Torres, R. (2003). Linkages between tourism and agriculture in Mexico. *Annals of Tourism Research*, *30*(3), 546–566. doi:10.1016/S0160-7383(02)00103-2

Tosun, C. (2006). Expected nature of community participation in tourism development. *Tourism Management*, *27*(3), 493–504. doi:10.1016/j.tourman.2004.12.004

Tranfield, D., Denyer, D., & Smart, P. (2003). Towards a methodology for developing evidence-informed management knowledge by means of systematic review. *British Journal of Management*, *14*(3), 207–222. doi:10.1111/1467-8551.00375

Travingdy, A. (2017). *Thirty years on the front line - the inside story of Tourism Concern*. Available at: www.travindy.com

Compilation of References

Truong, V. D., Hall, C. M., & Garry, T. (2014). Tourism and poverty alleviation: Perceptions and experiences of poor people in Sapa, Vietnam. *Journal of Sustainable Tourism, 22*(7), 1071–1089. doi:10.1080/09669582.2013.871019

Tseng, M.-L., Lin, C., Remen Lin, C.-W., Wu, K.-J., & Sriphon, T. (2019). Ecotourism development in Thailand: Community participation leads to the value of attractions using linguistic preferences. *Journal of Cleaner Production, 231*, 1319–1329. doi:10.1016/j.jclepro.2019.05.305

Tshomo. (2018). *Study finds positive impact of ecotourism on local communities*. Available at:www.kuenselonline.com

Türk, M., & Gök, A. (2010). Yeşil pazarlama anlayışı açısından üretici işletmelerin sosyal sorumluluğu. *Elektronik Sosyal Bilimler Dergisi, 9*(32), 199–220.

Turner, S. M., & Troiano, C. S. (1987). Notes. *The Cornell Hotel and Restaurant Administration Quarterly, 28*(3), 25–27. doi:10.1177/001088048702800311 PMID:29583616

Turpie, J., Lange, G., Martin, R., Davies, R., & Barnes, J. (2004). *Strengthening Namibia's system of national protected area. Subproject 1: Economic analysis and feasibility study for financing*. Ministry of Environment and Tourism.

UN. (2018). *From MDGs to SDGs*. https://www.sdgfund.org/mdgs-sdgs

UN. (2020). *The Sustainable Development Goals report*. doi:10.18356/214e6642-en

United Nations Conference on Trade and Development (UNCTAD). (2010). *The contribution of tourism to trade and development*. New York: United Nations. (TD/B/C. I/8.)

United Nations Conference on Trade and Development (UNCTAD). (2013). *The impact of trade on employment and poverty reduction*. Geneva: UNCTAD. (Note by the UNCTAD secretariat, 17-21 June.)

United Nations Conference on Trade and Development (UNCTAD). (2017). *Economic development in Africa report 2017*. Geneva, Switzerland: UNCTAD.

United Nations Conference on Trade and Development. (UNCTAD). (2020). *COVID-19 and tourism assessing the economic consequences*. Geneva, Switzerland: UNCTAD.

United Nations Report. (2018). *Sustainable development goals*. New York: United Nations.

United Nations World Tourism Organisation (UNWTO). (2005). Making Tourism More Sustainable-A guide for Policy Makers. Madrid, Spain: UNWETO.

United Nations World Tourism Organisation (UNWTO). (2015). Understanding tourism: basic glossary. Madrid, Spain: UNWETO.

United Nations World Tourism Organisation (UNWTO). (2016). Tourism highlights: 2016 edition. Madrid, Spain: UNWETO.

United Nations World Tourism Organisation (UNWTO). (2017). *2017 results: The highest in seven years*. Madrid, Spain: UNWETO.

United Nations World Tourism Organisation (UNWTO). (2018). *Tourism and the Sustainable Development Goals - Journey to 2030*. Madrid, Spain: UNWETO.

United Nations World Tourism Organisation (UNWTO). (2019). *Exports from international tourism hit USD 1.7 trillion*. Madrid. Spain: UNWETO.

United Nations World Tourism Organisation (UNWTO). (2019a). *Exports from international tourism hit USD 1.7 trillion*. Madrid, Spain: UNWETO.

United Nations World Tourism Organisation (UNWTO). (2019b). *International tourist arrivals reach 1.4 billion two years ahead of forecasts*. UNWETO.

United Nations World Tourism Organisation (UNWTO). (2020). *International tourist numbers could fall 60-80% in 2020*. Madrid, Spain: UNWETO.

United Nations World Tourism Organisation (WTO). (2007). *World tourism day*. WTO.

United Nations World Tourism Organization (UNWTO). (2011). *International tourists to hit 1.8 billion by 2030*. https://www.unwto.org/archive/global/press-release/2011-10-11/international-tourists-hit-18-billion-2030#:~:text=By%202030%2C%20arrivals%20are%20expected,friends%20and%20family%20every%20day

United Nations. (2014). *Millennium development goals*. United Nations.

United Nations. (2020). *About LDCs*. UN-OHRLLS. https://unohrlls.org/about-ldcs/

UNWTO & UNEP. (2005). *Making tourism more sustainable: A guide for policymakers*. UNWTO, Madrid and UNEP, Paris. http://www.unep.fr/shared/publications/pdf/dtix0592xpa-tourismpolicyen.pdf

UNWTO. (1981). Saturation of Tourist Destinations. Report of the Secretary General, Madrid.

UNWTO. (2019). *Global report on women in tourism* (2nd ed.)., doi:10.18111/9789284420384

UNWTO. (2021). *Community based tourism training workshop - World Tourism Day (27)*. https://www.unwto.org/node/12238

Urala, N., & Lähteenmäki, L. (2007). Consumers' changing attitudes towards functional foods. *Food Quality and Preference*, *18*(1), 1–12. doi:10.1016/j.foodqual.2005.06.007

Ural, T. (2003). *İşletme ve pazarlama etiği* (1st ed.). Detay Yayıncılık.

Uran, M., & Juvan, E. (2010). The stakeholders role within tourism strategy development: The local residents viewpoint. *Organizacija*, *43*(5).

Usta, Ö. (1992). *Turizm*. Altın Kitaplar Yayınevi.

Üstünel, B. (2000). *Ekonominin temelleri*. Dünya Yayınları.

Compilation of References

Uydacı, M. (2016). *Yeşil pazarlama*. Türkmen Kitabevi.

Uysal, M., Woo, E., & Singal, M. (2012). The Tourist Area Life Cycle (TALC) and Its Effect on the Quality of- Life (QOL) of Destination Community. In M. Uysal, R. Perdue, & J. Sirgy (Eds.), *Handbook of Tourism and Quality-of-Life Research* (pp. 423–443). Springer. doi:10.1007/978-94-007-2288-0_25

Van Zyl, C. J. (2005). *The role of tourism in the conservation of cultural heritage with particular relevance for South Africa* [PhD thesis]. University of Stellenbosch.

Varela, J. M. (2021). *OMCV promove workshop para apresentação da carta europeia do turismo sustentável nas áreas protegidas*. INFORPRESS. https://inforpress.cv/omcv-promove-workshop-para-apresentacao-da-carta-europeia-do-turismo-sustentavel-nas-areas-protegidas/

Vargas-Sanchez, A., Plaza-Mejia, M. A., & Porras-Bueno, N. (2009). Understanding residents' attitudes toward the development of industrial tourism in a former mining community. *Journal of Travel Research*, *47*(3), 373–387. doi:10.1177/0047287508322783

Varinli, İ. (2012). *Pazarlamada Yeni Yaklaşımlar*. Detay Yayıncılık.

Varun, T. C., Kerutagi, M. G., Kunnal, L. B., Basavaraja, H., Ashalatha, K. V., & Dodamani, M. T. (2009). Consumption patterns of coffee and tea in Karnataka. *Karnataka Journal of Agricultural Sciences*, *22*(4), 824–827.

Vehkamäki, S. (2005). The concept of sustainability in modern times. In A. Jalkanen & P. Nygren (Eds.), *Sustainable use of renewable natural resources from principles to practices* (pp. 23–35). University of Helsinki Department of Forest Ecology Publications.

Veltri, F., Miller, J., & Harris, A. (2009). Club sport national tournament: Economic impact of a small event on a mid-size community. *Recreational Sports Journal*, *33*(2), 119–128. doi:10.1123/rsj.33.2.119

Walker, B., & Salt, D. (2012). *Resilience thinking: sustaining ecosystems and people in a changing world*. Island Press.

Walker, J., & Cooper, M. (2011). Genealogies of resilience: From systems ecology to the political economy of crisis adaptation. *Security Dialogue*, *42*(2), 143–160. doi:10.1177/0967010611399616

Wall, G. (1982). Cycles and capacity: Incipient theory or conceptual contradiction? *Tourism Management*, *3*(3), 188–192. doi:10.1016/0261-5177(82)90067-X

Wall, G., & Mathieson, A. (2006). *Tourism: change, impacts, and opportunities*. Pearson Education.

Walo, M., Bull, A., & Breen, H. (1996). Achieving economic benefits for local events; a case study of local sports events. *Festival Management & Event Tourism*, *4*(3), 95–106. doi:10.3727/106527096792195353

Walton, J. K. (2001). *The Hospitality Trades: A Social History*. Butterworth-Heinemann.

Ward, N. K. (1997). *Ecotourism: Reality or rhetoric. Ecotourism development in the state of Quintana Roo, Mexico* [Unpublished master's thesis, University of Portsmouth].

Wattanakuljarus, A., & Coxhead, I. (2008). Is tourism-based development good for the poor? A general equilibrium analysis for Thailand. *Journal of Policy Modeling, 30*(6), 929–955. doi:10.1016/j.jpolmod.2008.02.006

WCED. (1987). Our common future, report of world commission on environment and development. UN. http://www.un-documents.net/our-common-future.pdf

WCED. (1987). *Our common future*. Oxford University Press.

Wearne, N., & Baker, K. (2002). *Hospitality Marketing in the e-commerce Age* (2nd ed.). Hospitality Press. Available at www.osea-cite.org

Weaver, D. (2006). *Sustainable tourism*. Butterworth and Heinemann.

Weaver, D. B. (1989). The evolution of a 'plantation' tourism landscape on the Caribbean island of Antigua. *Tijdschrift voor Economische en Sociale Geografie, 79*(5), 319–331. doi:10.1111/j.1467-9663.1988.tb01318.x

Weaver, D., & Lawton, L. (2007). Twenty years on: The state of contemporary ecotourism research. *Tourism Management, 28*(5), 1168–1179. doi:10.1016/j.tourman.2007.03.004

Weber, I. (2018). Tea for tourists: Cultural capital, representation, and borrowing in the tea culture of mainland China and Taiwan. *Academica Turistica, 12*(2), 143–154. doi:10.26493/2335-4194.11.143-154

Weed, M. (2006). *Sports Tourism and the development of sports events*. Idrotts Forum. www.idrottsforum.org

Weed, M., & Bull, A. (2005). *Sports tourism: participants, policy and providers*. Butterworth Heinemann.

Welcome to the Experience Economy . (2018). Available at: https://hbr.org/1998/07/welcome-to-the-experience-economy

Weller, C. (2017). *The World Bank released new poverty lines: find out where your country stands*. Business Insider.

Wilkinson, C. (2012). Social-ecological resilience: Insights and issues for planning theory. *Planning Theory, 11*(2), 148–169. doi:10.1177/1473095211426274

Williams, J., & Lawson, R. (2001). Community issues and resident opinions of tourism. *Annals of Tourism Research, 28*(2), 269–290. doi:10.1016/S0160-7383(00)00030-X

Williams, T. (2012). Tourism as a neo-colonial phenomenon: Examining the works of Pattullo & Mullings. *Caribbean Quilt, 2*, 191–200. doi:10.33137/caribbeanquilt.v2i0.19313

Compilation of References

Wilson, R. (2006). The economic impact of local sport events: Significant, limited or otherwise? A case study of four swimming events. *Managing Leisure, 11*(1), 57–70. doi:10.1080/13606710500445718

Winters, P., Corral, L., & Mora, A. M. (2013). Assessing the role of tourism in poverty alleviation: A research agenda. *Development Policy Review, 31*(2), 177–202. doi:10.1111/dpr.12002

Winther, N., Nazer-Bloom, L., & Petch, V. (1995). *A comprehensive overview of development, the North American Indigenous Games and provincial/territorial*. Aboriginal Sport Bodies.

Wires. (2019). Historic 2019 Ironman Malaysia Sees Biggest Ever Participation in Langkawi. *Wires*. www.asiatri.com

Wisdom, J., & Creswell, J. (2013). *Mixed Methods: Integrating Quantitative and Qualitative Data Collection and Analysis While Studying Patient-Centered Medical Home Models*. PCMH Resource Center. Available at: www.pcmh.ahrq.gov

Witt, S. F., & Witt, C. A. (1995). Forecasting tourism demand: A review of empirical research. *International Journal of Forecasting, 11*(3), 447–475. doi:10.1016/0169-2070(95)00591-7

Wondirad, A., & Ewnetu, B. (2019). Community participation in tourism development as a tool to foster sustainable land and resource use practices in a national park milieu. *Land Use Policy, 88*, 104155. doi:10.1016/j.landusepol.2019.104155

Wondirad, A., Tolkach, D., & King, B. (2020). Stakeholder collaboration as a major factor for sustainable ecotourism development in developing countries. *Tourism Management, 78*, 104024. doi:10.1016/j.tourman.2019.104024

Wood, M. E. (2002). *Ecotourism: Principles, practices & policies for sustainability*. United Nations Publication.

Woo, E., Kim, H., & Uysal, M. (2015). Life satisfaction and support for tourism development. *Annals of Tourism Research, 50*, 84–97. doi:10.1016/j.annals.2014.11.001

World Bank. (1991). *The world development report 1991: the challenge of development*. Oxford University Press.

World Bank. (2001). *World Development Report 2000/2001: Attacking Poverty. World Development Report*. Oxford University Press.

World Bank. (2011). *The World Bank annual report 2011*. World Bank.

World Bank. (2017). *Economic growth for Sub-Saharan Africa looks set to pick up to a modest 2.4% earlier this year, but a big improvement on 1.3% in 2016*. World Bank.

World Bank. (2022). *Poverty*. https://www.worldbank.org/en/topic/poverty/overview

World Heritage and Indigenous Peoples . (2019). Available at: https://whc.unesco.org/en/activities/496/

World Tourism Organisation (WTO). (2002). *Tourism and poverty alleviation*. World Tourism Organisation.

World Tourism Organisation (WTO). (2004). *Tourism and poverty alleviation: recommendation for action*. WTO.

World Tourism Organization (WTO). (2010). *Tourism highlights*. WTO.

World Travel & Tourism Council (WTTC). (2006). *Namibia. The impact of travel & tourism on jobs and the economy*. WTTC.

World Travel and Tourism Council (WTTC). (2015). *Travel and tourism economic impact 2015 Costa Rica*. WTTC.

World Travel and Tourism Council (WTTC). (2017). *Global economic issues and impact*. WTTC.

World Travel and Tourism Council (WTTC). (2019). *Travel and tourism: economic impact 2019*. WTTC.

World Travel and Tourism Council (WTTC). (2020). *Namibia key data 2019*. WTTC.

Worsdale, R., & Wright, J. (2020). My objectivity is better than yours: Contextualising debates about gender inequality. *Synthese*, *199*(1–2), 1659–1683. doi:10.100711229-020-02835-5

Woyesa, T., & Kumar, S. (2021). Potential of coffee tourism for rural development in Ethiopia: A sustainable livelihood approach. *Environment, Development and Sustainability*, *23*(1), 815–832. doi:10.100710668-020-00610-7

Xavier, M. D. (2018). *O trabalho da mulher em Arraias: Desafios e possibilidades para o turismo* [Degree dissertation, Universidade Federal do Tocantins]. Repositório Institucional da Universidade Federal do Tocantins. https://repositorio.uft.edu.br/handle/11612/2615

Xinhua, N. (2018, July 8). Art gives Namibian rural nomads a new lifeline. *The Namibian*.

Xu, H., Sofield, T., & Bao, J. (2008). Community tourism in Asia: an introduction. In Tourism and community development: Asian practices. Madrid, Spain: World Tourism Organization.

Yaman, A. R., & Mohd, A. (2004). Community-based ecotourism: A new proposition for sustainable development and environmental conservation in Malaysia. *The Journal of Applied Science*, *4*(4), 583–589. doi:10.3923/jas.2004.583.589

Yang, J., Zeng, X., & Yingkang, G. (2010). Local residents' perceptions of the impact of 2010 EXPO. *Journal of Convention & Event Tourism*, *11*(3), 161–175. doi:10.1080/15470148.2010.502030

Yang, X., & Hung, K. (2014). Poverty alleviation via tourism cooperatives in China: The story of Yuhu. *International Journal of Contemporary Hospitality Management*, *26*(6), 879–906. doi:10.1108/IJCHM-02-2013-0085

Yang, Z. (2007). Tea culture and Sino-American Tea connections. *Chinese American Studies*, *1*(2), 8–14.

Yeşil Oteller Birliği. (2015). *What are green hotels?* https://www.greenhotels.com/

Yetiş, Ş. A. (2018). Sürdürülebilir turizm kapsamında küçük ölçekli konaklama işletmelerinde yeşil pazarlama uygulamaları. *Gümüşhane Üniversitesi Sosyal Bilimler Enstitüsü Elektronik Dergisi*, *9*(23), 82–98.

Yonglong, L. (1996). Eco-tourism industry development-an alternative to sustainable use of landscape resources. *Journal of Environmental Sciences (China)*, *8*(3), 298–307.

Youell, R. (1998). *Tourism: an introduction*. Longman.

Yu, C. P., Cole, S. T., & Chancellor, C. (2016). Assessing Community Quality of Life in the Context of Tourism Development. *Applied Research in Quality of Life*, *11*(1), 147–162. doi:10.100711482-014-9359-6

Yuen, S. (2012) The business of sport in Hawaii. *Hawaii Business Magazine*. http://www.hawaiibusiness.com

Yuksel, A., Yuksel, F., & Bilim, Y. (2010). Destination attachment: Effects on customer satisfaction andcognitive, affective and conative loyalty. *Tourism Management*, *31*(2), 274–284. doi:10.1016/j.tourman.2009.03.007

Zacarias, D. A., Williams, A. T., & Newton, A. (2011). Recreation carrying capacity estimations to support beach management at Praia de Faro, Portugal. *Applied Geography (Sevenoaks, England)*, *31*(3), 1075–1081. doi:10.1016/j.apgeog.2011.01.020

Zakai, D., & Chadwick-Furman, N. E. (2002). Impacts of intensive recreational diving on reef corals at Eilat, northern Red Sea. *Biological Conservation*, *105*(2), 179–187. doi:10.1016/S0006-3207(01)00181-1

Zambezi Population and Housing Census. (2014). *2011 population and housing census: Zambezi regional profile*. Namibian Statistics Agency.

Zapata, M. J., Hall, C. M., Lindo, P., & Vanderschaeghe, M. (2011). Can community-based tourism contribute to development and poverty alleviation? Lessons from Nicaragua. *Current Issues in Tourism*, *14*(8), 725–749. doi:10.1080/13683500.2011.559200

Zeng, B., & Ryan, C. (2012). Assisting the poor in China through tourism development: A review of research. *Tourism Management*, *33*(2), 239–248. doi:10.1016/j.tourman.2011.08.014

Zeppel, H., & Beaumont, N. (2011). *Green Tourism Futures: Climate Change Responses by Australian Government Tourism Agencies* (Vol. 2). University of Southern Queensland, Australian Centre for Sustainable.

Zhang, Y., Li, X. R., Su, Q., & Hu, X. (2017). Exploring a theme park's tourism carrying capacity: A demand-side analysis. *Tourism Management*, *59*, 564–578. doi:10.1016/j.tourman.2016.08.019

Zhao, W., & Ritchie, J. R. B. (2007). Tourism and poverty alleviation: An integrative research framework. *Current Issues in Tourism*, *10*(2), 119–143. doi:10.2167/cit296.0

Zheng, W., Doyle, T. J., Kushi, L. H., Sellers, T. A., Hong, C. P., & Folsom, A. R. (1996). Tea consumption and cancer incidence in a prospective cohort study of postmenopausal women. *American Journal of Epidemiology*, *144*(1), 175–182. doi:10.1093/oxfordjournals.aje.a008905 PMID:8678049

Zhong, L., Deng, J., Song, Z., & Ding, P. (2011). Research on environmental impacts of tourism in China: Progress and prospect. *Journal of Environmental Management*, *92*(11), 2972–2983. doi:10.1016/j.jenvman.2011.07.011 PMID:21821344

Zhou, J. Y. (2010). Resident perceptions toward the impacts of the Macao Grand Prix. *Journal of Convention & Event Tourism*, *11*(2), 138–153. doi:10.1080/15470148.2010.485179

Zhouyiqi, C. and Tao, W. (2012). Application of special tea cultivars in landscape design of ecotourism tea gardens. *J. Crops, 2*.

Ziakas, V. (2010). Understanding an event portfolio: The uncovering of interrelationships, synergies, and leveraging opportunities. *Journal of Policy Research in Tourism, Leisure & Events*, *2*(2), 144–164. doi:10.1080/19407963.2010.482274

Zurick, D. N. (1992). Adventure travel and sustainable tourism in the peripheral economy of Nepal. *Annals of the Association of American Geographers*, *82*(4), 608–628. doi:10.1111/j.1467-8306.1992.tb01720.x

About the Contributors

Vipin Nadda is a competent, conscientious and motivated academic professional driven with well organized team spirit and goal oriented approach. Nadda is currently serving as Lecturer and Programme Manager (Postgraduate-tourism & Hospitality) with University of Sunderland in London. A science graduate with MBA (Marketing), MTA (Tourism) and PhD(Tourism Management), Nadda has more than fifteen years of Experience in academics and Industry. Besides this, also published two books and presented papers in various international seminars and Global conferences. Nadda also freelances as 'Education development consultant' for University of East London, Glyndwr University, Anglia Ruskin University, Director of studies for PhD with Cardiff Metropolitan University UK, 'Member of Academic Council' and Chief Examiner for Confederation of Tourism and Hospitality, London. As an experienced academician, Nadda has been Lecturing a variety of courses ranging from Marketing, HR in 'Business and Management' to 'International Tourism and Hospitality Management' in the UK as well as overseas.

Faithfull Gonzo is an innovative and ambitious individual with a high level of expertise within the hospitality, events and tourism industry. Before transitioning into academia, she has worked for large organisations such as Marriott Hotels. She successfully completed doctoral level research which focused on rural tourism development and poverty alleviation. Also graduated with a Master of Arts degree in International Tourism and Hospitality Management and a BA (honours) degree in Events Management and Hospitality Management. Has a passion and experience in teaching Hospitality, Tourism and Events management. She is currently working as a Senior Lecturer in Events Management at the University of West London. She has also worked in various academic institutions such as the University of Sunderland in London where she was a programme coordinator for Tourism and Hospitality Programme. She is an external evaluator for Malta Further and Higher Education Authority and an external examiner for North-West University South Africa. She has been lecturing on a variety of courses ranging from Events, International Tourism and Hospitality Management in the UK.

***

About the Contributors

Shuvasree Banerjee is a research scholar at Chandigarh University- UID-22YTH1002.

Rita Fernandes has a degree in Tourism from the University of Évora and a Master's degree in Tourism Management and Planning from the University of Aveiro. Her main areas of interest are inclusive and accessible tourism, cultural tourist experiences, development of strategies for the territory and creation of supply agents.

Gülsüm Kasap graduated from Gazi University, Faculty of Commerce and Tourism Education, Department of Travel Management and Tourism Guidance Teaching (2013). She received her master's degree from Nevşehir Hacı Bektaş Veli University Tourism Management Department (2017). She is an Lecturer at Isparta University of Applied Science, School of Eğirdir Vocational. Her main fields of study are tourism and tourism marketing.

Ezgi Kırıcı Tekeli graduated from Nevşehir Hacı Bektaş Veli University, Faculty of Tourism, Department of Tourism Guidance (2014). She received her master's degree from Nevşehir Hacı Bektaş Veli University, Tourism Management Department (2016), and her doctoral degree from Nevşehir Hacı Bektaş Veli University, Tourism Management Department (2020). She is an Assistant Professor Dr. at Karamanoğlu Mehmetbey University, School of Applied Sciences. Her main fields of study are tourism and tourism guidance.

Latif Oztosun is working as a lecturer and Programme Coordinator at University of Sunderland in London. Experienced Travel Specialist and Travel and Tourism Lecturer with a demonstrated history of working in the tourism and hospitality industry. Skilled in Leisure Travel, Sales, Tour Operations, and Customer Satisfaction. Strong operations professional with a Degree in Education and Training focused in Teaching from Canterbury Christ Church University. Additionally, a Masters in International Tourism and Hospitality Management from the University of Greenwich.

Rita Pereira has a degree in Tourism from the Faculty of Economics and Management of the University of the Azores and is a Master's student of Tourism Management and Planning at the University of Aveiro with a specialization in Management/Economics. Her areas of research interest are regenerative tourism, development and strategic planning of destinations, regional development, and island destinations.

About the Contributors

Vitória Plácido has a degree in Languages and Business Relations from the University of Aveiro and is a Master's student in Tourism Management and Planning at the University of Aveiro. Her research interests center on education in tourism and how it affects working conditions in the tourism area.

Isabella Roveri holds a degree in Tourism from the Federal University of São Carlos in Brazil and a Master's degree in Tourism Management and Planning from the University of Aveiro. She has carried out research in the area of community-based tourism, which she investigated in her dissertation. She currently works on the relationship between tourism and student mobility.

Wendy Sealy is a Reader in Graduate Employability at the University of Chichester, UK. She grew up and was educated in Barbados playing many traditional Barbadian games as a child. On graduation, Dr Sealy embarked on a hospitality career working in several international hotels where she experienced the 'behind the scenes' workings of the industry first-hand and experienced how the business models of trans national companies cause damage to local communities. Dr Sealy draws on her intimate knowledge of Barbados' tourism sector and indigenous sports to offer community-based tourism solutions.

Ravi Sharma is currently working as an Assistant Professor in the Department of Energy and Environment with Symbiosis Institute of International Business (SIIB) under Symbiosis International University, Pune, India. Masters of Science in Zoology with Environmental Sciences and Toxicology as specialization in 2003 and Ph.D. in Forestry under discipline Forest Ecology and Environment from Forest Research Institute University (FRIU), Dehradun, India. He was also awarded Junior Research Fellowship (2003-2005) from University Grants Commission (UGC) during his research tenure with Indian Institute of Forest Management (IIFM), Bhopal. Academic area of interest is in subjects of Zoology, Environmental Sciences, GIS, and Ecology. The academic experience at higher education level is more than 12+ years. His research focus is Environmental Impact Assessment, Ecotourism and Sustainability, Ecological Risk Assessment and Environmental Monitoring. He is engaged in research and academic activities at University level. IRCA approved Lead Auditor for ISO- 14001:2015.

Nina Szczygiel is a professor of Management at the Dept. of Economics, Management, Industrial Engineering and Tourism of the University of Aveiro, Portugal. Her research interests include well-being in societies, organizations and individuals, human mobility and integration, and networks. She is particularly interested in psychosocial and emotional aspects of work.

Mehmet Tekeli graduated from Nevşehir Hacı Bektaş Veli University, Faculty of Tourism, Department of Tourism Management (2014). He received his master's degree from Nevşehir Hacı Bektaş Veli University Tourism Management Department (2016), and his doctoral degree from Nevşehir Hacı Bektaş Veli University Tourism Management Department (2021). He is an Assistant Professor Dr. at Karamanoğlu Mehmetbey University, School of Applied Sciences. His main fields of study are tourism and tourism management.

Paul Wheeler is Senior Lecturer and the Programme Coordinator for the BA (Hons) Sport Management (Business) degree. His research expertise is the history of sport: His doctorate critically analysed the evolution of Golf Tourism on the South Coast of England from 1880-1939. Paul is part of various sports history-related research projects, independently and in collaboration with colleagues within this university, other universities and non-academics. Paul liaises with community groups and local partnerships to provide them with expert sport management advice that will assist them in the operation and organisation of projects and facilities.

İrem Yıldırım graduated from Nevşehir Hacı Bektaş Veli University, Faculty of Tourism, Department of Tourism Management (2014). She received her master's degree from Nevşehir Hacı Bektaş Veli University, Tourism Management Department (2017), and her doctoral degree from Nevşehir Hacı Bektaş Veli University, Tourism Management Department (2022). She is an instructor Dr. at Nevşehir Hacı Bektaş Veli University, Ürgüp Sebahat and Erol Toksöz Tourism Vocational School. Her main fields of study are tourism and tourism marketing.

Index

A

All-Inclusive Resorts 274-276, 294, 296

C

Caribbean Tourism 273, 275, 295
Carrying Capacity 47, 95, 185-191, 193-194, 196-197, 199-211, 253, 257, 263, 265
Clean Technology 51
Community Tourism 4, 83, 106, 123
Community-Based Tourism 1-2, 4, 8, 10, 14, 16, 100, 102-103, 106, 116, 143, 151-155, 159
Consumer Behavior 118, 268

E

Ecology 27, 50, 52, 58, 97, 168, 194, 201-202, 205-206, 209, 211, 250, 255, 259-260, 271-272
Economy 1, 7, 20-21, 24-25, 27, 36-38, 46, 72-73, 75-76, 78, 81, 83, 85-87, 95-96, 98-99, 105, 113, 118, 120, 123-124, 127, 135, 142, 146, 150, 160-161, 164-165, 181, 211, 214, 224, 226-227, 251, 254, 262, 274-275, 279, 291
Eco-Tourism 4, 20-21, 24, 26-48, 82, 100, 105-106, 150, 165, 167, 178, 181, 184, 186, 194, 196-197, 199, 207, 250-251, 254-255, 257-272
Ecotourists 32-33, 36, 40, 45, 260-261, 263, 267, 272
Entrepreneur 9, 19

Entrepreneurship 1-4, 7-9, 11, 13-19
Environmental Awareness 49-52, 54, 59, 62, 258
Environmental Sustainability 11, 52, 82-83, 94, 132, 254-255, 266

F

Female Empowerment 2, 7, 9, 14, 18

G

Gender Equality 1-2, 6-7, 9, 11-15, 17-19, 82, 132
Gender Inequality 1, 5-6, 13-18
Global Tourism 73, 76, 95-96, 121, 126, 129, 142, 148, 160, 201
Green Hotel 62, 69
Green Marketing 49-57, 61-63, 65, 67, 69
Green Place 55, 57, 69
Green Price 50, 55-57, 69
Green Product 55-57, 62, 69
Green Promotion 50, 55, 58, 69
Green Technology 69

H

Homestay 11-12, 15, 122, 160, 244
Hospitality 12, 19, 48-50, 53-54, 56, 58-60, 62, 64, 66, 68, 96, 100-101, 106, 151-154, 161, 163, 165, 168-169, 171, 180-181, 183, 212-214, 216, 218, 220-222, 224, 226-228, 231, 234-235, 244, 246, 271, 292, 295

Index

I

Indigenous and Tribal Tourism 107-111, 113-114, 116-119, 121-123
Indigenous Sport Tourism 283, 285, 288-289, 291
Inequality 1, 5-6, 8, 13-19, 99, 103, 110, 126-127, 143, 147, 153, 252, 258
Infrastructure Development 38, 71, 76-77, 110

L

Least Developed Countries 75, 77, 129, 142, 156
Local Communities 4, 13, 24, 28-31, 33, 37, 48, 70, 89, 100-101, 112-113, 117, 120, 125, 154, 165, 216, 220, 234-235, 241-242, 254, 256, 261-262, 272-273, 284

M

Marketing Mix 49, 55, 57, 65, 70
Marketing Strategy 32, 66, 124, 163
Multiplier Effects 13, 71, 86, 117

N

Nature-Based Tourism 80, 114, 124, 152, 194-195, 260
Niche Tourism 101, 107, 109, 114, 118, 121, 124, 277

P

Poverty 1-2, 4, 6, 8-9, 11-12, 19, 28, 35, 72, 76-77, 81-83, 86, 89, 92, 96-97, 101-104, 106, 110, 125-137, 139, 141-159, 163, 252, 254, 265, 282
Pro-Poor Tourism 125-126, 136, 142, 148-157

Q

Quality of Life (QoL) 5, 39, 72, 81-82, 85, 88, 90, 95, 127, 137, 139, 168, 212, 220, 228, 232, 234-240, 242-248, 281-282, 291

R

Responsible Tourism 26, 30-31, 34, 47, 82, 85, 149, 181, 234, 259
Rural Development 14, 46, 81, 89, 132, 137, 143-144, 184
Rural Tourism 11, 13, 16, 26, 31, 46, 72, 77, 80, 83, 104, 143, 152, 183, 195

S

Stakeholders 15, 30, 32, 36, 40, 48, 53-54, 62, 71-72, 83, 109-112, 118-119, 131, 133, 139, 143, 148-149, 151, 163, 171, 176-177, 183, 201, 203, 212, 220, 222, 224, 263-264, 266, 288
Sustainable Development 1-4, 6-7, 12, 15-19, 24, 27, 29, 33, 37, 41, 43, 47, 54, 82-83, 94, 99, 101, 106, 108, 110-112, 132-133, 135, 150, 152, 154-155, 157-158, 161, 165, 176, 181, 194, 196, 204, 229-230, 234, 250-255, 257, 264-266, 270, 272, 276-277, 296
Sustainable Development Goals 2, 6, 12, 17-18, 33, 110-111, 133, 135, 150, 152, 155, 157-158, 254, 277
Sustainable Tourism 11, 17-18, 21, 31, 45, 49-50, 55, 66, 68, 70, 97, 100-101, 104, 107, 120, 124, 132-133, 136, 143, 150-151, 153-154, 157, 165, 177, 183, 188, 194, 197, 199-202, 206-214, 229-232, 236, 242, 246, 250-251, 255-257, 265-273, 291-293

T

Tea Tourism 160-164, 166-171, 173, 175-178, 180
Tourism Development 4, 17, 26-27, 35, 37-38, 40-41, 71-73, 75, 77-78, 83-86, 96, 98-101, 103-106, 108-110, 120, 130-132, 137, 139, 141-144, 146-149, 151-155, 169, 180, 199-201, 204, 206, 208, 212-213, 220, 228-229, 231-232,

Index

234-243, 245-248, 254, 260, 268-270, 273-274, 283

Tourism Impacts 84, 93, 99-100, 134, 139, 229, 237-239, 243-245

Tourism Management 4, 15, 19, 45-46, 48, 66, 68, 96, 98, 100, 104-106, 124, 149-150, 152, 177, 179, 182-184, 194-195, 201, 206-211, 229-231, 244-245, 247, 268, 270, 277, 293, 295

Tourist 1, 8-9, 11, 13, 20-22, 24-34, 36-41, 71, 73-78, 80, 83, 85-89, 91-93, 95, 99, 101-102, 105, 113, 129, 136, 138, 144, 146, 158, 161-163, 165-170, 172-176, 179, 181-182, 186-187, 199-200, 202, 207-209, 211-212, 214-215, 218-220, 222, 225-226, 234, 248, 251, 255, 257, 261, 263-264, 266, 274-275, 277, 290-291, 294-295

Recommended Reference Books

IGI Global's reference books are available in three unique pricing formats:
Print Only, E-Book Only, or Print + E-Book.
Order direct through IGI Global's Online Bookstore at www.igi-global.com or through your preferred provider.

ISBN: 9781799887096
EISBN: 9781799887119
© 2022; 413 pp.
List Price: US$ 250

ISBN: 9781799874157
EISBN: 9781799874164
© 2022; 334 pp.
List Price: US$ 240

ISBN: 9781668440230
EISBN: 9781668440254
© 2022; 320 pp.
List Price: US$ 215

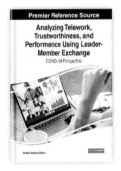

ISBN: 9781799889502
EISBN: 9781799889526
© 2022; 263 pp.
List Price: US$ 240

ISBN: 9781799885283
EISBN: 9781799885306
© 2022; 587 pp.
List Price: US$ 360

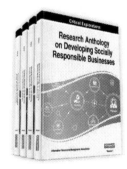

ISBN: 9781668455906
EISBN: 9781668455913
© 2022; 2,235 pp.
List Price: US$ 1,865

Do you want to stay current on the latest research trends, product announcements, news, and special offers?
Join IGI Global's mailing list to receive customized recommendations, exclusive discounts, and more.
Sign up at: www.igi-global.com/newsletters.

Publisher of Timely, Peer-Reviewed Inclusive Research Since 1988

IGI Global
PUBLISHER of TIMELY KNOWLEDGE

www.igi-global.com | Sign up at www.igi-global.com/newsletters | facebook.com/igiglobal | twitter.com/igiglobal

Ensure Quality Research is Introduced to the Academic Community

Become an Evaluator for IGI Global Authored Book Projects

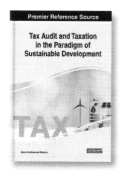   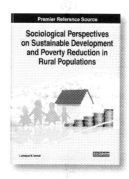

The overall success of an authored book project is dependent on quality and timely manuscript evaluations.

Applications and Inquiries may be sent to:
development@igi-global.com

Applicants must have a doctorate (or equivalent degree) as well as publishing, research, and reviewing experience. Authored Book Evaluators are appointed for one-year terms and are expected to complete at least three evaluations per term. Upon successful completion of this term, evaluators can be considered for an additional term.

If you have a colleague that may be interested in this opportunity, we encourage you to share this information with them.

Easily Identify, Acquire, and Utilize Published Peer-Reviewed Findings in Support of Your Current Research

IGI Global OnDemand

Purchase Individual IGI Global OnDemand Book Chapters and Journal Articles

For More Information:
www.igi-global.com/e-resources/ondemand/

Browse through 150,000+ Articles and Chapters!

Find specific research related to your current studies and projects that have been contributed by international researchers from prestigious institutions, including:

- Accurate and Advanced Search
- Affordably Acquire Research
- Instantly Access Your Content
- Benefit from the InfoSci Platform Features

It really provides an excellent entry into the research literature of the field. *It presents a manageable number of* highly relevant sources *on topics of interest to a wide range of researchers. The sources are* scholarly, but also accessible *to 'practitioners'.*

- Ms. Lisa Stimatz, MLS, University of North Carolina at Chapel Hill, USA

Interested in Additional Savings?

Subscribe to
IGI Global OnDemand *Plus*

Learn More

Acquire content from over 126,000+ research-focused book chapters and 33,000+ scholarly journal articles for as low as US$ 5 per article/chapter (original retail price for an article/chapter: US$ 37.50).

7,300+ E-BOOKS.
ADVANCED RESEARCH.
INCLUSIVE & AFFORDABLE.

IGI Global e-Book Collection

- Flexible Purchasing Options (Perpetual, Subscription, EBA, etc.)
- Multi-Year Agreements with No Price Increases Guaranteed
- No Additional Charge for Multi-User Licensing
- No Maintenance, Hosting, or Archiving Fees
- Continually Enhanced & Innovated Accessibility Compliance Features (WCAG)

Handbook of Research on Digital Transformation, Industry Use Cases, and the Impact of Disruptive Technologies
ISBN: 9781799877127
EISBN: 9781799877141

Handbook of Research on New Investigations in Artificial Life, AI, and Machine Learning
ISBN: 9781799886860
EISBN: 9781799886877

Handbook of Research on Future of Work and Education
ISBN: 9781799882756
EISBN: 9781799882770

Research Anthology on Physical and Intellectual Disabilities in an Inclusive Society (4 Vols.)
ISBN: 9781668435427
EISBN: 9781668435434

Innovative Economic, Social, and Environmental Practices for Progressing Future Sustainability
ISBN: 9781799895909
EISBN: 9781799895923

Applied Guide for Event Study Research in Supply Chain Management
ISBN: 9781799889694
EISBN: 9781799889717

Mental Health and Wellness in Healthcare Workers
ISBN: 9781799888130
EISBN: 9781799888147

Clean Technologies and Sustainable Development in Civil Engineering
ISBN: 9781799898108
EISBN: 9781799898122

Request More Information, or Recommend the IGI Global e-Book Collection to Your Institution's Librarian

---

For More Information or to Request a Free Trial, Contact IGI Global's e-Collections Team: eresources@igi-global.com | 1-866-342-6657 ext. 100 | 717-533-8845 ext. 100

Are You Ready to Publish Your Research?

IGI Global — PUBLISHER of TIMELY KNOWLEDGE

IGI Global offers book authorship and editorship opportunities across 11 subject areas, including business, computer science, education, science and engineering, social sciences, and more!

Benefits of Publishing with IGI Global:

- Free one-on-one editorial and promotional support.
- Expedited publishing timelines that can take your book from start to finish in less than one (1) year.
- Choose from a variety of formats, including Edited and Authored References, Handbooks of Research, Encyclopedias, and Research Insights.
- Utilize IGI Global's eEditorial Discovery® submission system in support of conducting the submission and double-blind peer review process.
- IGI Global maintains a strict adherence to ethical practices due in part to our full membership with the Committee on Publication Ethics (COPE).
- Indexing potential in prestigious indices such as Scopus®, Web of Science™, PsycINFO®, and ERIC – Education Resources Information Center.
- Ability to connect your ORCID iD to your IGI Global publications.
- Earn honorariums and royalties on your full book publications as well as complimentary content and exclusive discounts.

Join Your Colleagues from Prestigious Institutions, Including:

Australian National University
Massachusetts Institute of Technology
Johns Hopkins University
Harvard University
Columbia University in the City of New York

Learn More at: www.igi-global.com/publish
or by Contacting the Acquisitions Department at: acquisition@igi-global.com

Individual Article & Chapter Downloads
US$ 29.50/each

Easily Identify, Acquire, and Utilize Published Peer-Reviewed Findings in Support of Your Current Research

- Browse Over **170,000+ Articles & Chapters**
- **Accurate & Advanced** Search
- Affordably Acquire **International Research**
- **Instantly Access** Your Content
- Benefit from the **InfoSci® Platform Features**

THE UNIVERSITY
of NORTH CAROLINA
at CHAPEL HILL

" *It really provides an excellent entry into the research literature of the field. It presents a manageable number of highly relevant sources on topics of interest to a wide range of researchers. The sources are scholarly, but also accessible to 'practitioners'.* "

- Ms. Lisa Stimatz, MLS, University of North Carolina at Chapel Hill, USA

Interested in Additional Savings?

Subscribe to
IGI Global OnDemand *Plus*

Learn More

Acquire content from over 128,000+ research-focused book chapters and 33,000+ scholarly journal articles for as low as US$ 5 per article/chapter (original retail price for an article/chapter: US$ 37.50).